Praise for *The T*

'At a time when it is easy to lose fai
kind, and ultimately celebratory boon by ....
perfect global antidote to restore that faith. Clearly written with
a deep love for humanity, and with humility and appreciation to
boot, this triumph of positivity takes you across latitudes, aiming
to answer the fundamental question: who are we and what is our
role in it all?'

www.NomadMania.com – Directory and hub for the world's
most widely-travelled people

'Michael Richards has travelled widely and thoughtfully,
accumulating not only miles but insights. *The Travelling Ape* is a
heartfelt, illuminating, and frequently humorous examination of
the human passion to see and understand the world.'

Thomas Swick, author of *The Joys of Travel: and Stories That
Illuminate Them*. Contributor for *The New York Times Book
Review*, *National Geographic Traveller*, and *Smithsonian Magazine*

'Michael Richards has lovingly explored our planet like few
others. His fun, inspiring (and sometimes alarming) adventures
will persuade you that the urge to travel is in our DNA.'

Charles Wheelan, author of *We Came, We Saw, We Left*
and *The Centrist Manifesto*. Contributor for *The Wall Street Journal*
and *The New York Times*

'A wicked read by a restless globetrotter who manages to combine
his own exciting experiences with in-depth info and thought-
provoking commentary. This book will inspire any traveller to
hit the road.'

Gunnar Garfors, author of *198: How I Ran out of Countries* and
Elsewhere: A Journey to the World's Least-Visited Countries. TEDx
speaker, first person to visit every country in the world twice

'At once a bible for us dromomaniacs and a persuasive polemic for why you should become one, Michael Richards's impassioned travelogue is an inspired antidote to the petty nationalism that divides us. This witty and highly readable Travelling Ape paves a much-needed way forward toward a cosmopolitan interconnectivity – without which, we're surely all doomed.'

Travis Jeppesen, author of *See You Again in Pyongyang*. Contributor for *The New York Times* and *The Wall Street Journal*

'Written with humour, optimism, and light-hearted introspection, *The Travelling Ape* takes readers on a journey through the joys and challenges of travel itself. It's a broadly upbeat look at the world that reminds readers that – although global society is not without its challenges – most people are kind, curious, and good. *The Travelling Ape* is a compelling travelogue that reminds us we've got more in common than we think.'

Kim Dinan, author of *The Yellow Envelope: One Gift, Three Rules, and a Life-Changing Journey Around the World*, contributor for *Backpacker Magazine*

'A journey across the globe and the mind. Mike weaves in politics, economics, and philosophy alongside rich anecdotes drawn from visits to over 150 countries. Mike makes you think about your travels, and inspires you to roam further. A travel book like no other.'

Matt Walker, author *Europe United: 1 Football Fan. 1 Crazy Season. 55 UEFA Nations*, contributor for *The Guardian*

'It is so reassuring and refreshing to discover that a world traveller, so much younger than me, has made the same central discoveries about our Larger Home: The world is better than you think; most people are kind, helpful, hospitable; we are all world-citizens who have more things in common than differences. Mike has been to over 155 countries, which in itself is a great achievement for his age. From Saudi Arabia to Japan, from Myanmar to Ethiopia, his adventures, observations, and studies are documented in this admirable book that oozes love for travel, cultures, the human race, and most importantly learning.'

Nicos Hadjicostis, author of *Destination Earth: A New Philosophy of Travel*, included in *Business Insider*'s '18 Travel Books to Feed Your Wanderlust'. *Huffington Post* contributor

'*The Travelling Ape* goes way beyond your typical 'travel hack' books. It brilliantly shows us the transformative power of travel, while intriguingly connecting geopolitics and personal growth. Mike's storytelling is both amusing and thought-provoking, making the book an absolute delight for any wanderer seeking the true essence of their travel journeys.'

Freeman Fung, Global citizenship and TEDx speaker, and best-selling author of *Travel to Transform: Awaken the Global Citizen in You and Thrive in the Modern World*

'A truly engaging book, told with great humour. It gives a great understanding of what it's really like to travel to off-the-beaten-track destinations, as well as giving fascinating insights into geopolitics, the deeper meaning of travel, and much more.'

Lupine Travel, experts of off-the-beaten-track travel

'This book is both a joy and a tonic for anyone who has ever wondered about the value, or otherwise, of travel. Michael Richards, the self-styled 'Travelling Ape', has visited over 150 countries, and his relentless positivity and curiosity about the world shines through on every page. His introspective travel memoir brims with humanity and happiness – a good thing, these days – and the writing zips along with humour and honesty. It's a great read, I loved it.'

Jules Brown, author of *The Born to Travel Collection: Tales From a Travel Writer's Life* and *Rough Guides* contributor

'Trapeze around the world through amusing and thought-inducing stories bound to tickle your lust for travel. The author leaves the reader with a refreshing and positive outlook on our shared humanity.'

Bhavana Gesota, author of *The Art of Slow Travel: See the World and Savor the Journey On a Budget*

'An important reminder to get out there and experience the world while you still can... A must-read for everyone who's ever felt that unquenchable thirst to see the world up close and unfiltered... A fun and insightful romp around the globe!'

Christopher K. Oldfield, author of *The Dogs of Nam: Stories from the Road and Lessons Learned Abroad*

'An engaging cocktail of anecdote, opinion, self-deprecating humour, and refreshing optimism. I found it an unusual and thought-provoking read.'

Mick Webb, co-host of the *You Should Have Been There* podcast alongside Simon Calder

'Michael's passion for adventure and desire to experience other cultures really comes through in his writing. If I had my way, *The Travelling Ape* would be required reading in all secondary school and university geography and world history classes. It kindles a passion for learning about other places and will make the reader want to take a trip around the world.'

Greg Ellifritz, author of *Choose Adventure: Safe Travel in Dangerous Places*

A NOTE ON THE AUTHOR

MICHAEL MACKAY RICHARDS is a global economic and political research analyst from London, UK. Prior to this, he completed undergraduate and postgraduate degrees in Politics and International Relations from the University of Bristol in England. His passion for global affairs extends to travel. He's visited 155 out of the world's 195 countries according to the United Nations (UN) definition, documenting his travels and views on his website:

www.thetravellingape.com

Michael is also a certified meditation instructor with the British School of Meditation, with a few thousand hours of meditation practice and several silent meditation retreats under his belt. He also wrote this blurb about himself in the third person.

Michael Mackay Richards

the
Travelling
Ape

What Travelling (Nearly) Everywhere Taught Me about Humanity, Geopolitics, and Happiness

FUZZY
FLAMINGO

First published in 2023 by Fuzzy Flamingo
Copyright © Michael Mackay Richards 2023

Michael Mackay Richards has asserted his right to be identified as the author of this Work in accordance with the Copyright, Designs and Patents Act 1988.

ISBN: 978-1-7393669-5-7

Editing and design by Fuzzy Flamingo
www.fuzzyflamingo.co.uk

A catalogue for this book is available from the British Library.

For Mum and Dad.

Without your support, I'd never have had the courage to pursue my dream of a life filled with travel. I can only now, with a child of my own, fully appreciate how much you must have worried about me when I was holidaying in failed states or war zones. So for this, I say sorry. And also thank you, for all that you've done for me.

DISCLAIMER

The views expressed within this book are the author's alone. They don't necessarily reflect the views of any organisation or individual mentioned in the text. While the book's content is meant to be informative and thought-provoking – so much so that you might be tempted to believe literally everything inside it – readers should form their own judgements based on their own research. The author doesn't guarantee the accuracy or completeness of all of the information contained in the book, and notes that any mistakes within the text are solely his own.

The author takes no responsibility for any damages arising from reading the book, including but not limited to, paper cuts, feelings of wanderlust, or choosing Iraq as your next holiday destination. You've been warned.

Contents

Introduction

It was early, but already stiflingly hot. I'd arrived late the night before and, still groggy, wasn't ready for the early-morning assault on my senses that I was about to experience. The streets were chaotic. Full of cars, people, and *bajas* (local tuk tuks). The city echoed with the sounds of honking horns. Not quite ready to submit ourselves to the maelstrom of the morning rush hour, my friend Alex and I decided that food and coffee were a good idea.

We ducked into a dark little coffee shop. Its wooden panels and dim lighting didn't fill us with too much hope. But this was Ethiopia – its capital Addis Ababa, to be precise. Coffee production here dated back centuries. This is where arabica coffee originates. So perhaps appearances could be deceiving. The coffees arrived, thick and black. They tasted wonderful. Not only because of their rich and sweet flavours, but also because of their alluring scent. Coffee in Ethiopia is like rocket fuel. It felt like the caffeine was actively widening my eyes and pulling me out of my lethargic state.

Before we left, a waiter plonked a strange-looking flatbread in front of us. That we hadn't asked for. Filled with hundreds of tiny holes, its surface looked like a cross-section of a beehive, with a smooth, beige underside. Piled in the middle was a large clump of rich red lentils, which as we'd discover shortly, was at the absolute limit of tolerable spice.

'This is *injera* bread and *messer wot*. It's the local delicacy, you have to try it!' the waiter told us. We gobbled it down. The *injera* bread had a bitter kind of aftertaste, and was denser than the traditional loafs I was used to back home in England. But it was delicious, a sign of how we'd eat in Ethiopia over the next few weeks. Although we'd end up living off the stuff for the rest of our trip, we learnt that mixing spice and caffeine so early in the morning was potentially unwise, and something our digestive systems didn't altogether agree with.

Feeling refreshed – or wired, more accurately – we hailed a *baja*. We hopped in the back. The rusty little cabin was painted a rich blue and dotted with delicate ornaments. The dashboard was covered in stickers, many emblazoned with the Ethiopian horizontal tri-colour flag of green, gold, and red.

After we'd settled in, the *baja* driver smiled and looked back at us.

'How are you guys doing? What are your names?' he said, in good English.

'Mike and Alex,' I replied, my voice only just audible above the rattling engine and hectic streetscape.

'Oh cool, my name is Alex too.'

Whether or not this was something the *baja* driver did with all tourists, we'll never know. But in any case, 'Alex Two' seemed friendly. In fact, he seemed unable to stop chatting to us. As we weaved through the crowed roads

Introduction

of Addis, with the smell of diesel in our nostrils, he spent more time looking at us than the road. If this wasn't disconcerting enough, he was more than happy to drive as fast as possible too. He regularly veered into lanes with oncoming traffic, darting between cars, escaping collisions by mere inches. And we couldn't help noticing that his eyes were bloodshot, his pupils as big as dinner plates.

'Are you guys okay? Having a good time?' he kept asking us. In fact, he repeated this phrase so many times that I wondered whether he was really asking himself this question, given his slightly erratic state.

In between swerving and swaying, we noticed that he was munching ravenously on a bag of leaves, something I wasn't used to seeing, it has to be said. Noticing our confused faces, he said, 'Ah, this is *chat*. You guys want some?' I'd read that *chat* is a common legal stimulant, and people use it all over Ethiopia.

We didn't want to seem rude. And I felt pretty sure that accepting drugs from strangers was actively encouraged by mothers worldwide (right?). Plus, I figured I may as well enjoy the final moments of my life before we crashed and died, so we duly obliged. The leaves tasted bitter and starchy. Eating them required copious amounts of water to make them in any way palatable, and Alex Two said we'd need to eat a whole pack before it did anything.

But after quite a bit of munching, we eventually understood where our driver's misplaced confidence on the road came from. We felt wired and alert, even more so than after our earlier strong coffee. And fittingly, very chatty indeed. For the remainder of our frenzied journey through the streets of Addis, we happily nattered away, barely noticing the latest near miss.

Addis is a pulsating place. As we traversed the city's loud and busy streets in the *baja*, the faint outline of the Ethiopian Highlands was only just perceptible through the city's hazy and polluted skies. Low-rise structures appeared to have been hastily constructed using concrete or sheet metal, while the skyline was peppered with a slew of striking new skyscrapers. A sign of the city's – Africa's fourth largest, and the continent's administrative capital – growing influence and confidence.

Eventually, we reached our destination. We bade Alex Two farewell. He zoomed off into the distance, about to submit some other clueless tourists to one of the most intense experiences of their lives. The building we'd been dropped outside didn't look like much. Another concrete box. The only thing which signified that this place was located in Ethiopia was the beautiful Ge'ez script adorning the entrance of it, a local form of writing that rejects the Latin alphabet and has its roots in Egyptian hieroglyphics. Still swinging between euphoria and feelings of fairly substantial anxiety – my heart was beating much faster than I'd ideally have liked, due to the caffeine and *chat* – we stepped into the unremarkable-looking structure. Which upon entry, revealed itself to be no less drab.

The corridors were dark and dank. The whole building was dilapidated, a '60s relic which had presumably seen better days. Though its brutalist architecture might not have even looked good when it was completed decades ago. Nonetheless, I ventured further inside. There was

Introduction

only one reason why I was there in the first place. To meet a relative.

After further minutes spent getting lost in the maze of corridors and mouldy-smelling rooms, she came into view.

'Is she supposed to be this small?' I said to Alex. And then, 'To be fair, she actually looks pretty good for her age. She doesn't look a day older than 3.2 million years.'

'Did you think of that one on the journey over here?' Alex said.

'Maybe, but you get my point.'

I was in the crumbling National Museum of Ethiopia. In front of me was the skeleton of 'Lucy', one of the oldest surviving fossils we have of Australopithecines. These tiny apes – just three feet tall* – were actually early humans. At the time of discovery in 1972, Lucy was the oldest found potential ancestor for every known hominin species.

As I stood looking at her miniature skeleton, thoughts whirled around my head: 'This is where we all came from. She looks so fragile, so small. So insignificant. How far we've come.' I then read that Lucy died falling out of a tree. 'So she must have been pretty damn clumsy.' After mentally mocking Lucy's clearly sub-human coordination capabilities, I took my phone out of my pocket to get a picture. But proceeded to ungracefully drop it and crack the screen. If Australopithecines knew karma, I'm sure Lucy was (rightly) laughing at me right there and then.

It had been quite a journey for me to get to Africa and stand in Ethiopia. But for Lucy and her chums, it took a

---

★ As a Briton I'm compelled by nature to use imperial measurements.

few more million years to get on their feet here. Evolving bigger brains and bigger bodies. Becoming more and more human. And then deciding to travel. *Homo sapiens* left Africa around 60,000 years ago. By 50,000 years ago, they'd spread across Asia and reached Australia. By 40,000 years ago, they'd reached Europe. And finally, by 15,000 years ago, humans had crossed the Bering Strait and populated the Americas. A truly epic journey.

A couple of thousand generations after humans first left Africa, there I was. Standing in Ethiopia with a friend. Fumbling with a bit of space-age technology. Internally moaning that my 'legs were tired.' And disappointed that the museum coffee shop was closed, with the effects of the *chat* wearing off and lethargy starting to creep in once again.

We trudged out of the quiet museum and back into the buzzing streets, hopping into a (real) taxi this time. As the cab moved off, I reflected to Alex that, like our ancient ancestors, perhaps travel was also in my DNA. After all, I'd been all over the world. Ethiopia was the 140th country I'd visited at the time. But unlike my prehistoric relatives, I'd been able to travel across Africa, Asia, Australasia, Europe, and the Americas in just the 30 years I'd been alive at the time. 'Roughly 44,970 years quicker than our ancestors,' I smugly boasted to myself while struggling with the maths.

Like Lucy and her descendants, I too was a travelling ape. A bewildered primate, stuck on a large rock, hurtling through the endless vastness of the universe. But how different was I to these earlier iterations? Perhaps in our ancestors' case, their desire to explore reflected a simple

Introduction

need to find resources and increase their chances of survival. For me, my desire to explore started from less admirable beginnings.

Initially, my passion for travel was based on an interest in drinking lots of beer on beautiful beaches with my friends. But as the trips and countries started racking up, something changed. My travels became less about fun and more about learning. I wasn't sure quite why, but I felt like I *had* to experience everything this small planet located in one of the spiral arms of the Milky Way galaxy, had to offer. I was keenly aware that I only had one chance to explore this particular rock. And I felt compelled not to waste it. So I vowed to see as much of the world as I possibly could. And in this respect, I've had a decent crack at it over the past 15 years or so. I've been to 155 countries. Roughly 80 percent of the total.

In fact, I've actually seen more of the world than almost anyone in history. A back-of-the-envelope calculation suggests I've spent over five years of my life abroad and travelling in some form or another. I'm one of around just 400 people to have visited more than 150 countries according to *NomadMania's* UN travel ranking.[1] And all of these people have done it since the dawn of aviation (obviously). This puts me in roughly the best-travelled 0.0000000001 percent of humans who have ever lived. Hopefully, these statistics alone give credence to the haughty claim made at the start of this paragraph, which might have appeared to stink of hyperbole.

As months spent on the road turned into years, the things I held to be true about the world started to collapse under closer scrutiny. My world view frayed at its seams. Having spent my career writing as an economic, political, and country risk analyst, I thought I knew a decent amount about our planet. But I kept noticing how things on the ground were often quite different to what I was reading or writing about at work. Nothing compares to direct experience, I realised. Travelling was changing my understanding of so many things. And changing me as a person as well. Not only were my travels rich, rewarding, and highly enjoyable, but I noticed that seeing so much of the world – for myself – was giving me profound insights into the nature of humanity, geopolitics, and happiness.

This book is my attempt to share these insights with you. One insignificant ape's humble effort to come to terms with the world and his position in it. My hope is that in reading this book, you'll be left wanting to pack your bags and explore. You'll learn some neat stuff about this planet, and in doing so, become more curious about it. You'll hear stories and anecdotes from some lesser known, 'off-piste' travel destinations. You'll laugh (with me sometimes, at me mainly). And most importantly, you'll be left feeling positive that our home – this rock – is a truly remarkable place filled with a mostly good species of primate.

The book has four main sections. The first looks at what my experiences across the world have taught me about the concept of travel itself. It examines why we enjoy it and why it's so important. The second looks at what lessons travelling holds about humanity. How good is the modern world that we've created, and is it really in as bad a place as some seem to think? The third section examines what

Introduction

I've learnt about geopolitics and international relations as I've criss-crossed the globe, being exposed to some of the biggest challenges the world faces. The final section looks at how travel has transformed my understanding of happiness. For me personally, as well as revealing why our collective happiness perhaps hasn't improved as much as our circumstances have.

Before we get going, it's also right that I offer you a few caveats. My story isn't an 'against all odds' triumph. That I was able to visit so much of the world reflects many things entirely out of my control. I'm a straight, white man. I was raised in a nice part of South-West London. I got sent to good schools. My parents loved me. While my head is huge,* the brain within it functions okay. I was born in a Western, democratic, and industrialised nation, giving me a passport that makes it easy to visit almost anywhere. I'm able bodied. I get paid in a currency which is strong and makes travel cheap. I can do my job remotely on my laptop from anywhere. The list goes on.

This book should've really been called *Privileged Western Man Uses Fortunate Life Circumstances to Gallivant around the World, Then Writes Preachy Book about the Experience.*** While that's sort of a joke, it was too close to the bone to use. Plus, it would've deprived you of the Travelling Ape branding, which by now you're enjoying thoroughly

---

* Friends' nicknames for me include 'skip head', 'boulder head', and 'fat head'. All of which I assume are (somehow) affectionate.

** I was tempted to use the even more literal *Ink on Finely Sliced Bits of Tree about the Big Rock We All Live On*. But I figured it might have been a little harder to market.

The Travelling Ape

(an ape travelling around the world in a plane is a funny concept, okay?). I know I've been incredibly fortunate. And this book is my attempt to give something back.

This book has limitations. Some names have been changed to protect people's identities, lest they suffer the trauma of having to be associated with me in print for eternity. Other names have been changed because I met so many people travelling that I've simply forgotten some of them. With such a broad scope and so few pages, there are many things I've left out that I would've liked to talk about. This doesn't mean I don't care about them. It's just that it would have been hard to write a book about *literally* everything in the world.

On top of this, to cover such a wide array of issues I'll make some generalisations which some of you might disagree with. So it's worth reminding you here that the opinions held within this book are subjective. Everything I say is up for debate. Obviously. This book doesn't hold within it all of the objective truths of the universe.* Just my views on the world, which have been informed by extensive exploration. So if you disagree with them, that's totally fine.

I'll just try to be true to what I feel and what I've seen. Suffice it to say, being able to see so much of the world has been one of the true privileges of my life. I feel fortunate that our ancestors weren't all as clumsy as Lucy, and managed to leave Africa to settle across the world. And as a result, this modern-day Travelling Ape has had the chance

---

* I'll leave that for my next book.

Introduction

to explore the world in his one, fleeting lifetime. I'll do my best to share what I've learnt on my travels with you in the coming pages, and promise not to grandiosely refer to myself in the third person again.

Let's go.

PART I

Travel:
Expand Your Horizons and Your Mind

1

Why Do We Travel?

Travelling is a strange pastime. What's so alluring about packing your bags and then traipsing around the world?

I stepped onto the tarmac. My stomach was churning. It was a grey, humid day, the air thick in the lungs. Palm trees flanked the shabby-looking runway, filled with potholes. My sense of foreboding only increased when our pilot – who was (somewhat unusually) walking us to the plane – pointed out what was soon to catapult us into the air. A tiny, bright yellow plane was parked up in front of me. It had a minuscule propeller and miniature doors, and barely looked big enough to fit an adult. It looked like a toy plane, something I would've found funny if I hadn't spent good money trusting my life with it. And if the pilot hadn't looked about 10 years old.

'The technology used to design this plane hasn't really changed since World War II,' the young boy told us cheerily in a French accent. There wasn't even a hint of facial hair on his youthful and cherubic face. He looked like a child who had dressed up as a pilot for Halloween.

The Travelling Ape

'How long have you been flying?' I asked as nonchalantly as I possibly could. Ever keen to impress strangers for some reason (as we all are), I wanted to maintain an illusion of calm in front of the four other passengers, despite the possibility that we would all soon be resting peacefully at the bottom of the Pacific Ocean.

'I qualified last week in New Zealand. Many Europeans get their pilot licence over there. This route in Vanuatu is often given to pilots like me who've just got their wings.'

'Oh, that's really, er, cool,' were the words I heard coming out of my mouth. I started mentally saying goodbye to my family and friends.

I clambered into the tiny cabin and buckled the seat belt really tight, as if this would do anything if we plunged into the water at hundreds of miles an hour. The engines fired up. The whole plane vibrated and rattled furiously. And we started to charge down the runway, with the plane twitching and wobbling as it went. Soon enough, we were airborne. Soaring high above the crystal clear waters of Efate, the main island of Vanuatu, leaving behind its white-sand beaches and tropical rainforests. Before long, we could see nothing but the dark blue hues of the Pacific. We occasionally banked to avoid the odd cloud or two sitting ominously in the skies.

I'm not sure whether it was comforting or not. But there was a novelty in sitting directly behind the pilot. There certainly wasn't a door separating us, and I could see exactly what he was doing. It was demystifying to observe how he was actually flying the plane. That, and I was keeping an eye on his piloting, as if my misspent youth playing *Flight Simulator* would help in any way if something went wrong. But nothing did, fortunately. And as the time passed, I felt more relaxed.

After about an hour, a veritable eternity in some ways, another island became visible on the horizon. Remote Tanna. Squinting, I could just about make out its vertiginous hills, green with dense rainforest. Its empty, picture-postcard beaches. And then, what I'd flown all the way to this remote Pacific Island to see, Mount Yasur. One of the longest continually erupting volcanoes in the world.

We got closer and closer. The lush rainforests gave way to grey, charred earth, devoid of any vegetation. And the sky became filled with thick smoke. It was at this point that a thought popped into my head, which I matter-of-factly raised with the pilot.

'Weren't all flights in Europe cancelled for a few days when a volcano erupted in Iceland, due to fears over how the volcanic ash would affect the planes?'

'Yeah. Crazy, right?' he said unhelpfully, as we made a beeline for the volcano's crater.

'Perhaps the laws of physics don't apply in Vanuatu?' I optimistically thought to myself.

We got closer to the crater, until it felt like we were right on top of it. We circled around a few times, the plane banking sharply. This gave us a direct view right down into the belly of the beast. It was an exhilarating experience. Seeing the ash clouds billowing into the sky and the sheer power of nature, I felt truly alive. Nothing else seemed to matter, only the present moment. That said, I also felt glad and grateful when we landed safely about five minutes later.

The Travelling Ape

The airstrip here was nothing more than a thin ribbon of dirt, cut out of the forest in the shape of a ruler. There was no discernible terminal building and certainly no control tower. The plane was directed to its parking space by a man wearing flip-flops and a vest top, with bracelets on both of his arms. Remembering that this was Vanuatu and not a Full Moon Party in Thailand, I reasoned he was employed by the airport and probably wasn't a lost backpacker, despite appearances.

I cheerfully said goodbye to the child who'd successfully flown us here. He said, 'See you guys on the return flight in a couple of days.' Oh dear. A driver picked us up, we dropped our bags at the hotel, and headed straight for the volcano. This wasn't easy. There were no tarmacked roads in Tanna, just black and muddy tracks which snaked through the rainforest. We spent much of the trip sliding sideways, or having to reverse out of muddy puddles.

Our driver told us about the island. It had just 12,000 inhabitants and was served only by a few propeller flights a week. It was cut off from the rest of Vanuatu, let alone the rest of the world, he explained. He also said that, despite its size, 12 languages were spoken here, and for this reason, he couldn't communicate with more than 90 percent of the people on the island. Locals here lived subsistence-based lives, governed by village chiefs in small collectives.

Driving through a few villages, he didn't appear to be wrong. It felt like I'd been transported back into a different epoch. Bar a few things – the presence of a motorbike or two – it felt like nothing had changed here for centuries. Basic, single-storey structures made out of straw were embedded in clearings in the suffocatingly thick jungle. Locals wore colourful clothing, while younger kids tended not to wear anything at all. Some, but not all, of the villagers wore traditional reed dresses. The villages we passed were all bustling with activity.

Smiling faces greeted us wherever we went. People waved and children screamed as we passed them. Optimism and friendliness had greeted me throughout my trip to Vanuatu, and this only seemed to increase the further away we headed from the rest of the modern world in Tanna. Our driver told us that in parts of the island people believe in the divinity of the late Queen Elizabeth's deceased husband Prince Phillip. Two villages believed him to be a descendant of a powerful spirit, a feeling that was only strengthened when he visited Tanna in 1974.[1] Although I couldn't guarantee I'd be viewed with quite the same degree of reverence after my visit, I still felt deeply privileged to be experiencing life in such a remote and special part of the world.

Modern Explorers: An Easy Ride

Indeed, I was keenly aware that the human ability to travel the world has only existed for an infinitesimally small amount of time in the context of human history. To be sure, there were some early precursors of travel as we know it. Two millennia ago, the wealthy elite of the Roman Empire enjoyed escaping the capital, pursuing pleasure at their holiday villas in the Bay of Naples.[2] But where I was now,

The Travelling Ape

Vanuatu, didn't see a European until 1606. It took months for Portuguese explorer Pedro Fernandes de Queirós to get here,[3] losing many of his crew to scurvy on the way. One of the first Britons to arrive in Vanuatu was Reverend John Williams. He confidently strode ashore in 1888, and was promptly eaten.[4]

While explorers once faced horrendous conditions on board and death by scurvy, shipwreck, or worse, I was able to get here in less than a day. In an airborne metal tube.

We cannot fathom how much air travel has revolutionised the way we perceive the world. So much so that as I stood in Vanuatu, I realised that I had probably seen more of the world than legendary explorers Vasco da Gama, Marco Polo, Christopher Columbus, and Captain James Cook. Combined. I'm not trying to boast. This is just a fact. My scratch map of the world would trounce their scratch maps. Who cares that they helped draw those maps in the first place? (Presumably lots of you, but there we go.)

For most of human history – and indeed still for billions today – people lived, worked, and died without ever straying far from the place they were born. Like some of the more remote residents of Tanna, you were unlikely to meet or have much knowledge of anyone not in your clan. The rest of the world was an impossibly vast, uncharted mystery. Many of the explorers whose names we know today were the true daredevils of their era, leaving familiar, safe(ish) homes just to see what was out there.

Stunningly, today, the world can be circumnavigated by anyone who can afford a plane ticket in around 24 hours.

Why Do We Travel?

Cumulatively, I've done this several times in my lifetime. I've often tried to convince myself that, in many ways, being on a plane for ages is the purest form of travelling that exists. Indeed, the *Cambridge Dictionary* defines travelling as: '1. The activity of making journeys. 2. Moving from one place to another.'

I often try to imagine myself as some sort of Marco Polo of the skies, intrepidly navigating the atmosphere on an epic quest through the open blue. But sadly, the reality of long-haul flights is hard to ignore. I sit on my arse for an exceedingly long while, watch lots of terrible films, which all usually feature Dwayne 'The Rock' Johnson for some reason, and get covered in crumbs from various meals I fail to eat graciously. Not quite buccaneering on the high seas.

Travelling is now ubiquitous. It's seen as a rite of passage for privileged Westerners (like this writer).* Prior to the pandemic, there were around 45 million backpacker trips taken worldwide each year according to the WYSE Travel Confederation.[5] The proportion of backpackers aged over 30 hovered at just 10 percent.[6] It's no wonder that my 19-year-old self enjoyed judging 'the weird 30-year-old guy' staying at the hostel. There was usually at least one. And I always pitied their failure to grow up. Willing cognitive dissonance means that I've since written an entire book on why backpacking aged over 30 is the ultimate sign of a life profoundly well lived.

---

* When I travelled around Thailand aged 19, there was at times more likelihood of me bumping into someone from a rival Surrey school than an actual Thai person.

The Travelling Ape

A Brush with Earth's Majesty

But still. I'd made it to Tanna in a propeller plane that was a bit sketchy. This was surely up there with the exploits of the best historical explorers, at least in my head. After a few more hours in our 4x4, the rainforest eventually started to clear. The greenery quickly transformed into a desolate landscape. It looked like the surface of another planet. A black desert, overshadowed by the menacing presence of Mount Yasur, far in the distance.

We ploughed onwards and, as we did, it started to rain. Or did it? What looked like grey snowflakes flittered slowly down to the ground. They settled gently on the windshield, before the wipers smeared grey dust all over the glass. 'Volcanic ash,' our driver said. We drove on, about halfway up the volcano. Our car parked, and we began the short hike to the summit. It wasn't easy. My feet sank deep into grey sand. The volcanic fumes temporarily transported me back to Beijing and Karachi, two of the most oppressively polluted cities I'd ever visited.

Even though I'd seen Mount Yasur from the air, I wasn't quite ready for what greeted me on its rim. The noise was deafening. Explosion after explosion rattled my eardrums to the point of pain. It was like being surrounded by searing cracks of thunder. There was also the metronomic thud of rocks as they thumped into the charred, black earth beside me. Some were too close for comfort. All I'd been given by my guide to 'keep safe' was a yellow hard hat and flimsy plastic safety goggles. I felt they might not be a match for the giant lumps of magma which were being flung high up into the sky, and then falling violently back to Earth again. I peered down into the hell-like crater below, where bright orange lava gurgled and spat angrily.

I was scared. And yet I couldn't help but be spellbound by the majesty of what I was witnessing. Here I was in Vanuatu, a tiny country in the Pacific Islands that's mostly famous for being one of the countries people can't name in pub quizzes. I was standing atop a volcano which had been erupting for thousands of years. In most places in the world, health and safety rules wouldn't allow you to do this.

I stood there, transfixed. My inability to take my eyes off the unfolding chaos down to a combination of awe at seeing one of the world's true wonders, and the desire not to get squished by a flying lump of magma. The unsurpassable might of nature was too much to take in. It had flattened me (less dramatically than a massive rock would have, I concede). In moments like these, my senses appeared to be turned up. Colours, sights, and sounds seemed more 'real', more vibrant. And as I took in the strange circumstances of my current surroundings, I felt time slow down as my mind ached to capture every fine detail of the spellbinding scene.

In between feeling like I was communing with nature and also thinking I was definitely about to die, I had a realisation: until recently, I knew little about Vanuatu. I hadn't even heard of Mount Yasur, and that ignorance astonished me. 'Just how many other hidden gems are out there?' I wondered. 'My God, this is what travel is all about. This is why its's so special. Christ, that one was really close.'

The Travelling Ape

Back at the hotel a few hours later, I sat peacefully in my basic wooden hut, looking out at the ocean. The waves gently lapped against the shore, giving me what I now knew to be an unrealistically tranquil view of the natural world. Having seen the volcano, I was finding it hard to forget about the reality of the predicament of life on Earth. Wherever you are in the world, there lurks beneath you boiling and violent magma. And this truth becomes only too evident when you visit places like Tanna, where the hellish underbelly of our planet is so clearly doing its best to explode out into the human world.

My experience at the volcano was so enthralling, so memorable. It made me feel fortunate for all my travels. At the time, Vanuatu was country number 89. Each of these countries, each trip I'd taken, was another lesson in why I loved travel so much. After all, there's truly nothing that compares to the feeling of arriving in a new place. You've read the *Lonely Planet*, planned an itinerary, and seen pictures. But the sensory experience of touching down in a new, different, and foreign land, it's truly gripping. The beguiling smells, the alien-sounding language, the brightness of the colours. It's as if life itself becomes more vivid. For a short time, I'm captivated by the present moment. Completely immersed in the unfamiliarity of my surroundings. You become one with nature, and nature one with you…

Okay, okay. I'm not going to go full hippie here. Put simply, spending time in different cultures and unfamiliar surroundings can effect mental change. And as I sat in the middle of the Pacific Ocean – a world away from 'normal' life and the everyday – this, I thought, might be why I and so many others feel compelled to do it.

The Science of Travel

The feeling I got on top of Mount Yasur, that travel 'turns up' conscious experience, is actually backed up by science. Neural pathways are influenced by our environment and routines. New sounds, tastes, sensations, sights, and smells spark different synapses in the brain.[7] To some extent, things seem more vibrant when you're travelling because *they are more vibrant.* Your brain considers new information to be important, so it begins to pay more attention to what's happening around you. And this gives life the fresh feeling that I – and so many others – get when they travel.

Travelling also has an impact on how we perceive time. Our brain encodes new experiences, but not familiar ones, into memory.[8] This means that our retrospective perception of time is partially based on how many new memories we create over a certain period. By engaging in new and novel experiences, like travel, you can in theory slow down the perception of time passing.

Does this resonate with you? It made perfect sense to me, as I sat watching the waves lap against the shore in Tanna, sipping on a bad coffee, and writing in my journal. I'd been on the road for around 12 months at this stage, having previously had a stable life for about five years in London. During those years, I'd worked in the same job in the same office. I'd lived in the same apartment, hung around in the same social group, and spent lots of time at the same bars and restaurants. Those five years are a blur.

As a result of this stasis, I decided I needed a big change at 27, to make more memories and to slow down my life. I told people I was leaving full-time employment to travel. Eyebrows were raised. Curious statements about 'the future', 'settling down', and 'running away from responsibility' were common. When I told my boss of the plan, she offered me a promotion to tempt me to stay. It was to the role of global analyst. I'd not expected to reach this position for a decade or so. It made the decision harder.

I sat motionless in her office, a short while after the job was offered to me. But then, I roused myself, chuckled and walked to the door. Turning around with a wry smile, I said, 'I'm sorry, I'll have to turn down the role… I've got some of my own *global analysis* to do.' With that, I strode out of the room. A colleague told me that I had the swagger of a man who was clearly about to go travelling. As I reached the exit, several members of the team were in tears. A slow clap started as I walked out the office door, never to return.

Unfortunately, none of that actually happened. I thought of the laboured 'global analysis' quip while writing this book, years later. In reality, I asked my boss if I could think about it for a few days. Days that were mostly spent feeling anxious, constantly questioning my decision, and calling my mum a lot. But in the end, I held strong. And thanks to technology, I'd still be able to work remotely as a freelancer while I explored the world. Ideal.

Since leaving London to work remotely and to visit as

many countries as humanly possible, things completely changed. By the time I was in Vanuatu, memories of the past year on the road felt longer than the preceding half decade in London. I could still track what I did on an almost daily basis during my travels, working out which new country or city I was in, and deducing my day-to-day activities from this. So travel, it seems, is a way to build stronger memories. And, in some ways, to slow time down itself. Do my trips therefore make me some sort of time-bending alchemist? I'll leave you to decide.

My Name Is Michael and I'm a Dromomaniac

A rush of dopamine accompanies fresh experiences.[9] Put simply, novelty makes us feel happy,* and travelling throws up plenty of novelties. Indeed, there are few things on Earth as novel as visiting a new and unexplored land. Perhaps, then, my love of travel is simply an addiction to dopamine? Had I been blindly charging around the world, looking for my brain's next hit?

Well, if my compulsion to travel is an addiction, I'll take it. There's even a name for it, 'dromomania', which is usually defined as 'an exaggerated desire to wander'.[10] It's a registered medical condition. And an affliction that legendary British comic and traveller Michael Palin says

---

* Not all the time, obviously. The novelty of losing your job for the first time, or falling down a flight of stairs, is unlikely to engender a sense of underlying peace.

he suffers from.[11] It's probably better than being addicted to crack, even if a travel addiction might actually be more expensive.

For me, the addiction began in earnest in my early twenties. A friend showed me a 'scratch map' app.[12] I realised I'd been to a third of the countries in the world already, sort of by accident. I'd backpacked through Southeast Asia, South America, Europe, and India. I'd driven across the US, from New York to San Francisco. (If you're imagining me hitting the open road in a drop-top Ford Mustang, you'd almost be right. My friends and I cruised across the States in a dilapidated, beige, Mazda people carrier, which we felt had its own kind of appeal.)

Once I'd seen the scratch map, the damage was done. Having got so far, I felt I may as well keep going. What better way to understand the world than to encounter it first-hand? To visit the vast array of nations and cultures the world has to offer for myself? It seemed like something I simply *had to do*, a true calling. And conveniently, it was a calling I felt I'd be able to boast about for the rest of my days (hence this book).

While I was travelling because of a compulsion I felt, other people I met had other reasons for doing so. By the time I was sitting in Vanuatu, I'd probably met thousands of different people in hostels and on my travels. Not all were dromomaniacs, but several key themes emerged:

- **Fun**: Most people who travel regularly suggest that it's the most enjoyable thing you can do as a human. I'd agree.

Why Do We Travel?

- **Escapism**: Many say there's nothing like getting away from the daily grind to new and exotic parts of the world.

- **Weather**: Not too surprisingly, people who live in cold and wet countries travel more regularly than most. Anyone who lives in a sun-starved country where vitamin D deficiencies are common can blame their footloose hunter-gatherer ancestors for leaving sunnier climes. (And have to go somewhere hot to correct that.)

- **Connection**: It's much easier to meet people while travelling. Walking into a hostel bar and striking up a conversation with strangers is actively encouraged. If I walked up to a stranger in London for a chat, they'd think there was something wrong with me. Being able to connect with locals is also a big plus for many travellers.

- **Education**: You learn so much more about the world by seeing it, rather than being told about it at school or online. Travel truly broadens the mind.

There are doubtless many more reasons why we travel. But these are the five that came up again and again on my trips. And combining these factors together, travel can permeate into improved health and greater overall satisfaction with one's life.[13] If travel were a pill, doctors would surely prescribe it to everyone. But alas, I don't expect medical professionals to start prescribing trips to erupting volcanoes anytime soon.

The Travelling Ape

Back on the Road: The Other Side of Travel

As the next few days would show me, however, travel isn't always fun. Or enjoyable, in the traditional sense. I packed my bags in Tanna, feelings of dread rising as I realised my life would soon once again be in the hands of a child, flying a plane built by a toy manufacturer. This time, the flight was much less eventful. As has been every flight I've ever taken since then, given their comparative lack of life-threatening, volcanic action.

We touched down in Port Vila, the tiny capital of Vanuatu. Compared to Tanna, however, Port Vila felt like a veritable metropolis. There were cars, bars, and a smattering of Australian tourists. A traffic-clogged main street, flanked by stalls and markets selling tourist 'tat' (as I and many others like to call it). Port Vila overlooks a picturesque cove, ringed by palm trees and pretty beaches. 'This,' I thought, 'is probably what people imagine when they think of the Pacific Islands.' Laid-back and paradisiacal, and a very pleasant place indeed to spend time. With an agreeable lack of visible tectonic action to boot.

I spent a few days eating too much food, lazing around on pretty beaches, and trying to forget what lay beneath me (and all of us, really). Much sooner than I'd have hoped, it was time to pack my things again, and head over to my next destination, Papua New Guinea. I wasn't exactly sure what to expect. Before my visit, I'd loosely imagined Papua New Guinea to be a forest-cloaked and rather magical place. A land of enchanted jungles. Of ancient and nomadic cultures, whose way of life hadn't changed for centuries. A place where the tentacles of Western civilisation had failed to reach into its impenetrable interior, and eating humans wasn't something consigned to horror movies.

The early signs were good. From the plane window, I saw mile upon mile of undulating rainforest, mist shrouding its canopy, the entire scene bursting with life. In my mind, I imagined myself to be Sir David Attenborough. In one of the clips of him from the 1950s when he was young and fit and a bit of a heartthrob, to be honest.[*] A true explorer, about to plunge into uncharted territory, armed only with a walking stick and shorts that were too small. But as the plane came into land in Port Moresby, the capital of Papua New Guinea, these preconceived ideas faded. Endless rows of corrugated iron roofs spread out beneath me. Roads were made of dirt in most places, with large open landfills occupying empty plots of land. The scene hummed with despair.

I clambered into the back of a taxi at the airport, feeling uneasy. My driver had just happily told me he wouldn't be stopping at traffic lights, to reduce the chance of 'carjacking'. He delivered this unsettling news in an airy tone. It was an unnerving start.

As we drove into town, I didn't feel any better. We passed acres of shanty towns. I can still vividly remember the putrid smell of burning plastic. There was litter everywhere. The streets were filled with men who looked sinister. Nowhere to

---

[*] Looking back at pictures, I can see that I had a shaved head and horrible, thick black beard at the time, and so most definitely failed on every single count to achieve Attenborough-ness.

be, and nothing to lose. Arriving at my hotel was only a slight relief. The level of security there made me in some ways feel even more nervous. It was surrounded by high walls, a barbed wire fence, and iron gates. The hotel had an expensive prison kind of vibe. Why was the security so extreme?

I was advised by the receptionist not to go out 'after sunset'. And also to avoid walking around the city 'in the daytime'. I pointed out this left precisely zero minutes in the day when leaving the hotel was advised. She paused thoughtfully for a second and then said, 'Yes, best not to leave the hotel if you can.' I was taken aback. Port Moresby had quite a posh-sounding name. Regal, even. And as for Papua New Guinea overall, I'd expected Edenic jungles and pristine beaches. I'd not expected a sense of dread.

In retrospect, perhaps I should have. A family friend who'd been told me that Port Moresby was without question the worst place he'd ever visited. 'Nah, he's probably just exaggerating,' I thought. 'I'm a hardcore traveller, he's probably just too soft.' I also knew Port Moresby had regularly been ranked as one of the least liveable cities in the world by the Economist Intelligence Unit (which I freelance for).[14] Its failure to develop economically pointed to some of the wider issues facing Papua New Guinea. The nation has few roads, challenging geography, and a widely dispersed population, which has made effective state-building difficult.[15] This has been made worse by corruption and the ongoing legacies of decades of colonial rule.

I connected to the wi-fi and was promptly able to read online that it's one of the most dangerous cities on Earth, racked especially by murders and violence against women.

Why Do We Travel?

As I bravely explored the city in the following days – sitting in the back of a taxi decked out like an armoured car – I felt there were few redeeming features about the place. Port Moresby seemed like a sad microcosm of many of the world's problems. Urban decay, violence, and fear hung in the air. While having this thought and being stuck in traffic, I sat and watched a carjacking unfold about three cars ahead. An armed man rapped on the window, and the terrified female driver darted out of the car with her hands up. The assailant hopped in the car, and sped off. No one on the street batted an eyelid.

'Yep. This is officially the worst place I've ever been,' I thought. And also, 'Wow, this is quite terrifying.' It was like I was trapped in one of those *World's Most Dangerous Places* TV shows. Port Moresby in fact provided the kind of doomsday image I'd see on rolling news about the world outside the West before I travelled.

Despite the carjacking, we persevered. I didn't think that sitting in my fortified hotel would teach me anything about this city or nation. And there were a few interesting things I got to see, which certainly involved less adrenalin than witnessing a crime. The Bomana War Cemetery is the final resting place of thousands of Australians who died in the South Pacific during World War II. I strolled around row upon row of identical white tombstones, surrounded by lush vegetation and the gentle rolling hills of outer Port Moresby. The Port Moresby Nature Park was also a highlight, full of local flora and native animals. But driving between these places I saw constant reminders of the troubles facing the city, and many others like it in the world.

The Travelling Ape

Later on that evening, I sat in the relative safety of my hotel. Unable to leave, and still in a state of mild shock following the carjacking. A strange thought popped into my head: 'I'd rather not be anywhere else. I'm right where I need to be.' This seemed odd. It was easy for me to explain to others why I enjoyed travel when visiting places like Vanuatu, but perhaps less so in places like this. How had I found myself on holiday in somewhere like Port Moresby? It was at times like these that I realised my relationship with travel probably wasn't 'normal'. Even more perversely, I knew by then that I tended to look back on these less favourable travel experiences with a sense of real fondness, and they often became 'highlights' of my trips abroad.

Sitting in a quasi-failed urban area, after many months on the road, I understood that I travelled not because it was easy but precisely because it was sometimes hard. Travel was a vehicle to take me out of my comfort zone, and come face-to-face with challenging places and situations. To grow. To push myself. And in some ways, to embrace the many challenges I and so many other travellers faced on the road. After all, these challenges paled into insignificance compared to those faced by the people who actually lived in certain parts of the world.

When travelling, there'll be daily practical annoyances. Lugging a huge bag around in boiling and humid countries is quite testing. As is getting on a bus with a driver who doesn't speak your language and stinks of booze. And often feels compelled to drive while mainly checking his phone.

You'll lose belongings. You'll have stuff stolen. Public

transport will be late or won't turn up. Getting visas to some countries will often be as hard as applying for full citizenship, or at least it will seem like it. Sleeping in dorm rooms with people who insist on snoring, farting, and unpacking and zipping and re-zipping their bags repeatedly at 4am will get tiring. You won't be able to drink the tap water in many places. You'll get ill. If you're travelling alone, you'll undoubtedly get stuck with people who you think are awful, but with no one else around, you'll probably just put up with them. And narrowly avoiding carjackings can be an occupational hazard.

Type Two Fun

Although this might make travel sound terrible to some, this is where the concept of 'Type Two Fun' comes in. For me, and doubtless others, this is a further reason why travel is so irresistible. Type Two Fun refers to experiences that are objectively bad at the time. Like most of my stay in Port Moresby. But later on, you peculiarly view these experiences with much fondness, and they become treasured memories of your trips abroad.

Several years before I'd found myself holidaying in the world's worst city, I was swimming in the Red Sea, enjoying the last few days of a trip to beautiful Israel with my good friends Ant and Sandy. The turquoise sea was utterly resplendent. With a few gentle kicks of my diving flippers, I serenely sliced through the clearest water imaginable. I gazed at shoals of luminous, tropical fish, in awe of their simple beauty. As I swam, the usual chatter of my busy mind hushed to a whisper. Paddling around in the deliciously inviting sea, I felt completely at peace.

'Er, guys, I can't find our bags,' said my alarmed friend Sandy as I returned to shore. He looked shell-shocked. We'd left our luggage in the boot of our comically small rental car while we swam.

'What do you mean you can't 'find' them? The bags are massive, they barely fit in the boot! They're either there or they aren't, surely?' I said without conviction. We ran to the car to suss out the situation.

Denial is a funny thing. When we arrived at our car – a vehicle barely big enough to fit a human – the boot was clearly open. Where the luggage had been, there was now only a gaping, empty hole. Not wanting to accept reality just quite yet, we stayed calm and proceeded to methodically check all of the other parts of the car where the 'bags might have got to'. Under it. On the roof. In the wheels. Behind the steering wheel. In the glove compartment. Despite our valiant efforts, after five minutes of collective delusion, we accepted reality. 'Okay, so someone's taken all of our stuff,' I said, in between a barrage of expletives.

I do really mean *all* of our stuff. We were now wearing our only remaining belongings: swimming trunks. Our passports, money, computers, and clothes had all gone. After a futile trip to the police station, we cut our losses and began the long drive back to Tel Aviv. We passed beautiful and desolate scenery as we trundled through the Negev Desert. We saw camels, canyons carved into rock by millions of years of wind erosion, and sandy desert vistas.

Why Do We Travel?

It was by any measure a wonderful place for a road trip.

But, perhaps understandably, the atmosphere in the car couldn't have been much worse, aside from moments of occasional nervous laughter about where the hell we were going to stay that night. Or how we were going to pay for it. There's something about driving almost naked that feels wrong. Four hours later, the desert gave way to suburbs and then the modern tower blocks of Israel's capital. We parked up and plodded into the British Embassy, topless and barefoot. I caught a glimpse of my face in a mirror, and my worst fears were confirmed: I was sunburnt, sweaty, and wore an expression that screamed: 'Please feel sorry for me.'

Like all brave and intrepid explorers, the first thing we did in the embassy was call our mums in a panic. We begged them to send us some money so we could clothe ourselves and return home. They obliged (thanks, mums). We touched down in London the next day, having spent six hours without anything to do on an easyJet flight that pushed the boundaries of 'short-haul' cabin comfort. We arrived in a foul mood. It was many weeks before we could laugh about the experience. And if I think about it, this change in attitude coincided with the insurers saying they'd pay out for the loss of all our worldly belongings. But today, this memory is something we laugh about and, in some ways, treasure.

A few years after this, I found myself on a dusty 'road' (a raked bit of sand) in the Namib Desert, where we had broken down. Without any mobile phone reception and in 100°F (38°C) heat. The Namib Desert feels so scorched and dry that you get a sense of how hostile our planet can be. Each inhale was a struggle, with the hot and thick air singeing my lungs. The horizon stretched out endlessly; there was nothing to see other than perfectly flat sand. We were short on water, and hours passed without seeing another soul. It was scary. I somewhat dramatically made my life flash before my eyes, through conscious effort. It'd be six hours until a car appeared and we were saved.

But now? This pathetic near-death story seems like great wholesome fun. Like the other stories, this roadside trouble (somehow) stands out as the highlight of my Namibia trip. Whenever I meet up with those I shared these unfortunate experiences with, it's the most unpleasant and testing times that we talk and laugh about.

The whole point of travel is to be pushed beyond your normal limits. And while being robbed or breaking down probably isn't a prerequisite here, experiences that are difficult or challenging will be what you remember the most. In the 100 or so countries that I've visited since Israel, I've always tried to keep the concept of Type Two Fun at the front of my mind. Ready to be deployed when, inevitably, things don't turn out to plan. It was this attitude that helped me see value in experiences like the one I was having in Port Moresby. And, oddly, why I kept choosing to pack my bags and set off for the next off-piste destination.

Time for Some Type One Travel

After a couple more days in Port Moresby, I was back in the sky. And after a three-hour journey across the Philippine Sea, I spotted land. Appearing through the aeroplane window, sidling into view, was Palau.* 'This is more like it,' I remember thinking. Rounded, curvy hills dropped into some of the clearest water I'd ever seen. Piercing strips of white sand divided green from turquoise. I could see coves and bays. And none of the disorder and decay of Port Moresby. 'Good.'

We touched down and taxied to the airport terminal. It looked more like a large hut than a major transit hub. It had a large red roof, thronged on either side by lazily swaying palm trees. Palau has just 21,000 inhabitants, making it the fourth smallest country in the world by population. It's so small, in fact, that I was sitting in the row behind the country's president on my flight. I didn't know it was the president until the border officials started rushing around frantically on landing, and the locals started to murmur. For a brief, delicious moment, I thought they may have been pulling out the proverbial red carpet for the arrival of the Travelling Ape. Obviously, I was wrong. One day.

Entering the terminal, I noticed signs everywhere about conservation. Posters telling visitors 'What not to bring into Palau'. To 'Keep Palau clean', and such like. All visitors pay US$100 on arrival for conservation. Before leaving the airport, a border guard checked my bag. He confiscated sunscreen (yes, really) because it can damage coral if you swim wearing it.

The owner of my guesthouse collected me in his

---

*   Writing this chapter would have been much easier if the country had just called itself Paula, which is what my spellcheck has been incessantly changing it to.

27

car. He was a short, plump man called Reng. The slow pace of island life clearly suited him. He was laid-back. Figuratively (his personality) and literally (his car seat was reclined so far that I wasn't confident he could see the road). We certainly weren't in a hurry to get anywhere. We weaved, incredibly slowly, along picturesque, winding roads. To be fair to Reng, he was driving with the steering wheel on the wrong side, so maybe caution was needed. Palau switched from Japanese to American rule after WWII. The Americans declared that cars should drive on the right once they arrived, which they still do today. Not considering that Palau imports all of its cars from Japan, which drives on the left. So all its cars have their steering wheels on the wrong side, to this day.

Reng's leisurely driving allowed me to take in the tropical beauty of the place, with hundreds of shades of green on show. The roads sliced and slithered through dense rainforests. We were driving slowly enough that, with the windows down, I could hear crickets and birds and other sounds of nature, rather than the car's engine. Efforts to conserve these islands were clearly working. Palau was spotless.

I chatted to Reng. He told me some short snippets about the history of Palau. 'Our history is defined by Japan and America. Our language is a mix of Japanese and indigenous dialects. While our favourite food here is sushi.'

'Ah, I love sushi,' I said, telling him about my trips to Japan and its fish markets.

'Yeah. Also Spam is really popular here, which came from America. I love it,' he added enthusiastically.

Why Do We Travel?

I chuckled. But backtracked when I realised his face looked deadly serious and he wasn't joking. I guess he had never watched *Monty Python*. I didn't have a travel anecdote about Spam,* so I just said, 'Er, yeah, it has a really, um, distinct flavour, doesn't it?'

Reng showed me into the guesthouse. A basic structure, with white walls and a veranda with a tin roof above it. But, my word, what a location. Perfectly situated on the edge of a white cove in the pleasing shape of a wineglass, and with sand like salt. After chowing some lunch down – noodles, not Spam, fortunately – Reng pulled his boat onto the crumbling jetty outside. We set off for the Palau National Marine Sanctuary, the country's immaculate national park. On our little wooden vessel, vibrating wildly as we chugged onwards, we meandered through seemingly endless pristine limestone and volcanic islands. Giant slabs of rock jutted high into the sky, topped with little pockets of rainforest that looked like tufts of hair. We cruised through shimmering turquoise lagoons. There were no cars to hijack here. This most definitely was Type One Travel.

Reng asked me if I'd like to snorkel at a dive site called 'Shark City', which was part of the marine sanctuary. I did. After bravely swimming with the sharks – albeit very small ones – I set off on a kayak. I had one of Palau's beautiful lagoons all to myself. And reasoned that there were few

---

★   Until now.

places on Earth that have beaches as gorgeous as those in Palau. If you've been to Koh Phi Phi in Thailand or El Nido in the Philippines, you'll get the gist. But Palau's are remote and empty.

After a short while, I stopped paddling. I was alone. Left only with the sounds of the kayak rhythmically slapping against the gentle waves, and with a warm breeze rushing past me. It presented an opportunity to reflect on my trip through the Pacific. And what it had taught me about travel itself.

'Perhaps,' I thought, 'we venture abroad in the name of fun, escapism, better weather, connection, and education.' Or maybe we're just unsuccessfully battling nasty cases of dromomania. Whatever the reason, floating in paradise, in a place many people haven't even heard of, I figured there were few pursuits like travel. That help you engage with the planet. Know it. Get a sense of its scale. Its majesty. Its beauty. As I'd experienced it in Vanuatu and again as I paddled through the almost too-beautiful-to-be-true lagoons of Palau. Travel can truly leave you with an imprint of what the world and its regions are actually like. And with that in mind, let's kayak over into the next chapter.

2

A Brief Guide to the Planet

*Travel showed me just how much this incredible
planet has to offer. Where to start?*

The sky was an oppressive shade of grey. Bleak. It was freezing. Snowing lightly, in fact. Not quite what I'd anticipated. Even though my old, slightly damp-smelling helmet offered me some respite from the elements, it was clear I was completely underdressed for the occasion. Chilled to the bone, I started to pedal. Aiming the handlebars of my bike down what I felt to be an unnecessarily steep looking trail. 'At least it's tarmacked,' I thought.

I followed a group of other cyclists along the twisting, winding road. It snaked its way through a barren landscape, dotted with clumps of snow and ice. I'd love to say that it was a peloton sort of situation going on. But we were – clearly – all amateurs. Even though the road was smooth (for now), not all of us looked particularly stable on some of the more aggressive hairpin bends. This didn't exactly bode well for later. In the brief moments when I looked up, I saw crisp mountain peaks. Gnarly exposed rock. And a hell of a drop to the valley below.

The Travelling Ape

For this particular ride, we'd been driven to the top of a mountain in Bolivia. And, fortunately, from there we wouldn't need to do much in the way of pedalling as we cruised downhill for the rest of the day. My body started to warm, slowly but surely, as we lost altitude. The chattering of my teeth soon giving way to my visor fogging up and my palms becoming sweaty. The pleasing paved road transitioned into a narrow, uneven gravel track. Perfectly timed, I felt, as the visibility dropped to just a few yards as we hit clouds. I could only just make out the cyclist in front of me. I started to understand why this particular route had been jovially nicknamed 'Death Road' for decades. (I promised my mum I'd never do it. Sorry.)

Luckily, the clouds cleared. And I didn't die (evidently). Once below the clouds, however, the sheer scale of the drop at the edge of the road became even more visible. How on Earth workers managed to cut a road into the at times almost vertical cliffside, I'll never know.

The icy, barren landscapes from the start of the ride were soon a distant memory. Instead, they were replaced by lush, dense rainforest. Trees and shrubs somehow clung to the almost vertical mountainside. Vines seemingly preventing some rock from falling into the abyss. Small streams periodically soaking us, like miniature showers from above. And still, the valley. The drop. Ever present. I removed more layers as the humidity ratcheted up. And continued gingerly navigating my way down the track. Every now and then my confidence would increase. I'd feel the wind on my face, the ground rushing beneath me. Sense the adrenaline. I'd start to pick up the pace, take an apex closer to the cliff edge. Before remembering I liked my life. And paying money to optionally die on something called Death Road might make me look a little bit stupid in my obituary.

Our guide, José, was a stocky man whose physique didn't strike me as that of a traditional cyclist. But he certainly showed no qualms about doing athletic tricks on the edge of the precipice. He did wheelies and bar spins, right at the edge, laughing loudly as he went. Not setting the best example to the wider group in health and safety terms, it has to be said. For hours, our group of non-mountain bikers continued onwards, losing still more altitude. I was now down to a T-shirt and shorts, completely dripping with sweat. The humidity was oppressive.

As we reached the bottom of the valley, we were greeted by the hum of the rainforest. We were thankful not to be dead. And we could now look up at the giant, towering mountains we'd just cycled (well, freewheeled) down. We'd reached the edge of the Bolivian Amazon rainforest. It was incredible to think we'd been up near glaciers just a few hours ago.

Upon completing the ride, José said, 'We've dropped down from almost 16,000 feet to around 4,000 feet in the last few hours. Well done for staying safe, all. Now for some drinks!' On the drive back up to Bolivia's administrative capital, La Paz, José and his biker guide friends proceeded to consume a quite spectacular amount of rum. Our minibus driver declined, thankfully. Their tongues loosened as the journey went on, as we navigated yet another hairpin bend climbing steadily upwards. They started to tell us about all the people who had recently died on Death Road. The general theme was: 'The people who died probably deserved it. They were taking selfies and messing around.' A touch harsh, perhaps. But then again, I'd chosen to do Death Road with a company called Mayhem Tours, whose slogan was 'No wimps'. I should've figured health and safety was probably low down on their list of priorities.

Also, as I failed to mention at the start of this chapter (the reason escapes me as to why), Death Road is much safer than it used to be.

'There used to be 200 to 300 deaths a year on North Yungas Road [its official name]. But this was when it was open to traffic, and cars and lorries regularly used to fall off the edge. Fatalities are much rarer since Death Road closed to cars and trucks,' José said. The 'occasional' tourist death still made it seem a bit sketchy to me. But also was part of its appeal. The ride was a truly spectacular experience.

José and his pals dropped me off at the hostel, a converted Spanish colonial structure. It had yellow walls, ornate wooden balconies, and a grand-looking entrance. I dropped my bag, and took a short walk to dinner, which, given that La Paz is one of the highest cities in the world, felt more like an alpine trek. It was strange being surrounded by roads, cars, and the normal buzz of urban life. While at the same time being constantly tired and out of breath.

I sat down in a local *cocina* and ordered some *salteñas* – baked Bolivian pastry turnovers, which always seemed quite dry to me – in broken and limited Spanish. And loudly discussed what had just happened on Death Road with my friends Andrew, Alex, and Matt, whom I was travelling with at the time. We all ordered a Pacenas, a local beer, which tasted as if sand was a not insubstantial ingredient. The beers never stopped frothing after being opened, an indicator of the thinner air in La Paz. And I can tell you, hangovers at 15,000 feet are even less fun than at sea level.

Bolivia is a relatively small nation; its population is only around 12 million. But in two weeks there, I'd been treated to a stupendous amount of variety and natural beauty. The shimmering, otherworldly salt flats of Salar de Uyuni, the world's largest, where horizon and sky merge above endlessly repeating polygonal patterns of salt on the ground. The ramshackle and sprawling city of La Paz, filled with cavalcades of vendors and diesel-spewing cars. The glaciers and snow-capped peaks of the Cordillera Real. And the humid Amazon rainforest. Having so much in one small nation pointed to an even greater revelation about the diversity of this beautiful, awe-inspiring, incomprehensible* planet we all live on.

The rich diversity of Bolivia – and so many other countries – has changed me. Before I travelled, I took the world for granted. After all, it'd always been there. At best, the world had played a supporting role in the very 'me-focused' narrative of my life. But by experiencing so much of Earth's beauty first-hand, as in Bolivia, I've begun to appreciate our smallness. The world's greatness. Its true wonder. So, in this chapter, I'm going to try and give you

---

* Hopefully less so for you once you've finished this book.

the briefest taste of what this place has to offer. The briefest of brief travel guides to the world.

Understanding Our Place in the Cosmos

To do this, we first need to understand one thing. We actually live on a planet. A tiny, mostly blue orb, dangling delicately in the eternal cosmic nothingness of space. You might say you understand this, but I don't think enough of us do. Most of us rarely think about the fact that we're on a big rock, orbiting a giant thermonuclear furnace at around 67,000 miles per hour. Or that a tiny 10-mile sliver of atmosphere separates us from the impossible vastness of the universe. Standing atop Mount Yasur in Vanuatu, it was impossible for me to ignore these uncomfortable truths. Similarly in Bolivia, the strange contortions of Earth's crust, which created so many of its geological masterpieces, made our planetary existence more apparent to me.

Most of us aren't confronted by volcanoes, or earthquakes, or the fragility of Earth on a daily basis. We're too busy taking close-up pictures of our own faces. For those who travel, however, we're given countless opportunities to step back and consider how remarkable this rock we're all on really is (and also to take close-up pictures of our own faces). We can begin to appreciate how strange it is. How beautiful it is. To travel is to fall in love with Earth's natural splendour and enthralling humanity, time and time again.

Getting a holistic view of our planet is hard – except for those fortunate enough to have viewed it from space.

A Brief Guide to the Planet

Astronauts talk in almost religious terms about the experience of looking back at the world. American James Irwin, the eighth man to walk on the moon, said viewing Earth from space was so profound he went from being a lukewarm Christian to a devout one.[1] Canadian astronaut Chris Hadfield talks about seeing the planet from space in similarly evangelical terms (minus the Jesus part). He said he only truly understood Earth's beauty once he'd been to space, circumnavigating the planet every 92 minutes while on the International Space Station.[2] He felt more connected to humanity when he was up there, recognising the commonality of our shared existence.[3] Other astronauts agree. A survey of 39 of them found spaceflight had positive effects on the psyche, particularly in appreciating Earth's beauty.[4] Author Frank White interviewed 29 astronauts and cosmonauts for a book called *The Overview Effect*, which describes the life-changing impact that being in space had on astronauts.[5]

Obviously, space travel isn't an option for most of us. Unless you're a billionaire, it seems.[6] But travel offers ample opportunity to gaze up at the cosmos. Shortly after my trip to Bolivia, I went stargazing in San Pedro de Atacama, in Chile. It was one of the most special experiences of my life. San Pedro has some of the best night skies on the planet, given its altitude and the fact it never rains. I remember seeing the Milky Way (our celestial cul-de-sac) for the first time. It was an explosion of impossibly bright, twinkling stars. There are no words to describe the beauty. The whole sky was illuminated, glistening, with ethereal cosmic wonder. I had the strange sensation of *feeling* like I was on a planet, floating through space. I could sense the gentle rotation of Earth, as the Milky Way sidled up and over the horizon. It's something I've never forgotten.

I got told to point the telescope towards a small, seemingly uninteresting 'cloud'. As I zoomed in, I remember audibly saying, 'Woah,' something that seems lame in retrospect, as I write. It was Andromeda. Another galaxy located 'just' two million light years away. It was bursting with more stars than my eyes could take in. It's not a surprise, really, there are a trillion stars in the galaxy. Later that evening, I learnt that there are an estimated two trillion galaxies and 10,000,000,000,000,000,000,000,000 planets in the universe. This might seem like just a big, unpronounceable, meaningless number. So a simpler way to understand it is that there are at least 10 times more planets in the universe than there are *grains of sand on the world's beaches*. Or, put another way, there are more planets in the universe than there have been words and sounds uttered by *all* the humans who've ever lived.[7]

Travel helps remind me about our peculiar planetary existence. It helps give Earth a sense of scale, at once both enormous and minuscule, against this cosmic backdrop. It's altered my understanding of the preciousness of this tiny blue speck we all live on. For me, there wasn't any other option than to explore and experience as much of it as possible in the minute sliver of time that I'll have the privilege to live on it. Each of our magnificent continents is a universe of humanity and natural beauty in and of themselves, just waiting to be explored. What are they like? What do they offer?

Europe: An Unparalleled Depth of History

Let's start with Europe, a continent that once received an aggregated TripAdvisor score of 2.7 stars (out of 5). I've been to each of Europe's 44 countries and for the life of me can't understand why some people feel this way. There's no continent on Earth that has been so immeasurably shaped by humanity. There are few truly 'wild' parts of it left. Almost every snippet of land here's been changed by agriculture or civilisation. But what it lacks in remoteness and raw natural beauty, Europe more than makes up for in the depth of history and culture on show. It's unsurpassed, anywhere.

Where else on Earth do you have cities as great as London, Paris, Barcelona, Berlin, and Rome, all within two hours of each other? Where else offers so many different cultures and countries in such a small space? And where else can you experience ancient fairy-tale castles brushing uncomfortably against the relentless march of modern urban living? It's the physical reminders of Europe's long, rich, and complex history that allows us to glimpse the civilisations that forged this continent. The small scale of cars, roads, and most buildings, with chaotic and unplanned streetscapes, a reminder that this continent was built long before motorcars and electricity.

Europe is a tiny continent in some ways. It squeezes 740 million people into an area half the size of Australia (where only 25 million people live).[8] Such is the ease of travel here, it's quite possible to visit some of the world's most famous and historic cities, sunbathe on stunning beaches, and visit the Alps in days or weeks rather than months.

The Travelling Ape

This is what makes Europe so unique. Indeed, even the islands of Malta, a few specks of land in the Mediterranean Sea, pack in a remarkable collection of ancient architecture and history considering their diminutive size.

Starting in the south with Malta, you're in the centre of the vibrant Mediterranean. In Spain, Southern France, Italy, Greece, and Portugal (culturally if not geographically part of the Mediterranean), people focus on living the good life and family takes centre stage. There's a fairly strong correlation between wealth and weather in Western Europe, with incomes generally decreasing the further south you head.[9] As the weather gets better, clearly, the need to slave away working to enjoy life decreases. Indeed, living on the cheap is easier to do on stunning beaches, with an endless supply of delicious food.

As you head further east, things become less Western. The spectre of the USSR still looms large over the region's culture and politics, despite its collapse over three decades ago. In the Balkans, you have a strange mix of Western European and Asian influences, with a layer of brutalist Soviet architecture on top. Russia offers visitors something completely different: faded imperial grandeur mixed with the harsh realities of persistent socioeconomic decline. For all President Vladimir Putin's[*] posturing on the international stage, this is a poor country. It's not surprising he decided to invade Ukraine in 2022 against this backdrop. Military strength is all he has, and even this looks greatly diminished.

---

[*] Phonetically pronounced 'Poo-tin'. A hidden metaphor, perhaps.

A Brief Guide to the Planet

Head up through the forward-looking, technological trailblazers of the Baltics – Estonia, Lithuania, and Latvia – and it's only a short ferry ride over to the Nordics:* Sweden, Norway, Finland, and Denmark. These are the best functioning societies on the planet, with beautiful people and robust democratic principles. If only daylight wasn't such a precious commodity during winter months. And people weren't all so effortlessly stylish and good looking (I'm not bitter).

Venture west to Northwest Europe. You have the British Isles, made up of Ireland and the UK. The latter, my home, is steeped in history and natural beauty. Ireland, on the other hand, has a much smaller population and is much more untamed. A rural and beautiful land with an astonishing history too. Also in Northwest Europe are Belgium, the Netherlands, Luxembourg, and Germany, where economic pragmatism and social restraint reigns culturally supreme. Jet further north to Iceland and enter a curious and geologically fascinating country. A place of ice, lava flows, and waterfalls. It doesn't feel of this Earth, but is strangely familiar to anyone who's spent hours of their life being titillated by violence (and needless nudity) in *Game of Thrones*.

Travel to Europe may seem familiar, even to those who haven't visited before. If you're from the global 'West', even if you live in the Americas or Australia, you're still living a

---

* The Helsinki to Tallinn ferry has effectively been a booze cruise for Finns for decades, although Estonia's use of the euro has now dented its low-cost appeal.

life framed by European values. From politics to language, to religion, to social and economic norms. Europe grew and then spewed itself all over the planet, for better or for worse. And for me, its familiarity means it doesn't offer quite the same level of excitement as destinations further afield. (That, and it's stupidly expensive.)

Asia: An Explosion of Humanity

One place where travel awe and unfamiliarity are not lacking whatsoever is Asia. Describing Asia as a continent seems a bit silly. Over 4.6 billion people live here, almost 60 percent of the world's population. To highlight this, draw a circle on a map of the world, with the perimeter being India to the west, Indonesia to the south, Japan to the east, and northern China at the top. Know that more of the world's population live *inside this circle than outside it*. Twice as many people live in China alone than in the continent of Europe. So, it would seem more accurate to describe Asia as its own planet, one that is so diverse as to make the mind boggle.

Asia is an explosion of human life. Tiny Bangladesh is roughly the size of Greece. Greece squeezes 10 million people into its craggy landscapes and islands, and it feels pretty 'full' when you visit. Bangladesh, somehow, fits an astonishing 170 million people into the same area (not far from the population of the UK, Italy, and Spain combined). Most of the world's fastest growing countries are in Asia. Estimates for 2050 show that three of the four largest economies in the world (China, India, and Indonesia) will be in Asia.[10] If the past is Europe's and the present is America's, then the future is Asia's.

Most travellers – like yours truly – cut their teeth in Southeast Asia. A trip to Thailand, Malaysia, Laos, and Vietnam was where I picked up the travel bug, aged 19. The cuisine is cheap and delicious, the locals are friendly, and the beaches are idyllic. Cities like Bangkok give you the chance to experience Asian megacity mayhem at its purest – while not being so intense as to make the novice traveller never want to leave their home country again.

Asia's two monoliths usually follow for those who caught the bug in Southeast Asia.* Travelling in China is a shocking experience. First, when you realise you've landed in a new world superpower. Second, as you struggle with the terrible air quality. Third, as you experience its depth and diversity. Cultural differences in cities outside Westernised places like Hong Kong and Shanghai can be striking, and sometimes incomprehensible.

Then we have India. I've been three times. But the assault on my senses – noise, humidity, the smells of food and pollution – never fails to catch me off guard. It's like being dropped into a completely different reality. India changes you; it touches the soul. Everyone would benefit from experiencing the radically different way in which such a huge chunk of the world's population lives. If you

---

* I'm going to stop using the travel bug analogy. With this book being written in the age of COVID-19, it seems to cut too close to the bone.

are unsure about India, go to Sri Lanka. If you find this too much, you're probably not ready for India yet.

Then we have the more off-piste Asian destinations. Starting with the 'stans' of Central Asia: Kazakhstan, Turkmenistan, Uzbekistan, Kyrgyzstan, Kirkukstan, and Tajikistan. A gold star to anyone who noticed the made-up country. For those who were duped, you should've paid attention in geography class.* To be fair, these are some of the least-visited and lesser-known countries in the world. The visitor who does make it here is rewarded with a mismatch of Soviet influences and stupendous Islamic architecture.

You also have the Caucasus. Azerbaijan, Armenia, and Georgia are a peculiar mix of Eastern and Western influences. Soviet undertones make you feel like you're still in striking distance of Russia's orbit. While at the same time, remote monasteries in the stunning Greater Caucasus mountain range can transport you to a simpler time of centuries past.

The Middle East rarely figures on travellers' itineraries, excepting the holiday destinations of places like the United Arab Emirates (UAE), the beautiful beaches of Oman, and Jordan, which of course has Petra, the half-sunken ancient city carved into windblown orange canyons. But the region has so much to offer outside these options. Israel is one of the best small-country destinations on the planet, despite its ongoing political challenges. Saudi Arabia is

---

*   Kirkukstan doesn't exist, for those who couldn't even be bothered to get their phone out to google it.

modernising at a pace that has to be seen to be believed (albeit from a staggeringly low and illiberal base). And then there's fast-paced Beirut in Lebanon, with its culinary delights. It is one of my favourite cities on Earth, even if it too remains a deeply divided and unsettled place.

All said, it's Asia's size, variety, and low cost that blows the mind. As well as its deep history. While Europe was a backwater millennia ago, parts of India and China were developing truly advanced civilisations, the remnants of which can be glimpsed if you go. I've visited 44 of Asia's 48 countries, and if I could only travel in one continent again, it would be that one. Part of this bias reflects the ace it has up its sleeve: Japan, my favourite country on Earth, as it is for so many people.

I could write a book about Japan one day, such is my love for this enchanting country. There's something mystical about this land. On paper, it shouldn't work. There are 125 million people squeezed onto a small, earthquake-prone archipelago mainly made up of mountains. But those people play a huge role in its allure. They are the most polite, friendly, and courteous you are likely to ever come across. While stereotypes are often lazy, the ones commonly thrown at Japan are at least almost universally positive. An online poll of overseas visitors found that the five most popular adjectives to describe the Japanese are: polite, punctual, kind, hard-working, and respectful.[11]

Their appreciation of nature is legendary too. There are few other countries that suggest *shinrin-yoku* (forest bathing) to relax, or have specific words for the sunlight splintering through trees (*komorebi*), or the cold that lets us know winter has arrived (*kogarashi*).[12] For these reasons, Japan feels like visiting another world. For me, every trip to these islands has been profound. It's the jewel in Asia's crown, and I'll talk more about it in the next chapter.

South America: A Haven of Natural Wonders

South America has a special place in my heart. My mum lived in Uruguay until age 21. Unfortunately, a stubbornness on the part of almost everyone in the Anglosphere (including me) to learn another language means my Spanish could be better (it couldn't really be worse, if I'm being honest). This is something that became painfully apparent when I visited Uruguay with my mum, only to see confusion on the faces of all her old friends when they found out I couldn't communicate with any of them.

I once journeyed up from the southern tip of Chile (where my grandfather was born) right to the rainforests of Guyana and Suriname in the north of the continent. It truly stirred the soul. And gave me the feeling that South America is all about space, epic scenery, and the power of nature, on a giant scale. You have the vast glaciers of Patagonia. You have San Pedro de Atacama, which as well as having the best stargazing on the planet has lunar landscapes that make you feel like you're actually in space yourself. Then there are the otherworldly landscapes of the Bolivian Salt Flats. The angular, vertiginous peaks of the Andes. The unparalleled fauna of the Galápagos Islands in Ecuador, where you can snorkel with turtles and sea lions. Countless Inca ruins, including Machu Picchu in Peru. The lush rainforests of the Amazon. And the white-sand beaches of Colombia's Caribbean coastline. It's true to say that South America is the most beautiful continent on Earth if you love nature (and who doesn't?). The scale of the landscapes, the epic emptiness, and the clarity of the crystal clear night skies make you feel exceedingly small.

The wilderness is a recognised source of transcendent emotion for human beings. Various studies have demonstrated nature's power to induce intense emotions such as awe and inspiration.[13] There's no better place than South America to bathe in nature's presence, and to be pleasantly overwhelmed by what Edmund Burke described as the 'delightful horror' of scenic vastness, our smallness, and the majesty of nature.[14]

Time spent on the continent's east coast feels more urban, and more Portuguese, for that matter. Almost half of South America speaks Portuguese, not Spanish, all in Brazil. A trip to the picture-perfect landscapes and playful mountains of Rio de Janeiro is on most travellers' 'to do' lists, and it doesn't disappoint. It has the same natural beauty of the wider continent, but sitting amongst Rio's urban vitality. Also on that list is a visit to one of the world's largest waterfalls. Iguazu Falls are so massive they straddle the borders of three countries: Brazil, Argentina, and Paraguay.

Dipping your toe into the snooty Argentine megacity of Buenos Aires is a fast-paced, high-octane experience. Even though as an English person you might not be particularly popular there. I got spat at twice for my apparent role in the war over what they called 'Las Malvinas' (the Falkland

Islands). A war that began seven years before my birth. I wanted to explain to the perpetrators that citizens shouldn't be held accountable for decisions made by politicians – especially when they are yet to exist – but then I remembered: I can't speak Spanish. And that was that.

North America: Full of Surprises

Strangely, the countries of Central America and the Caribbean are technically part of North America. Given that Central America offers visitors compelling insights into the impacts of Spanish colonial history, and remains truly Latin in most respects, its inclusion in South America would probably make more sense. Central America could be described as South America for beginners; it's small, at least compared to its Latin cousin to the south. I've been to every country in Central America. You probably could do that too if you gave yourself a month or so.

Here, you have exquisite Spanish colonial architecture in Nicaragua, in towns like Granada and León. Stupendous volcanic peaks dot the landscapes, and loom threateningly over the region's horizons. Remnants of the Maya and Aztec empires reveal themselves in Mexico. Stunning beaches aren't hard to find in Belize, El Salvador, Panama, and Honduras. There is so much to see – and all in a fairly small sliver of land. Homicide rates in the region are among the highest in the world.[15] But this shouldn't necessarily put you off. Just don't linger in rough areas of capital cities. In any case, you aren't far from the paradise islands of the Caribbean. Cuba, the Bahamas, Barbados, the Dominican Republic, Jamaica, St Lucia, and St Vincent and the Grenadines all have screensaver-worthy tropical beaches. They'll hurt your wallet, however.

So then, we come to Anglosphere North America: the United States of America, and Canada, a bit. While Canadians will forever resent being confused with Americans, they should take solace in the fact that theirs is a better – if colder – society than their much bigger brother to the south. There's so much beauty in Canada, and so much space. Having driven from Quebec to Vancouver, I know how vast this land is. But also how it's filled with some of the politest and friendliest people on Earth. As well as some exceptional cities, from bustling and multicultural Toronto and francophone Montreal in the east, to nature-infused Vancouver in the far west. It's great. And also if you like funny accents, some of the most whimsical in the world are on the east coast. A sort of fusion between British and American accents, with sing-songy inflections, and a historic bent.

Then we have America itself. The United States. It's popular to dislike Americans. But then again, it's also popular to hate the best sports team or the biggest pop star. Well, I'm going to shock – and potentially annoy those in the anti-America camp – by saying that I love America. Deeply.

Ignore the politics, as hard as that may be. While Japan is my favourite country, America comes a close second. If I could only visit one nation ever again, it would be America. By a mile. Surprising? Well, it shouldn't be, really.

The Travelling Ape

Nowhere else on Earth has as many awe-inspiring metropolises. New York and San Francisco are just the tip of the iceberg. I've visited 40 of the 50 states; each has its own unique identity and idiosyncrasies. Few nations have as much natural beauty, and certainly none have as many fantastic national parks – indeed, the US created the world's first. If California alone were to be a country, it would be one of the most beautiful on Earth. It would also, stunningly, be one of the most powerful. California, a mere state in the United States, would have the fifth largest economy in the world, ahead of the UK, France, and Italy.[16]

Statistics like these allude to the true nature of America: it's more a continent than a country. Think of America as 50 different countries, each with unique characteristics and widely differing views on how to live. Citizens of New York and North Dakota are likely to have little in common, particularly when it comes to politics or religion.

In fact, there are only two things that appear to hold this behemoth together: the English language and (the enforced) worship of the Stars and Stripes. The language giving the sense of sameness across this divided place, the flag reminding all that they are supposed to be one. It's no wonder, then, that the national anthem is sung the whole time, children pledge allegiance to the flag every day, and the sight of a flag flying outside someone's home is perfectly normal. (Whereas in Europe, such behaviour could suggest a propensity towards football hooliganism.)

When people argue that the United States doesn't work as an entity, I disagree. I highlight the more miraculous fact that a constitution written in 1787 has essentially managed to hold together 50 different countries for over 200 years. And for that matter, produced the most powerful nation the world has *ever* seen. When you're in America you feel like you're in the centre of the world. Because you are. We refer to those from the United States as 'Americans', even though anyone hailing from the Americas could do the same in theory. It highlights the United States' dominance over the region, and indeed the wider world.

Australasia: The End of the Earth

For any Brit, Australia and New Zealand are oddly familiar. Cities have roads named after British streets, places, and famous people. Red postboxes dot street corners. The Queen's profile adorns currency, at least before King Charles gradually replaces her on coins and banknotes. Both nations also love sports generally regarded as odd by the parts of the world that avoided becoming part of the British Empire (cricket). It makes travel here familiar, but perhaps less exciting as a result. That said, there are some things that take a while to get used to, particularly in Australia. The first few times I was asked, 'How ya going?' I replied, 'In a car, mainly,' before realising I was simply being greeted.

These are two of the best societies on the planet. Australia is a gem of a country, which offers space, beaches, and scenery as beautiful as anywhere on Earth. New Zealand is perhaps even more beautiful. Islands that generate images of romantic mysticism, due to the striking marriage of British and Māori culture across this mountainous, fern-covered treasure of a place. I can see why Silicon Valley types have been drawn to buy property here, believing this isolated country would make the perfect escape to ride out an apocalypse.

Beyond the region's largest destinations, out in the seemingly endless blue, you reach the 11 nations of the Pacific Islands. Here, you feel profoundly disconnected from the rest of the planet. Despite being home to just 2.3 million people (0.0003 percent of the world's population), the Pacific Islands are scattered across an area equivalent to 15 percent of the world's surface.[17] You're truly isolated here. One wonders what it would've been like before the internet. The vast majority of people here will never take a step off the tiny speck of land on which they were born. The end of their small island effectively demarcates the end of their world.

Some, like Fiji, Samoa, Palau, and Micronesia, offer you the kind of tropical paradise you'd expect to see in this part of the world. Untouched white beaches, swaying palm trees, and inviting turquoise water. Micronesia has Nan Madol. It's a 2,000-year-old ancient settlement made up of vast slabs of basalt that have become enveloped by trees and other vegetation. My guide told me that local legend has it that Nan Madol was built by 'spirits'. I didn't have the heart to tell him that it was probably built by slaves (like most ancient monuments), and lots of them.

Other Pacific Island nations offer cautionary tales about some of the biggest problems facing the world today. The atolls of Kiribati and the Marshall Islands are only a few yards above sea level at their highest points, and are slowly being submerged by rising seas. Others, like the Solomon Islands, are blighted by crime and a lack of economic opportunity. Given their isolated location, out of sight and out of mind of most of the world's media, they're likely to remain low on the global list of priorities.

Africa: The Mother of All Continents

Africa. The cradle of humanity. The birthplace of humankind. A truly majestic continent. And there's much more of it than perhaps you think there is. Flat maps distort the size of continents, shrinking those near the equator, such as Africa. You probably won't believe this, but Africa is larger than China, India, the United States, and Europe. Combined.[18] Only with this knowledge can you begin to understand the true scale and wonder of this stupendous continent.

Africa is likely to play an even more important role in the world in the coming century. While population growth turns negative in Europe, and grinds to a halt across much of the developed world, Africa will be an exception. More than half of all global population growth between now and 2050 is forecast to come in Sub-Saharan Africa. The population is set to double to 2.5 billion.[19] So we would all do well to learn as much as we possibly can about Africa.

The problem is, it's the hardest and most expensive continent to travel in. It's the continent I've been able to visit the least, having been to 24 out of its 54 countries. Africa is served by fewer flights than any other continent. Backpacking infrastructure is in some countries non-existent. Visas for many places are hard and expensive to get. And safety is a larger consideration than in most other continents. In many African countries, like Kenya, the tourism sector remains high-end and expensive.

A good way to travel here is overlanding, where around 15 people travel together in an off-road-ready coach, camping along the way. I did one such trip from Cape Town to Zanzibar in 2017, through South Africa, Namibia, Botswana, Zimbabwe, Zambia, Malawi, and Tanzania. Covering 3,300 miles is no mean feat, especially if you saw the quality of the roads (or dusty tracks) we were driving on for much of it.

The southern and eastern parts of the continent are the usual starting points for travel. In several places, you can see the Big Five game animals – lion, leopard, rhino, elephant, and African buffalo. You can enjoy unearthly sand dunes in Namibia's Namib Desert, the majestic Victoria Falls in Zimbabwe, gorilla trekking in Rwanda, and the stunning coastlines of South Africa, Mozambique, and Zanzibar.

Some like to combine a trip to the southern part of Africa with a visit to the idyllic island nations of Mauritius and the Seychelles, which I confess I've visited several times but not in a backpacking capacity.* They are both as close as it's possible to be to the tropical island haven of your dreams.

---

*   On family holidays, I'm loath to concede, lest it further dent my already limited credibility in backpacking circles.

A Brief Guide to the Planet

Wild, unique, and dramatic, Ethiopia, located on the eastern Horn of Africa, is my favourite country to visit in Africa. It has a distinct history and culture, and it's the only country on the continent that Europeans failed to colonise. Moving west, things get more challenging. The central and western parts of Africa are some of the hardest to visit for logistical and safety reasons, but trips to Sierra Leone and Côte d'Ivoire in 2020 gave me a taste of vibrant West Africa.

Moving above the Sahara, it's a different ball game entirely. There's good reason why the Middle East is usually lumped in with North Africa (hence the MENA acronym) in the world of geopolitics and global macroeconomics. Here you have the bulk of Africa's predominantly Muslim nations, which are culturally and ethnically a world away from the rest of the continent. There's plenty that dazzles here. The souks of Marrakech in Morocco; the well-preserved Roman ruins in Tunisia; the truly awesome Pyramids of Egypt. There is a lot to see. And if you live in Europe, no other African countries offer the potential visitor such an enthralling change of culture, such a short hop from home.

Travelling nearly everywhere has made it clear to me just how much this little planet has to offer. The world and its nations are a marvel, and travel shows you this underlying magnificence. It's hard to say which continent is the best. So let's just say they all have a huge amount to offer.

The Travelling Ape

After all, they are *continents*. Anyone who says, 'I don't like Europe,' or, 'I didn't really like Asia,' clearly has high standards. If continents of hundreds of millions of people, each containing untold natural beauty and cultural riches, are not good enough for you, then I'm not quite sure what will be.

If you're planning a trip, then the best thing you can do is work out what your priorities are. Whether it's personal growth, meeting new people, learning a language, cost, or a multitude of other potential factors, deciding what you want to get out of a trip can be key to its success. But for me, there's one part of travel that excites above all others: diving headfirst into the fast-paced, frenetic cradles of civilisation that we call cities. And it's to this topic that our attention will now turn.

3

Lessons from Urban Travel

Urban areas are a physical embodiment of humanity, whose melancholic beauty is revealed to those who travel.

The jet lag was still painful. I'd only flown in the night before, but, desperate to get out and explore, I set my alarm and woke early. I pulled back the curtain on my sleeping pod – something fairly unique to Japanese hostels. Even in a dorm room, interior design in Japan is thoughtful and considered.

I set off on foot. I'd been warned that Tokyo in July is punishingly hot and humid. But it still took me by surprise. Having showered about five minutes ago, I soon felt this had been a completely pointless endeavour. I grabbed an iced coffee. Temporary relief. The coffee shop oozed style. It had polished concrete floors. Dark wooden panels. Devil's ivy houseplants dangling from the ceiling. The barista serving me couldn't have been more polite. Finishing our transaction with a singsong of '*arigato*'s, I thought, 'I bloody love Japan,' and was so pleased to be back.

The Travelling Ape

I was staying in the Asakusabashi district. Which, much like the rest of Tokyo, is filled to the brim with densely packed concrete and glass buildings and wide roads. It had a small river – the Kanda – but even this had seemingly been completely urbanised. Roads on either side of it. The river walls fortified. There were few signs suggesting it had once belonged to nature. As I strolled onwards, I wondered whether, on the face of it, many visitors would view Tokyo as a pretty city. But I found it all strangely beautiful. Above me, the mangled, birds-nest-like mess of Tokyo's cables and power lines buzzed and hissed. They're ever present. And exist almost in direct opposition to the order and calm which defines much of urban life in Japan, and its culture too.

In Tokyo, you're never far from serenity, despite its at times domineering scale. I strolled down a few of Asakusabashi's backstreets. The city's alleys are for me where Tokyo really shines. I walked down a single-lane, empty road. There were no cars. A few elderly people pottering around. Perfectly manicured plants sat aside simple, two-storey houses. Tiny restaurants without signage looked inviting. Unlocked bicycles were propped up against shop fronts. These unassuming alleyways have a life of their own. It felt like I'd landed in the backstreet of a simple Japanese village. And then I took another turn, and was back in chaos. People. Cars. Huge tower blocks. Tokyo.

I attempted to get my bearings. I tried to remind myself of the Tolkien quote turned travel platitude, 'Not all those who wander are lost.' But I'd forgotten to charge my phone overnight and it was out of battery. All the signs were in Japanese. And while I tried to look as cool as possible (leaning against a wall casually), it was clear I was lost. But seemingly, the polite citizens of Tokyo will do anything to help a lost-looking passer-by.

A kind-looking, well-dressed man approached me. He was about 50 years old, wearing a crisp suit. On his commute, by the looks of things. I think he asked where I was going. But didn't speak English. So, after a short game of charades, the high point of which involved me pretending to be a train, he understood and started walking me towards the nearest train station. Directions or pointing would have sufficed, but no. To my astonishment, he proceeded to accompany me all the way to the station. A 10-minute walk. Once there, he stood smiling and waving until absolutely sure I'd got my ticket and passed through the barriers. Only then did he turn around and walk back to where we'd met. This sort of stuff happens a lot in Tokyo. Unlike some other major cities, where locals would rather do virtually anything than strike up a conversation with a stranger.* It's the atmosphere and friendliness, among so much more, that makes Japan's capital so great.

After about five minutes or so on Tokyo's impeccably clean and punctual subway, I arrived at Oshiage Station. At this stage, I noticed my belly rumbling. In my excitement this morning to be out in this great city I'd forgotten to eat breakfast. I was desperate, so grabbed some sushi from the nearest place I could find. Which happened to be a shabby-looking stall in a poorly lit underpass near the station.

---

*   This is most definitely the case in London.

The Travelling Ape

The sushi was so fresh. So tasty. The ratio of fish to rice was probably four to one. As opposed to the reverse which I was used to when eating sushi outside Japan. 'Even sushi in underpasses is exquisite,' I thought. Strangely, I didn't attempt to morally justify my eating fish to myself, even though at the time I'd recently become a vegetarian. It reminded me that this city is, surely, the culinary capital of the world. The food here is on another level.

Hunger satiated, I craned my neck and looked up. My destination towered above me. Twisted steel reaching towards the sky. I bought a ticket, hopped in a lift, and sped upwards. The doors pinged open, and I stepped out. I took a few steps forward, and then gazed out across the horizon. Concrete. As far as my eyes could see. Thousands of tower blocks stretched into the distance. The city didn't appear to end. The faint, perfectly triangular outline of Mount Fuji was just visible through the smog. I was at the top of the Tokyo Skytree, viewing the city from the world's third tallest structure. In some ways it felt like an out of body experience.

My eyes struggled to accept what I was seeing. While others seemed happy to take selfies, talk loudly (too loudly, perhaps?), and leave after a few minutes, I stayed up there for hours. I was looking at the largest urban area ever created by a human civilisation. A staggering 40 million people live in the Greater Tokyo Area, more than the entire population of Canada. There was barely a tree or a park in sight, only the grey, angular, and metallic constructions of humanity.

I peered around the observation deck. I got the

impression that most people took it as a given that Tokyo had always existed. Whereas to me, I was gobsmacked by the fact that less than 500 years ago this was a small town called Edo with less than 10,000 people. It seemed like a miracle that from nothing, humans had designed and constructed almost everything I could see (Mount Fuji probably being the only exception). And it's in moments like this – nerding out on my own atop an observation deck – that I feel most alive when travelling. Few things generate such a sense of awe for me as seeing humanity's greatest physical creations: cities.

To some, they are polluted, too busy, and not fit for human life. American author Christopher Morley said that 'all cities are mad: but the madness is gallant. All cities are beautiful: but the beauty is grim.'[1] It would be fair to say this about Tokyo in its grey, rectangular oppressiveness. But as I surveyed the skyline, I felt a firm belief that cities are a testament to the ingenuity of human beings. I knew there was *something* special about them, but had perhaps never thought about why, until that day. I pondered. Why can travelling in cities feel so impactful? What can it teach us about humanity's past and future? Of all the world's thousands of cities, which could claim to be the best? And crucially, what has compelled me to ask so many questions? What better place to answer these questions than in a chapter of this book (rather than in my head while up a skyscraper in Tokyo).

As a brief side note, when I wasn't considering deep philosophical questions about urban areas while surveying Tokyo like a slightly deranged king looking out over his empire, I was mainly thinking, 'I really hope the "big one" doesn't strike when I'm here,' something I selfishly think about whenever I'm visiting a city prone to massive earthquakes. Being in an earthquake in Malawi was scary enough – despite the fact that I was camping outside with nothing to land on me but lions, hippos, and rhinos. (The probability of this happening was quite low, I realised only after the initial panic of the event.) But looking at the millions of tons of buildings surrounding me in Tokyo, it didn't feel that safe. You can tell me again and again that these buildings are engineered to withstand earthquakes, but the primitive part of my brain and my nervous system doesn't buy it.

The Lure of Urban Travel

Urban areas are often the first port of call for any traveller. Part of what makes travelling so exciting is the feeling you get when arriving in a new and foreign city. You're instantly plunged into the madness of urban life. You gain an immediate insight into the soul of a nation. For all its merits, natural beauty doesn't provide the same window into a country's people and customs as cities do. Immediately, you're exposed to how people talk, dress, and socialise. You get a flavour of the country's cuisine and culture. And in often a very short time indeed, you mentally start painting a picture of what the country and its people are like.

I'll never lose the love for arriving in a new city,

especially when wandering with no destination. Pockets of solitude punctuated with areas of life so vibrant it appears to explode out from crammed city streets, like in Tokyo and its alleys. Often fantastic. Often heinous. Cities are both good and bad, uplifting and disheartening; the personification of humanity itself, perhaps.

We were once fragile apes. Hunter-gatherers living nomadic existences. But now, over 50 percent of the world's population live in urban areas. This goes up to over 75 percent in the West. Cities are expected to house two-thirds of the world's population by 2050. In 1900 this figure was just 13 percent.[2] What a bizarre change, in such a short time. For most of us who live in cities, almost everything you set eyes on was built by other humans.

Cities like Tokyo are the spasmodic accumulation of hundreds of years of independent human development. They may look planned. But really, they're the result of generations of unplanned chaos. Much like a spider's web is the physical embodiment of the consciousness of arachnids, cities are a projection of the creativity of human minds, brought into the physical realm in the most fantastic manner. We'd do well to remember how astounding they are.

Peering into Our Past

After a few hours spent gazing at the strange beauty of Tokyo, I shuffled back into the lift. Back to sweet (still very earthquake-prone) street level. It was just a 15-minute walk to my next destination. Rare in Tokyo, a city four times the size of London. I wandered down a few more charming, quiet backstreets. Watching happily as local Tokyoites got on with their daily lives. With such a sense of calm, grace even.

Still on foot, I plodded across the Sumida River. Slightly grey, reflecting its surroundings. Lined with tall tower blocks, guarding it like tightly packed bookends. Crossed by multiple rail and road bridges. Riverside highways seemingly squeezing the river inwards from either side. As I strolled onwards, the *newness* of Tokyo became apparent; built at a time where transit and infrastructure took precedence over nature. Few buildings looked more than 50 years old.

It came back to me that Tokyo was flattened by an earthquake in 1923. Tokyoites valiantly rebuilt it. Only for it to be flattened again in World War II. An estimated 100,000 people died in March 1945 from US bombing.[3] It's a little-known fact that more people perished during these attacks than from either of the atomic bombs dropped on Hiroshima and Nagasaki, which ended the war. Tokyo was almost completely destroyed. The capital's post-war rebuild defines the modern city. Lots of concrete. A great deal of boxy and utilitarian-looking buildings, but with some architectural gems among them. Roads and urban highways snake through small gaps, struggling to find clear paths through unrelenting urban sprawl.

After a few more minutes' walking, however, I was pleased to see how small parts of this city's storied history remain. Somehow surviving brutal assaults from both nature and humans (the most dangerous part of nature sometimes). I'd arrived at Sensō-ji, Tokyo's oldest temple complex, completed in 645 CE. I followed charming Nakamise-dori Street up to the temple, a narrow alley packed with pretty little wooden stalls on either side. With shop names in ornate Japanese script, as if written by hand with a fountain pen. As I walked further, the main temple, Asakusa Kannon, became increasingly prominent. It had blood-red wooden beams. Proudly holding up its intricate, curved, tiled Karahafu gable roof. This divine little design, a swooping roof seen on dozens of castles and temples, in many ways defines traditional Japanese architecture. This building, too, was decorated with gold Japanese script. Positioned within it were a few shining, golden Buddhas. Giant lanterns hung from its centre, while a perfectly formed five-tier pagoda sat to the side.

The whole thing felt like the most Japanese thing I'd ever seen. Almost too Japanese, in a way, a cartoon-like version of it. When confronted with ancient architecture it can sometimes feel like you're in a theme park. We've all been exposed to this. Poor attempts at recreating historic buildings as backdrops for log flumes or rollercoasters. But this was the real thing. And it was beautiful.

I sat on the steps, my legs already starting to feel heavy. Craning my head to the left, I could see Tokyo Skytree in the distance. It felt like a new form of pagoda for Tokyo, looming over the entire city and the elusive snippets of Tokyo's past. Especially here, it was possible to imagine what it might have been like to live in the ancient village of Asakusa. Living a simple, Buddhist lifestyle. With perhaps a few hundred other people. On the banks of a sluggish Sumida River. Connected to nature. And surrounded by trees. Rather than by 40 million other humans.

I've had experiences like this in many of the world's great cities. And feel they can give us access to the achievements of former civilisations. It's tempting for us to view anyone who isn't alive now as some sort of ignoramus. And it doesn't help that black and white films or photographs give us the idea that people who lived just decades ago lived in some sort of 'turned down' reality. But this certainly isn't the case. Tokyo's devastating twentieth century means just a few precious buildings, like Sensō-ji, stand as insights into its history.

Other cities have far more physical reminders that help us understand their past. And none more so than Rome. Indeed, you can't really start anywhere other than Rome for its depth of history. The words I'm typing are partially in a Roman script (Latin). The city I live in was founded by Romans. And there are probably some Roman branches in my family tree. When I visited the Italian capital for the second time,* I gained a real sense of just how great this city and civilisation used to be (and still is, to be fair). And as a means of embracing the past, I decided to embrace a (more) recent form of travel and bounce around town on a Vespa.

---

* I was 18 when I first visited. And while not a complete philistine, Rome's incredible history was at the time evidently much less interesting to me and my friends than listening to repetitive, monotonous house music for four days straight. So we rushed through the sightseeing there, in our haste to get to a music festival in Croatia. To be young.

Lessons from Urban Travel

What better way to see historic Rome than on a classic, iconic Italian moped? The mental image I had was of me serenely and elegantly cruising through town. I'd be wearing a crisp Italian suit, stopping to drink an espresso from time to time. And just generally looking like an unrealistically handsome man from an Italian aftershave ad.

The truth was slightly different. If I was being kind, I'd say that Italians drive 'passionately', making the roads quite a hostile environment. And, crucially, I'd never ridden a moped before. I wobbled nervously around town, covered in sweat, apologising profusely to the latest driver who'd almost run me over. Rome's streets are cobbled. Not ideal for any moped rider (let alone one with no experience like me). A particular low point saw me doing one of those slow, sideways, stationary falls while at busy traffic lights. While on my side, moped on top of my leg, I laughed and smiled to concerned-looking bystanders. Excessively and jovially repeating, 'I'm fine!' way too many times. As we all do, when faced with gut-wrenching humiliation in front of people you'll never see again. But still, I rode a Vespa around Rome, and that was my boastful party line to friends and family (until I revealed the truth in this chapter).

I was just about competent enough to drive the Vespa around Rome and see its incredible sights. The Colosseum is breathtaking in its size and splendour. A stadium so advanced it even had a retractable roof, offering shade for those below it. Swap watching gladiators kill each other for people kicking footballs and it was easy to see the links running from this civilisation to ours. Nearby, the city's Forum and ancient underbelly might be crumbling, but is well preserved enough for you to get a sense of what living here would've been like millennia ago. The scale and regal splendour of its architecture pointing to how advanced this civilisation once was. How the wealthy elites probably lived lives not too dissimilar from modern Romans. But hidden out of sight and from these monuments, their gilded lives were propped up by the suffering of slaves.

Later in the trip, I drove down to Naples (in a car, wisely). In Naples and much of southern Italy, it sounds like everyone is talking to each other as if they're having a massive argument. I strolled into Da Michele, allegedly one of the oldest pizzerias in the world. I sat down. Looked at the menu, a paper one, which doubled as a placemat. I ordered a pizza, which seemed to be a fairly reasonable thing to do. Only to then be met with a stinging rebuke and angry face from the Neapolitan waiter, who minutes later plonked a pizza down in front of me with all the care of a man throwing his rubbish away. An Italian friend based in London had warned me about the style of conversations here, and assured me these types of interactions were just a sign of 'Neapolitan passion'. Just how people here communicated. Not totally convinced, I devoured the soft, chewy margherita. It was wonderful. Belly full, I resolved that I wasn't just here for pizza and being shouted at in Italian, I was here to see Pompeii. So off I set.

The excellently preserved city (thanks, Mount Vesuvius) oozes sophistication. I strolled around its cobbled streets. There were perfectly conserved villas with ornate pillars and tiled roofs. I ambled, like the Romans would have, down Pompeii's perfectly grid-like system of streets and alleys. All the while, the triangular peak of the volcano whose eruption destroyed the city back in 79 CE loomed above me. The rich blue sky pierced by the silhouettes of Cyprus trees. As I continued to explore this huge archaeological site, I learnt that people bathed here, used to watch sports, and had dogs. One house had a mosaic that said '*Cave Canem*' – 'Beware of the dog'. For all our modern advancements, seeing things like this reminded me that even two thousand years ago, people's lives weren't so different from ours today. We mistake how 'primitive' historical civilisations were, that the people weren't 'ignoramuses'. And urban centres such as Rome and Pompeii amply illustrate that.

This understanding isn't just limited to my experiences in Italy. I've felt it countless times in other cities. Walking the marble streets of Dubrovnik in Croatia; admiring Spanish colonial architecture high up in the Peruvian Andes in Cuzco; strolling through Prague's dark and dramatic streets, filled with Gothic, Baroque, and Renaissance architecture. Urban travel transports you back to the hustle and bustle of these historical times. Great, ancient cities imbue a sense of wonder about our past. And what about the present? What do our great cities teach us? Which are the modern world's greatest cities?

What Are the Greatest Cities on Earth?

After a few more hours ambling around Sensō-ji, it was time for me to move on. I hopped back on the Tokyo subway. I disembarked at Harajuku, a trendy part of

The Travelling Ape

Tokyo, full of hipsters, and popularised in the West by an incredibly annoying Gwen Stefani song. In Harajuku, my preconceived notions that most Japanese people are largely reserved went out of the window. As I strolled its colourful streets, peppered with coffee shops and tattoo parlours, I passed more than a handful of people with luminous green or pink hair. And sometimes both. Wearing brash, fluorescent outfits, the sort you'd have seen at 'nu rave' parties back in the UK in the late noughties. Or at children's parties now. Or to put it another way, lots of people were wearing really stupid, bad clothes. They seemed to be having fun though, so good luck to them.

Surprised at my catty thoughts about people's fashion – perhaps I was hangry – I headed back down onto the subway, my desire to see this well-known part of town satiated (unlike my hunger). The subway was filled with sombre people wearing boring clothes and suits. I don't know why I felt more at home here, but I did. What a sad soul I must be. A stop or so from Harajuku, I arrived at Shibuya. A Tokyo icon. The world's busiest pedestrian crossing. Thronged on all sides by towers of neon lights and garish, multistorey arcades. And now, seemingly, made much busier by tourists like me, who proceed to cross and recross the junction for 'fun'. Never had crossing a road been so thrilling for so many, including me.*

---

*   Apart from maybe at the Abbey Road crossing in London. Which is either a really annoying traffic bottleneck, or spiritual meeting place for Beatles' worshippers. I'm in the latter camp (but I don't really drive in London, so might be biased).

Lessons from Urban Travel

After my fourth or fifth crossing, I thought, 'That's probably enough.' I'd met a couple of people at my hostel the previous night, and we'd agreed to meet for a coffee. The coffee shop had panoramic glass windows with stools overlooking the junction. So we could sit and watch the little ant-like humans parade back and forth across the junction at will. It was oddly mesmerising, like watching a wave building before crashing over the junction.

I was joined by Randeep, a friendly and outgoing Sikh man from India; he was burly and dressed in expensive-looking clothes. And also by Agnes, a blonde girl in her mid-twenties from Copenhagen, Denmark. We chatted at length about how much we were all enjoying Tokyo, how special Japan is, and how the city is quite unlike anywhere else on Earth.

'It's just insane here. There's so much to do. I think it's the best place I've been, surely the best city in the world, no?' said Randeep.

'Yep, I'd agree. Copenhagen's much more relaxed and probably a more comfortable place to live. But in terms of excitement and the sheer scale of the place, Tokyo is for sure my favourite city,' concurred Agnes, excitedly.

'Hmm, it's definitely up there,' I said. Keen to bolster my ego and credentials in backpacking circles, I explained that I'd been fortunate enough to visit almost all of the so-called Alpha Cities of the world.[*4] These are said to be the world's

_____

★   I completed the list only for Riyadh and Guangzhou to be added after I'd had the conversation. After later chapters in this book, you might see why I'll be reluctant to visit China or Saudi Arabia again in a hurry.

most important economic, political, and cultural cities. There are 49 of them. With London and New York being designated Alpha ++, and Beijing, Hong Kong, Shanghai, Tokyo, Dubai, Paris, and Singapore being Alpha +. (For the remaining cities see the Notes. I didn't bore Randeep and Agnes by listing all of them, even if I then did choose to bore them with my upcoming 'best city in the world' spiel.)

'I think Tokyo's definitely one of my favourites. But would maybe come second place in the world for me, behind London,' I said, cautiously. As I spoke, I remembered that I regularly decried the naivety of people who believed that where they happened to live was ever so conveniently the best place in the world. Indeed, this is the basis of nationalism, effectively. 'Paris is prettier. New York's skyline gives it a bigger 'wow' factor. Sydney has its beaches. But no other city comes close to offering London's astonishing diversity,' I continued. 'London can be a million things to a million different people. It's steeped in history, but punctuated with modernism. It's quintessentially British, while being the most culturally and ethnically diverse city in Europe. It's snooty and stuck up, while being bohemian and edgy.'*

Randeep and Agnes looked at me, as if unconvinced. So I persisted. 'It's best to think of London as 100 different villages mulched together, each with completely different architectural, cultural, and historic characters. It's a mess

---

*   Despite working for large corporations and being painfully middle class, I naively like to put myself in the latter category because I drink artisanal coffee and like street food.

from a city planning perspective, having grown organically over the past two millennia. You see churches next to skyscrapers, warehouses next to quaint village high streets, and regal splendour next to '60s brutalism.

'I spent a day once which perfectly summed up why I love London so much. It started with a stroll along the winding and lazy Thames. I grabbed food at Borough Market, which has sold produce from all over the world since 1850, though it's thought that a market has been at this location for over a thousand years. I strolled past Shakespeare's Globe and St Paul's Cathedral, two icons. Crossing over Norman Foster's Millennium Bridge, I glanced at the new London. The towering, space-age City of London skyline, with the church-steeple inspired Shard just across the river.'

'I've seen the Shard, it's cool, but the top kind of looks unfinished,' said Agnes, questioningly.

'Er, something to do with aviation regulations, them having to shorten the spire,' I responded vaguely, keen to get back to my perfect day story. 'So I continued onwards, diving through swinging Soho. I grabbed brunch with a friend on Carnaby Street, surrounded by mods. I felt like I was back in the '60s.'

I took a sip of my coffee and a pause for breath, still loosely aware of the tides of people rushing around below us at Shibuya Crossing. 'I passed the iconic Houses of Parliament and ambled into the regal splendour of St James's Park, famously overlooked by an old lady's house,* Buckingham Palace. With the rows of Union Jacks and

---

* And to a much lesser extent, her son.

perfectly manicured lawns and flowerbeds, I felt like I'd slipped back into Victorian England with all its pomp. I jumped on the Tube, and set off to Craven Cottage, to watch my local team, Fulham, play in a Premier League football match. The stand I sat in was crumbling and wooden, built in 1905. I sat alongside hordes of aggressive, burly men, who seemed to get very cross indeed whenever a ball didn't go where they wanted it to. As their fathers did, and their fathers probably did before them too.[*]

'After watching my team lose – as is customary and indeed perceived an honour in England – I grabbed dinner. Delicious Ethiopian food. I met up with some friends and partied in a giant abandoned printing factory, which pointed to the grim reality of London's industrial past. Do you think there's any other city in the world where you could have a day like that? My feeling is probably not, which is why London I feel is the best,' I concluded.

Randeep and Agnes sort of nodded. But maybe weren't totally persuaded. So, at risk of being accused of bias by them,[**] I also mentioned that London has been rated as *Time Out*'s best city in the world for the past five years running, so I'm not alone in this line of thinking. That after over 30 years living there, I still got butterflies exploring it. I said that I'd probably spend the rest of my life trying to get to a point where I finally 'know' London but would likely run

---

[*] I've been to hundreds of football matches in England and across the world. And would still estimate men usually make up at least 90 percent of football crowds, for whatever reason.

[**] But fortunately, not at risk of being accused by readers that it surely isn't possible to remember quotes that long verbatim.

out of time as it keeps changing. I thought of the famous Samuel Johnson quote from 1777: 'Sir, when a man is tired of London, he is tired of life; for there is in London all that life can afford.'[5] But stopped short of quoting it out loud, for fear of looking too pretentious. If I didn't already.

I'm not sure Agnes and Randeep were prepared for how much I loved my home city. But they seemed to get my point. They'd both visited, and kind of understood. Randeep backed Paris over London, and Agnes again gently suggested Copenhagen also might have a shot at being the most liveable city in the world.

'How biased and jingoistic is she?' I caught myself thinking, despite the lecture I'd just given her about my home city's greatness.

'New York's definitely up there, though. So, my top three would be London, Tokyo, and then finally New York,' I said. Both had also been to New York, and also loved it. We all shared our experiences of visiting the world's most famous city. I went for the first time as a child, and so began my obsession with all things urban, and skyscrapers in particular. I talked of arriving, age nine, at New York's John F. Kennedy International Airport. Glimpsing the Manhattan skyline for the first time. Seeing the vertical walls of steel and glass looming over the horizon. A sight which has stayed with me forever, and began a decades-long (and still very much alive) obsession with tall buildings.

After about 20 or so more minutes – and definitely not because I'd been boring them – Agnes and Randeep said their goodbyes. They were off to the Ginza district. I felt

The Travelling Ape

I'd done enough walking in, talking about, and pondering the nature of urban areas for one day. So I headed back to my hostel, closed the curtain on my little capsule, and went to sleep.

A few days later, it was time for me to move on from Tokyo. I packed my bags and made tracks for Tokyo Station. The building itself looked slightly out of place. A red brick structure with an imperial feel. All prominent pillars, dramatic and ornate windows. Topped with an angular, pitched roof. Opened in 1914, the design is speculated to have been inspired by Amsterdam's Centraal Station, upon request from Emperor Meiji before his death. Even if only a rumour, I could see the similarities, and felt briefly transported back to Europe. Inside, my feet squeaked on the perfectly polished marble floors. I headed further into the deep underbelly of this sprawling monster of a station, filled with a labyrinth of tunnels and passageways, and reached my platform. To be greeted by the pointy, space-age nose of one of Japan's iconic Shinkansen trains: the bullet train. I was back in Japan.

The doors weren't open. I looked through the windows and could see that all of the as-yet-empty seats had the ability to swivel around (I'm guessing facing backwards at high speeds isn't a lot of fun). Eventually, the doors opened, I entered, and rushed to get a window seat. Soon after, we were off. The train silently accelerated. The ride was as smooth as treacle. The cityscape of Tokyo slipped past, gradually at first. It was only as we reached the edge of the metropolis that the burners were put on. At speeds of 200mph, Japan serenely glides past you on a bullet train. You're treated to a perfect montage of the country's unique loveliness. The concrete blocks of Tokyo giving way to verdant paddy fields, framed by the slightly blurred backdrop of the angular Japanese Alps. Into a tunnel. Out again. Over a valley, and quickly into a tunnel again. And on. The Shinkansen is an engineering marvel. You float through the scenery as if you're barely touching the ground.

I spent the next week immersing myself more in this wonderful country, travelling by Shinkansen as much as possible. I marvelled at the stately Edo-era palaces and gardens of Kanazawa. Visited Takayama, an historic, alpine village. All rickety wooden houses, Meiji-era inns, pretty streams, and hillside shrines. And then visited Kyoto, filled with 2,000 temples and shrines, and leafy, quiet boulevards. And then it was one final, short jump to my next destination and another metropolis – Osaka.

Back to the Future

From Osaka Central Station, I grabbed the train to Nagahoribashi Station. The train tracks were raised above the city streets, right up at the level of its messy and mangled cables, giving peeks into offices as we went. I arrived, and awkwardly weaved my way around throngs of commuters, with my large backpack brushing people, making the turnstiles hard to navigate. Back down on street level, I headed for my hostel. It was only a few blocks away. Just a short stroll.

Osaka – like Tokyo – wasn't pretty in the traditional

sense. But it had something about it. Something hard to put your finger on. The appeal of Japan's cities is more of a feeling than something that can be easily described. Osaka's slightly bland architecture was more than made up for by buildings being cloaked in dazzling neon billboards, with busy streets below. Thronged with pedestrians.

Hostel reached and backpack dumped, I ventured out without delay. Evening was approaching. I was excited to explore the city, which I hadn't visited before. The prospect of a stroll round an unknown destination is like being offered a portal into a new world. It had become cloudy as the day progressed, with gusty, warm winds periodically blowing in my face like a hairdryer. Osaka seemed even more urban than Tokyo (which is saying something). Around 20 million people live in the Greater Osaka area, so this was another giant metropolis. I walked beside a canal over which city planners had decided to build an expressway. It meant the sky was completely obscured from view. Concrete pillars emerged from and were reflected back in the dark water. It shouldn't have been pretty but I found it to be so. In a strange sort of way.

The canal continued, and eventually the sky appeared as the raised motorway tacked away from it. The canal cut through the centre of Dotonbori, Osaka's lively nightlife district. Like with the pillars before, the canal acted as a mirror for the towers of flashing lights, neon screens, and chaotic Japanese script which sat above it. The wakes of tourist boats blurring it, ever so slightly. Being in Dotonbori felt like being in a video game or a cartoon, where the hues and saturation had been turned up to unrealistic levels. It reminded me of dystopian cityscapes from *Blade Runner*. For a moment, fleetingly, it felt very strange indeed to be alive. The oppressive weather and cityscape. It all felt slightly unreal. The weight of my very existence weighed on me. A feeling which was at once exhilarating and melancholic. How peculiar, that we, these little apes, had created this slightly twisted environment. And that one day, I wouldn't be here to experience any of it.

Shrugging off my brief existential meltdown,* I proceeded to have quite a wonderful night out in Dotonbori. I munched on some of the best street food in the world, hoovering up *gyoza* and tofu *karaage* buns. I chatted to locals, a surprising number of whom spoke good English; Osakans appeared brasher and more jovial than Tokyoites. The streets hummed with activity and laughter. But one thing was strikingly similar. After a few hours, some of the streets became littered with people (mainly men) slumped on corners, having had about seven drinks too many. I'd seen this in Tokyo, where work drinks would descend into a kind of chaos on Friday nights. In Tokyo, there was something strangely poetic about seeing men with perfectly made suits and ties splayed on the ground like starfishes, but still valiantly clutching onto their expensive European leather briefcases.

For all of Japan's modernism, there is something slightly *off* about it. Cities like Osaka have this outwardly futuristic feel. But they point to a vision of the future

---

★   I think I was reading the basically incomprehensible works of Jean-Paul Sartre at the time.

which is now dated. The country's cities are like the '80s or '90s view of what the future might be like. So for all the shining lights and signs, some of the buildings themselves don't look space-age. They're concrete boxes from the '60s. They're filled with things that people in the '90s thought would probably take over the world but haven't. Like vending machines which serve hot food. Toilets that talk to you, and have a million flush functions. Capsule hotels. All great, sure. But they hark back to a time when Japan was the world's economic poster child, and dominated the tech scene in the '80s. Its economy has stagnated since the '90s, thanks to its declining population. And it has been in some ways left behind.

What Does Urban Travel Say about the Future?

My trip through Japan and its cities helped me peer into Japan's urban past. Its present. And its probably unhealthy relationship with booze. A few days later, I'd travel somewhere that would teach me more about the future of our cities than Osaka did, with its ahead-of-its-time and yet also outdated feel. I grabbed a flight to Singapore.

Up in the sky, I reminisced about my last trip to this tiny city-state. It had been over a decade before. I was only 19. And to be honest, my friend Josh and I weren't particularly enamoured with the place when we visited. It was too straitlaced. Grey. Regimented. Expensive. Boring. That, and there was this underlying sense of urgency that we should make quick haste to Thailand, or 'Thailash' as

Lessons from Urban Travel

Brits who planned on partying in the country cringingly called it. (But definitely not us. Probably.) The most exciting thing we did in Singapore was take a picture of ourselves topless in one of the pods of the Singapore Flyer Ferris wheel. In retrospect, this was neither funny nor wacky. We also stuck a middle finger up to the city's strict laws[*] by jaywalking once (repeat offenders can be jailed, rather insanely). And by chewing gum. YOLO.

A decade later, I disembarked at Singapore Changi Airport. The airport gave clues as to the miraculous transformation the city had undergone since my last visit. The place was covered with verdant, living walls. With tropical flora flanking travelators. It even had the world's largest indoor waterfall, cascading from a gaping hole in the airport's glass, almost wave-like roof. The water plunged into a dark abyss below, surrounded by lush vegetation. It felt more rainforest than airport. Like Cornwall's Eden Project, but on a much grander scale. Urban greenery would be a theme I'd see all over Singapore.

I took a taxi into town. Singapore's roads were spotless (no jaywalkers in sight – perhaps they'd all been jailed). They were flanked by flawlessly manicured trees, which arched overhead. It made it feel like I was driving through a tunnel made of a natural canopy. Singapore appeared more like a giant, urban botanical (urbanical?) garden than a standard city. I saw skyscrapers covered in trees and vegetation. More living walls that stretched 30-storeys high. Palm trees growing happily, 300 feet in the sky. If

---

[*] But definitely not to an actual policeman.

you've ever watched a post-apocalyptic movie, where trees and grass have overrun a once bustling metropolis, that isn't too far from what Singapore offered. It was truly marvellous. I was genuinely thrilled to be there. Which would have been hard to believe a decade earlier.

'Have I got more boring while Singapore has stayed the same? Or is Singapore actually a more exciting place than it was ten years ago?' I wrote in my journal later that evening. 'After all, in Tokyo, I found crossing and re-crossing the road at Shibuya junction thrilling in some ways. Perhaps my threshold for excitement has just fallen through the floor, if road-crossing is a thrill for me these days.' I stopped writing and pondered the relentless march of ageing, and maturity. Before finishing: 'Who knows. But in any case, Singapore is what the *real* future will look like.'

In the coming days, I noticed more remarkable changes all over the city. As I learnt, these mainly pointed to the so-called Garden City's desire to be the greenest in the world. Urban planners were weaving nature into the city's fabric. New developments must all now include plant life, in the form of green roofs, vertical gardens, and living walls. As someone who loves contemporary architecture and living walls, Singapore is now a favourite destination of mine.

I felt confident that this place would be a template for cities all over the world in the coming decades. Studies show that even having house plants or views of greenery can reduce stress and boost positivity.[6] So it's a good thing that the biophilic city movement is gathering steam, aiming to incorporate more nature into architecture and urban planning.[7] In travelling to countless other cities

Lessons from Urban Travel

worldwide, I've seen how urban greening is a trend that's already catching on. Boston's 'Big Dig' buried its major highways, replacing them with large parks that are lovely to stroll through. Clever urban green spaces like the High Line in New York (built on an abandoned railway) or the Millennium Park in Chicago (replacing old rail yards) are also a sign of things to come.

Urban greening looks like it'll be the tip of the iceberg as cities become fundamentally better places to live. Improved technology and a shift to remote working should lead to less overcrowding on commutes. Fewer cars on the roads will allow for greater pedestrianisation of cities, more cycle lanes, and other things that will make cities generally much nicer places to be. The cars that remain will be electrified. This means city dwellers won't all live as if breathing through an exhaust pipe. I've got no doubt that the Londons, New Yorks, and Shanghais of 2100 will be much more pleasant places than they are today.

A study in 2020 estimated that all things human-made – known as anthropogenic mass – now weigh the same as all of the planet's living biomass.[8] That figure has doubled in just 20 years. It might double again. So we'd do well to be like Singapore, and make greening our urban spaces a central part of their growth if we want to maintain any connection with nature at all as we move into the future.

I reflected on all of this on my final evening in Singapore. I went to watch the sunset on the impossibly large SkyPark

The Travelling Ape

Observation Deck. Raised up 56 storeys, it straddles three buildings and stretches over 1,000 ft. It's the world's largest cantilevered platform and has on it the longest infinity pool anywhere. Singapore's skyline spread out in front of me. Glass skyscrapers twinkling, and turning pink as the sun set. Verdant canopies covering major roads. The air felt warm and damp. Hundreds of cargo ships bobbed out at sea, stretching across the horizon. I'd bookended my trip to Japan with another cityscape. I felt so grateful to have had the opportunity to visit so many of the world's great metropolises.

Urban travel has given me so much. It's made me marvel at what we've been able to create, and made me believe our cities are humanity's most obvious legacy on Earth (assuming we don't nuke ourselves to death). It has allowed me to delve into ancient civilisations, into the essence of the world's best modern cities, and given me clues as to what the future might hold for them. I knew when visiting these urban centres that being surrounded by millions of tightly packed apes would never be as relaxing as lying on a tropical beach. But I felt that to learn about a nation's history, culture, and soul, one has to experience its greatest cities.

Little did I know that I'd later feel grateful for simply having been able to travel so much in the year 2019, including to Japan and Singapore. Before 'you know what' happened. A period which, more than anything, made me certain that those dismissing travel as a trivial pursuit were misguided.

4

The Importance of Travel

Few things on Earth have the ability to engender
perception change in humans more than travel.
It's not to be scoffed at.

A s the plane came into land, it banked. And I could see that the 'runway' was merely a strip of tarmac cut into dense jungle. Its canopy was criss-crossed by dusty-looking orange tracks. Interspersed among the trees were small, single-storey houses with rusty corrugated iron roofs.

I stepped off the plane. It was unbearably hot. The terminal was a swooping concrete structure. It had a modern silhouette, but its finish was rough around the edges, with paint cracking and a battered old sign telling arrivals that we were at 'Freetown International Airport'. I sought refuge from the heat inside, hoping for sweet, sweet air conditioning, but there was none. At border control, the other passengers and I formed an orderly queue. I felt tired. A bit groggy. And after many hours' travelling, just wanted to check into my hotel and collapse in a heap on my bed.

The Travelling Ape

The border guards, as tends to be the convention almost everywhere on Earth, were dour and unfriendly. But for the first time in my life when I arrived in a new country – this was my 151st – I was also greeted by an altogether more unusual sight. Several people wearing hazmat suits. I had my temperature taken. A man forced me to rub enough alcoholic hand gel on my hands to make me drunk through osmosis. I had to dip my feet in a footbath, something I thought was meant for cows.

After a slow slog through immigration and border control, I jumped in a minivan which took me and a few other passengers to a covered pier. A dilapidated and corrugated structure, parts of which appeared to have already collapsed into the sea. 'Hmmm, I hope the boat is in better nick,' I said nervously to one of the other passengers, hoping for a wry smile but instead getting a blank-faced response. He must not have spoken English. Or perhaps the many hours of travel had made him grumpy too.

I stepped onto the boat undeterred (and with no other options – this was only way to get to the centre of Freetown). As we chugged across a wide and imposing estuary, the hilly terrain of vibrant Freetown came into view. I was in Sierra Leone. A thick layer of smog hung menacingly over the city. It actually gave the scene an even more dramatic feel. The sky had a hazy, blurred quality. The outline of Freetown's giant hills almost merging into the sky above. In the foreground, a few large buildings sprinkled the shore. Behind them were thousands of small houses, mainly painted in pastel yellows, greens, and pinks. Little blotches of colour trying to shine through the haze.

The Importance of Travel

The scene reminded me of some of the favelas that I'd seen in Rio de Janeiro. Even the outline of Freetown's aforementioned hills took me back to Rio, with their curved and sweeping profiles. A major difference being that Freetown lacked a comparable Copacabana beach, at least from what I could see. And also, I couldn't remember smelling quite so much burning plastic in Rio. The boat 'captain' – a local man drinking a beer and not appearing to take his nautical responsibilities too seriously – told me that Freetown gets much of its electricity from an offshore 'floating power plant'. This 'power plant' was in reality an old cargo ship that had been altered to burn coal, the fumes of which were being blown by the prevailing Atlantic winds right into town. It dominated the skyline.

I checked into the hotel. As is the case across much of Sub-Saharan Africa, travel wasn't easy here. I knew not to expect cheap hotels or hostels. Places like Freetown get few visitors who aren't government officials or non-governmental organisation (NGO) staff, so you're often forced to stay in terrible value 'international hotels'. Like this one in Freetown. It had a depressing feel, with dark corridors and a massive, empty conference hall. You had to go through airport-style security each time you left and came back. At once making you feel safer, but also more nervous.

I had a short nap. The sort that feels amazing when you drift off to sleep, but where you feel utterly disorientated upon waking a couple of hours later. Then, I grabbed a local taxi and went for a tour around Freetown; I'd hoped to walk or take a bus but was advised there was limited transit infrastructure in the capital.

The Travelling Ape

The city was frenzied but charming. It hummed with activity and vibrancy. The hills and mountains offered stunning views of the sea, but also the challenges it faced. Infrastructure was basic at best; few roads were tarmacked, and rubbish lay strewn across some of its streets. Given what I could see, it made sense that Sierra Leone's average earnings were among the ten lowest in the entire word, with 60 percent of the population living below the poverty line.[1] On one point, however, the authorities had their act together: there were hand sanitation stations on almost every street. Volunteers were handing out flyers, warning of an impending virus.

At this stage, I'd visited enough places like Sierra Leone to understand how fortunate I was to grow up in a developed, democratic, and relatively wealthy country like the UK. Where 'remaining alive' is not one of the main things on people's 'to do' lists. Where poverty is not the norm.

Travelling in places like Freetown reminded me why travel is so important. To help me put my fortunate position in the world into context, and giving me regular opportunities for humility. It helped me realise that many of the problems and issues I complained about back home were trivial. Embarrassingly so, when visiting places where clean water, basic sanitation, and electricity were lacking for some people. Somewhere like Freetown always puts my 'problems' into much-needed perspective. And while some may decry this as 'poverty porn' travel, I personally think we in the West have a duty to see how so many others in the world live. I know many people who've travelled to

South Africa. They witnessed the vast racial and economic inequalities that exist in the country. Many reported that it made them uncomfortable. But these inequalities exist on a global scale. It's just easier to blank them out in the Western safe havens in which most of those reading this book will live in. Unless, of course, you travel.

The Antidote to Nationalism?

The taxi drove me higher and higher into the hills of Freetown. Vegetation got sparser. The space between corrugated-roofed, concrete-walled houses got wider. Exposing the bright orange Earth beneath it, reminding me of the Australian outback. We continued gaining altitude. The battered old taxi wasn't a 4x4. Its wheels slipped and spun as the tarmacked roads gave way to orange tracks. Eventually, we reached the summit of one of the tallest hills that overlooked the city. I got out and spent a few moments enjoying the spectacular vistas of the Atlantic Ocean far below. Humanity, here it seemed, had managed to squeeze itself onto steep rises and into narrow valleys. I looked out over beautiful palm-tree-covered sandy beaches. Which later, I'd sadly realise, were covered in litter. Sunlight shimmered off the ocean waves, tiny white horses dancing on the horizon.

We weren't far off half a mile high, above the thick layer of smog. The sky had returned to its more natural shade of blue. Up near the peak, there was a small hut. It looked like a toilet block; it definitely wasn't big enough to be a home. On one of its damp walls someone had painted a Union Jack. I picked a few flaws in it – 'The diagonal cross doesn't have the thin red strips which represent the saltire of St Patrick, and thus of Northern Ireland. The shade of blue isn't dark enough' – before wondering why on Earth I was even raising these pedantic points purely to myself. It wouldn't be the last Union Jack I'd see in the city.

The legacy of British colonial rule was certainly still notable here; Sierra Leone was ruled by the British from 1808 to 1961.* My slightly depressing 'international' hotel was in a part of the city called Aberdeen (few places on Earth bear less resemblance to that grey, Scottish city than this part of Freetown). It was a few minutes down the road from the palm-tree-lined Lumley Beach, a surname not uncommon in the UK. Earlier, we had passed a settlement called New England. The viewpoint where I was currently standing was in Leicester Village. A ramshackle urban development clinging impossibly to steep, bright orange hills. It, too, bore no resemblance to its British namesake.

Sierra Leoneans speak a creole version of English, given that their ancestors were slaves from London, Nova Scotia, Jamaica, and other parts of West Africa. When my driver told me of this uncomfortable fact as we descended from the peak – as has happened to me in some other former colonies of the British crown – I never quite know what to say. 'Er, yeah. Sorry about that,' is usually the best I can muster.

---

* Britain established Freetown as a haven for liberated slaves in 1787, but had been involved in the transatlantic slave trade before then.

The Importance of Travel

It was at times like these, even squirm-inducing times like these, when I could recognise one of the most important benefits of travel – its ability to expose you to new perspectives and to dismiss preconceived ideas and home-grown prejudices. Exposing you to new points of view, outside the echo-chamber of your home country. Indeed, the nationalist myths that define the lives of so many people quickly unravel the more you travel. Through travel, I better understood that my country's history had both good and bad in it (like all countries' pasts). I could feasibly feel lucky to be from somewhere that has spread democracy and the rule of law. That has given the world so many of its most popular sports, most important inventions, and biggest music stars. But equally, travelling in places like India, Pakistan, and Myanmar (among many other former colonies) directly exposed me to our darker colonial history. The suffering it caused, much of which still reverberates in these countries and many other places. Had I rarely left my home country, I might have never truly witnessed for myself differing views on history, and indeed how the world works. And might have been more prone to a kind of narrow, unhelpful nationalism.

An Incredibly but Unintentionally Environmentally Unfriendly Mini Break

I got the taxi driver to drop me at the beach in Aberdeen. It had a pleasing, curved profile, white-ish sand, and turquoise water, with an awful lot more plastic than you'd hope to see. But on the plus side, the slightly damp and oppressive greyness of its Scottish counterpart was certainly not on show here, as I soaked up the sun. I sat down in a beach bar, overlooking the ocean. It had bright red plastic seats, wonky wooden pillars holding up the roof, and multiple television screens loudly showing English football. It was a beautiful setting.

I enjoyed the sounds of the gently crashing waves, a soft, warm breeze. I was being given the chance to commune with nature for a brief while longer. But instead, I did what almost all of us do. And connected to the wi-fi. To be fair, needs must, particularly in this case. It was March 2020. Just that morning, I'd flown in from Sydney, Australia, where I was living at the time (and it's a bloody long way away, I can tell you). My original aim was to travel overland from Sierra Leone through Guinea, Guinea-Bissau, The Gambia, and Senegal over a four-week period. (If you can place all of these countries on a map, give yourself a pat on the back.)

Before I set off, I dismissed growing talk of a 'pandemic'. As an economic, political, and country risk analyst, a few friends and family asked me for my take on what might happen. 'This madness will all be over in a few weeks,' I confidently asserted. I also ignored my dad's advice not to travel at all, which I internally dismissed as 'helicopter parenting'. I felt that everyone just needed to calm down a bit and let me go on my holiday. Everything would be back to normal soon enough. Right?

I looked at my phone. A few messages from my dad here. A few articles saying the US and many European countries were starting to close their borders there. The UN declaring that COVID-19 was a pandemic. An email from my overlanding group to say our trip across West Africa had been cancelled. A meme where some people had put boxes of 'corona' beers on their heads, claiming to have 'corona' virus, which I presume were deleted as the death toll rolled into the millions. Another message from my dad.

I put my phone away and gazed out to sea. Probably, I felt, it was time for me to pull my head out of the sand. Did I want to be stuck in Sierra Leone during a pandemic? Did I want the Australian borders to close, separating me from my then-girlfriend-now-fiancée Sophie? Would people judge me for getting my predictions about the pandemic wrong? Probably not.* So I looked on Skyscanner. I took a rather large hit to my wallet (and my pride) and booked flights back to Australia. Or in other words, I ran away, as most intrepid explorers do. I spent a night in Freetown, then reluctantly hopped back on a plane to Sydney (my choice, not because my dad told me to) and completed one of the most expensive, long-distance, and environmentally unfriendly weekend 'mini breaks' in human history.

After about 24 hours in the sky, I touched down at Kingsford Smith Airport. Almost as soon as I'd landed, Australia closed its borders. I'd made it by a few hours. I took the train to Circular Quay. Despite having been based

---

*   The great thing about working in the 'prediction' business, as I do, is that when you get predictions wrong you simply remind everyone that predicting the future is, in effect, impossible. But when you get your predictions right, you take full credit for them.

here for six months, the sight of the Harbour Bridge and the Opera House never got old. Sydney has to have the most delightful natural harbour on the planet. The iconic yellow and green ferry to Manly was already waiting at Wharf 3. I made it just in time and clambered up the stairs to get my usual seat at the side of the boat. It allowed me to gaze at Sydney's simply wonderful bays and beaches as we chugged across the water to the Northern Beaches.

As I sat there, wind in my hair, sea spray lightly covering me whenever we ploughed through a big wave, I took stock of the last few days. Having my trip drastically curtailed by factors outside my control didn't feel good. 'Not being able to travel sucks,' I thought. Little did I know that Sierra Leone was to be the last new country I would visit for two years.

Despite the borders closing, it was a few weeks before lockdowns started in earnest. Eventually, with my visa running out, I had to return to the UK. But before my departure, I spent a few more idyllic weeks walking Sydney's dramatic beaches and cliffs. Having overpriced coffees in affluent Manly, enjoying the sunshine. Occasionally, I'd chat to some Sydneysiders about my travels. They couldn't understand why I'd want to go to somewhere like Sierra Leone. And for that matter, many couldn't understand why anyone would want to leave Australia at all. Ever.

In the local coffee shop I often visited to write my daily freelancing articles, I chatted to the owner, Paul. A friendly man who must have said 'g'day' about a thousand times daily to his many loyal customers.

'I don't know why you'd wanna go somewhere like Sierra Leone, mate,' he said. 'We got the weather, the beaches. It's like every day is a holiday here. This is the best city on Earth, in the best country. Africa can wait for another time.'

'Yeah, Sydney's definitely up there,' I replied. 'I love it here. Just curious, though, if Sydney's your favourite city and Australia's your favourite country, what are your second and third favourites? Which places can you compare it to?'

'Don't know, mate, haven't seen much of the rest of Australia. But we're the lucky country, you know, so I'm pretty sure the rest of it's beaut too.' To Paul, Australia *was* the world, and the rest of the actual world simply wasn't on his radar. If you watch local Australian news, you'll see this same attitude repeated.

I can't tell you the number of times I've had discussions like this with locals. In countries ranging from Australia to Thailand to Iraq. Where the theme rests on, 'Isn't where I live the best place in the world?'* Normally, I nod along to develop an element of rapport with whomever I'm talking to, particularly in places where I feel uneasy.

Sydney, to be fair, is lovely. And Australia's a great nation. But if forced to leave the confines of their home country, many people, including Aussies, might realise that where they were born probably isn't the best place in the universe. There could well be places with better food, weather, and scenery. And for that matter, even if they did

---

* The astute among you might now be crying hypocrisy, given that I chose London as my favourite world city. But I'd counter that with: a) I've at least seen almost all the other world cities for myself, b) this is my book so if I want to be a hypocrite I can.

live in the actual best country in the world (Norway or Switzerland, probably), travel might perhaps allow them to scrutinise why they were so proud of that fact. What have they done to contribute to the success of their nation? Aside from the fact that they were randomly born there – something they played literally no role in – where does the feeling of national superiority come from?

Is Travel Fatal to Prejudice?

Back in my hometown of London, the months of lockdown dragged on, and turned into years. I had plenty of time to look back on my travels. I tried to console myself that I was one of the lucky ones. I didn't lose my job during the pandemic. My family and I remained safe. But I still missed travel.

One of the things I had time to consider was whether the huge growth in travel in recent decades has coincided with a fundamental collapse in levels of global conflict in the second half of the 20th century? My experiences travelling make me confident that our ability to visit other countries, in person, played a role in this. The world is much less scary when you see it for yourself, rather than learn about it online. And indeed, during the pandemic it was sad to see how so many nations once again descended into jingoistic name calling. Could it be that seeing other countries and cultures *for yourself* makes you a more open person? Can travel help you develop a more empathetic view of people from other countries?

The Importance of Travel

American writer Mark Twain would say so. He said in his 1869 book *The Innocents Abroad*:

> Travel is fatal to prejudice, bigotry, and narrow-mindedness, and many of our people need it sorely on these accounts. Broad, wholesome, charitable views of man and things cannot be acquired by vegetating in one little corner of the Earth all of one's lifetime.[2]

It's only through exposure to the 'other' that you challenge your preconceptions. Indeed, in the social sciences, contact theory suggests contact between groups promotes tolerance and acceptance.[3] From personal experience, my views on the world have changed irrevocably because of travel. In my sheltered, pleasant childhood growing up in Southwest London, I fell into the trap of believing my country's people were 'the best'. Like many people still do, I also believed sweeping claims about Americans being brash, Germans being boring, South Americans being lazy. I'd not been to any of these places yet, of course. All I had to support my views were the views of other people living in my own country (most of whom were unlikely to have visited these places, either).

When I *did* get to these countries for myself, I was embarrassed by my lazy preconceptions. Most Americans are polite. Many Germans are funny (they have a dry sense of humour). South Americans are the opposite of lazy – you only need to go there to see how hard so many people toil just to exist in parts of that continent.

The Travelling Ape

There are millions of people in each of these places. Categorising 330 million Americans, 80 million Germans, and 422 million South Americans into narrow personality types is preposterous. And yet, most of us still do it. Had I sat 'vegetating in one little corner of the Earth' for the rest of my life, I doubt my views would have changed. Indeed, how could they?

I've learnt more on my travels than from any classroom or website or movie. I only wish travel could somehow be part of every person's education. I count myself lucky that it was for me. I know that travelling has made me a bit more open. Slightly less narrow-minded. And given me a staunchly positive view of humanity in general. I'm inclined to think this isn't just a one-off, given that I've met many other experienced travellers who feel the same way. And there is perhaps no one more experienced than Harry Mitsidis, with whom I sat down to speak on the subject.

Harry puts my globe-trekking exploits to shame. He is most likely the best-travelled person in human history. Although this is something he modestly denies, the statistics speak for themselves. Harry has been to every country, as well as 1,233 out of the world's 1,301 regions (which include things like states and municipal districts). He sits atop *NomadMania*'s master ranking for the best-travelled people on Earth. When we talked, I asked whether travelling had changed the way he sees the world. He replied:

> I've always believed that human beings are inherently good, and intense international travel

The Importance of Travel

has only strengthened my belief given that almost everywhere I have been, I have found helpful, open people who are as curious about me as I am about them. Though it may sound very clichéd, I think the greatest lesson is that we truly are more or less the same, with almost identical needs and desires, no matter the obvious differences in lifestyle, material conditions or beliefs about the world.

Harry and Mr Twain and I clearly agree on this[*]. But you don't need to take just our word for it. Science backs up our conclusions. One study showed that travel breeds greater openness. It examined German students – yes, many of whom were probably funny. One group of these students took a year to study abroad and the other group stayed home. Those who travelled showed increases in openness to new experiences and emotional stability compared to those who didn't leave the country.[4]

A separate study showed that trust in humanity was boosted by travelling to *multiple* countries. Its experiments showed evidence that there's a relationship between the breadth of foreign travel experiences and increases in trust in the benevolence of humanity.[5] The study author added, 'The more countries one travels, the more trusting one is. Breadth is important here, because breadth provides a greater level of diversity in people's foreign travel

---

[*] By including us all in the same sentence, I hope to subtly imbue the idea among readers that I'm Twain's literary equivalent and have travelled as much as Mitsidis. Which, in both cases, simply isn't true.

experiences.'[6] ('See, everyone, that's why Michael Richards has been to so many countries,' he forgot to add.)

Until we travel, we often fear the unknown.

Given the many important benefits of travelling, it's unfortunate that the majority of the world's population don't get the chance to do it. Globally, most people will never step foot outside the country where they were born. Even in two of the richest places on the planet, almost half of their residents have never left home soil. In the United States, the figure is around 40 percent of people,[7] compared to around 37 percent of those living in Europe.[8] Some 11 percent of Americans have never even left their own state. For most, this is because travel is too expensive. Anyone who gets to do it is in the privileged minority. So its advantages, sadly, will remain out of reach for the many.

It's worth noting that even if you haven't travelled much, however, you can still reap the benefits of travel later in life. It's now widely accepted that neuroplasticity – the ability of the brain to change over the course of its life – persists in some form throughout adulthood.[9] Michael Merzenich, known as the 'father of brain plasticity', argues that people who travel to new places and continue to experience new things into old age are far less likely to develop cognitive decay.[10]

Even if travel abroad isn't feasible, the benefits of vacationing should not be understated. One study found older men who took regular vacations were 32 percent less likely to die from heart disease.[11] Another discovered that women who holiday every six years or less had a much higher chance of having a heart attack compared to women who vacationed at least twice a year.[12] These studies accounted for income levels and pre-existing poor health. Taken together, all of the studies we've looked at imply that travel probably offers the same sort of physical and cognitive benefits as crossword puzzles. With the added bonus that you don't have to bore yourself with endless crosswords. Perfect.

It might sound clichéd, but travelling the world has shown me that the village, town, or city you were born in isn't really your home. The world is.* It would be a shame to get so pulled into the daily grind that you don't stop to consider the wonders that this planet has to offer. Heed the advice of Brazilian lyricist and novelist Paulo Coelho: 'If you think adventure is dangerous, try routine, it's lethal.'[13]

You only have one life. There's only one Earth. Travel is more than a pastime. It's a way to connect to the world, to the lives of others, and to a common humanity that prevails even though it's so often obscured from view. Few things can shift your perceptions as profoundly as travel. I've seen a fair bit of what this world has to offer, and can say that exploring it has been the privilege of my lifetime. It's not always pretty or comfortable. But the journey changes you, and that's quite a profound thing.

We've now looked at what travelling nearly everywhere

---

*   I'm not sure I can bring even myself to believe my own platitudes. I accept that your home is your actual home. But you get my point.

has taught me about the concept of travel. We do it because it feels good and expands our minds. My travels have shown me just how much this staggering planet has to offer us, and it has helped me fall in love with the urban areas that so many of us call home. It's shown me that travel could be a potential antidote to nationalism and narrow-mindedness, and for this alone, it's a much more important pursuit than we give it credit for. Hopefully, some of this might convince you to book your tickets to somewhere.

If more proof is needed, though, of the importance of travel, then indulge me by reading one more anecdote that demonstrates its positives. This time, from Central Asia.

I remember once travelling in the stunning and jagged peaks of Tajikistan, up in the Pamir Mountains (did I mention I travel?). I was nestled among some of the highest peaks in the world outside the Himalayas. I grabbed some lunch; fresh fish from the alluring lake I was sitting beside. I munched on the fish, and then gazed periodically upon the rich, turquoise waters of one of Tajikistan's Seven Lakes. Snow-capped peaks pierced the jet-blue sky. I was tired; I'd been trekking for most of the day. Altitude is a killer.

I'd not seen a tourist for days, and that had been back in the leafy capital, Dushanbe. Certainly, there were none in the tiny, remote mountain settlement where I was currently staying, next to Kuli Marghzar lake. There wasn't any electricity. The locals lived simple, rural lives, most of them as shepherds or farmers. Their lifestyles looked like they hadn't changed much for decades, if not centuries.

The Importance of Travel

As the sun set, I left the lake and went for an evening stroll around the village. There were little green fields with goats in them. Collapsing walls, made of little local stones. It was charming, in an unfamiliar and yet alpine kind of way. The surrounding behemothic mountains felt as if they were almost on top of the village. Protecting it in some way from the outside world and modern civilisation. A smiling local popped out of his house, a basic, one-storey structure built into the rock, called a *chid*. He was wearing a beige tunic on top of an ornate lilac undercoat. His face was weathered and wrinkled, but kind, with large laughter lines at the edge of his eyes. He wore a dark grey skull cap, called a *tubeteika*.

He initially looked shocked to see me. There was a brief moment when we just stood still, about 15 feet away from each other. Him staring and me trying to make myself blend into the local environs (incredibly unsuccessfully). But then he smiled and frantically beckoned for me, and I duly approached. He spoke no English. For this reason, I didn't even catch his name. Years ago I might have been cautious, but I'd seen enough of the world to know that in these situations, people's motivations are almost always overwhelmingly positive. And I was right.

I stayed for dinner. I sat with the local Tajik shepherd whose name I didn't know, his family, and a bunch of other villagers (or 'the old gang' as I mentally called them). We ate Tajik bread, a circular, puffed out loaf, large as a pizza and thick as a cake. We ate (as you'll eat for most meals in Central Asia) *plov* – meat, onions, and carrots, served with rice on a single platter in the centre of a communal table.

The Travelling Ape

I tried to scoop out the meaty parts of the *plov* on the sly, which I'd feed to the local dogs later, not wanting to offend anyone for not eating all of the meal.

It's strange. In situations like this – in a remote corner of Tajikistan – I was always struck by how much of a bond you can build with strangers. Despite the minor inconvenience of not being able to communicate with them. At all. We drank. We laughed. We ate (some questionable) food. It was a great evening. And as I sat there, I realised I hadn't felt uncomfortable at any stage during the entire meal. There was no fear. I'd been in enough situations like this to know they almost always end well. From being a slightly insular, nervous, and risk-averse child while growing up, travel had changed me into someone who sees that humans are mostly good, the world is safe, and we don't need to be afraid of people from other places. Travel had given me so much, and nothing more than insights into the nature of humanity. Which is what we'll be looking at in the next section of the book.

PART II

Humanity: There's More to Celebrate than Lament

5

The World Is Better
than We Are Led to Believe

*It's nowhere near perfect, but travelling has
shown me that we humans have created a
modern world our ancestors would be envious of.*

I flung my backpack into a taxi and set off for my
guesthouse. I could see lots of hills and mountains
stretching out to the horizon. Muddy roads snaked
around volcanic landscapes. Terraced farms clung
precariously to steep hillsides. It looked strikingly verdant,
even though we were most definitely in an urban area.
I was immediately taken by this little slice of the world
called Rwanda.

Most people tend to think of only one thing when
they hear the word Rwanda – genocide. And certainly I
felt a little apprehensive. As if my mind was about to be
exposed to constant, visible signs of the suffering that once
occurred here. As I peered out of the taxi window, I was
almost actively looking for confirmation that this was a
tragic and scarred place. But I saw nothing of the sort.

Driving around the capital Kigali and its surrounds, I

soon noticed it was one of cleanest places I'd ever been to. Certainly the cleanest city in Africa. Buildings were still a little rough around the edges, but the streets were spotless. Houses were immaculately painted, often in bright colours. There was barely a blade of grass out of place outside the civic buildings. There was a feeling of order that made me feel serene while in this city too. I soon learnt that there was good reason for how aesthetically pleasing Kigali was. It was Saturday. People were busy cleaning and beautifying the busy streets. And not just a few people. Seemingly everyone.

My guide Claudine explained, 'By law, *everyone* in Rwanda must help clean up on the last Saturday of each month. It's called *Umuganda*.'

'Do people like it?' I asked, struggling to hide the surprised look on my face.

'Most of us. It's helped communities come together, and heal our past. It's helping Rwanda have a brighter future.'

Claudine was in her mid-thirties and had a kind and friendly face. Like many who I'd meet on my trip to Rwanda, she was upbeat. Disarmingly so. As she explained how much she enjoyed being forced to clean up once a month, we passed a police checkpoint, there to check *Umuganda* was being adhered to. We got pulled over. I wondered whether I'd have to jump out, but the policeman soon realised there was a tourist on board, and happily waved us on. The policeman's smiles and friendliness did nothing to counter my guilt. The idea of being a 'spoilt Westerner' never seemed more accurate. At the same time, I knew that tourism was one of the key drivers of the country's now fast-growing economy.

The next morning, after a night's sleep that wasn't long enough, we drove northwest. The scenery was spectacular. Rwanda is known as the Land of a Thousand Hills. And it was easy to see why. We wound our way up, around, and down hill after hill, with sweeping views of the countryside. The tropical vegetation peppering splashes of bright green over the soggy and orange ground. I could smell the moist earth and the wet grass and felt connected to nature in a way so often absent in my hometown of London. Agriculture appeared to have crept into every arable acre. And this made sense. Around 12 million people are squeezed into this country, which occupies an area not much bigger than Wales (which has a population of just over 3 million). There was barely a patch of land that I could see which hadn't been in some way manipulated by humans to feed Rwanda's ever-growing population.

The scenery became wilder as we approached the border with Uganda and the Democratic Republic of the Congo. Perfectly formed little volcanoes dotted the horizon, towering above the fertile agricultural land below. It was getting cloudier and colder, a sign that we'd been gradually gaining altitude. Eventually, the farmland gave way to thick and, ostensibly, impenetrable jungle. We hopped out of the 4x4. I dropped my bags in the lodge we'd arrived at and was told to prepare to 'get wet' by Claudine.

Claudine introduced me to our wider tour group, of about ten people. We were met by a park ranger called Shema. She was wearing green combat trousers and a camouflage jacket, accessorised with a rather large gun. She looked more soldier than park ranger. The only thing giving her away was a bright red backpack (which negated any of the camouflage offered by the rest of her outfit). That and she was also softly spoken, making me feel less like I was about to set off to hunt jungle-based militias. She asked our small group to follow her, and to take care with the slippery earth and soaked undergrowth.

After seeing the skeleton of one of our earliest extinct ancestors in Ethiopia,* I'd come to Rwanda to contact some of our closest *living* relatives. The rain was torrential; Claudine's warning wasn't wrong. We spent two hours or so slipping and sliding around the muddy Volcanoes National Park. The ground was so sodden that even a minor incline was impossible to climb without grabbing on to trees or vines. And as we trudged further into the park, I felt a real peace coming over me. I was grateful to be out in the forest, connecting with nature.

Shema said we were getting close, and to keep talking to a minimum. Then, all of a sudden, there they were. We'd stumbled into a gorilla nest. We appeared to be almost surrounded by these amazing animals we'd trekked to see. Some of the gorillas were so deeply embedded in the lush undergrowth that I could only see their faces poking out. Strangely familiar, so very human. They grabbed leaves off trees, and stuffed them into their mouths, absent-mindedly. Their jet-black hair and shiny hands and faces stuck out against the many green hues of the jungle. The

---

*   Lucy, for those of you not paying attention in the Introduction.

air, so thick with humidity, was also tinged with the musky, pungent smells of these great creatures.

At that moment, I knew that my life was completely at the mercy of these wild animals. Our guide had told us that gorillas can be *nine* times as strong as humans. (I like to call it eight, otherwise my lifetime of vainly doing bicep curls in the gym has been a complete waste.) It was perhaps the most enchanting experience of my life.

We were supposed to keep a 10-yard distance, and to remain still if the gorillas approached us. But this was impossible. The gorillas had other ideas. A silverback ominously ambled closer. The sheer power, muscularity, and dominance of the creature was palpable. Had he wanted to, he could have ripped us apart with his bare hands. He grunted, moving slowly. His arms were gigantic, his back enormous. Standing next to a professional bodybuilder, the silverback would still look ginormous. No amount of bicep curls or gym memberships would make a difference against these beasts.

After sizing us up, the silverback let us be. He walked on all fours, on clenched fists, and slowly brushed past us, as if we were just a minor irritation, like a fly. His fur had the smell of damp human hair. He took a seat a few feet away from us, surrounded (aptly) by what seemed like a throne of bamboo and vegetation. After he had seemingly given us humans 'the okay', a playful infant came to curiously inspect the new human toys that had just arrived. The way this young gorilla moved, the way they all moved, the life behind their eyes and their vitality, was so remarkably human.

The Travelling Ape

One looked me straight in the eye and brushed my head with its hand. It was like I'd seen this face and gaze before, that this was somehow a familiar encounter. Like we could see each other's souls. That gorillas share 98 percent of our DNA made perfect sense to me.[1] I felt connected to natural selection and evolution – our real creator – in that moment. Feeling awe. And a reverence for the frankly unfathomable truth that this gorilla and I were distant relatives.

I spent the next few days reliving the experiences at the gorilla nest. Witnessing these primates with my own eyes, I found it hard to believe that we humans – essentially humble apes too – had created the modern world that we live in today. The gorillas were majestic in their beauty, and being around them in their natural habitat was a true privilege. I'll treasure those memories for the rest of my days.

But. The strength and power of the apes stood in direct opposition to their fragility. They've been as close to extinction as it's possible to be over the past few decades. All of the mountain gorillas in the world live in a 174-square-mile region of volcanoes, on the border between Rwanda, Uganda, and the Democratic Republic of the Congo. In 2010, they numbered fewer than 500, with numbers increasing only slightly in recent years.[2] I'd seen one of the few families that still exists in the world.

Planet of the Apes

We humans have gone in an altogether different direction from the gorillas that had captivated me in Rwanda, whose way of life hasn't changed for millions of years. They remain in the jungle, as they always have been. Humans and gorillas split from a common ancestor a 'mere' 10 million years ago. Or if you imagine the world as just a day old, around three and-a-half minutes ago. We share even more in common with bonobos and chimps (99 percent of their DNA), branching off from a common ancestor around four to seven million years ago, again, in Africa.[3] This was just one minute and 45 seconds ago.

What is our nature as humans, then, and how similar are we to our primate relations? One of the world's leading primatologists, Frans de Waal, has spent his life studying the behaviour of chimps and bonobos. He argues that we can learn a lot from our nearest genetic cousins. He says we do have the selfish, mean, and violent tendencies of chimps, as told in Jane Goodall's horrifying accounts of inter-group chimp violence. Goodall described the invaders 'cupping a victim's head as he lay bleeding with blood pouring from his nose and drinking the blood, twisting a limb, tearing pieces of skin with their teeth.'[4] Chimps have also been known to murder members of their own group, abuse their dead, and even eat them.[5]

But de Waal also argues we have the loving instincts of bonobos, which are largely peaceful creatures. They live in harmonious, matriarchal communities where they use complex vocal sounds to communicate with each other.[6] They have sex almost constantly, demonstrate empathy to strangers, and generally seem like a much less scary bunch. De Waal argues we are both chimps and bonobos, and are split down the middle.[7] The generosity of spirit witnessed between countrymen in wartime, compared to the violence these same people will show towards the enemy. Or perhaps the friendliness of the local Rwandans smilingly enjoying *Umuganda*, juxtaposed with the horrendous violence which engulfed the country in 1994. We humans are capable of the sublime and horrendous.

What we've achieved since our days spent first as apes in jungles, and then as early nomadic humans, is nothing short of remarkable. We've created culture, language, economics, and gone to the moon and beyond. We've created democracy and governments to bring order to what would ultimately be a messy and violent existence. We've built skyscrapers, dammed rivers, felled forests, and moved mountains; changing how the world looks both around us and from space. And then there are the arts. Can you imagine a world without music, film, and literature? Or theatre?*

And then there's technology, which most of our ancestors would believe to be the work of magic. We've gone from being chased by rhinos to microwaving burritos. From creating cave paintings to photo-realistic, 3D computer worlds. Then there's electricity itself. Do you ever stop to think about how incredible it is? Conceptually, most of us still don't understand how it even works, me included. But we take it for granted, a constant in our lives as much as the sky is blue and trees are green.

Clearly, we humans weren't content eating leaves in the

---

* Actually, I can imagine a world without theatre, and it's a perfectly good one.

jungles of Africa. Being personally exposed to our rather primitive beginnings in the Volcanoes National Park, I felt it was fortunate that our evolution didn't incline us to remain in the jungle. And it's from this starting point that a discussion about our progress as a species and analysis of the modern world must begin.

Jungle Life

A few days after seeing the gorillas, I took a short flight down to Dar Es Salaam, in Tanzania. The hectic, traffic-filled city, Tanzania's largest, would be the start of an overlanding trip right across Africa, ending in Cape Town. Over a couple of months, I'd travel through Malawi, Zambia, Zimbabwe, Botswana, Namibia, and finally, South Africa. I'd travel over 3,000 miles on our overlanding bus – often on painfully slow and bumpy 'roads' – all the while camping and cooking for myself (and travel companions) each night. When not busy crapping in holes in the ground or fixing broken tyres, I'd also continue to learn a great deal about humanity's humble beginnings. And be exposed to our undeniable advances in recent centuries.

For example, camping each night helped me adjust to life without luxury, in places where humans were more exposed to the forces of nature. As we had been for most of our existence. Camping wasn't always easy, particularly when we were bush camping. In these scenarios, there was no electricity, no running water, no toilets. A typical day involved waking when it got light; dismantling our temporary homes; packing up our things, and moving on to the next destination. When we arrived at our next camp, we'd have to assemble everything. Again. Go and collect firewood; find a source of water. We had limited food supplies, so hunger became more of a reality than it normally was in my daily life (where it was not a reality at all, and usually satiated as soon as it came up). We'd wait for it to get dark, so we could go to bed. And then do it all over again.

I was often profoundly aware that I was surrounded by things that could kill me. In Zambia, a genuine worry was hippo attacks, as we were located on the banks of the hippo-infested waters of the Zambezi. In the Okavango Delta in Botswana, we were twice awoken by the minor shock of elephants trundling through our camp. I could hear them breathe. I could smell their scent, as they stood only feet away. All it would've taken was a clumsy misstep from one of them, and I'd have ended up looking like a half empty tube of toothpaste. That we find the dark so naturally terrifying as children finally made sense to me while we bush-camped across the wilds of Africa. And this also perhaps explained why going to the toilet in the bush was so unnerving at night – being scared of the dark serves the evolutionary purpose of helping us not being eaten at night.[8] Anthropologists estimate that roughly one in sixteen of our ancient ancestors ended up as food for large predators,[9] so for those ancestors, that fear I temporarily felt must have been a real and all-consuming issue.

Now look, I like camping as much as the next person (which means I sometimes love and sometimes hate it. It usually depends on the weather). But having to build my 'home' each night, and this home being made out of felt, certainly made me appreciate so many of the comforts we take for granted in our modern world. I'd often internally moan to myself on nights when I struggled to sleep: 'This roll mat doesn't do anything. An inch of foam is not a bed. How camping firms have successfully marketed them as such is beyond me.'

But I'd then remember that many of our historic predecessors would probably have given an arm and a leg just to have a roll mat. Or my sleeping bag. Or tent. Let alone my torch, toiletries, or phone. My camping experience would have been like a luxury holiday compared to how hunter-gatherers used to live. We sometimes forget that for 99 percent of human existence, we lived as hunter-gatherers.[10] And it was only in situations like this, while travelling with none of the niceties of my usual life, that I was better able to understand the acute improvements in humanity's way of living in recent centuries. And it made me less likely to moan about some of the problems we face, particularly in the West (most likely the freest, most advanced civilisation ever to exist). It helped me realise just how blessed we are to have been born in this era, and not back then. It made me think that the roughly eight billion people alive today have more to be happy about than the 100 billion or so people who lived before them.[11]

The Travelling Ape

Peering into Our Past (Again)

The first few weeks of the trip across southern Africa passed in a blur of colour and noise. We saw the Big Five game animals in Tanzania's Serengeti National Park. We camped on the peaceful shores of Lake Malawi, a body of water so vast it seems like an ocean. We kayaked down hippo-patrolled waters of the Zambezi, one of the most exciting but probably stupidest things I've ever done in my life. Hours spent trying to avoid bobbing hippo heads and even the occasional elephant. We crossed Zambia's border to Zimbabwe – an epic arched bridge with views of the monumental Victoria Falls. The way the spray billowed upwards from the falls reminded me of Mount Yasur, back in Vanuatu. Another example of nature's true might, its true majesty.

We watched some ridiculously cute meerkats in dry and desolate southern Zimbabwe. The meerkats lived in little holes in the cracked earth, looking tiny against the uninterrupted expanse of dry grasses and sand. They'd sporadically pop their heads out of the holes. Standing bolt upright, anxious as hell, looking to the sky, trying not to be eaten by eagles. From what I could see, the life of a meerkat was thus: spend every waking moment being petrified of death for a few stressful years, and then actually dying. This is what life is like for most animals, and perhaps our own ancestors. I was glad that life for the vast majority of modern humans was no longer a terrifying battle for survival. And we could now instead moan about being 'bored' or not having enough 'fun'.

The World Is Better than We Are Led to Believe

A few days later, we arrived in Bulawayo, Zimbabwe's second largest city. We stayed on the outskirts of the rather chaotic place, enjoying the relative luxury of being allowed to sleep on someone's front lawn. That of a seemingly wealthy (and white) Zimbabwean family, who lived in a well-maintained villa. While many white Zimbabweans had left in recent years, those who had stayed still appeared to control much of the country's limited wealth.

Our hosts were a middle-aged couple, with two small children and, more importantly, a friendly golden retriever we could play with. Their hospitality did seem a touch conditional on us agreeing to convert to Christianity, however. Over dinner, I was asked if I could pass the rice and almost at the same time told, 'While you have sinned, God will forgive you if you repent.'

'Hmm, delicious,' I replied. After being reminded of my evil nature for about the thirtieth time, I headed for bed. At daybreak, we awoke, hopped in a convertible 4x4 (a nice change from the overlanding truck), and set off for the day.

It was a two-hour drive through dense and undulating terrain. Our battered old Land Rover trundled and clattered aggressively along orange, slippery, muddy tracks. Huge granite boulders jutted proudly out of the jungle below. Some defied gravity, with one unfeasibly teetering on top of another, looking destined to topple. We zoomed past zebras and giraffes. Eventually, we were told to hop out of the vehicle.

We were led deep into the undergrowth by our guide for the day, Zimbabwe's infamous 'Rhino Man'. Part man, part rhino, this strange creature was one of the most peculiar sights I've ever witnessed. Not really. He's just a white Zimbabwean man who really likes rhinos. His name is Ian (doesn't sound quite so exciting now). He was tall, lanky, and tanned. And spoke with a thick Zimbabwean accent. It was clear from his dusty clothes and leathery skin that this was a person who spent most of their life outdoors.

Ian is a living legend. I'd never met anyone who's so passionate about the natural world. And, of course, rhinos, which he described as 'his children,' while we stood in a clearing between the trees. When he told us this, I laughed at first, thinking this was for comedic effect. But Ian was being deadly serious.

'I'm connected to these great creatures,' he said in a low drawl. 'They are my family, my life. It's my job and life's work to protect the endangered African rhino. And you can see a few of them in front of you now.'

We stood in the clearing, surrounded by tall grass. A group of four rhinos – a 'crash' according to Ian – stood motionless, sheltering under a lone tree. There are few things on earth that look so prehistoric. Their thick hide, sheer bulk, and mottled faces would've seemed much more appropriate a few hundred million years ago, I felt. And also appropriate would be not having them standing just a few feet from where I was currently located. Somewhat inevitably, the rhinos started to charge (walk slowly) towards us. Ian told us to not move quickly, and act in a 'deferential' way. It reminded me of similar advice I was given when gorilla trekking in Rwanda: 'If a huge thing that could easily kill a human tries to attack you, just remain calm and don't panic.' Simple.

The World Is Better than We Are Led to Believe

To be fair, we did feel safe with Rhino Man at our side. They waddled up to us, and to Ian in particular. He was able to stroke and pat them, inviting us to do the same. Which some of us did, very gingerly indeed. It was a captivating experience, one of many we'd had in this most ancient of continents over the past few weeks.

We bundled ourselves back into the Land Rover. The relief of being out of reach of the rhinos was only marginally offset by how bumpy the ride was. After some time – enough to know I passionately didn't want to be shaken like a cocktail any longer – we arrived at our next destination. A giant cave lay ahead of us. It was impressive, sure. But I didn't yet see what the fuss was about. It effectively looked like a big hole in a cliffside. But as we advanced further in, with the sandy hues of the rocks enveloping us, it became clear why we were here. We'd come to learn about another animal. A less prehistoric one this time. Us, human beings.

The inner walls of the cave were covered in a vast array of paintings, in a range of reds, browns, and yellows. The images were a snapshot into ancient human life. There were figures, sometimes eating, often arranged in complex but ordered scenes. There were drawings of giraffes, zebras, monkeys, and rhinos. If I was being picky (which I was), I felt some of the compositions were a tad 'basic'. I mean, the humans weren't much more than stick figures. 'I could've probably done better when I was six,' I boasted to myself internally. Perhaps I should have been kinder. These paintings were drawn by hunter-gatherers. Over 13,000 years ago.

Ian told us what he knew about the caves and their

occupiers – located in what is now called Matobo National Park – crouching down and speaking in hushed tones for some reason: 'These caves were inhabited by the San people, or Bushmen, as they are sometimes called. The paintings suggest that three or four families would've lived together in a cave like this one, feeding on antelope and using the animals' skin to make clothing. It was a simple, but probably challenging existence. Likely with the threat of predators looming. At all times.'

I stood there, taking in Ian's words and my surroundings. Looking at the cave paintings made me melancholic. I wondered what life would have been like back then for these people. What did they think about? Did they have hopes and dreams, like we do today? How often did they think about getting eaten themselves? The paintings depicted a life so far removed from ours that I found it hard to comprehend that these drawings had been done by the same species. But they had. Crazy. And yet our brains and bodies have barely changed since this ancient graffiti was splashed onto these cave walls.

The paintings we saw were evidence that human beings had been here as long as we could even call them 'human beings'. Most scientists think that people who look like us – anatomically modern *Homo sapiens* – have existed in some form for around 130,000 years.[12] If we again imagine the world has existed for 24 hours, the cave paintings in Zimbabwe were drawn just 0.2 seconds ago and human beings have only been around for 1.7 seconds.

Humanity Goes Boom

But what a 1.7 seconds it's been! Created fire, drew some cave paintings, left Africa, spread all over the world, invented the wheel, spent most of the time killing each other, created bombs big enough to destroy the planet, travelled into space, and, finally, invented the selfie. It's been quite a ride.

Until 1900 – or 0.001 seconds ago – the world remained mostly empty. Just a billion or so humans were spread across its surface. Fast-forward to today, and there are around 7.9 billion of us squeezed onto our little rock, with improving agricultural techniques, the spread of fossil fuels, and better healthcare leading to our recent explosive spread. The population is set to rise to around 10.9 billion by 2100.[13] A truly scary statistic given the environmental pressures we already face, made only marginally less scary by the fact I won't be around then.

We humans multiplied exponentially, and completely changed the world before we even had time to blink. While the other animals I'd zoomed past on the way to the cave paintings still restrict themselves to mating and eating, we've gone a lot further. I'd seen first-hand on my travels just how much we've changed the world since our modest beginnings. We've shaped nature in our image. We've multiplied relentlessly. We've spread to every corner of Earth. So much so that in all my travels it's been rare to be somewhere where I couldn't see at least *some* evidence of humans or human activity.

As I gazed at the cave paintings – a window into our

primitive origins – these truths swirled around my mind. Once I'd stopped childishly mocking ancient hunter-gatherer painting skills, that is. I realised that no one planned any of the leaps we've taken since our days in the cave. The world I'd seen on my travels was simply the result of a spasmodic and disorderly explosion of human life over centuries and millennia. Of humans making trillions and trillions of decisions over generations. There wasn't some grand overarching plan. We've been running around like headless chickens for thousands of generations, and have accidently created a planet-encompassing society of human beings.

'How have we done it?' I thought. 'Has the world really changed for the better since these paintings were drawn? Are we moving in the right direction as a species, or would we be happier living as hunter-gatherers? Is this modern world our species created mostly good or bad?'

Seeing so much on my travels has made me feel confident that the average inhabitant of Earth lives a life infinitely better than those lived by our early ancestors. Although we're more disconnected from nature than we used to be – something I'd become acutely aware of spending time in Africa – we on average enjoy longer, safer, healthier lives than we did in the past. And life for the majority of us is no longer a short and often brutish struggle for survival. I for one could attest to being happier in a world where we no longer live in caves, and the majority of humans enjoy comforts like electricity and a roof over our heads, among many others. I was deeply pleased not to be a roaming hunter-gather or cave-dwelling painter in ancient Zimbabwe. Or simply, a different species of ape sitting in the jungle.

Cave art appreciated, we hopped back in the Land Rover, once again rattling through the dusty, windy tracks of Matobo National Park. We passed through a local village. Children screamed and waved as we drove past, chasing us for as long as their little legs could muster. The village was fairly basic, but there was a school, and a local shop filled with produce. Buildings were made out of concrete with metal roofs, all painted colourfully. Some of the local men had dragged a TV outside, and were watching football while enjoying beers. It was simple, modern life. But still, this Zimbabwean village offered comparative luxuries the likes of which the cave painters couldn't even have conceived.

We drove onwards. Out of the village and back into thick undergrowth. Eventually, it started to clear. Trees becoming scarcer. As we gained altitude, more of the granite bedrock became exposed, much of it streaked by bright orange and yellow lichen. We pulled up. And after a short walk atop a vast, wind-sculpted granite slab, we were greeted by a strange sight. It seemed completely out of place. A shiny black grave with writing on it, surrounded by several almost perfectly circular boulders. 'Here lie the remains of Cecil John Rhodes,' it read.

Compared to History, Life Today Seems Rather Good

British imperialist Cecil Rhodes set up the British South Africa Company, which colonised much of the region in the 19ᵗʰ century. Zimbabwe used to be called Rhodesia (and also included Zambia). The name gives you clues to his influence. Rhodes famously pushed for the construction of a railway through British territory from Cape Town to Cairo, which was only ever partially completed. When Rhodes scaled a granite peak in what was then called Matopos in 1896, he chose it as his resting place.

Like most people involved in colonialism, Rhodes is controversial (i.e. not a popular historical figure, to say the least). He was a white supremacist who explicitly believed in the superiority of white English people over Sub-Saharan Africans. He's perhaps mostly famous now for the 'Rhodes Must Fall' campaigns to remove statues of him from across the world. Rhino Man Ian told us there was a movement to remove his grave from Matobo National Park too, which was facing some domestic opposition given its importance to the local tourism industry. At the time of writing, the grave still remains there.

Like at this grave, the uncomfortable echoes of Britain's colonial past were hard to avoid in this part of the world. A few days before, we'd been at 'Victoria' Falls (there are over 150 towns worldwide also named after Britain's second longest-serving monarch). Though named in the nineteenth century after the British queen, the falls were obviously well known to locals before Europeans arrived. Ian explained that they called them 'Mosi-oa-Tunya', which means 'the smoke that thunders'. To me, this seemed much more suitable than naming it after a woman who lived thousands of miles away, but there you go.

I sat and watched the sunset over Matobo National

The World Is Better than We Are Led to Believe

Park, the sky turning pink, with dashes of orange. The stifling heat was gradually replaced by a refreshing coolness, and the soothing sound of leaves and tall grass blowing in the wind as the air pressure changed. The unusual rock formations cast long shadows over Rhodes's grave. With beauty like this on show, and having seen so much in the past few weeks, my mind was whirring. It was like I'd been given brief snapshots into different human epochs, and was struggling to know what to do with this information. I'd already figured that I'd rather live in the modern world than in the jungle eating leaves, or as a hunter-gatherer, or as a cave dweller. But seeing remnants of our more recent history on my travels – such as this monument to colonialism – highlighted just how grim life used to be for most humans throughout history, even if you peer back just a short distance into our past. In contrast, at home it was completely normal for me to read articles that decried the state of the modern world, as if yearning for bygone eras. Having seen what I'd seen, it made me wonder which eras exactly these people felt were better than the current one?

Was the world better in Neolithic times? I once visited Skara Brae, a small and remote settlement in the Orkney Islands in Scotland which dates from around 3000 BCE. To get there, I took a short and choppy ferry ride from John O'Groats, and then a minibus through green rolling hills filled with thousands of sheep. The sky was grey, and the houses were grey. It was like viewing everything with the saturation turned down. I passed towns and small villages with Norse names, a reflection of the fact that these islands were actually part of Norway and Denmark until the 15th century. Hence, place names like Quoyloo, Burray, Orphir, and famously, Twatt.

I arrived at the Bay of Skaill, and got my first glimpse of Skara Brae. Stone ruins were cut into the ground, with mounds of grass and earth on top of them. It looked like those World War II bunkers you can see on the coasts of Europe and the UK. Situated way up here in the North Atlantic, life here five thousand years ago must have been grim. The primitive settlement probably offered some respite from the elements. The ancient people had dug trenches for their homes, using grass and earth to make roofs. But still, life must have simply been one cold, wet, and short struggle to survive.

Our tour guide, Doug, was a funny man. He looked a touch dour, and had a sarcastic and morose sense of humour. Like many Scots. In between sardonic jokes about how boring living on Orkney was, he told us that many Neolithic locals would have spent entire lifetimes digging ditches for pretty stone circles. While we were told they had great social and religious meaning, they seemed a little pointless to me. One such example was the imposing Ring of Brodgar, situated a few miles down the road. Twenty-seven huge stones arranged in a circular formation, with a diameter of over 300 feet. Each stone was dark and weathered, sitting imposingly against the grey skies and craggy hills of Orkney. 'It is like a better version of Stonehenge,' I thought. But mainly, I felt grateful not to live in a time where life was not just a struggle to remain warm, spent toiling to build superstition-inspired monuments.

The World Is Better than We Are Led to Believe

Or was life better during the time of the Romans two millennia ago, when people used to watch people kill each other for fun? An empire built on slavery, and awash with violence and sexual exploitation. You wouldn't even want to swap places with the emperor. Marcus Aurelius had 13 children. Five survived to adulthood. We tend to be dazzled by the might of Rome, by its stupendous architecture, which I've seen in Italy, Algeria, Greece, France, and England. But this lasting legacy hides the fact that being an average citizen would have sucked. As a 'pleb' you faced poor living conditions and a good chance of being forced to die in a pointless war somewhere. And this was a damn sight better than what life was like for slaves.

Or what about during the time of the Aztecs and Maya? Let's say you were born in Central America around 500 years ago. Ahuitzotl, the eighth emperor of the Aztec royal dynasty, wisely used to make tens of thousands of human sacrifices a year so the world wouldn't end.[14] On a visit to Chichén Itzá in Mexico, I also learnt a great deal about the ancient Maya civilisation. The city of Chichén Itzá was vast and grand, sitting in a clearing cut from the surrounding thick jungle and dominated by huge flat-topped pyramids. A feeling of mystery shrouds these and its other many ancient monuments, built out of hulks of ornately decorated limestone.

I learnt how the Maya were an advanced civilisation. So much so that El Castillo – the main pyramid – had been built to project shadows at specific times of year. Every spring and autumn equinox, a shadow in the shape of a snake appears to move down the steps of El Castillo. Fairly impressive, to say the least.

I then got shown a court made of stone where the Aztecs played a sport innocuously called *Pok-A-Tok* (the 'ball game'). It wasn't too dissimilar to basketball; even the stone court looked kind of familiar. There was a grass rectangle in the middle. Although here, the edges of the court were imposing stone walls. The 'hoops' were made of stone and angled vertically, rather than horizontally. The other slight difference was that while the winners of major basketball games get millions of dollars, sometimes the 'winners' of the 'ball game' at Chichén Itzá were rewarded by having their heads chopped off.[15] Lovely.

Maybe the world was better during the rip-roaring days of European imperial expansion, when powers including Portugal, Spain, France, Belgium, and Britain rampaged around the world, pillaging as they pleased? It's hard to travel almost anywhere without seeing the impacts of colonialism, just like I had in Zimbabwe. You feel like you've been transported to Spain in some parts of Latin America, or Britain in Australia and North America, simply because they did such a good job of exporting their culture abroad.

What about the United States in the years following its foundation in 1776, breaking free from the rule of the British? I've visited the at times comically patriotic National Constitution Center in Philadelphia where I learnt so much about this country's history, almost all of which was noble and great (phew!). The minor blemishes of slavery and burning tepees were hard to find anywhere in the museum.

The World Is Better than We Are Led to Believe

In the 20th century, we proceeded to kill over a hundred million of ourselves in two stupid world wars. I've seen World War II cemeteries in Australia, Papua New Guinea, and all over Europe. The haunting holocaust museum in Berlin. All are colossal monuments to how terrible things have been even in the recent past. Until very recently, if you were a man, you'd have been forced to fight and die in any war your government thought was a really good idea. While for women and minority groups, you were basically second-class citizens. Both historical options don't appeal.

Seeing evidence of our more recent past on my travels has made me certain that not only is the world improving, but now is the best time to be alive. Ever. Bar none. It's not even a contest. But because of social media, negative news coverage, and our inability to appreciate historical context, often this truth is obscured to us. But thankfully, seeing things for yourself can change your view.

Heading in the Right Direction

My trip to Rwanda also highlighted some of the progress that's been made in recent times. After I'd seen the gorillas (and before my overlanding trip began), it was a three-hour drive back to the capital from Volcanoes National Park. There was something relaxing about watching the scenery passing by: bamboo forests, perfectly maintained plots of agricultural land, rolling hills. This seemed such a harmonious little nation. It was almost impossible to believe that this place had seen one of the worst atrocities in human history, only a couple of decades before.

Tentatively, I asked my guide Claudine about her take on what had happened during the genocide in 1994. Her normally bright facial expressions became sombre, sorrow etched across her face.

'It was a horrible time. I had 10 siblings at the time of the genocide. We had to hide in the jungle for several months to keep safe, just living off any food we could find. Not all of us survived. But I know many families where the situation was much worse, and they were completely wiped out.'

I mumbled something like, 'Oh my, that must have been terrible, I can't imagine,' not being truly able to comprehend what she must have been through.

'But that's in the past now. Rwanda is unified. We must move forward. We are healing our scars, to make this country better for ourselves and our children.'

In 1994, 500,000 to 800,000 of the Tutsi minority ethnic group were killed by the ethnic Hutu majority in the country's darkest hour.[16] I'd written my dissertation about the genocide, so I had a reasonable understanding of the facts. But the reality of it and its impact on individual people really struck home talking to Claudine.

We arrived back in Kigali, at the same guesthouse I'd stayed in on my first night. After dumping my things and having a coffee, Claudine asked if I fancied doing some sightseeing. I did and we set off. After about 20 minutes, we arrived at the Genocide Memorial. Over 250,000 people are buried in this small plot of land. The building itself was fairly unremarkable, looking something like a dated sports pavilion. But it was what was held within that was humbling. Long lists showing the names of the murdered. Photographs of families and victims. Letters from the distressed calling for help. Evidence of the global community turning its gaze away, even as UN envoys begged the West to step in and stop the bloodshed. Along with Auschwitz in Poland and Pol Pot's killing fields in Cambodia, it was one of the most sombre places I'd visited. As a person who likes to view humanity through a broadly positive lens, places like this make me feel confused and melancholic.

But there was a disconnect as we left the memorial and started touring the city again. Everywhere I looked, there were smiling people. Hutus and Tutsis going about their business, working together, living among each other. There appeared to be a deep sense of community spirit and a desire to move on from the past as a united country. The capacity for forgiveness was awe-inspiring.

Not only this, but I felt a sense that Rwanda was going places. New office blocks and international hotels were being erected all over the city. The streets buzzed. I learnt that Rwanda is now the success story of the region. It's one of the fastest growing economies in the world, one of the least corrupt countries in Africa, and is becoming its leading regional information and technology hub. Not bad for a country that in 1994 was in effect a failed state, made up of mostly uneducated guerrilla fighters (and a few real gorillas too). A sign of how much progress societies can make in a pleasingly short space of time.

The truth is, success stories like this are commonplace. A century ago, the world was a collection of imperial possessions and some failed states, with a few better-functioning ones in Europe and North America (which again had massive issues). But now, according to the *Bertelsmann Transformation Index,* there are ten failed states in the world: Afghanistan, Syria, Yemen, Libya, Somalia, Sudan, South Sudan, Central African Republic, Democratic Republic of the Congo, and Haiti.[17] These are places riven by violence, poverty, and conflict. Yes, these countries sadly contain millions of people, representing roughly 3.4 percent of the world's population.[18] However, out of 195 countries in the world, having ten or so classed as failed looks better when you consider our violent history. Your chances of being born in a non-failed state today are roughly 96.6 percent. If life was a lottery – and indeed it is – I think most of our ancestors would take those odds.

Most of the countries I've visited have been democracies, and if they aren't, the bulk have been reasonably well run. That I was able to visit them as a tourist is also a sign of progress. Not too long ago, vast swathes of the world were 'off limits' to travellers, due to regional conflicts or disputes. Think the Soviet Union up until its collapse in 1991, China until recent decades, or even Europe in the first 50 years of the 20th century, which twice turned into the world's bloodiest ever battleground.

In Defence of the Modern World

Rwanda isn't an exception to the rule. Across the world, my travels have shown me that the vast majority of countries have been on an upward curve in recent decades, and that most people born today enjoy a much better quality of life than their parents and certainly their grandparents did. I just needed to compare the democratic and charming Europe of today to the Europe of the 1950s, split by an 'iron curtain', racked in places by communism, and flirting with dictatorships. Or the divided but free US of today to the America of the '60s, with racial segregation and young men being forced to die in Vietnam. The rapid development of modern China, while not democratic, has pulled almost a billion people out of poverty since 1970. South Korea, Japan, Taiwan, and Singapore – four of my favourite places to visit and some of the most futuristic places on Earth – have been transformed from low-income nations to some of the richest in the world.[19]

The societies we've created from our primitive beginnings should – on the whole – be celebrated rather than condemned. When I land in a new country, I would be very surprised if I didn't find there to be some form of governing authority, which (notionally) wants the best for its citizens. And assists in the provision of education, law enforcement, healthcare, infrastructure, energy, and housing. Indeed, in the over 150 countries I've visited, I can count on one hand the number of times I've noticed the absence of any of these things. For most of our history, these positive aspects of civilisation haven't existed. We now take them for granted.

Much suffering remains and many problems need to be solved, and these will be touched upon in detail in later chapters. I'm not arguing that the world is perfect, or that we can rest on our laurels. But it's important to acknowledge our progress, if only to prove to ourselves that we can continue making the world a better place in the decades ahead. Most people have an overly negative view about the state of the planet, but experienced travellers always seem to have a much more positive take on the state of affairs.

Bad news sells, and creates an overly negative picture of the world and humanity. Stories of gradual improvements in global poverty, living standards, equality, literacy, economic well-being, education standards, and collapses in global violence simply do not.

'Over the last 25 years, more than a billion people have lifted themselves out of extreme poverty, and the global poverty rate is now lower than it has ever been in recorded history. This is one of the greatest human achievements of our time.' World Bank Group President Jim Yong Kim said this in 2018.[20] I hazard a guess that this didn't make headline news where you live.

My travel-inspired belief that the world is mostly good and improving has also been backed by an ever-growing body of statistics. Renowned academic and statistician Hans Rosling makes the absolutely compelling case that not only is the world the best it's ever been, but that the pace of our progress is increasing rapidly.[21] Let's look at some comparative statistics from 1900 to the mid-to-late 2010s, from Rosling and a number of other sources.[22]

The World Is Better than We Are Led to Believe

Five Good Things Improving

1. **Global literacy:** Has improved from 12 percent to 86 percent.
2. **Democracy:** The share of the world's population living in democracies has risen from around 10 percent to 56 percent.
3. **Female suffrage:** The number of countries where women have the right to vote has risen from just 1 to 193 (out of 195).
4. **Global life expectancy:** Has *doubled* from around 35 years to 72.
5. **Electricity coverage:** Negligible in 1900 and restricted to wealthy individuals in the United States and Europe (just 6 percent of UK homes had electricity supply in 1900). By 2016, 87 percent of the population of the *entire world* had access to electricity.

Five Bad Things Happening Less

1. **Child mortality:** The proportion of children dying before their fourth birthday has fallen from over 40 percent to under 4 percent. If you had three children a century ago, more than one would have died before adulthood on average.
2. **Global extreme poverty:** Has fallen from over 90 percent to below 10 percent. A century ago, 9 in 10 of us

would have lived in extreme poverty. Now only one does.

3. **Deaths from conflicts:** Over the course of the 20th century, human violence was responsible for about 5 percent of all deaths, a share which had fallen to just 0.009 percent in 2010-2017.

4. **Hunger:** The global death toll from great famines was over 40 million between 1900 and 1910, compared to less than 1 million so far in the 21st century.

5. **Deaths from natural disasters:** The annual global death rate from natural disasters has fallen by a staggering 95 percent since the 1920s.

There are enough positive statistics like this to fill a book, so I just picked a handful. While life is still very tough for millions, these statistics (and most others) imply it would have been much worse for almost everyone 100 years ago. Let alone 1,000 or 10,000 years ago. Statistics like these and the knowledge gained during my travels have left me certain that we should be proud of the direction we're heading in.

I reflected on the modern world and all of our progress as I watched the sun set over Matobo National Park in Zimbabwe. I felt glad to live in a time when humans have mostly restrained our seemingly instinctive desire to colonise other countries[*] (only five countries globally

---

[*] Russia's invasion of Ukraine being a sad and pointless recent aberration to the rule.

were never conquered by Europeans at some stage during colonisation). And, more broadly, to have been born in an era so much better than that of the cave painters and those who were colonised in African nations like Rhodesia.

I clambered back into the Land Rover, prepared to be shaken to bits again on the drive back to Bulawayo. I felt conflicted. While travel helped me see how much better the world was, so many others remained perpetually negative about modern life. And as we slowly trundled into Bulawayo, I could see why. My rose-tinted 'the-world-is-awesome' glasses were quickly knocked off my face. We passed rickety shanty towns, where 'houses' were built from discarded trash. Litter was strewn across many of the streets. The air was thick with fumes from dirty old motorbikes and cars. There were long queues at ATMs, some over 100 people deep (Zimbabwe's hyperinflationary crisis was still ongoing). Clearly, there remained much suffering in the world. Ian talked of the daily hardships so many people faced here, often struggling to find clean water and enough to eat. It was chastening to hear.

Clearly, the world isn't perfect. And for some, it's tempting to believe that in places facing challenges like this, it hardens people. They become meaner, more dangerous. But from what I could see, the citizens of Bulawayo were very much like the rest of humanity at large. Kind. Welcoming. As we stopped in town to pick up supplies, we saw friendly and helpful faces. People welcoming us to their country. Asking us about our trip. Offering us their help. Some even offering us their limited food and supplies. Living in Bulawayo would surely be enough to make anyone bitter. But people here weren't. They were kind and friendly.

And this is a trend I've noticed across the world.

So my advice? See the world for yourself. You might notice that humans aren't a nasty bunch, hell-bent on destroying the planet and indeed each other (at least not intentionally). Because for all our flaws and idiosyncrasies, it might shock you to learn that the vast majority of us are *good* people.

6

Most People Are Nice

*Seeing the world for myself makes me
confident humanity isn't doomed. A small
proportion of the world's people are messing
it up for the rest of us.*

The sky was a rich shade of blue. The air outside had a crisp, dry, pleasing heat. I was sitting inside a rusty old bus, with a handful of other 'tourists', if that's what you could feasibly call them. Especially given our destination. We'd been driving for hours. The scenery at the start of the journey had felt quite Mediterranean. Gentle rolling hills, peppered with olive trees, brown rivers, and little farms. But as the hours rolled by, the olive trees got sparser. The green gave way to brown and beige scorched earth. Mottled, rocky outcrops protruded out of the increasingly desolate and parched ground.

We pulled over at a petrol station that had seen better days. It was once painted in bright shades of red and blue, but decades in the sun had seen these fade to a peeling light pink and grey. The fuel pumps were filthy. About 15 of us clambered out of our coach, hoping for sustenance. And

The Travelling Ape

we were in luck. There just happened to be an old man inside, bearded and dishevelled, who was selling *baklava*, the dangerously moreish local dessert. A filo pastry filled with dates and nuts, and, crucially, absolutely drenched in honey. Excellent.

We exited the petrol station, and I visited what had been described by the person at the till as a 'toilet'. To me, it merely seemed a shockingly unclean and dank room, with a small hole in the ground (which most patrons hadn't bothered aiming at). My relief at being outside again was palpable. That is, until a convoy of four jet-black tanks appeared on the horizon, heading in our direction. They produced a metallic and industrial cacophony, one as far removed from the noises of nature as it's perhaps possible to. The tank chains became louder, the diesel engines gurgling, as they approached.

Eventually, the tanks pulled into the petrol station car park. Their scale was unsettling. They simply towered over the surrounding cars and people. Their solidity. Their weight. Their sinister feel and appearance. They looked primed and ready for action. The red Turkish flag was emblazoned on the side of one, appearing like blood against the tank's dark metal skin.

We kept our heads down and clambered back into the bus. We knew where they were going. In the distance, I could see a shoddy fence made of corrugated metal, topped with rusty barbed wire. It was the Syrian border. Dark plumes of thick black smoke – the type I immediately knew wasn't just from a bonfire or something less malevolent – rose ominously up into the sky. It was 2019, and Turkey had

142

begun air strikes on its southern neighbour in preparation for a ground offensive. The stated aim was to create a 'safe zone'* extending 20 miles into Kurdish-held northeastern Syria, an attempt to expel Kurdish forces from near the border.[1] As we sped away, I wondered whether the tanks I saw would head across that border and into the fray, as indeed they did.

Fortunately for me, I wasn't going to head over the border with the tanks. I was sitting near a Scottish mother and son, an American postgraduate student, and a couple from Italy. We agreed on how bad we felt for the people of Syria. And also that we felt fortunate Syria wasn't where we were going. But it then quickly dawned on me that our next destination was hardly Orlando, Florida. It was Iraq. Iraq, which not only neighboured Syria but which was also most definitely Iraq. Erbil was the first stop on our trip. I grabbed my phone and looked at a map of where we were going. On one side we had the war in Syria. Just 30 miles away we had Mosul in Iraq (which had been recently held by ISIS). And then we had Iran to the east. I shuddered as a thought popped into my head: 'Disney World Orlando might actually be more appealing than this.'

We reached the border a few hours later. But not before seeing more sinister plumes of smoke on the horizon than I'd ideally like to see on a road trip. A beige structure with tiny windows lay ahead, with border guards and soldiers milling around it. I remember my heart rate

---

* Most wars are ostensibly fought in the name of the very thing they decimate: safety.

picking up. My hands trembled as the guards boarded the bus and asked to see our passports. Meanwhile, below, two German Shepherd dogs were happily scrambling around in the bus's underbelly, hoping to find a treat. Or, from the perspective of humans, a belonging that could lead to the incarceration of its owner. Passports checked and dogs disappointed, the doors were closed, and we crossed into Iraq. The warnings of friends and family rang in my ears.

'Iraq isn't a very good place to go on holiday, is it?'

'Isn't Iraq still a touch ISIS-y at the moment?'

'You have a death wish.'

All they'd heard were negative things about the country and its people since the beginning of the Iraq War in 2003. So it was no surprise they were worried. And, being honest, I was too. What the hell was I doing here?

We drove on. Through craggy deserts. And sandy, flat plains that stretched out beyond view, interrupted by the occasional oil pumpjack, bobbing away. The sun began to set as we reached the outskirts of Erbil, turning orange and then pink and then red. I'm not sure what I was expecting to see. But I guess the stereotypes I'd heard about Iraq had infiltrated my subconscious. What I didn't expect to see were glitzy new skyscrapers with large LED signs and fluorescent lighting on them. Bustling shopping malls. Expensive cars, driving on well-maintained four-lane roads. But this is what Erbil had. In abundance.

The tour group dumped our bags at the hotel and walked into town. The streets were busy, mainly filled with men (as is the norm in this part of the world). Shisha bars overflowed with customers enjoying the temperate nighttime weather. There was a pleasing hum of voices, happily laughing and chatting away. Kebab shops and *baklava* outlets numbered in the tens – we seemed never more than a few feet from one. It was all so, well, normal. I started to feel a bit embarrassed about my little meltdown at the border a few hours ago. At least I hadn't verbalised it.

About 10 of us sat down at a shisha bar, a busy place with seats outside and large televisions showing Premier League football. I ordered a beer, which I was not only allowed to do, but something I did quite enthusiastically. After a worrisome day, I felt that my nervous system could do with a little calming down. A smiling local man walked over to our table. He was dressed in black jeans, a crisp white shirt, and had a well-groomed beard and a sharp haircut. He looked like someone you'd see in any Western bar.

He'd come over to welcome us to Erbil and to Iraq. As, for that matter, had many other people in our short few hours in the city. On the walk to the bar, people smiled at us, came to get photos with us,* and to cheerfully say how happy they were to see tourists here.

'I can't believe how friendly you all are here,' Lydia, the Scottish mother, said to the well-dressed man (like many people here, he spoke great English).

'Why are you surprised?' he said with a big grin. 'Just because we're in Iraq you thought we'd all be evil or something? You thought it'd be a warzone everywhere?'

---

*   Again, early hopes that these were avid Travelling Ape fans were indeed seriously misguided.

The Travelling Ape

She laughed nervously, but he'd pointed to an interesting truth. Media coverage of places like Iraq is almost wholly negative in the West. But everyone here so far couldn't have been more kind, friendly, and helpful. And indeed this was not the exception to the rule. By the time I ended up in Erbil, travelling the globe had already shown me that people were mostly nice, wherever I'd been. I'd come across thousands of curious, helpful, and polite locals on my journeys. And only a handful of jerks (many of whom were other travellers). Could it be true that we humans really aren't such a bad bunch? And that most people are good?

Our Warped View of 'The Other'

In our home countries, most of us expect everyone to be polite and courteous. Particularly in places like the UK. Why, then, do we tend to have a much bleaker assessment of the goodness of other people when we consider humanity as a whole? We know scores of good people personally, but when we think of the entire world, we're inclined to have a more negative view of the goodness of humans. Or, as Dutch historian Rutger Bregman argues, people instinctively trust those in our immediate communities, but this attitude changes when applied to people as a whole.[2]

The media is the biggest cause of this. I mean, look at all the horrible things happening abroad on the news. Whether it's about some mass killing, terrorist attack, or brutal war, the implied narrative is that people outside your nation are malevolent and dangerous. 'Best not to leave at all, then,' is the subsequent conclusion of millions in the developed world who see no reason to abandon the safety of their home nation.*

We're now *overwhelmed* by bad news from around the world. You wake up and almost immediately you get your first hit of negativity. Admit it. You check your phone before your eyes are even properly open, don't you? You check the news or social media or both. You might then read or listen to the same depressing stories again, in various formats, as you travel to work. You then punctuate the rest of your day with sporadic helpings of bad or irrelevant news (from social media), checking your phone incessantly. Americans check their phones 80 times per day on average.[3]

Just before bed, you turn on the news (which you now know like the back of your hand). You then hear someone list, solemnly, all the terrible things that are happening around the globe. All the horrible things horrible humans have done. Some of the UK news programmes even begin with ominous gongs, as if to ram home the sadness of all the things you're about to hear.

You might then wait to watch the local news after this. Here, another serious and solemn person tells you about lots of other bad things that have happened. This time on a smaller scale. But still worrying because these bad things are happening nearer to where you actually live. Although

---

* Particularly Americans, despite living in a country where around 15,000 people are killed each year by gun violence alone.

you missed the exact location of where the murder happened because you were also looking at cute dog videos on your phone at the same time in a likely doomed attempt to wedge some joy into your day before bed.

Compare this to almost all of human history. We had no access to any sources of news *whatsoever*. Millions of people could have died in an earthquake, and you'd have been none the wiser. Your knowledge of 'the world' extended no further than walking distance from your clan. Just a couple of decades ago, our hits of bad news were limited to a daily bulletin or perhaps one morning read of the paper. Now, any tragedy that takes place anywhere in the world gets beamed to us from a million different sources. And you'll consume it, ravenously, throughout your day. Warping your view of the world and the people in it.

I've met people from almost every country on Earth. And you know what? The negative view we hold about others couldn't be less true. One of the most emphatic takeaways from travelling nearly everywhere has been that most people on this planet are nice. Most people are *good*.

An example comes to mind. In Uzbekistan, a man in one market kept shaking our hands and telling us, 'You are very welcome in this country.' He really was at pains to tell us how happy he was that we'd decided to visit. So much so that it became a problem. He followed us back to our bus. He wouldn't stop telling us how welcome we were, to the point where he was chasing us and bellowing it through the window as we drove off. This might sound extreme, but for me, stories of overwhelming friendliness like this outnumber the negative 100 to 1.

Most People Are Nice

The generosity I've been shown across the world has also been staggering at times. In Namibia, a man smilingly undertook a two-hour round trip to get us help when our vehicle broke down in the desert. He didn't need to do this. In some places, people offered to feed or house me for the night, even though they clearly didn't have much to give. In Malaysian Borneo, I stayed with a local family who insisted on cooking me a feast, despite my protestations. In India, I was given free food and tea as I walked the streets of Jodhpur.

And then there have been the countless times when, while standing around looking like a lost and confused tourist (and in fact being one), I wasn't mugged. Instead, people pointed me in the right direction or asked if I needed help. I've yet to be the victim of any great injustice or crime so far on my travels. You could call this luck. Or being a man. But this is common among experienced travellers, especially those who travel to 'dangerous' places.

At the shisha bar in Erbil, conversation quickly moved on to everyone's travel adventures. Our tour of Iraq had been organised with Lupine Travel. It's a fantastic travel company that specialises in arranging trips to left-field destinations that most people would pay good money to avoid. A slight downside, at least on a personal level, was the type of person a tour like this attracts. They're harder to impress. I sat back and relaxed, waiting to pull my 'North Korea' trump card out of the bag. As I usually do, I reeled off a few destinations I'd been to in recent years, dropping North Korea into the mix as nonchalantly as humanly possible. Like it was a package holiday to Benidorm.

The Travelling Ape

I waited for the inevitable dropped jaws, barrage of questions, and a nice dopamine hit from being the centre of attention. I got nothing. Of the 15 or so people on my tour, ten had also been to North Korea, I discovered. Mostly with Lupine, as I had. I had to up the ante. I revealed my attempt to visit as many of the world's countries as possible, certain that this would do the trick. 'Iraq is country number 140,' I said, as casually as I could. Checkmate.

Or so it seemed. 'Oh, that's nice, I've been to 190,' said an 80-year-old Spanish man called Rafael. He planned to finish the lot later that year. 'I'm on 160,' an American lady called Jane, who hadn't let her use of crutches stop her travels, interjected. A lot of the group had been to at least 100 countries. While most were older than me, it still took the wind out of my sails. On the positive side, it meant I had some seriously interesting people to spend time with. From being arrested in Angola to visiting Baghdad during the 2003 war, anecdotes from the Lupine group were certainly never boring.

Did the others seem worried about coming to Iraq? 'Not really,' seemed to be the overwhelming feeling in the conversation that followed. In fact, most agreed that they'd not come into much trouble *at all* on their travels. One thing we could all agree on – aside from the benefits of taking vacations in war zones – was the goodness of most people we'd come across, all over the world.

Rafael had seen more of the planet than us all and had lived the longest. He was a bit frail, with leathery skin and white hair, but still had passion and vitality in his eyes. He said, 'Most, maybe 99 percent, of people are simply doing their best. Trying to be good people, parents, and human beings. Often in challenging situations. This is the main lesson I'll take to the grave from my travels.'

'I agree,' I said. 'Being a human is utterly bizarre if you really think about it. Our shared predicament is in many ways stranger than fiction. We're made up of the contents of exploded stars. Trapped in a body, with a life, and on a planet, for seemingly no reason. These simple facts should be enough to make everyone go crazy. But somehow, miraculously, almost everyone doesn't.'

I noticed a few raised eyebrows as I spoke. I don't think anyone was in the market for my existential chat just yet. So I pulled the theme back to travel.

'From what I've seen on my trips, most people go about their daily business, doing their best to get by, without any dramas. And on the whole, they do this while being as kind and friendly as they can. I've very rarely seen rage spilling over into physical violence, or been shocked by the behaviour of a stranger on my travels.'

In these situations, where you're speaking to a large number of people, it can sometimes seem like your mouth's moving, words are coming out, but you're not really in control of what's happening. Despite my best intentions to keep the theme on travel, my philosophical assumptions were getting the better of me. I continued.

'To me, it's a minor miracle that people don't feel the urge to run through supermarkets naked, screaming their heads off, covering passers-by in milk they've just stolen from the dairy aisle…'

There were a few seconds of silence. 'Um, yeah,

I guess,' was the muffled response from a few people. Eventually. One or two looked embarrassed. I might have lost them with the supermarket freak-out.

Which Are the Friendliest Countries in the World?

As it got later, a strange thing happened. Erbil's streets got busier and busier. The shisha bar, which in most other cities would normally start emptying around 10pm, started to fill up. The road was closed to traffic, and eventually became truly packed with people (read: men, again). Shopping, chatting, drinking tea, and appearing to have a rather good time. In places as hot as this, it's not surprising that after dark is often the best time of the day to get things done. Or to stuff your face with local honey-glazed pastries (in my case, at least).

We all chatted about how safe Erbil seemed, and how friendly the locals had been. It made us excited for sightseeing in the next couple of days. Rafael spoke again, raising the question: 'What do you think is the friendliest country in the world?' This again kicked off a debate within the group. I wanted to get involved. But I was stuffed with *baklava*, tired, and conscious that everyone probably thought I was a weirdo after the 'milk in the supermarket' gaffe. So after a long day of travel and worrying that I might say something odd again, I left everyone to it and headed to bed.

I woke early with a 'Christ! I'm in Iraq' feeling of panic. I was instantly awake, body full of cortisol. I knew I was safe, but had to do something with the excess energy. With last night's question about 'friendliest countries' swishing around my head, I grabbed my old, black, scruffy journal. I opened it on a clean page, and headed it with the question: 'What are the three friendliest countries in the world?' I scribbled down some barely legible notes, which got less legible as I drank more and more strong local coffee. But I've since managed to decipher the general thrust of what I wrote that morning:

> By some margin, Algerians are the friendliest people I've ever encountered. This is surprising to most, who usually don't know much about Algeria, notwithstanding that the capital is Algiers or footballer Riyad Mahrez hails from there. There's good reason for this. Algeria's very hard to visit. Its visa is one of the most laborious to secure in the world.

> Algiers feels very French, a legacy of colonial rule. I walked the streets, sipped coffee, and ate from local patisseries, as the locals did. Algiers' narrow and crumbling backstreets were chaotic but juxtaposed pleasantly with the city's wide French-built boulevards and elegant apartments.

> Architecture aside, I was bowled over by the Algerian people. Everyone I met couldn't have been more welcoming and hospitable. People smile more in Algeria. They want to know where

you're going, where you're from, and more than anything, will bend over backwards to make sure you're having a good time. This friendliness was especially impressive given that my Algerian visit coincided with the largest protests held in the country for decades, in 2019.

Millions took to the streets each Friday for months. But the protests remained completely peaceful. It's a testament to the Algerian people. They'd been calling for an end to the 20-year term of President Abdelaziz Bouteflika, who had angered protesters by seeking a fifth term. He was a sprightly 82, and had barely been seen in public since having a stroke in 2013. There were rumours he couldn't even talk, which is probably a prerequisite to running a country of over 40 million people.

But the protests remained calm, especially the one I attended in Oran (my dark features and beard helped me fit in; many thought I was Algerian). People came wrapped in Algerian flags and sang songs. Car horns beeped. Smiles abounded, the atmosphere was jubilant and celebratory. It felt like Algeria had just won the World Cup, and certainly not like they were demanding regime change. The protesters came armed only with flowers, which they handed to the police. Many I spoke to were happy to see tourists, and hopeful more would come when the country's government allowed it.

Most People Are Nice

I was also struck by the friendliness of the people in Tonga when I visited. I got a proper insight into life in the slow and relaxed Pacific Islands (I also got to hang out on white, sandy, paradisiacal beaches). I learnt that Tonga is referred to as the 'Friendly Islands' by many, and especially on the Tonga Tourism Authority website. When discovered by Captain James Cook – a sailor who mapped most of the Pacific – in 1773, local Tongan chiefs cooked him a feast. Cook had a great time. So much so that he coined the term the Friendly Islands to describe the country's people in his journal. I guess it stuck, and for good reason.

Cook didn't realise the feast was actually part of a plan to cook and eat him, which was abandoned at the last moment. And several centuries later, a man writing in his journal in Iraq was frustratingly denied the chance to deliver a punchline along the lines of, 'Cook gets cooked at friendly feast.' Cook was later violently murdered by natives in Hawaii, in circumstances that don't appear to have been particularly friendly or funny. In any case, Tongans are a friendly bunch today. The slow and gentle pace of life allows Tongans the space and time to smile at all who pass, and they spend much of their time laughing and joking with friends. You have more time to smile when you slow down, clearly.

Then there's Pakistan. For anyone who's been lucky enough to have travelled there, they'll know what I mean. Pakistani hospitality is famous. As a foreigner, I was treated as nothing less than royalty. Pakistanis consider guests a gift from Allah, and treat them accordingly. In megacity Karachi, moving around on foot was often slow, and not just because of the horrendous congestion. I kept being offered free food or tea from friendly locals, and being stopped by people who wanted to talk to me about cricket. Given the way it's perceived in the media, Pakistan completely defied my expectations.

Once I'd finished writing, I spotted common themes in my analysis. First, people are often friendliest in economically poorer countries, where we're led to believe they have less to be happy about. Second, many of the countries perceived in the West as 'evil' are in fact filled with perfectly nice people. Who knew?

I packed away my journal. After a satisfying breakfast of fresh cheese, tomatoes, bread, and vegetables (washed down, of course, with some more *baklava*), we set off for our tour around Erbil. The highlight of the day was unquestionably the city's impressive citadel, which is said to be the oldest inhabited in the world. It's been lived in for over 6,000 years. It sits like a sentinel. A circular little village proudly crowning a large mound, surrounded by imposing clay walls. Just below it, we wandered around the frenetic, thriving bazaar, filled with little alleyways, nooks and crannies, and peppered with tea spots and places to eat. Despite a population of over one million people, the city (outside the bazaar) was quite serene for this part of the world in the daytime. Car horns were notably absent. Taking your time for leisure seemed to be the order of the day.

After a few more days exploring Erbil, our group headed east, up towards the border with Iran. After many hours driving through flat, arid scenery, we started to climb. We'd reached the Zagros Mountains, which straddle the Iraq-Iran border. We passed giant gorges and canyons. Snow was just perceptible on a few of the mountain peaks, glistening in the sun.

Beautiful scenery aside, we enjoyed a frankly bizarre interlude at a quasi-abandoned theme park in Rawanduz. We were the only people there. And got to ride a self-driving roller coaster. Each train held just one person and, somewhat alarmingly, we were individually responsible for braking. The track followed undulations in the terrain. I swooped down valleys, the track shaking and warping as I went. It turned sharply, just before I felt I was about to drop into the gorge below. I'm fairly sure it wouldn't have passed even the most basic health and safety checks back home. But still. Zooming around on roller coasters wasn't something I expected to do while in Iraq.

From the mountains and gorges of Rawanduz, we drove past the beautiful Dukan Lake. It had perfectly still azure water, surrounded on each side by craggy hills and scorched yellow grass. We then moved on to the second largest city in the region, Sulaymaniyah. We rolled into town on a busy, raised highway. Brand new infrastructure was sprouting up in almost all directions, cranes lining the horizon. The city was ringed by desolate, rolling mountains. Streets were thronged with busy stalls and restaurants. Despite a feeling that things were going well for Sulaymaniyah, this part of Iraq would soon give me more of an understanding of the country's much more challenging recent history.

Our bus approached the Red Museum. It was a decrepit structure, with tiny, barred windows, fortified by towering walls on either side. A few sand-coloured tanks sat outside it – these ones, fortunately, were only for show. We traipsed into a building that had largely been left as it was during the rule of Saddam Hussein. The part of Iraq I was visiting, Iraqi Kurdistan, has its own identity. Kurdistan straddles parts of Turkey, Syria, Iraq, and Iran. While never a formal state, the region has an identity that has persisted throughout rule by the Roman, Safavid, and Ottoman empires. This is the identity that Saddam Hussein's regime wanted to crush. Locals allege this museum was once a place where Kurds supporting greater autonomy for Iraqi Kurdistan were imprisoned, tortured, and killed.

We walked through tiny cells. The smell of damp was palpable. A depressing, earthy scent. Some cells were barely big enough to fit a double bed (not that prisoners were given the luxury of even a sleeping mat). We were told that sometimes tens of prisoners would be crushed into one of these rooms. Being in there for half an hour was enough for me. I couldn't comprehend what it would have been like to be stuck in there. Since US intervention in 1991, the Iraqi Kurdistan region has enjoyed a degree of autonomy, setting up its own administration in 1992 and declaring itself a federated state.[4]

People Are Nice, Even in 'Evil' Countries

The Red Museum and so many other places I've been on my travels have highlighted the worst side of humanity. Most people just want to get on with their lives, and don't care much for power. But those who do, what we'd call 'politicians', can cause an incredible amount of damage, as Saddam Hussein did in Iraq before his toppling in 2003. These people are driven by nothing more than ego and a desire to control others. Almost all wars can be traced back to ego-driven people like this; they've existed as kings and leaders throughout human history. For this reason, I think we should be wary of voting to give politicians more power over us. Indeed, I think the desire to be president should, frankly, disqualify you from that very role.

My travels had shown me that while 99 percent of people are indeed nice, the remaining 1 percent often choose to be politicians and the like. They can drum up nationalist fervour. They can use the media and (mis)education to drive their population to hate outsiders. They can declare war on other nations, condemning millions to die in wars they didn't want to fight.

Lots of countries have terrible leaders. But we shouldn't confuse the behaviour of a country's leader with the characters of those living within it. Even in so-called 'evil' countries, the people can be good. No one has any control over where they were born. You may disagree with the policies of a government – such as the one led by Saddam Hussein in Iraq – but it's not fair to blame the average citizen of that country for such things.

People can still be nice, even if they support ideologies you disagree with. Let's say I was born in Russia, was educated at Russian schools, and was indoctrinated to love Vladimir Putin from birth. It would be fairly miraculous if I grew up to be the vegetarian, millennial stereotype that I currently am. Just because someone in Russia supports a leader who couldn't be less popular in the West, this doesn't preclude them from being generous, or loving their family, or being helpful in their community.

When I visited Russia myself, I was surprised at how open and hospitable Russians were to overseas visitors. They were actually friendly. They didn't, as I had subconsciously assumed, spend their days acting suspiciously, plotting the downfall of the West. Russians do without the use of words like 'please' and 'thank you' when they speak their language, which leaves us with the impression they're being rude when they speak English and omit those words too.[5] But this is just how they speak. They can't be blamed for the actions of their government, or, really, for being duped by the propaganda that permeates almost every aspect of Russian society.

I've met plenty of friendly and kind people in other 'difficult' places too. Even in North Korea in very trying circumstances. Lots of Americans won't like to hear this, but on a road trip through the US's Trumpian Deep South, I found people to be hospitable and warm. I've met many

Most People Are Nice

Americans who said they won't speak to anyone who voted for Trump. They prefer to forever deem these 67 million people as fundamentally 'evil', rather than trying to find common ground. And there is common ground; America is a nation filled with kind people. But tribal politics – driven by divisive politicians – means the country is practically on the cusp of a second civil war. It's utter madness.

The World Is Safe

After a few more days in Iraq, I bode the Lupine tour group farewell. I'd travelled in Pakistan just prior to Iraq. And before that was probably the first single person in history to travel to the Maldives, where being on a honeymoon appeared to be a prerequisite to getting a visa. So I felt I was ready to spend a bit of time in a more 'normal' backpacker spot. As the Turkish intervention in Syria gathered pace and regional tensions flared, I booked flights to Bali, Indonesia. I intended to lie on idyllic beaches. Drink Bintang beer. And gleefully boast of my intrepid global adventures (without more experienced travellers there to steal my thunder). Bliss.

On the flight, I pondered my trip to Iraq. A place so different to what I'd anticipated. I realised that despite my visiting so many of the world's allegedly worst and most dangerous countries, I'd always remained safe. And again, I'd got round Iraq without incident. I looked out of the window. The plane skimmed wispy clouds. I looked down at the shimmering ocean, far below. And thought,

'If people weren't mostly nice, I would've surely run into trouble in some of the 'evilest' countries on Earth by now. But I haven't.* And neither had any of the other Lupine travellers, despite their apparent fondness for danger tourism.'

I concluded that the world is safe because most people are good. Being a man helps. But for both genders, statistically, the chances of getting caught up in some form of unrest or even a terrorist attack are fairly low, even in destinations we deem to be the most dangerous. For example, according to the University of Maryland's Global Terrorism Database, there were 564 terrorist attack deaths in Iraq in 2019.[6] Although these figures might seem high (and are definitely tragic), they're less so when you consider the country's population. Iraq is a huge country, of almost 40 million people. The part I visited – Iraqi Kurdistan – with its oil money and Western backing, is relatively safe compared to neighbouring regions (I'm feeling less brave now that I've included this extra information). Indeed, there's even a border separating it from the rest of the country.

People thought I had a death wish when visiting. For them Iraq equals that big war after September 11th. It's easier for people to write off an entire nation as 'dangerous' than to consider the nuanced societal and geopolitical differences that exist within that (and all) nations. But as in

---

* The worst things I've faced on my travels have been witnessing the carjacking in Papua New Guinea and getting my belongings stolen in Israel. Not bad in over five years on the road, I'd say.

many of the world's unstable places, life goes on as normal for most people in Iraq, without any violence or drama. In any case, 'safe' destinations like India and the Philippines were not far behind Iraq in terms of terrorist attacks, with 277 and 284 deaths respectively in 2019.[7]

The truth is some people already have an irrational fear of terrorism. In 2021, one poll showed 36 percent of Americans were either 'very' or 'somewhat' worried that they or someone in their family would be caught up in a terrorist attack.[8] And this is domestically. So, I don't doubt this fear rises substantially when people consider visiting countries they expect to be more dangerous. In 2020, there were around 530,000 deaths globally from human violence.[9] This might sound like a lot, but it's a tiny number. This suggests deaths from human violence only accounted for 0.8 percent of the 63.1 million deaths registered that same year.[10] In comparison, snakes kill about 100,000 people each year,[11] a statistic which makes me profoundly more scared of snakes.

Human violence doesn't even make the top 10 causes of death, with road accidents killing almost three times as many people each year.[12] And yet, we don't think twice about visiting a country with a poor road safety record. It has never even crossed my mind, to be honest. Which is peculiar, because road accidents are far, far more likely to kill you than human violence or, indeed, anything else on your travels. Each year, 1.35 million people are killed on the roads globally.[13] But do you think twice about getting in a car? Maybe you should.

Being on the road has probably been the most

dangerous part of any of my trips abroad, even if I didn't realise this. In Myanmar, many old taxis and cars still have the steering wheel on the wrong side. The government changed from the left- to right-hand side of the road driving a few decades ago, making journeys on perilous mountain passes even more terrifying.

If you spend more than a few hours on the road in India, you'll likely have more than a handful of near misses. You are *eight times* and *10 times* more likely to die on the roads of India and Thailand respectively, than in the UK.[14] Statistically speaking, letting little Jimmy go on his gap year to Thailand or India is far more likely to end badly than if you let him go to North Korea, Russia, or Iraq. And yet, people like me are free to go on their 'woo-woo' spiritual quests to India without their sanity being questioned (at least from a personal safety perspective).

Our collective goodness should be celebrated. After all, we evolved from primitive creatures who don't appear to be genetically predisposed to niceness all of the time.* As Anne Frank so famously said, 'In spite of everything, I still believe that people are truly good at heart.'[15] Travelling has shown me that this adage is emphatically true.

I had a much more negative view of humanity before I travelled. It was only when I saw the world for myself that I

---

* Read the bit again in Chapter 5 when the chimps drink each other's blood for a little reminder.

grasped an underlying truth: good people overwhelmingly outnumber bad. Despite the world's dizzying array of nations, societies, and subcultures, we still manage to produce mostly good people with similar basic values. Evolutionary psychologists like Robert Wright argue that our evolutionary design explains why we see so many repeating patterns in politics, family, friendships, and morality, across ostensibly different nations.[16] While we may bang on about the primacy of individuality, travelling has shown me the opposite. We're much more similar than you think.

7

We Aren't So Different After All

Our underlying sameness becomes startlingly
apparent the more you travel.

I spent a week or so in Bali, decompressing after my tour to Iraq.* And after a lovely time spent doing not a great deal, I realised I'd had my fill of backpackers. Had my fill of Bintang. Had my fill of 'relaxing'. It was time to go back off-piste. But first I took a short flight to Singapore and had a few days to once again amble around one of my favourite cities. Then I was back in the sky. A kind of happy place of mine. Gone were the days when, as a child, I was too scared of flying to even want to step foot on an aircraft. Thankfully, hypnotherapy works. (Not the type where people pretend they've been hypnotised into thinking they're a chicken; the type where your negative mental associations are reframed.)

I looked out the window at the clouds hovering below me. The sky was a deep shade of blue, a reflection of our

---

* Which made it sound like I'd bravely fought there, rather than merely visiting on holiday.

proximity to space. Being up in a tube in the sky never fails to amaze me. Air travel's astonishing. I wondered what people from decades ago would think of our ability to be up in the sky. Above the clouds. Watching movies. Connected to the internet. All things that would have been dismissed as impossible, or even unimaginable, a couple of centuries ago.

I returned to my reading. The book I was devouring had also got me thinking about how futuristic so many things were in the modern world that we take for granted, like flying. Aldous Huxley guessed at what the future might be like. A future devoid of differences between nations and indeed people. In the prophetic *Brave New World,* published in 1932, Huxley envisaged a genetically engineered future, where nations have disappeared, and everyone's governed by a so-called World State.[1] People wear similar clothes, and all conform to their own social grouping. There are no lasting romantic relationships; everyone is said to belong to everyone else. Children are created outside the womb and cloned to increase the population.

'Huxley seems to have predicted where the world was going,' I thought (even if the more outlandish visions haven't materialised – yet). More globalisation, the erosion of cultural differences, the fraying of nuclear family arrangements, and the early stages of genetic engineering. The themes of narrowing differences between people and nations were particularly salient. Especially as I disembarked the plane.

I'd flown from Singapore to Ulaanbaatar, the capital of Mongolia. I'd crossed huge landmasses and nations, and travelled more than 3,000 miles. I was now in a place that, on the surface, seemed markedly different from Singapore, and from places in the West like my hometown of London.

Elements of the place certainly did feel outwardly alien. I'd arrived at Genghis Khan Airport, a faded, rusting old terminal surrounded by rolling hills on one side and polluted urban sprawl on the other. Before hopping into a local taxi, I grabbed some Mongolian Tugrik notes from an ATM. All crumpled, limp, and faded. And with pictures of Genghis Khan on them.

The taxi ride into town was quite shocking. The green hills I'd seen quickly gave way to a not especially photogenic city. I passed huge coal power stations. All dark, with their towering chimneys dominating the cityscape and belching out thick fumes. The sky was overcast and foggy. I could taste the pollution and each breath felt dense, constricted. I could see how this was one of the most polluted cities on Earth. Large Soviet-style buildings rolled past me. So rigid. Square. So inhuman in their scale and design.

Eventually, we reached the centre of town, and I got the taxi to drop me in the central square, outside the Government Palace. My initial feelings were that it was a strange building. It looked a bit like a Las Vegas or Disneyland attempt to copy historic buildings of centuries past. It had grand white columns. A wide, imposing profile, a touch Greco-Roman. But they'd used modern green glass in some places when they'd renovated the building in 2006. It also looked like it was clad in cheap-looking plastic, which was meant to look like stone but had missed the mark. It reminded me a bit of a shopping mall. In front of it was a statute. Of a man riding a horse. A man called – you guessed it – Genghis Khan. This black statue, on inspection, was a less than flattering one. It implied that he perhaps enjoyed his food a little too much later in life (maybe he put on weight when he spent less time pillaging in old age).

In any case, the continued reverence for Genghis Khan here did make me think. Clearly, the Mongolian authorities were proud of this man's all-conquering exploits, with the Mongol Empire in the 12th and 13th centuries stretching across the entire Asian continent and all the way to Europe.[2] As many countries in the West grappled with their colonial legacies, it seemed this wasn't happening in Mongolia. To be fair, I felt Genghis would have been well placed to take advantage of the nationalist tide sweeping the West when I visited in 2019. For starters, his rampaging exploits made Mongolia 'great again'.[3] His followers could have worn local hats, *loovuuz*, with catchy slogans like 'Yes we Khan!' or 'Surrender or we'll murder everyone in this village', which would've been a more accurate depiction of the brutal rampaging that the Mongol Empire was famous for.

'Okay, so maybe the politics is a little different here. Back in the West, in the current climate, reverence for violent imperialism is rather frowned upon these days,' I thought as I walked on from the square and past several more statues of the great man in quick succession. However, all over the world, characters with chequered histories are often given central importance in nations' identities. Huxley's insights continued to weigh heavily on me as I explored Ulaanbaatar. The city had a number of industrial buildings, visible in the distance. Lots of angular, repetitive housing blocks. Interspersed, ever so occasionally, with beautiful Buddhist temples and shrines.

It felt different from Singapore, and indeed from London. But was it really so? In both cities, there were large roads, concrete housing blocks (the ones in Singapore were a bit nicer). Shops selling similar things, restaurants, cars everywhere. Ulaanbaatar was surrounded by nature, whereas Singapore had nature incorporated within it. But still, the basic fabric of these places had much in common.

I continued to stroll Ulaanbaatar's streets, craning to take as much of it in as possible. I'd been told to see some Mongolian throat warbling while in the country. So I bought a ticket and walked into a theatre that had red velvet seats and an ornate lobby. I sat down. The noises created by the singers were truly bizarre, utterly inhuman. A male singer stepped into the centre of the stage. He was dressed in a *deel*, a folded tunic made of blue cotton. He opened his mouth and produced a noise which didn't seem possible. Like a woodwind instrument, with two pitches being produced at the same time. A low rumble and a whistle-like tone. It was compelling and strange. But how different was this to gigs I went to at home in London? Far fewer people in Mongolia appeared to be 'off their heads', it had to be said. But the venue wasn't too different. People clapped when they were having a good time, had come to have an enjoyable evening with friends or family. Again, despite cosmetic differences, the similarities here seemed to comfortably outnumber the differences. Music is a truly global, human-wide love affair.

We Aren't So Different After All

From what I'd seen at this stage in my travels, I'd become accustomed to how similar most major world cities are and how people in them behave in (largely) familiar ways. For someone who has visited so many countries, it's rare for me to feel like 'an alien' when I touch down in a new land. Why?

Pondering this as I left the throat warbling and trudged to my guest house, I thought, 'How different are we all, really? How distinct are our countries? Do we lead such different lives? I'm really hungry, there must be a hot pot place around here. Could it be true that our differences are all only skin deep?' Spoiler alert: the world is underpinned by a quite staggering sense of sameness, wherever you go. One of the many reasons that makes travel worthwhile is that you notice both these commonalities and the superficial differences that make new lands exciting. We humans are the same species of animal, evolved from the same common ancestor, and with the same genetics. Indeed, one in 200 humans alive today is a direct descendant of Genghis Khan, so successful was his raping and pillaging.[4] Given that we have the same mental operating systems, it would surely make sense that the societies we've created are also mostly the same.

Later that evening, I went for dinner in the capital. The restaurant was dimly lit, giving it an unintentionally seedy vibe. There were wooden tables that looked like they'd been scuffed up to make them look older than they were. There were other attempts to make the restaurant appear 'old' and 'authentic'. But a bit like the Government Palace, it didn't quite hit the mark. The grey tiled floors, television screens mounted on large white pillars, and cavernous size of the place exuded more of a conference hotel restaurant feel. But the food was good, at least. A Mongolian hot pot. A large, metallic bowl was placed in front of me, filled with a gurgling broth. As well as some plates of vegetables to dunk in it. It felt like a novelty. The kind you only get at a 'do it yourself' restaurant. Places that, weirdly, ask you to pay for the privilege of doing the very thing that you'd hoped to avoid by eating out: cooking.

Towards the end of the meal, my guide arrived. He was called Narantuya, and would be taking me into the wilds of Mongolia. He looked young, like a boy almost – all fresh-faced, with rosy cheeks – but he told me he was in his mid-20s. He wore Western clothes. He had thick, spiky black hair, and had one of the happiest and sweetest demeanours of anyone I'd ever met. Laugh lines prominent on his smiling face. And a youthful innocence that was utterly infectious. We talked at length about the plan for my upcoming trip. But also, quickly, the conversation moved on to his life. His hopes and dreams. He was educated, and spoke impeccable English.

'I like living here in Ulaanbaatar,' he said with a sigh, 'but there are still challenges.'

'How so?' I replied.

'Meeting girls here is hard. I keep striking out on dates. And also my career is kind of at a turning point. I like guiding, but I'm not sure this is what I want to do forever. I spent some time in New York and that was amazing. So, I guess I want to travel a bit, work abroad maybe. And then hopefully settle down, have a few kids. But it's hard knowing what the right path is.' Narantuya paused, the inner conflict etched on his face.

Relationship and career worries. A desire to travel. Hopes, dreams for the future. These were not conversations any different to those I had in London with friends, and yet, I was supposed to be somewhere very different indeed to back home. The old refrain that there's more that unites us than divides is as true as it is preachy and annoying.

'Ah man, that must be tough. To be honest, I think I want the same kind of things one day. A family maybe. But I'm not sure my constant travelling is making it easy for me to meet someone right now,' I added.

We chatted for around 20 minutes or so. Then Narantuya said he had to head off to meet an American couple who'd be joining us for our trip. I was alone again. With time on my side and no pressure to say anything, my mind, as it so often does, started to drift off. It seemed strange – but also marvellous – that we'd just had a conversation like that. One that speaks to our common humanity. All over the world, perhaps thousands of times, I'd had conversations like this in whichever country I happened to be in. People everywhere have almost identical desires and hopes, regardless of their nationality or culture. Human dreams, you could say.

To highlight this, it might at this point be worth engaging in a little thought experiment. Let's take the residents of tower blocks in New York, of the rickety stick-built villages of Western Madagascar, the vast social housing blocks of North Korea, and the remote mountain settlements of Tajikistan's Pamir Mountains. I've been lucky. I've had conversations with people from all of these places (with varying degrees of success, given language barriers). I noticed that they spoke different languages, wore different clothes, followed different customs, and looked physically different in some ways. Sure.*

If a resident from each of these places met at a fictitious cocktail party, they might first notice those differences. But it's true to say that these people I've met on my travels – a New York cabbie, a coffee farmer from Madagascar, a tour guide in North Korea, and a cotton picker from Tajikistan – are almost all genetically identical. They are in fact related to each other, like all of you are. Distantly, of course, but it still counts. Related to Genghis too, perhaps.

At our imaginary cocktail party, let's imagine that our guests from across the world can communicate via wearable translators. Not from *Brave New World,* these already exist.[5] Without the artificial barrier of language, our guests would start to get to know each other.

Have you ever noticed how people who live in Anglosphere nations or Spanish-speaking nations seem to get on so well with each other when you see them abroad? We like to think this is because we have unique cultural bonds, which to some extent we do. But the main reason is that we can communicate easily – and because we can, we realise we aren't so different. Shock! Striking similarities emerge because of this. In Britain, people like to joke that

---

*   Don't worry. I wouldn't have included these disclaimers unless I was about to obviously refute their relevance in the following paragraphs.

We Aren't So Different After All

British people always talk about the weather. But this isn't a British thing, this is a human thing done in every country.

But back to the party. The guests would say they like to spend time with friends, and make jokes at their expense. They like to meet in groups, share food, drinks, and stories. They – and particularly the men – would reveal an unhealthy reverence for the most popular sport in their nation (each nation presumes their own national sport is 'the best'*). They'd grudgingly concede they like a good gossip. They'd talk of the primacy of their families in their lives. They'd outline how they all try their best to raise their children, despite challenges.

They'd reveal hopes for the future, regrets about the past, and that they are, to some degree, haunted by the daily chattering of their busy minds. Like us all, they'd reveal a lingering sense of dissatisfaction in their day-to-day lives. They all know and feel emotions that are universal to all humans. They worship some kind of god.

Against this backdrop, they live their lives day by day. And try as best they can to be good people. For the most part, they succeed. With the cocktail party at risk of becoming slightly heavy, I interject (I've been sitting at this fictitious party in silence, taking notes): 'It's remarkable, isn't it? Wherever people come from, it's our common humanity that always shines brightest. When you scratch

---

★   Even the Irish and Australians, who in maintaining that Gaelic and Aussie football are the best sports in the world, are implicitly suggesting that 99.5 percent of the world's population who live in countries where the sports haven't taken off are wrong.

The Travelling Ape

beneath the surface of appearances, the character of almost all humans and our societies is so very similar. The cultural idiosyncrasies we cling to are only skin deep. The old adage couldn't be more right – we aren't so different after all.'

Our cocktail party guests swiftly ask me to leave for making 'ill-timed, grandiose, and culturally vacuous statements' which 'disrupted the flow of an otherwise lovely evening.' With that, I stand up, grab my coat, and write this sentence on my laptop, bringing the imagined evening to an end.

I'll bring some more substance to the table.* By the time I was in Mongolia, I'd experienced every continent (apart from Antarctica). I'd encountered a myriad of languages, customs, and cultures. The full spectrum and complexity of ways in which humans choose to live on this planet. With all my travelling, I'd expected to be left feeling overawed by the diversity of humanity. Feeling that our differences define us. Instead, I felt precisely the opposite.

So much so, in fact, that the thrill of arriving in new countries has slightly diminished as the number of countries visited has racked up. Nothing *truly* surprised me anymore. There's nowhere on Earth where I land and now feel overawed by any gobsmacking paradigm shift in the way that humans live. Nowhere where people wear pants on their heads, use shoes as gloves, or ride unicycles instead of bikes. A few places, like Japan, feel different, but the similarities outnumber the differences a hundred to one.

---

* The notional table of this chapter's argument, not the cocktail party. I was asked to leave, remember?

We Aren't So Different After All

This isn't to say that I don't love travel. It's still essential. Learning we're all basically the same is a fundamentally important discovery. An antidote to the depressingly narrow-minded tribal views of the world that appear to have taken hold in recent years. Where people choose to define themselves in opposition to different imagined identity groups. Where people believe that their skin colour, nationality, political affiliation, or religion are useful tools to divide us into groupings of 'us' and 'them'. Choosing to favour those inside the group, and hate those outside it. But I've now seen enough of the world to know what to expect wherever I land: a 'different' grouping of people, adhering to almost exactly the same rules as in every other country on the planet. We talk about globalisation as an ongoing process, but the truth is, it's already happened.

Is Globalisation Complete?

The next day, I lobbed my bags into the 4x4, said hi to Narantuya, and got introduced to the aforementioned American couple. Mark, who'd lived in England the first half of his life (so he'd been left with this odd-sounding northern English accent, suffused with a Texan drawl) and his wife, Brittany. They were both in their fifties. They looked as if they'd seen some stuff. Mark had big bags around his eyes, wore a leather jacket, and was covered in tattoos. Brittany wore a lurid pink trucker hat, had bright blonde hair, and massive sunglasses that appeared to cover around 99 percent of her face. I mentally questioned whether they'd booked flights to the wrong destination. But we said our greetings, and they seemed perfectly agreeable.

We set off, passing the same grey suburbs of Ulaanbaatar from the day before. Until housing blocks gave way to single-storey houses and sheds. And an increasing number of white, circular *ger* huts (yurts). Then, after a surprisingly short while, there was nothing. Just green rolling hills. A few dirt tracks heading off into the seemingly endless horizon. The occasional horse here, *ger* there. Massive skies above us, filled with the odd white fluffy cloud. A sense of melancholy in the air. It now became obvious that we were in the least densely populated country in the entire world. Half of Mongolia's three million residents live in the capital, Ulaanbaatar. The remaining 1.5 million live largely nomadic lives in rural areas.

Hours rolled by. My eyes gazing, transfixed, through the car's open window. Not listening to any music, just taking in the subtle majesty of the Mongolian steppe. The occasional large eagle, floating serenely on thermals above us. Herds of horses, here and there. Grasslands and hills and not much else. They had a simple beauty. It was also deeply refreshing to take a break from looking at or touching the small rectangular object I carry around with me at all times. 'I doubt people here have smartphones,' I figured. What joy. In some ways. It's hard to comprehend that repetitively watching funny dog videos or checking the football results won't ultimately make you happy, unless you look up at the world around you occasionally. As we drove onwards, I felt that the Mongolian wilderness was a justifiably good reason to do so.

In England, sitting in a car for hours can feel like a lifetime. In Mongolia, watching the scenery roll by for hours is part of the experience. Which was fortunate, because as we left the tarmac we realised our pace of progress would now be glacial. It would be dirt roads and muddy tracks for the next ten days or so.

As we bumped and slipped around, the car's wheels jerking occasionally in slippery spots, I started to chat more to Mark and Brittany. They seemed perfectly nice, despite a slightly 'hard' exterior. We talked about travel, our lives, and other such things. They asked what I did for a living and, perhaps unwisely, I told them that I was an economic and political risk analyst.

'Oh I see,' said Mark. 'So what do ya think of Trump then?' in a slightly loaded way. He and Brittany both seemed to sit up, and lean forward.

Everything about how they spoke, where they lived, and indeed their personalities, made it very clear they were likely to be fans of his. Which they were entitled to, but which also filled me with unease. I was about to spend 10 days with them. And years later, I'd write a chapter in a book that said we shouldn't write people off just because they had different political views to us. So I had to be diplomatic.

'Um. Yeah, well he's kind of unhinged, isn't he? Not very presidential. Childlike. He makes me worried. But I understand that a lot of Americans really like him,' I said, trying to find a point of shared understanding at the end.

The Travelling Ape

'Yeah, he's pushing back against this constant drive for globalisation from world elites,' Brittany said, matter-of-factly, head bobbing around as we navigated more bumps. 'Look. I love travel. I've been to over 50 countries. I love experiencing different cultures, seeing the world. But I feel like in America we're being made to feel ashamed of *our own* culture. Ashamed to be American. I'm proud to be from the States. Even if Trump is slightly crazy, we voted for him. He's the only candidate who seemed to be looking out for people like us.'

Talking politics is rarely a good idea. I knew then – as I always have – that you have about as much chance of changing someone's political views as trying to convince a devout Christian that there's no God. So I paused and listened; not bothering to try to change their views on Trump. And then tried to steer the conversation away from the US president of the day. The 4x4 bounced on. We'd now practically slowed to jogging pace, as we undertook yet another river crossing.

'On the globalisation point, don't you think the horse has already bolted a bit?' I said tentatively, wondering whether my phrasing had something to do with the number of horses we'd seen on the drive so far. 'I mean, you must have seen it in all your travels too. I just feel like the world is already globalised, the differences between our nations aren't anywhere near as big as the media makes out. We're basically all the same, right? And globalisation is simply humanisation, with, hopefully, the barriers between us getting smaller over time?'

Mark and Brittany looked at me for a moment.

We Aren't So Different After All

They looked at each other. They then responded with long monologues about 'elites'. How globalisation was a conspiracy, and we weren't as similar as politicians made out. Given that it was a two-on-one situation, I just vaguely added, 'Haha, yeah, but what do I know, anyway?'

'Quite a lot actually,' I said to myself mentally, looking out of the window as the conversation subsided. One of the best things about writing a book is that there are no Marks and Brittanys to push back against my ideas. No dissenting voices to interrupt my stream of conscious thought. Indeed, you're currently being forced to read whatever words I write. Even if I write something that makes no real sense. Fizzy shoes. You'll still read on. You have no ability to respond if you disagree with me. Ah, wouldn't life be easier if all debates were like this?

Had I had the courage, or had I been less tired after eight hours of being buffeted around in a 4x4, I perhaps would have continued. 'Mark, Brittany, I actually disagree. The world, its countries, and its people are much more of a homogenous gloop than we think they are. Although the fauna, flora, and landscapes vary hugely between countries, the people within them are much less different.'

I'd recently written some notes on globalisation, which I planned to put on my blog. Had I felt braver (or bothered enough at the time), I'd have then taken out my journal and started to read from it – which of course would have been an insanely pretentious thing to do in real life. The journal entry highlighted the sense of sameness I noticed in recent trips to four places.

The Travelling Ape

Let's examine my trips to Tonga, Taiwan, Trinidad and Tobago, and Tanzania. Many people probably think these places wouldn't have much in common apart from beginning with the letter 'T'. After all, they're not even in the same continent. But the reality is different. Even if we look at something as simple as travelling from the airport to my hostel.

We begin. I land at an airport. They're different sizes, and some are more modern than others. The one in Taipei is space-age, while the one is Trinidad and Tobago is nothing more than an airstrip with a large shed attached to it. But the runways and flight control regulations are uniform enough for my plane to safely land there. All pilots and air traffic controllers communicate in the world language: English.

Shortly after landing, I see some rectangular pieces of colourful cloth on poles or signposts. Each is the same size, but the colours and patterns are (slightly) different. Three of these flags are mainly red, while Tanzania's is blue, green, and black.

I reach border security. A person wearing a military-inspired uniform (looking surly) puts a stamp in my passport. This is a document that is recognised wherever I am in the world. I sign an immigration form, which mostly looks the same and always asks pointless questions about which hotel I plan to stay in. Why bother when they'll never check? If I haven't booked anywhere, I sometimes put 'City Hotel, 123 Fake Street' and have never got so much as a raised eyebrow.

I take some pieces of colourful paper from an ATM. They have pictures of royalty or some other important historical character. I walk up to a vendor. I hand over some finely sliced bits of tree from the last country I visited, which allow me to buy goods and services, and receive a coffee in return (a drink available everywhere).

I hail a taxi. They're different colours and sometimes drive on the other side of the road – Taiwan drives on the right – but the process of driving is the same. Apart from in London, taxi drivers (for some reason) never seem to have even a basic knowledge of the city they work in, so they check on their smartphone. I enter the address on Google Maps for them, but still not a flicker of recognition. Know the feeling?

As we set off, I notice that almost everyone we pass is glued to a small device the whole time. I wonder whether they are browsing specific websites available only here. Then I remember that apart from in Mainland China and a few other countries, chances are the strangers are all browsing the same websites as everyone else in the world. And even in Mainland China, they're simply browsing the Chinese versions of the websites the whole world is addicted to.[6]

The road quality varies, but this aside, being driven in a car is strikingly the same everywhere. Taiwan is slow and steady. Tonga even slower. In Trinidad, my taxi driver asked if we could stop at what looked like a shop, which turned out to be a pub. He nailed a pint, and on we went. Driving in Tanzania is fast, hectic, and dangerous. It has one of the worst road safety records in the world. Fortunately, I've always reached my destination.

But still, these are cosmetic differences. Some of the road signs are in a different language, but still provide largely the same messages in each country. Regardless, each carries a translation in English. Adverts on billboards peddle exactly the same products as everywhere else; the only difference is that some developing countries are team Pepsi and some are team Coke.

My driver asks where I'm from. I say 'London'. 'Oh, England! Manchester, Chelsea, or Arsenal?' That's how it usually goes. There's barely a country on Earth where I can't keep up to date with the football.

We Aren't So Different After All

I arrive at the hotel or hostel, connect to the wi-fi. And all of a sudden feel like the distance between me and home has evaporated. Everyone at the hotel speaks the global language.[7] I eat dinner. The content of which differs country-to-country. Each has its own national dish and Tongan food isn't anything to write home about. But dinner is a ritual followed in each of these countries (and indeed the world).

I head to bed, flick through some of the TV channels. The languages are different. But local news, sports, reality TV, and drama are easy to recognise anyway. As is the pervasiveness of international news channels, which you can get in almost every country on Earth. I fall asleep, ready to take on the next day of sightseeing.

There's nothing that truly shocks me when I arrive in a new country these days. When Captain James Cook landed in Tonga in 1773, for the locals it would have been like aliens landing. People who looked quite different, using technology they would have thought impossible, with customs that would have been truly strange.

After my no less significant arrival in the annals of Tongan history, I chatted to the taxi driver in English about rugby and talked about global current affairs. I was on the other side of the planet, in the middle of the Pacific Ocean. But distances are now irrelevant in the tiny, globalised world we live in.

To step foot in another land in the modern world is to simply see your home country, albeit with a few subtle differences: the humidity, temperature, and scenery. A different flag here, different coloured money there. A strange-sounding language, buildings that look slightly unfamiliar. Don't get me wrong, there are superficial variances in how some countries appear. Bur the underlying foundations upon which all countries have built their societies are strikingly similar. And so it goes that our lives are as well. These similarities speak of no conspiracies, merely that we are all human.

But alas, and to my shame, all I did say was, 'Haha, yeah, but what do I know, anyway?' Maybe Mark and Brittany are reading this book. And if they are, they now know how I really felt.

A World of Few Surprises?

Let's spell these common themes out in more detail to ensure you don't think this is a sanctimonious globalist rant. (Well, it is a bit, but it might just have some truth to it.) Of the 155 or so countries that I've been to, every one is structured by the following principles:

We Aren't So Different After All

Government: Every country has some form of governing authority. These can range from the excellent, democratic governments of the Nordic countries to the corruption-riddled ones of West Africa. Over half the world's countries organise themselves in a democratic system.[8] Just under half are run by monarchies or one-party systems, with varying degrees of success. The systems may differ, but the general idea is the same: an authority exists to administer the country or territory in question.

Work: The Greek legend of Sisyphus highlights the reality of most humans' working lives.[9] Sisyphus was condemned by the gods for eternity to repeatedly roll a boulder up a hill, only for it to roll down again once he got it to the top. While everyone's boulder is different, this is an achingly accurate depiction of how almost every person on Earth lives.

From the paddy fields of Bangladesh and the boardrooms of Frankfurt to the spice markets of Istanbul, the jobs differ but the concept is the same: we all spend most of our lives toiling away each day to make ends meet. And then start it all over again the next day. There are few, if any, exceptions to the rule here.

Education: As a species, we've decided that school is a great idea. I used to think this was just for learning. But it conveniently offers parents around the world respite – childcare – for a few heavenly hours on most days of the week. Genius. A few countries have rejected this idea for girls, often because of their god. Some others can't attend because they are too far from a school. Despite this, globally just nine percent of primary age children don't attend some form of school.[10] Overwhelmingly, the basic structure of children's lives is exactly the same in every country and revolves around education.

Socialising: We're social animals. This is apparent wherever you are in the world. People like to sit around – drinking tea or alcohol usually – talking, chatting, and laughing with friends. The location varies. In the West, it's mainly in bars and pubs. In Southeast Asia, it's more likely to be in street markets and small restaurants. In the Middle East, it'll probably be at shisha teahouses. In West Africa, it's more likely to be in people's homes. The settings differ, but the ritual doesn't. We all have a strong desire to spend much of our lives in the company of those we hold dear.

Family: Families, and children in particular, provide perhaps the deepest meaning to the lives of the largest number of people on Earth. If this wasn't the case, the concept of the world being overpopulated wouldn't exist. You have helicopter parenting in the West, and children being allowed to roam free in much of Africa. You have parents spoiling their children in China (after all, many only have one per couple due to the legacy of the One Child Policy). The desire to have children and a family is strong everywhere. It's like it's programmed into our DNA or something.[11]

We Aren't So Different After All

Urban living: As mentioned previously, there's been a huge shift to urban living in recent decades, a trend that will only accelerate in the years ahead. And within these cities, the fabric of daily life is often very similar indeed. In much of the world, cities look so similar now that you'd be hard-pressed to know what country you were in just by walking its streets. Let's say someone is blindfolded and flown around the world in an expensive and extremely strange experiment. Every time they arrive in a new city, they get dropped in the centre of town and are allowed 30 seconds to work out where they are without their blindfold.

How easy would this be? Let's say they can't read the Latin alphabet. Plonk them in Toronto, New York, or Melbourne, and they'd struggle. Similarly, how about Paris, Cologne, or Copenhagen? It wouldn't be immediately clear where they were, save for any obvious monument. While urban areas in less economically developed countries might look different, the structure and infrastructure of cities are the same. Grid-road systems exist where possible, shops and restaurants pepper city streets, and buildings get denser and taller towards the town centre.

Patriotism: Wherever I've been, people have held a love and reverence for their nation. Almost everyone overstates their nation's greatness. Nationalism and patriotism are key features of human societies almost everywhere. It looks slightly silly when you travel extensively. Loving your nation – and disliking your nearby rivals – is as ubiquitous in this world as having a family and eating breakfast.

The Travelling Ape

Economics: Almost every nation accepts the basic tenets of economics, in particular capitalism. The idea that money is used as a store of value which can then be used to buy goods and services exists in pretty much every nation on Earth. Even in North Korea, as I'll touch upon, despite its communist ideals.

Sport: I've yet to visit any place where sport is not an obsession for much of the population, especially for men. In most of Europe, South America, Africa, and Southeast Asia, football is king. In Europe, hooligans will fight and even kill each other to protect the honour of the mostly foreign millionaires who kick a ball towards a net for their local team. The sport itself, to some degree, is irrelevant. Whichever country you're in, there'll be at least one sport that is revered above all others, and occupies an almost comically important position in that society.

Technology: Our access to technology once differed according to economic development. But the spread of smartphones has changed all that. Almost wherever you go in the world, everyone's glued to a screen. Particularly in the poorer parts of the world, it's been a godsend, allowing people access to things like online learning and banking. Mainly, though (of course), people use this technology to take close-up pictures of their own faces and laugh at videos of other people getting hit in the groin by footballs. This goes for people in India and Indiana, and South Africa and Switzerland.

We Aren't So Different After All

Music: In a few places, like Iran, music is controlled, but this really is the exception rather than the rule. As I'd noticed watching the throat warbling in Ulaanbaatar, music plays a central role in almost every country I've been to.

Few Places Left Untouched by Globalisation

The next few days in Mongolia were quite, quite wonderful. I saw just a fraction of this massive nation, but still felt like we were covering vast, uncharted distances each day. Hiking in the wilderness around the Tsenkher hot springs was a delight. Trekking up to and around the Khorgo volcano was challenging – and made worse by having had a karaoke disco in a *ger* the night before, which had involved cheap vodka and local dancing.* Staring into the volcano's black and red crater made it worth it, though. I was pleased it was dormant.

I went on almost daily solo treks. Into the mountains. Yomping (yes, yomping) through sweeping, empty vistas where I could see no evidence of humanity. No roads, or people, or buildings. Just nature, as it'd been for millions of years. It was probably the most isolated I'd ever been from 'civilisation' at large, and I was loving it. We visited the historic city of Karakorum. It had red and white buildings, with ornate green roofs with golden details, in the traditional Buddhist style. All contained within a

---

* Narantuya taught us. Badly, if one was to judge our dancing skills.

large perimeter wall. It was the old capital of the Mongol Empire, and was filled with crumbling tombs and ruins. It's one of the few places in the country where you can still find artefacts from the empire. Their nomadic way of life means there are few surviving monuments compared to other great empires.[12]

We mainly stayed in *ger* camps over the course of the trip, where we'd burn logs or coal to keep warm. Often overheating things. To the extent that I'd wake up boiling at 2am, fling open the *ger*'s entry flap and stand outside in my boxers. In these moments, my sweat-covered body being cooled by the crisp wilderness air, I'd get to gaze at the skies above. The shimmering, ethereal clouds of stars that make up the Milky Way. A glimpse into the cosmos with no light pollution.

We had one final *ger* stay before I'd set off for my next destination. We were to spend a few nights with a local, nomadic family in Khorgo-Terkhiin Tsagaan Nuur National Park. We rolled into their small, ramshackle settlement, situated by a small stream and surrounded by pleasingly curving green hills. Horses and yaks wandered around happily. The family waved and smiled as we exited the car. There was a couple and their two small children. A few chickens that looked like dinosaurs* – the kind you mainly see in Asia – were running around their feet. They were all wearing traditional Mongolian *deel* (the humans, that is).

---

*   Amazingly, chickens share genetic makeup with the tyrannosaurus rex.

We Aren't So Different After All

The six-year-old boy was called Arban. He had rosy cheeks and a mischievous smile. And also, as I'd witness, the rather incredible ability to herd yaks alone on his horse, as if he'd done it for decades. I watched as his father, Baasan, rode with his two-year-old daughter Gerel sitting in front of him. They certainly start them young here. From what I could see, you can practically ride before you can walk in the wilds of Mongolia.

At dinner time, we all huddled into the cosy *ger*. It didn't look like much on the outside – a circular tent covered in a white sheet, with a little rusty metal chimney coming out of the middle of it. But inside, it was much more inviting, filled with red, wooden furniture, and with ornate Buddhist artefacts on the walls. We sat on a thick red and green patterned rug, a crackling fire in the stove warming us. Narantuya – translating – told us that the family had lived the same way for generations. Off the land. During winter, when temperatures drop to -40°F (-40°C), their diets were made up almost entirely of meat, given that growing anything becomes almost impossible for many months of the year. They moved location around four times annually, they said.

'Wow,' I said to Mark, Brittany, and Narantuya. 'They live lives that are so different to the way we live back in cities, and...'

But at almost exactly the same time as I was delivering what I thought was a perceptive insight, Jargal, the mother, pulled out a bloody iPhone. She flicked through it nonchalantly, tapping away.

'Please don't tell me her mind's been hacked by social

media. She surely can't spend her days looking at inane memes and dog videos?' I groaningly pleaded, I'm not sure for whose benefit.

No, she wasn't. But she was playing Candy Crush. And apparently, incredibly, could get 4G connection here. We were four hours' drive from the nearest village. Modern technology had still permeated here, to the remotest of places. Jargal passed her phone to Narantuya. Who then proceeded to take selfies of all of us, for her to presumably upload to her social media later. I felt stunned.

Even though Mongolia is one of the poorest countries in Central Asia, things were changing here. Fast. You could even say that the country was taking a 'steppe' in the right direction, if you were a fan of bad puns. I'd seen motorbikes replacing horses to herd yaks. Almost every car we saw was a Toyota Prius – they apparently made up an astonishing 60 percent of car imports most years. Many *gers* had satellite TVs, such as the one I was sitting in. I'd kicked a football around with Arban earlier, and he'd keep saying 'Cristiano Ronaldo? Messi?' clearly amazed by my football skills. Or more likely, gesturing as to which I preferred. I wondered how the hell he'd even heard about them. But then saw the TV and his mum's smartphone.

This was one of the remotest places on Earth, and yet it was well and truly part of our interconnected world. We struggle to realise how the internet, like air travel, has led to an even greater figurative collapse in the size of the world. And that these days it's hard to find destinations that are truly different. To do so, you'd most likely have to travel far into the rainforests of the Amazon or Papua

We Aren't So Different After All

New Guinea. Estimates vary, but there are only around 100 'uncontacted' pockets of people left in the world, most of whom are located in those two regions.[13]

These 'uncontacted' groups are the only people on Earth you could rightly argue live uniquely different lives from the rest of us, a hunter-gatherer existence that no longer survives elsewhere. For example, the Amondawa people in the Amazon have no concept of time. All their language is in the present tense.[14] Some people suggest that the Korowai in Papua New Guinea still practise cannibalism,[15] a pastime deemed generally 'not cool' by the rest of the world. These are extreme examples, but highlight how little of the world has been left untouched by globalisation.

I once camped in the Okavango Delta, in Botswana. We were bush camping, and so deep into the wild that lions' roars could be heard. Local villagers came to perform some of their rituals at our campsite one evening. It felt authentic. They danced around the fire, sang, and were dressed in beautiful clothing. It was wonderful. I felt like Bruce Parry on the BBC show *Tribe,* where he'd spend a month living with some of the most remote peoples on Earth. But the illusion was quickly shattered. All the members came into our campsite after their performance and they spoke perfect English. I'm Facebook friends with many of them to this day. They mainly preferred Messi.

Almost 70 percent of humans are expected to live in cities by 2050.[16] Those living in rural areas today rarely live so remotely that they haven't been untouched by globalisation. It's no wonder that the world is so much more homogenous than many realise. Travelling has demonstrated to me just how samey the world is, and how we're all much more alike than we think. Globalisation is something that's already happened. While superficial cultural and historical idiosyncrasies are sure to persist, the unrelenting march of homogenisation looks set to continue.

After a couple of days spent doing the nomad thing, it was time to move on. We piled into the 4x4 for another slow but beautiful drive. Ambling over dirt roads, with bumps and lumps, and at times simply meandering through fields of lazily swaying tall grass. I'd loved Mongolia. And watching the serenity of the steppe rolling by, I was sure that its welcoming people, greener-than-green landscapes, and endless big sky vistas would stay with me forever.

By the time I visited Mongolia, I felt I'd seen enough of the world to gain a sense that things on this planet, on the whole, are much better than we tend to think they are. Watching fluffy white clouds hang above us as we drove onwards, I remember feeling a sense of gratitude. Subtle joy, even, that I was alive and that I'd been born in the world of today. I was certain that the modern world, while imperfect, is the best world there's ever been. I'd been shown that the vast majority of humans are good. And had noticed an overwhelming sense of sameness, wherever I went. Which I felt was a good thing. A sign of our common humanity.

We Aren't So Different After All

The more we recognise our similarities, I felt, the less inclined we'll be to murder each other for having the audacity to be born in a different country. I figured it should be perfectly possible for every nation to hold on to the unique aspects of their language, architecture, customs, and way of life. As I'd seen in Mongolia and so many other countries, while at the same time belonging to a much bigger whole: humanity. Who knows, perhaps we'll one day band together to solve common global issues. And Aldous Huxley's prophetic 'World State' will become closer to being a reality (without the dystopian stuff, hopefully).

The sun was going down in the vast open sky. Suddenly, after days of being buffeted around like we were in a plane experiencing heavy turbulence, we finally turned onto a tarmac road. The first in over a week. 'Sweet, sweet, tarmacked roads,' I thought. It was like we were hovering above the ground. Serenely floating above the asphalt, gliding like a bowling ball down an alley. Soon after returning to the rediscovered joys of normal roads, we began to pass a few *gers*. And then a few permanent houses. And then more. A petrol station. And the beginnings of a city, the first we'd seen since Ulaanbaatar. Civilisation.

This town wasn't pretty. It was one of the dustiest placed I'd ever seen. Mostly grey and brown. Quite bland. Houses had pink or blue tin roofs, the only flickers of colour in an otherwise sepia cityscape. Buildings were basic. A plethora of twisted, fizzing wires and cables connected each one to the electricity grid. After spending the past few days communing with nature (at least in my mind), it was jarring to be back in the urban world. And in a city, it seemed, that had many challenges.

As we trundled past a multi-storey car park – one of the larger structures in the town – I saw a rusting, dilapidated road sign, naming our location. It said 'Moron'. How apt. And coincidental.* I felt like one. When faced with places like Moron, my positive worldview seemed hopelessly naive. Towns like this give clear insights into the problems still facing the world. Many locals there looked like they were living in, or close to, poverty. Everyone in Moron burned coal to keep warm – and would die in the winter if they didn't – and so a thick smog hung over the city.** I saw few people wandering the desolate streets, which didn't even have pavements. Those I did see were mainly men, as is so often the case, speaking to the strict gender roles which still exist here and across much of the world.

The world definitely has problems to address. Problems like those on view in Moron, the sight of which was quickly replaced by Mongolia's green emptiness. Yet despite the misgivings I had, given what the sadder elements of Moron had aroused in me, I still believe we're

---

*   The city, amazingly, was indeed called Moron.

** As someone who's flown a lot, I'm absolutely the last person on Earth who can hector anyone about pollution or climate change. Racing driver Lewis Hamilton – who reportedly takes over a hundred flights in a private jet annually and drives around in circles for a career – might do well to take note here. I offset my flights, but know that this isn't enough. Hopefully the positive messages in this book in some way compensate for the damage I've personally done to the environment. Which is a lot, frankly. Sorry.

We Aren't So Different After All

heading in the right direction. Most likely, the world will get better still in the coming years. And this is something we should celebrate. To continue making progress, perhaps we need to realise how far we've come? A positive message to focus on. Something to believe in, you could say.

But as I'd learnt through travel, most humans don't have a problem believing in something. It's one of the things that makes us human. And it's to this topic that we now turn.

8

God's Planet

God is seriously hot property right now. And getting more popular by the day, even though we in the West wouldn't think it.

Saudi Arabia was always one country that I thought I'd struggle to visit. Indeed, it was impossible for tourists to visit for many years. But then Saudi's reformist leader, Crown Prince Mohammed bin Salman threw open the gates to tourists. And I made sure I was on practically one of the first flights. I arrived at Jeddah Airport, took a taxi into the centre of town, and swiftly went to bed. I had a full-on day starting the next morning.

I woke early – not my choice. The call to prayer reverberated around the city at 5am, when the sun was just about rising. I downed a coffee, wolfed down some breakfast, and then went to collect my hire car. In the very short amount of time I'd spent on the roads in Saudi Arabia – all of 15 minutes – I'd come to realise that *In sha'Allah* (if God wills it) is taken rather literally here when it comes to driving. If God wills that you'll crash, you'll crash. So why bother to indicate before merging lanes? Why bother looking at the road rather than texting on your phone? You simply don't need to sweat the small stuff (like driving incredibly dangerously).

I jumped in my miniature 4x4 (the kind that most definitely wasn't designed to go off road), and cautiously set off. Leaving Jeddah was a bit hairy. The city is notable for its many wide, busy, 10-lane freeways, full of drivers who felt they had limited agency. It was out of their hands whether they'd end the day as a lump of mangled flesh and metal in the central reservation. But, thankfully, after a short while, the roads became emptier. Buildings became scarcer. The motorway narrowed to just two lanes. I was making tracks into the desert.

With fewer cars, it was becoming an altogether more relaxing experience. But almost exactly as I had this thought, I looked at the fuel gauge. Empty. There weren't any obvious places to stop for petrol. I'd been driving for an hour or so and was kind of in the middle of nowhere. But then, fortunately, I saw a fuel station emerging on the horizon and pulled in.

A few things didn't seem right about the station. It was derelict and had boarded up windows, for starters. And the pumps were rusty and covered in cobwebs. I got out of the car and just stood there. Hoping that this situation – I had no fuel and this petrol station had clearly been closed for decades – would magically resolve itself with a little patience. 'Perhaps situations like this are what praying is for?' I mentally reasoned.

A massive black SUV pulled into the forecourt. It had a loud, rumbling engine. Tinted windows. Strangely, it pulled up right next to me (had my non-prayers been answered?). The windows rolled down to reveal no driver. For a millisecond, I thought the Saudis must have cracked self-driving cars. Before then looking down a bit further, I realised there was indeed someone behind the wheel. It was just that this someone was a child, who genuinely couldn't have been more than eight years old. He looked tiny in the massive seat, feet miles from the pedals.

Seeing such a tiny child drive a massive car looked like something from a comedy sketch. But with no fuel, no phone reception, and at the time not finding a great deal about the situation funny, I realised this boy was my best bet. He didn't speak great English. But he gestured and beckoned for me to follow his car. So we set off, in this very strange-feeling convoy.

Evidently, he must have been able to see over the steering wheel, as he led me and my car to an open petrol station. One run by his dad, it seemed. This must have been their business model: Send the child to pick up lost visitors or those running near-empty and bring them here. The father filled up the car and I went in to pay. The father and son were all smiles. And, like many of the locals I'd go on to meet in Saudi, were utterly polite and charming. I thanked them profusely. There was lots of handshaking and more smiling, a common theme I'd experienced in the Islamic countries I've been to. I said, 'Thank you,' and then departed.

Tank full of fuel, I drove into the desert. Into a smothering heat, luckily unnoticeable due to air con (whoever invented air con, thank you). The landscape was flat and arid, with the occasional boulder here, shrub there. Or a caravan of camels ambling along the side of the road like it was a totally normal thing. (Yup, a group of camels is called a 'caravan'.) Oppressive beige and yellow in all directions, sitting below a sky that was almost white due to the heat.

After about 20 minutes or so, signs of human activity appeared on the horizon. A dilapidated shop, a couple of houses. The single-lane road widened to a double, and then quickly into a triple. It became busy, as if out of nowhere. I was getting closer to Mecca. Islam's holiest city.

I reached the city outskirts and saw perhaps the strangest road sign I'd ever seen in my life. Emblazoned above two lanes on the left, a huge sign read, 'Muslims Only'. Next to it was a sign for a turnoff, 'For Non-Muslims'. I knew non-Muslims weren't allowed in Mecca, but it was still a shock to see this sign. I took the 'For Non-Muslims' lane, which skirted around the city, as I'd planned to.

Skimming around Mecca, there were wide roads and car parks. A truly incredible amount of transport infrastructure constructed to cope with the massive influx of pilgrims who come to the city each year for Hajj (the pilgrimage all Muslims are supposed to do once in their lives). Over two million people, I'd read. Once past Mecca, the roads narrowed again. As I continued towards my destination, the mountain retreat of Taif, my mind was busy, evaluating what had just happened.[*]

I had no problem not being able to visit Mecca as a

---

[*] The motorway turnoff, not the pathetic fact I had to be rescued by an eight-year-old. A memory I managed to successfully repress and not mention to anyone, until I wrote this book.

non-Muslim, given that it's viewed as a holy, spiritually significant place for Muslims. But I'd never seen anything this stark before. Where entry to a city was dependent on whether you believed a particular story or not. It was the strongest possible example of the power of ideas, and how they can manifest in the physical world. As the flat desert scenery gave way to craggy rocks, with steep and charred mountains beyond, I wondered what London would be like if on the M25 ring road you had a lane for 'Christians' and a lane for 'Non-Christians', who weren't allowed in the city. It was something so far removed from my reality back home that I simply couldn't imagine it.

At this stage, I'd spent most of my life in London. A mostly secular city in the mostly secular country of the UK. Before the age of 10, I sometimes recited the Lord's Prayer before bed. Mainly because I was scared of burning in the flames of hell for eternity if I was a 'bad boy'. But that was the extent of my own religious belief, which has been non-existent since then.

As I grew older, I began to question the morality of terrifying small children into worshipping the Christian God. And wondered about some of the supposed morality tales held in the Bible. Like flooding and killing almost everyone on Earth to teach humanity a lesson. And God telling Abraham to murder his son Isaac, only to say, 'Just kidding, just needed to see if you still loved me!' just before Abraham sank the knife into his child. Actually, God really said, and I quote, 'For now I know that thou fearest God.'[1] Which is probably even worse than my (equally fictitious) quote.

204

God's Planet

At school, my doubts continued. In history, geography, and physics classes, I was taught many things that directly contradicted the teachings of the Bible. And if Christianity was true, why were there other religions? I also likely sinned a lot, at least in God's eyes. Realising that God had not yet smitten me for my sinful ways – and all of my friends for that matter – any religious feeling I had dissipated. Being from a rich country, having suffered less than most perhaps, this made it less likely I'd want and need to believe in an afterlife. Indeed, there's an almost direct correlation between rising average incomes and falling levels of religiosity.[2]

In any case, a decade or two later, here I was. A grown man in Saudi Arabia, who would've probably defined himself as an agnostic-atheist, if pushed.* I couldn't say with 100 percent certainty what happens when we die. But agreed with most of the scientific evidence that suggests our brains will switch off and that'll be it.

I was pulled up from my distracted thoughts. The roads up to Taif changed from being rigid and straight to all of a sudden winding. As I started climbing the mountain shelf, the road became one of the most vertiginous I'd driven on ('Death Road' pipping it to the post, mind). Sheer drops on one side, carefree and reckless Saudi drivers on the other, mountain peaks above me, the temperature dropping as I gained altitude.

A large truck on the other side of the road careered past me, a little too close for comfort. In these moments,

---

*   Not before asking the questioner to stop pushing me.

I accepted life would be much easier if I just believed in a god and an afterlife. I'd be able to enjoy drives like this more. And maybe even enjoy my life more. But, alas, all I had for comfort in these moments were cold-blooded science and reason. 'Remember the billions of years before you existed and there was nothing?' I mentally reasoned with myself. 'Of course not. Well death will be like that again, almost certainly. That pre-birth period was fine, so, if a truck ploughs into you now, death probably will be too.' It was a less appealing story than one including eternal bliss. But it would have to do.

Up Into the Heavens

Taif was a rather strange place. Situated at almost 6,000 feet, it was much cooler than Jeddah. There were pockets of bright wildflowers and crusty mountain peaks surrounding the town, which was made up mainly of big, rather tired looking hotels. I'd heard that Taif is where Saudis come to escape the heat in the summer. I was there in October, and from what I could see, the place was pretty deserted. And nowhere more so than my hotel.

It was ten-storeys high, with a large, vaulted lobby entrance. Grand in some ways, but a little rough around the edges. I dumped my bags, and went to relax by the pool. I found myself, once again, completely alone. I lay on a sun lounger with perhaps the thinnest cushion in the world, and pulled out my battered old journal. To me, writing in my journal was a way to suck the chaos of a day out of my mind, transferring it onto the pages. Unburdening me of relentless rumination on what I'd done that day, while giving a semblance of order and structure to my thoughts.

After my skirting around Mecca, the concept of religion was still floating around my skull. And now spewing out onto the page in text form. Before I'd travelled extensively, I'd thought that believing in God was as unfashionable as wearing sunglasses indoors. I barely knew any religious people. Indeed, a 2019 poll showed that 52 percent of Brits don't belong to any religion, up from 31 percent in 1983.[3] The proportion of Christians fell from 66 percent to 38 percent in the same period. Former British Prime Minister Tony Blair had to hide his faith while in office, fearing it would make him unelectable.[4] It's perhaps no wonder that, in my younger years, I assumed religion was on the decline. Everywhere.

Having seen most of the world's countries, though – Saudi was number 145 – I shouldn't have been so surprised by the motorway turnoff in Mecca. In fact, I could now confidently assert that I was not only a little bit wrong about religion being on the decline. I was, unequivocally, barking-up-the-wrong-tree wrong. People still really, really, like God. Wherever I've gone, He's[*] been the talk of the town. The omnipotent kid on the block. So much so that I now felt that a belief in a higher power – or some form of God – was one of the defining features of our species. Of humanity as a whole. Predominantly non-religious places like Northern Europe, the east and west

_____

[*]   It's always a He.

coasts of the United States, New Zealand, Australia, Japan, and China to some extent* were the exceptions to the rule. And even then, there were still plenty of religious people in these regions, even if they were in the minority.

My travels had shown me that across most of the world, it seemed, religions still determined how people dressed, behaved, and ate. Opulent and impressive religious structures were often the centre-points of the world's major cities. Religion is probably the most important central pillar of community in most countries on the planet. I naively thought that the church of 'we're going to get eaten by worms and gradually decompose' was gaining some real traction. But I really couldn't have been more mistaken.

My suspicions were further confirmed in Taif when I grabbed my laptop and started analysing the data ('holidaying' with me is a real hoot!). I learnt that *84 percent of people globally* still define themselves as religious,[5] which seemed to chime with what I'd seen on my global travels. And gods are set to become *even more* popular in the years ahead. The proportion of non-believers will shrink, and the religious will grow in the decades ahead.

Some religions frown upon contraception, while others promote having children. Between 2015 and 2060, the Muslim population is forecast to grow by 70 percent, Christians by 34 percent, and Hindus by 27 percent.[6] The non-religious? By just 3 percent. The countries with the fastest shrinking populations on Earth are largely

----

*   I'd argue that the state is the national religion in China.

secular ones, with 18 in Europe.[7] Far more than any theist doctrines, these statistics predicting the demise of atheists quite literally put the fear of God in me. I closed my laptop and sat on my lounger, staring into space. Empty pool in front of me. The outline of Taif's mountains ringing my peripheral vision. The pinkening sky filled with a few fluffy clouds. It was odd to think that, unlike most humans, I thought that clouds (and perhaps a few birds) were the only other things looking down at me from above.

I spent a couple more days in Taif despite there not being a great deal to see; I think I'd gone at the wrong time. Eventually, I hopped back in my car and made tracks for Jeddah again. But not before I'd ticked off something I'd longed to see – a rather large crater in the middle of nowhere. I drove down the twisting mountain roads, and then, thankfully, onto flatter and emptier stretches below. After about three hours of driving through empty, largely featureless desert, I finally arrived at the Al Wahbah Crater.

I parked in the empty car park (I was literally the only person there) and strolled towards the crater's edge, where I was greeted by a truly breathtaking vista. The crater is over a mile-and-a-half wide and around 820 feet deep (about four-fifths of the height of the Eiffel Tower). The crater sides were dark, shadows accentuating each crevasse in the mottled rock. At the bottom, in the centre, was what looked like a giant, bright salt flat. It filled most of the crater, with white tentacles flowing out towards the edges.

I sat for an hour or so. Staring. Thinking. Feeling the sun on my skin. How mindboggling that a massive meteorite had caused this depression; the destruction it must have caused; the power and majesty of nature and the cosmos, and our planet's pathetically tiny place in it. Life on this planet. We're so helpless, truly enslaved by the forces of nature. Maybe the strangeness of our predicament is enough to make anyone believe in a god?

Finally, I'd had more than my fill of existential angst. I scrambled up and began slowly plodding back to the car park. I noticed there was a small structure, without walls but with a roof to protect me from the relentless solar radiation. I stepped in. It was largely empty. Not even a bench. There were at least a few information placards on the walls, detailing aspects about the crater. Two things caught my attention. First, the crater wasn't caused by a meteorite, it resulted from a massive underground steam eruption (so much for that cosmic angst meltdown). Second, there was a world map attached to one of the walls, made of black stone and showing the outline of the world's landmasses. It didn't include the borders we've invented to divide the world up, which is always refreshing.

I spent a few moments looking at the map. Given where I was and what I'd seen, I looked at it through the lens of humanity's fondness for religion. And it struck me almost for the first time: 'Isn't it convenient that all the world's religions are, generally speaking, popular in fairly well-defined regions?' I thought. 'How interesting that Christianity predominates in the Americas, Europe, the southern parts of Africa, and then Oceania. That Islam spreads in a well-defined band from Morocco in the west, across North Africa, the Middle East, through Pakistan, and then on to Indonesia. That Hinduism is neatly and mainly confined to India. That Buddhism predominates in South-East Asia. With believers in each region thinking that those who live in other regions are so hopelessly misguided in their beliefs.'

The Deep Spiritual Meaning (Provided by Territorial Conquest)

I had plenty of time to reflect on this on my three-hour drive back to Jeddah. And since then, I've seen the power of religious stories almost everywhere I've been on Earth. That the makeup of today's modern, religious world is owed mainly to geography and history, more than any other factor.

The modern boundaries of Islam are a perfect example. Arabia was unified in the 7th century, bringing Islam with it. The Muslim Rashidun and the Umayyad Caliphates then expanded beyond the peninsula into Syria, Palestine, Armenia, Egypt, and the rest of North Africa, taking Islam with them.[8] The religion was then spread to Southeast Asia by traders. Today, there are almost two billion Muslims in the world. And in places like Qatar and Kuwait, I've witnessed how a belief in these stories structured every facet of life and society, and provided those within them a deep sense of meaning in their lives.

Pakistan is one the friendliest places I've ever been. Islam plays a central role in daily life there too. I visited the mausoleum of the country's founder, Muhammad Ali Jinnah, in Karachi once. It was an otherworldly tomb, perfectly white and surrounded by shining marble floors.

The Travelling Ape

It had a domed roof with four giant entry gates on each side. Its perfect symmetry was the direct opposite of the rest of frenetic Karachi. As the only Western person (almost anywhere in the city from what I'd seen to that point), a few people came over to chat and get selfies with me while I was visiting. A tiny insight into how being a celebrity would be objectively quite annoying.[*]

Inside the mausoleum, I caught a glimpse of Jinnah's tomb. Made of white marble, with intricate designs carved into it, surrounded by an ornate silver-looking fence. A teenage boy – who'd been trailing me for the past five minutes – eventually worked up the courage to speak to me. Without introducing himself, he smilingly asked me 'Are you Christian?'

I said, 'No, actually, I have no religion,' as kindly as I could. I should have just said 'yes', in retrospect. I'll never forget the look on his face. His jaw dropped to the floor; he was genuinely gobsmacked. It was Earth-shattering to him. I had *no* religion. It was as if I'd told him that aliens had just landed, he had 10 seconds to live, or that Leicester won the English Premier League in 2016. The simple truth was that he – and 97 percent of the population of Pakistan[9] – derive deep, deep meaning from religion, in their case Islam. But had Arab armies under the banner of the Umayyad Caliphate not been sent to extend their rule into what is now Pakistan in the 8th century,[10] my conversation with this friendly teenager could have been very different.

---

[*] I'm aware I'm playing with fire writing this book. Hence the Travelling Ape alias.

God's Planet

In the same year as my Pakistan trip, I visited another building that made me consider how the world's religions have spread – the epic Hagia Sophia in Istanbul. I was transfixed by its vast domes and towering minarets rising majestically over the rich blue waters of the Bosporus. It's the pride of the city. But it didn't seem to bother anyone that the purpose of this building had changed hands like a hot potato over its history.

It was built as a Christian church in 537 CE during the Byzantine Empire.[11] It was briefly a Catholic church from 1204 to 1261, under the Holy Roman Empire. It then became a mosque in 1453, after the fall of Constantinople to the Ottoman Empire. In 1935, the secular Turkish Republic established it as a museum. In 2020, it was redesignated as a mosque as part of President Erdoğan's attempts to increase the Islamisation of Turkey. Hagia Sophia's changing religious association and that of the people of Istanbul over centuries past was due mainly to the tides of conquest and geopolitics. Unless, of course, Istanbul's population was spontaneously realising what the objective truth of the universe was. And then changing their minds every few centuries.

Buddhism emerged in the 6th century BCE.[12] It spread from India over the next thousand years or so across Southeast Asia, China, Japan, and beyond. I've seen giant Buddhas in Sri Lanka, Thailand, and Bhutan. The stunning Shwedagon Pagoda in Yangon and the 4,400 temples of Bagan in Myanmar. Prayer wheels dotted all over the stunning Himalayan kingdom of Bhutan. Orange-robed monks padding the leafy and quaint streets of Luang Prabang in Laos. And even the minimalist concrete museum of the Japanese Zen master DT Suzuki, in Kanazawa.

I'll argue that the Buddhist teaching of meditation is practical in later chapters. But most people I've spoken to in Buddhist countries don't actually practise meditation. Rather than strengthening their mental health through this secular modality, they instead worship the man himself, the Buddha. Interestingly, the Buddha himself dismissed religion. Probably the last thing he wanted was to be worshipped by anyone. If he could talk from beyond the grave, he'd probably just say, 'Damn it, guys, you promised you wouldn't worship me!' (perhaps in a more compassionate way). But we humans can't help ourselves, and Buddha-worship is common.

Christianity, Colonialism, and Missionary Work

The bulk of the places I've visited have been Christian. Most countries in Europe, the Americas, and Africa are Christian. Like Islam, it also has around two billion followers. Much of Southern Europe remains Catholic. I've marvelled at the many beautiful and ornate churches all over Spain, Italy, and Portugal. It's clear to me that religion plays a central – and sacred – role in these societies, particularly for older people. But none of them would feel this way had it not been for the exploits of the Roman Empire, under which, in 380 CE, all other religions were deemed heretical.[13]

God's Planet

Today, the head of the Catholic Church sits in, you guessed it, Rome. And Christianity spread, via Spanish and Portuguese conquest, to all of 'Latin'* America in the 15th and 16th centuries. There are a staggering 425 million Catholics living in Latin America to this day,[14] a much bigger number than the entire population of the Roman Empire (which most estimates put at around 60 million at its peak). And in my travels to Latin America, the degree of religious devotion was hard to ignore.

While religion has declined in Northern Europe, the remaining pockets of belief can be explained by quirks of history. In the 16th century, Northern European countries started to reject elements of the Roman Catholic Church and the Protestant Church emerged. English king Henry VIII was very keen to divorce one of his wives, so he broke from the Church in Rome to form the Church of England.[15] He also declared that he should be in charge of it. How surprising.

To this day, the C of E is the religion of 85 million people.[16] When I visited Northern Ireland, I could see that people's lives were still defined by this Catholic/Protestant split. In both Belfast and Derry/Londonderry, the cities are strictly divided into Protestant and Catholic sections.

In Belfast I hopped in a taxi and got taken on a tour of the city. My driver's accent was so thick I struggled to understand him. And also so different from the singsong, upbeat accents you hear in the Irish Republic. I saw many violent murals adorning walls and houses. In Belfast, a

---

★   Wonder where they got the 'Latin' prefix from.

huge wall – ironically named the Peace Wall – was built to separate the two fierce opponents. Who, lest we forget, actually believe in the same God. People here act as if the other side are from another planet, rather than compatriots who believe about 90 percent of the same religious stories. It's amazing, really. While a lot of vitriol stems from the unsettled status of Northern Ireland and British exploits in the region, religion is a defining characteristic of the split.

The religions Europeans once carried with them on their global voyages now define the lives of so many outside the continent. How so? Well, the British went on to conquer much of the world during the colonial period from the 18th to 20th centuries, including but not limited to: North America; Australia; New Zealand; and much of Sub-Saharan Africa. Converting the populations to Christianity was part of the deal.

Due to these colonial exploits, I've noticed that people in the Deep South of the US are still fervently committed Christians. I chatted to a businessman in a bar in Houston. He looked serious and professional. He told me his business decisions were outsourced to God. He was a stockbroker who said he asks 'the Lord to pick my stocks for me'. I had practically no idea what this meant. Across the Atlantic in Africa, I noticed Tanzania's, Uganda's, and Kenya's lush landscapes are dotted with Anglican churches. Religion still plays an absolutely central role in everyday life in much of the US and Africa.

Even at the Earth's geographical extremes, few places have been spared from the reach of Christianity and its missionaries. And none more so than the Pacific Islands.

God's Planet

From what I've experienced, these are some of the most intensely Christian places on Earth. Poor and isolated, they were viewed as ripe for conversion by the missionaries of centuries ago.

The London Missionary Society began sending missionaries to the region in 1795. The Wesleyan Missionary Society, founded in 1814, did the same. The indigenous beliefs the islanders held before the British arrived have since largely disappeared. Over 95 percent of Pacific Islanders are now Christian.[17] I saw this for myself; there are churches everywhere. Countries like Samoa and Tonga are probably the most Christian places I've encountered.

This devotion is slightly bewildering – at least from an outsider's perspective – given that the Pacific Islands are still a battleground for missionaries to this day. Whenever I saw a young, Western person in the Pacific Islands, I knew they weren't there to travel; they were there to convert. I'd see them, all perfectly presented and smartly dressed. In one particularly memorable incident, I travelled to the Solomon Islands, a country even named after the biblical king Solomon.

I touched down in Honiara, the ramshackle capital and hopped in a cab. I passed colourful and wooden houses on stilts, with some precariously clinging to Honiara's rolling hills. Many locals waved and smiled as I passed. The Solomon Islands weren't exactly paradise. Rubbish lay strewn across many of the streets. It seemed like a poor nation. Fertile ground for a belief in a higher power.

Eventually, I arrived at my home for the next few

nights. It sat atop one of the city's surrounding hills; the veranda had sweeping views of the bay and the city. I could see the thick rainforest giving way to the much less pretty urban sprawl of the capital. This reached a crescendo at the seashore, which was peppered with clapped-out cranes, rusty cargo vessels, and rundown warehouses. The guesthouse – as I learnt – was really just a local family home, with a few spare rooms. Inside, I was welcomed by a creaky wooden bed with an ill-constructed mosquito net. And no windows.

I heard a knock at my door. I opened it to find a white man in his mid-twenties, from America. He was flanked by two clones. They stood there, smiling slightly too much, smartly dressed in short-sleeve shirts, no ties but with the top button done up. Which, in my view, always looks a bit weird.

'Hi, friend! We just thought we'd drop by to tell you about the Lord. He's changed our lives, and could change yours too, if you'd…'

'Here we go,' I thought. I heard them out for a few minutes, trying to be as polite as possible. But they barely paused for breath. So finally I had to kind of interrupt with a few laughs, while saying sorry lots and closing the door at the same time, as if I was dealing with door-to-door salesmen. Which in a way, I was. These guys were selling God. And it wasn't just that one time. They were relentless for the duration of my stay.

When they weren't staying up late singing hymns as loudly as possible (not sure why they couldn't have praised God in the daytime), they tried their utmost to convert me. They'd start by talking about other topics like sport or food. Lure me in. But they'd then somehow steer the conversation in the direction of 'How damn great is our belief system? How clever are we for believing in Jesus? Wouldn't it be great if everyone in the world believed what we did?' (my paraphrasing).

My already limited patience for this stuff was wearing thin after a few days. In the kitchen, making breakfast, they started again. And so I just said, with a hint of frustration, 'I'm non-religious, and very happy for it. When I die, I'll get eaten by worms. So I'm going to live my one and only life here on Earth to the fullest.'

One responded smilingly, knowingly, and patronisingly. 'Well, God has of course given you the ability to have your own views and that's a great thing.'

'And clearly God's given *you* the ability to be an insufferable jerk and that's a great thing too,' I mumbled under my breath, barely minutes later (bravely making sure he was well out of earshot).

Christian missionaries are certainly determined. In one sad tale in 2018, 26-year-old American John Allen Chau tried to convert the indigenous population of North Sentinel Island in the Indian Ocean. He was warned he might be killed if he did so, from the Sentinelese no less. After years of meticulous planning and with God on his side (presumably), he strode confidently ashore. And was killed almost immediately, as predicted.

I could see why missionaries were targeting places like North Sentinel Island and the Pacific Islands: they're cut off, poor, and underdeveloped. And in the eyes of wealthy

US donors from the Mormon Church and, to a lesser extent, Seventh Day Adventists, incentives (bribes?) could be used to help people realise that the Christian God is the best.

In Kiribati, the Solomon Islands, and Samoa, in particular, I noticed that almost all of the most robust structures were built by Mormons. The schools they'd built had excellent facilities, including basketball courts and libraries. Altruism at its best. I asked a few locals about them. They all said that literally *anyone* is allowed to send their child there – as long as they accept the Mormon Church's theological story. Which many seem to be willing to do as the Church's work has been a success – around 30 percent of Polynesians are now Mormons. We humans want to believe in something. And missionaries and colonial explorers have always been more than happy to take advantage of this fact, spreading the world's modern religions across its surface in the process. Often at the tip of a sword.

Jeddah and Modern Saudi Arabia

Back in Jeddah, I had a couple of days to relax, explore the city, and, I hoped, not spend all my time worrying about mystical deities and their impact on the world. Before visiting, I'd been in touch with a Canadian traveller friend who'd agreed to put me in touch with one of her friends who lived in Jeddah. So in the morning, outside my hotel, I met him. His name was Fayez.

God's Planet

Fayez, like many of the Saudis I'd met by this stage, was incredibly kind and hospitable. He was short, wore Western clothes, and had a youthful face, looking younger than his 30 or so years. Despite my protestations, he basically demanded that he be my chauffeur for the entire day, driving around the city and showing me the sights. So, I didn't stop him; it meant that I could concentrate on the city more. Jeddah was not what I was expecting. Modern and not too dissimilar to large US cities like Los Angeles and Houston in some ways. Huge motorways and overpasses stretched out in all directions, punctuated by giant malls and fast food restaurants. New buildings were going up all over the place.

We went for a walk along the Corniche, the jewel in Jeddah's crown. It's where they now host the annual Formula 1 race. Skyscrapers overlooked a wide, palm-tree-flanked road, used by walkers, runners, and cyclists, who were all out in force. Always in view were the invitingly azure waters of the Red Sea. Few women wore *hijabs*. I knew that Jeddah was considered the more liberal part of Saudi, at least compared to the conservative capital, Riyadh, but I was still surprised at, well, how 'normal' the city seemed. It was nothing like my preconceptions of what Saudi Arabia might be like.

Fayez and I talked about all of the rapid changes his country was going through.

'What do you think of it all?' I asked.

'I think it's great. It's nice to see tourists. It's a positive step that women don't have to cover their hair and wear an *abaya* if they don't want to. And are now allowed to drive, obviously. These might sound like a crazy thing to outsiders, but for Saudis they represent massive changes. Lots of the older generation aren't happy about it, to be honest. They think the change is happening too fast,' he said, in perfect English with an American twang to it.

We continued strolling down the Corniche. The sun twinkled off the lazy waves; palm trees swayed above us, giving periodic – fleetingly glorious – moments of protection from the sun.

'Obviously he's controversial,' I said, 'but it seems like Mohammed bin Salman (MBS) is modernising Saudi in many ways. I'm glad it's possible for me to visit as a tourist, and things are liberalising in some ways.' Fayez agreed.

Saudi's reformist prince has shaken things up in recent years, opening the country to the world. Recent changes included the powers of the religious police being reduced in 2016, women being allowed to drive in 2017, a ban on music concerts being lifted in 2018, and the so-called guardianship system being relaxed, which previously made it hard for women to do many things without seeking permission from their male guardians. In the West, obviously, these things are rightly seen as basic and fundamental rights. But for Saudi, these are profound and rapid changes. Prince MBS said the reforms would return Saudi to a more open past: 'We are simply reverting to what we followed – a moderate Islam open to the world and all religions.'[18]

Once back in the car, Fayez and I drove down another of Jeddah's rather faceless, large, American-style freeways, full of American-style SUVs. This time, I paid careful attention to whether women were using their new-found 'freedom' to drive. Few appeared to be. Perhaps old habits die hard, perhaps it would take time for the culture to shift, especially given that women still face a number of obstacles to taking the road.

We pulled over and walked into a brightly lit restaurant. It was pink on the outside. Inside, it had shiny white tiled floors, TV screens on the walls showing football, and was filled with young people. Or more accurately, young men. I still hadn't got used to the gender separation in restaurants. Here, as elsewhere, there were separate entrances: one for families and women, one for men. I looked at the menu, a fast food style one situated in large font above the tills. No beers, from what I could see. Even though I'd pretty much stopped drinking beverages intentionally laced with poison at this stage of my life (which makes drinking alcohol actually seem quite stupid), it reminded me that this was a conservative nation. One still heavily influenced by Sharia law.

We were there to eat a truly bizarre meal. A local delicacy, according to Fayez. I paid my money, and was given a plastic container filled to the brim with cornflakes. Which had then (logically) been covered with melted cheese and dates. It was nice, however. Oddly so. So I hoovered down a second portion, which I almost immediately regretted. Most of the men in my side of the restaurant were young and hadn't seen many tourists before. So they came over to chat and take selfies. Most spoke excellent English. All were impeccably polite. Par for the course here.

The Travelling Ape

A Tension Between the Past and Future

There's a tension at the heart of Saudi. It has some of the most welcoming and friendly people on Earth. But then at the same time it has these rules, laws, or customs that are hard to understand. Across much of the world outside Saudi too, I'd seen that repression is often more common in religious places. And towards women in particular.

Across the globe, women tend to earn less than men. They're underrepresented in senior jobs and political positions of power. Their access to education is worse as well. In many countries, women still have far less influence over how important household decisions are made, and are overwhelmingly more likely to be the victims of sexual violence.

While things in Western countries are by no means perfect, substantial progress has been made.[19] In other places, less so. In 2014, there were still 22 countries where gender-equal inheritance did not exist.[20] A year later, there were still 17 countries in the world where married women didn't have equal ownership rights to property.[21] The 2020 *Global Gender Gap Report* suggests that at the current rate of change, the gender gap will be closed in the next century in most regions, apart from the Middle East, North Africa, East Asia, and the Pacific regions.[22] Which is quite a lot of regions, and a long time, to say the least.

I couldn't help but feel that this discrepancy has something do with religiosity. Most of the world's religious texts were written by men. Is it surprising, then, that these men decided to use these texts to enshrine their privileged positions in the world into law where they could? Orthodox Jews even forbid women to read their main religious text, the Talmud. As one rabbi representative of this view – or *hashkafa* – cheerfully explained, such scholarship 'is not congruent with the woman's role.'[23]

Even in the West, the biggest threats to the rights of women to have an abortion, to the equal status of homosexuals, and even the right of women to become priests, bishops, and the lot, come *from churches*. In the UK, for instance, the legislative body of the Church of England voted *against* allowing women bishops.*[24] Not 100 years ago. Not 50 years ago. In 2012. The Church reversed the decision in 2014. Hallelujah! But perhaps they are too far behind the curve. In 2018, just 1 percent of young Britons aged 18 to 24 identified as being members of the Church of England, which faces extinction in the UK within decades.[25] To this day, women can't be priests, let alone bishops, in the Catholic Church.

I'd also seen a particularly egregious example of men using religion to the detriment of women in a trip around the Himalayan kingdom of Bhutan. One day, I visited the Temple of Fertility, a series of white temples with ornate wooden roofs, surrounded by stunning blue skies and craggy mountain peaks. The temples were dedicated to a monk called Lama Drukpa Kunley. Otherwise known as the Divine Madman, he was a monk who lived over 500 years ago and is still revered by Bhutanese Buddhists.

He had a slightly unorthodox approach to his practices.

---

*   What were those women thinking?!

For starters, he selflessly told women they would be enlightened if they slept with him. He's alleged to have slept with over 5,000 women. He drank and smoked too. To this day, women still flock to the temple of the Divine Madman to increase their chances of becoming pregnant. To do this, they simply have to walk around the building three times, while holding a four-foot-high wooden sculpture of a phallus. Okay, then.

Back in Jeddah, we got back in the car and headed towards the Old Town. Fayez and I got chatting. The conversation moved onto relationships.

'I mean, despite the rules, there must be gay people here? I can't imagine it's easy for them, given that it's banned and persecuted here?' I said.

'Ah, like, there are obviously gay people here. I know one. They don't disappear just because of the rules. But I guess they have to be a bit careful, cover themselves,' said Fayez. 'Getting caught just isn't an option for them.'

'I see. Still sounds sketchy to me. It must be tough,' I added.

'The thing is, humans are all quite similar behind closed doors. People drink here too, despite it being illegal. Where there's a will there's a way. And often, there's a will, regardless of what religion says about it,' he said, shrugging his shoulders.

We sat in silence for a minute or so. I couldn't imagine what it must be like for his friend, to know that having sex could cost you your life. I shared a story with Fayez about a time I visited Uganda, where attitudes towards homosexuality seemed equally strict.

God's Planet

I took a tour around Kampala, Uganda's loud, chaotic, and vibrant capital. The city streets were crammed with people and cars, lacking any perceptible order. Most there passionately believe in Christianity (forced upon them by the colonising British). My guide casually said, 'I hear there is a problem in Britain. The population is falling. Nobody is having babies because everyone is gay.'

Surprised that this man had such a keen knowledge of British demographics, I simply said, 'No, this isn't true. Our population is growing. Are there any gay people in Uganda?'

He burst out laughing. 'No, no, no! Of course not! It is a sin, it is a sin!' In March 2023, the Ugandan parliament passed a law which stipulated that merely *saying* you are gay can be punishable with a life prison sentence.[26] As Jesus would have wanted, no doubt.

Fayez said, 'Wow, yeah, maybe not so different from here then. Maybe it's a religious thing, rather than anything to do with one particular religion.' (I learnt later that Fayez was right. There are 67 countries in the world where it's illegal to be gay. Most are in Africa, and almost all of them are deeply religious.[27])

I agreed with Fayez's view on the tension between religions and social freedoms. 'Largely atheist societies – like mine – still have a long way to go, though,' I added. 'And aren't perfect. A lack of guiding belief can make people in them rudderless, and a touch nihilistic.* But we're at least much freer. To love who we want. Choose

---

*   I like to use big words casually in conversations like this.

227

the life path we desire. And ultimately, to not have all our choices coloured by a constant fear of a hellish oblivion if we misbehave.'

'Yeah,' he said, 'it's kind of messed up. And what also frustrates me is how much religions divide us. Like, to some people, I'm a Muslim, and that'll be a problem to them. And for some people here in Saudi, anyone who's Jewish isn't going to be popular. The amount of hatred between people – who are the same in so many ways – generated by religion is just really, well, sad.'

This is a point that I not only agreed with, but had thought about at length in my life and while on the road.

Sewing Division across the World

From what I've seen, hatred, wars, terrorism, and genocide aren't tolerated in the modern world. But when it comes to religion, these things are still far too common. Unfortunately, all the wonderful community spirit generated within each religious group is counterbalanced by a just as robust dislike of those outside the group. Part of this reflects our tendency to form unhealthily close bonds with groups. We're compelled to belong to a group as if our lives depend on it, because it did when we were hunter-gatherers. If you were disliked and banished from your group back then, you were unlikely to survive. That ingrained instinct means we cling to our groups to this day.[28]

There are further unfortunate consequences of our need

to be part of a group. The main one is a tendency to detest anyone outside it. This is called 'in-group favouritism'. A famous experiment split boys into two groups.[29] Despite the boys knowing that they had been divided arbitrarily, it didn't take long for each group to believe theirs was the 'best', and to start having hostile feelings towards the other randomly generated group.

If it's easy to generate hatred for no good reason whatsoever, it's no wonder that loyalty to a religious group can become so dangerous. Especially when your religion explicitly tells you to favour your own kind at the expense of others. Over time, we depict those outside the group as less than human, with hatred of the out-group (non-believers or people of other religious beliefs), solidifying the self-worth of the in-group. Primatologist Frans de Waal suggests this behaviour is evident in chimps (99 percent the same as us, remember?), who detest the out-group to the point of 'dechimpization', leading to lethal violence between them.[30]

Organised religion – perhaps tied with nationalism – has probably been the main cause of human violence in history. A cursory look through our past reveals religious wars, crusades, and religion being spread by the sword. The Crusades, the Thirty Years War, the Spanish Inquisition. The 'civilising' and God-sanctioned colonial wars. More recently, you had Serbs, Croats, and Bosnians violently dividing themselves along Orthodox, Catholic, and Muslim fault lines.[31] I could still see the bullet holes in the crumbling buildings of Mostar in Bosnia when I visited.

And it's still an issue today (obviously). The treatment

of the Uyghur Muslims in China. The genocide of the Rohingya in Myanmar by supposedly peaceful Buddhists.[32] Terrorist attacks by Islamist extremists are part of life in Europe and the Middle East. This list goes on. A 2018 survey of 21,000 people rated religion 'as the primary source of global conflict today'.[33] Can you blame them for thinking that?

How do most major religions square the supposedly peaceful nature of their belief systems with all the violence they generate? Quite easily, as it happens. If you encourage someone to believe in the cosmic righteousness of their own religion, you shouldn't be surprised when a small minority take things the wrong way and fundamentalists start doing extreme things.

Recent research suggests there may be intrinsic aspects of religion that promote conflict. In a study, those who were told that a passage in the Bible condoned violence were more likely to be violent in a task afterwards.[34] One study argued that while most religious text is peaceful, the words can often be twisted to justify violence.[35] The study author argued that 'religious books are often incorrectly cited or cited in a way that serves personal prejudices'.[36]

Back in Jeddah, still in the car, I told Fayez of my experience in Pakistan at the tomb of Muhammad Ali Jinnah, and the boy whose brain exploded at the concept of my non-belief.

Shortly after shocking that boy, I told him that I flew from mostly Muslim Pakistan to mostly Hindu India. In both countries, everyone was predominantly pleasant and friendly. But when I mentioned my dark secret to people in India, that I'd recently visited their neighbour, their behaviour immediately changed. They sought reassurance that those across the border were as heinous as they believed them to be. They were quickly filled with hate.

At the time of my visit to both countries, in 2019, it was shortly after an Indian pilot was shot down and captured by Pakistani forces. The Indians I spoke to in New Delhi used this as a perfect example of the Pakistani people's inherent wickedness, with many Indians mentioning Islam as a possible explanation for this.

The Pakistanis I spoke to said that the authorities' excellent treatment of the pilot – who was subsequently released and treated as a war hero in India[37] – showed how Pakistanis were a kinder people than the Indians, and this was likely due to the former's faith. To be honest, I just nodded along with both sides. I knew the impacts of the mishandled partition of India played a role in their hatred,[38] but I felt a deep sadness that good people were again being driven to hatred by religion.

Fayez sighed. 'It's so stupid when you look at it like that. It sucks.' I went on to describe how other trips had likewise shown me the darker side of religions. I told him how I visited enchanting Sri Lanka once with my family. How we had a lovely taxi driver who spoke of his unending love for his two daughters and was unbelievably likeable. Unfailingly polite and a truly sweet person. Driving into the famous town of Kandy, surrounded by tea plantations, we passed a slum with some roadside stalls.

Out of nowhere, our driver smilingly said, 'Look at these dirty, smelly people. They're Muslims. They ruin everything about this country. Don't go near them.' I didn't mention that the poverty the Muslims lived in was a direct consequence of the systemic discrimination they face at every level of society in Sri Lanka by Buddhist nationalists.[39]

I talked to Fayez about a trip to Israel that had amply demonstrated how religion can have a pernicious impact on a nation's relations with its neighbours. On arrival, I had to get an extra page added and stamped on my passport. (Other countries in the region – such as Saudi Arabia – won't let you visit if you've been.)

My trip to Jerusalem was strange. As I walked around the city's ancient, cobbled streets, I could easily sense how important this place was to so many people. It contained sights holy to Christians, Jews, and Muslims. I saw minarets next to church steeples, and Hasidic Jews walking around with Christian bishops nearby. The small Old City was divided along religious lines. And although there's a sort of peace there, it felt like a fragile one. Armed police and soldiers patrolled the streets. I had to go through airport-style security to get near the Wailing Wall. While in some way an example of how religions can co-exist, for me, Jerusalem was defined by tension.

While words in religious books can seem abstract, the real-life consequences of religious belief can be shocking. Driving into the West Bank in Palestine was a chastening experience. We had to show our passports to be allowed through a giant concrete wall, malevolent in its scale, a scar across the landscape. Most Palestinians and Israelis aren't allowed to cross it, but tourists and those from overseas can, such is the distrust between both territories. On the other side of the wall, we were suddenly transported from a rich country to one riven by poverty. From Israel, wealthy and Jewish, to Palestine, poor and Muslim. Ultimately, this border and the tensions between Israel and Palestine are rooted in both sides claiming the same land in Israel as their ancestral homes, as crucial to their religious identity.[40] Military conflicts between both sides have been common throughout Israel's history. And given the vast ideological chasm between both sides, I expect tensions will remain high for the foreseeable future.

'I really want to go to Israel one day. Just to see for myself,' said Fayez. 'But I also feel like there's already a target on my back. I definitely don't need that stamp in my passport too.'

We both laughed. I guess you kind of have to in Fayez's situation. But despite all the limitations his country's religion imposed on him, quite amazingly he didn't begrudge it.

'For most people here, Islam has a massively positive impact on their lives. It helps structure their days, and gives people hope. Makes them want to be good people. I've spent a few years of my life in New York and London. And to be honest, I'm not sure the lack of religion there is making people any happier. In fact, it looked like it was making people less happy.'

'Hard to say, isn't it,' I replied, looking out the window. Despite its restrictions, I'd seen for myself the meaning Islam gave to locals here. 'Maybe my life would be simpler if I believed in one of the religions too. But I just can't do it.'

Popular for a Reason?

Travelling has taught me that geography and history explain the spread of world religions. But there clearly had to be more to their long-lasting impact than historical battles and territorial conquests. Religions probably wouldn't be as popular as they are unless they offered something spiritual to believers. Despite superficial differences – rituals, stories, and customs – most religions offer followers remarkably similar things. In particular, meaning, and comforting certainty about their lives and the universe.

Whoever did the marketing for them – God, probably – deserves a pat on the back. Consider what most religions provide the average bewildered ape who's trying to come to terms with their utterly irrelevant position in the vast cosmos.

Fearful human: 'I'm scared of death.'

God(s): 'Don't be, you'll live for eternity in paradise after you die.'

'My life is full of so much suffering. I'm so unhappy!'

'Don't worry. The more you suffer here on Earth, the better the afterlife will be for you.'

'Oh that's good. But in the meantime, I feel disconnected from others and am lonely lots of the time.'

'Come to worship me each week, there will be a ready-made community of others just like you. You can gain a new social support network.'

'But the world and life are so complex, how can I navigate the chaos? I lack direction.'

'Honestly, you have nothing to worry about. I've thought

about everything. We have more rules than you can imagine, and our knowledge of the universe is complete. So just follow the rules, accept our knowledge, and simplify your life!'

'Wow this is starting to sound amazing. But I also feel like there is a spiritual place in my life, for rituals and ceremony, that isn't currently being fulfilled.'

'We've got it covered. You'll have to wear particular clothes and practise certain rituals from time to time, to give you the sense of sacredness you desire.'

'So you're saying I'll live forever, that my suffering and life all have a higher cosmic purpose, and that you have devised a meticulous way of operating on a day-to-day basis to give structure to an otherwise chaotic universe?'

'I am indeed.'

'I'm sold. Thanks, God(s). You sound so wise and compassionate. Just to let you know, I'm a woman and I'm gay. Guessing I'll still have equal rights and stuff. I mean, if you're omnipotent, it wouldn't make sense to want certain groups to be discriminated against, right?'

'Um, yeah, about that. Just try your best not to be gay, or a woman, ideally. I'm also quite insecure and needy. You'll have to praise me constantly. Best not to ask where you'll go if you fail to do this.'

So religions give meaning to the suffering and lives of many. Most of the rules dished out by the various faiths appear to support behaviours which, on the whole, would be viewed as morally virtuous. Being religious often improves the behaviour and community-minded spirit of many people, at least, within their own religious grouping. It's just a shame that this spirit doesn't extend to those outside their own religion, and leads to so much division between them.

On a personal level, following a faith might just make people happier, too. A 2019 study found actively religious people were more likely than their less religious peers to describe themselves as 'very happy'.[41] In Mexico, for example, 71 percent of the actively religious were 'very happy', compared to 61 percent for the religiously unaffiliated. In Uruguay, the religious won by 43 percent to 33 percent in the happiness stakes, while in Estonia the difference was 20 percent to 11 percent. Notice that Estonia is the richest country of the three, and the least happy. It's like this almost everywhere. Religious people are also less likely to drink and smoke (which is probably good), and to be more democratically engaged.

Remember those compelling things religion has to offer. 'We promise you'll live forever, your suffering has a deeper cosmic purpose, and we'll provide you with a community and support network of like-minded individuals.' German philosopher Friedrich Nietzsche is widely attributed with the famous (translated) quote, 'If we have our own why of life, we shall get along with almost any how.'[42] In difficult circumstances, there's perhaps no better 'why' than religion.

Fayez and I spent our last few hours together strolling around Al Balad, Jeddah's Old Town. It appeared as if unchanged for centuries. Wonky white buildings were adorned with wondrously intricate and beautiful Arabian wooden balconies, doors, and window frames. Some left unpainted, others in rich shades of turquoise or blue or pink. We ducked down tiny little alleys.

'We'd be able to touch the walls on both sides if we outstretched our arms,' I said excitedly. Realising immediately this was a stupid idea and would block all pedestrians, I added, 'Theoretically.' It felt like we were walking through Saudi's distant past while being in the middle of glitzy modern Jeddah. I thanked Fayez for showing me around. And, mostly, for being so honest. And giving me a small glimpse into what life is like for people like him in this country.

Next morning, I was sitting in my freezing, air-conditioned hotel lobby thinking that maybe I could squeeze in a couple more tourist sights. So I set off on foot. First, the tallest fountain in the world, which soars to an incredible 1,025 feet. That's just shy of the Eiffel Tower at 1,083ft. (Why I'm so obsessed with comparing everything to the Eiffel Tower, I'll never know.)

I soon realised walking was a silly move. This is a city made for cars. And a bloody hot one at that. I strolled on pavements but also along the side of roads; the idea of walking here is so alien the authorities hadn't bothered to build pavements next to a great deal of them. I, at least, had a lot of time to consider my journey through Saudi. And what it and my global travels had taught me about religion.

I now knew that my agnostic-atheism is unusual in a religious world that will become more religious going forward. I'd seen how for most their chosen religion simply reflected quirks of geography and history. That religions hold back social progress and sow tension between nations. But also that they give people deep meaning. Deep purpose. And a reason to live. To be better people. I realised that our collective religious devotion is one of humanity's defining characteristics. Influencing nations, government policy, and international relations, the subject of which we'll examine in more detail in the next section of this book.

An hour passed. Slogging along on the side of highways and through nondescript urban sprawl. I finally arrived at King Fahd's Fountain. There was a sweep of sea, row upon row of palm trees, all topped with blue sky. But no fountain. Turned off for the day. 'It's not as if it has feelings and needs a rest,' I said under my breath. Damnit. Oh well, on to the next landmark, I figured, not wanting to let this setback defeat me. I set off and 30 minutes later, I arrived.

Truthfully, I couldn't help but feel emotional – the main emotion being frustration, however. As the largest flagpole in the world, my destination, came into view, I noticed that it was conspicuously lacking a flag. Was God taunting me? I asked a passer-by where the flag was. He told me it was being cleaned.

'The flagpole is as tall as a 50-storey building, so even that is amazing in its own right,' I told myself. 'But this is just over half the height of the Eiffel Tower. Without the flag, this walk has been a waste of time.' Even with my best intellectual acrobatics, I struggled to see the positives.

'Also, does anyone really, truly need a flag this massive? What the hell are they trying to prove here?' I asked myself.

God's Planet

At the time of my visit in 2019, this was indeed the tallest flagpole in the *entire world*, rising to 557 feet. 'I haven't seen flags this big anywhere back home, or anywhere in the West for that matter.'

My next adventure would show me that the tallness of this flagpole was no coincidence.

PART III

Geopolitics: The Drama Will Never End

9

Democracy: Flawed, but Dismiss it at Your Peril

The world isn't perfect. But it's more democratic than it's ever been, and democracies are easily the best places to live.

I had a few hours to kill at Jeddah Airport. They hadn't (yet) built a fancy new one to cope with the hundred million or so tourists Saudi Arabia optimistically aims will be visiting each year by 2030. It was still a low-ceilinged '60s affair. I grabbed a coffee and sat down on those uncomfortable black airport seats that you see all over the world. Sipping and 'surfing the web' (wasting the one life I have by googling lots of things), I started looking more into the concept of flags. And one of the first things that popped up was this immortal quote about flags from Calvin Coolidge:

> We do honor to the Stars and Stripes as the emblem of our country and the symbol of all that our patriotism means.

The Travelling Ape

We identify the flag with almost everything we hold dear on Earth. It represents our peace and security, our civil and political liberty, our freedom of religious worship, our family, our friends, our home. We see it in the great multitude of blessings, of rights and privileges that make up our country.

But when we look at our flag and behold it emblazoned with all our rights, we must remember that it is equally a symbol of our duties. Every glory that we associate with it is the result of duty done. A yearly contemplation of our flag strengthens and purifies the national conscience.[1]

Some of you might not know who Calvin Coolidge is. Well, he isn't just a man who really, really likes flags; he was the 30th president of the United States.[*] In any case, I felt this quote accurately highlighted the odd reverence with which we view our national flags. So much so that just a few days before in Jeddah, I learnt their main flag gets cleaned regularly and towered over all buildings around it.

In dozens of countries I'd visited, I'd seen how flags have a sacred significance. So much so that in many places it's illegal to 'insult' the flag.[2] I'd seen lots of flag waving in Europe during the football championships one year. But I only learnt later that desecration of the flag will result

---

[*] From 1923-1929. I'm going to be completely honest and concede that I'd not really heard of him either.

in a jail term in Germany, and a slew of other countries worldwide invoke the same punishment.[3]

When a 'Greater Albania' flag was flown by a drone into a football match between Serbia and Albania in 2014, it caused a fight among players, crowd trouble, and a full-blown diplomatic dispute between the countries.[4] India has lots of granular laws surrounding its flag. So much so that Indian cricket hero Sachin Tendulkar got in hot water in 2007. For burning the flag? No, for cutting a cake with the Indian flag on it.[5]

So maybe, I reasoned, Saudi wasn't the only outlier here. I continued clicking away. I discovered that Saudi Arabia was currently in 'pole position' when it came to having the world's tallest flagpole. And there were many more. The top five tallest flagpoles were in Saudi, Tajikistan, Azerbaijan, North Korea, and Turkmenistan.

Sub-par airport coffee inside me, I sat back and reasoned, 'While these countries have big flags, they aren't famous for being particularly free or democratic. Is this merely a coincidence?' In that moment, I realised there could well be an inverse correlation between how free a country is and the size of its main flagpole. I turned out to be right. The higher your flag, the less freedom. Here are the flagpoles and their heights:

1. Saudi Arabia   Jeddah 557 feet (150th)
2. Tajikistan   Dushanbe 541 feet (156th)
3. Azerbaijan   Baku 531 feet (134th)
4. North Korea   Kijong-dong 525 feet (165th)
5. Turkmenistan   Ashgabat 436 feet (161st)

I've added figures next to the heights to show the country's ranking (out of 167) in the Economist Intelligence Unit's Democracy Index in 2022.*[6] The countries rank similarly dismally in Reporters Without Borders' annual Press Freedom Index (2022), which in my view is a useful proxy for how free and democratic a country is.[7] Clearly, for all Saudi Arabia, Tajikistan, Azerbaijan, North Korea, and Turkmenistan have in terms of big flags, they lack in things like a liberal press and democratic freedoms. But how would this rather grim assessment match up with my experiences on the ground? Well, I'd already seen the first and fourth tallest flagpoles, in Saudi and North Korea (which I have a great deal to say about in the next chapter). And as luck would have it, I was about to take a flight to Baku, in Azerbaijan, before overlanding through Central Asia. I'd be able to visit them all. And in doing so, I hoped, would be able to see what lessons these big bits of cloth could teach me about freedom and democracy.

Baku to the Future

After a few hours spent in the troposphere in a pressurised aluminium tube, I touched down in Azerbaijan. Or the so-called 'Land of Fire', as many posters in the airport were at pains to point out. Apart from the fact that Azerbaijan

---

★   Although I write for the Economist Intelligence Unit, it's worth making clear that the Democracy Index's methodology is a little more sophisticated than the 'look at some massive flags' formula I've employed to devastating effect in this chapter.

is hot, and this could in theory cause fires, I wasn't sure the catchphrase made much sense. I learnt later that the country's ancient population used to worship fire, so modern Azerbaijanis could perhaps be descended from pyromaniacs.

Heydar Aliyev International Airport, named after independent Azerbaijan's first president, was at least wonderfully modern. It looked a bit like the spaceship from Star Trek.* All of it glistened. And this positive first impression continued. After collecting my bags, I walked out the front of the airport and was greeted by the entirely unexpected sight of a long line of London taxi cabs. The only difference is that these ones were purple rather than black. It reminded me of home. Even if they seemed completely out of place in the desert heat.

We set off, driving on wide, new, immaculately paved roads. The main highway taking us into town – the Heydar Aliyev Avenue – had clearly been completed in the not-too-distant past. New skyscrapers shimmered in the distance. Three of them even had the silhouettes of flames – the aptly named Baku Flame Towers. This was both impressive and disheartening. Clearly this 'fire' tag line was going to be pushed very hard for the duration of my trip. There were cranes and construction in all directions. The place reminded me a bit of Dubai. Development taking place on almost every available plot of land; glass and steel rising up out of the sandy desert. Azerbaijan was going places.

Before I'd even checked into the hotel, I got my taxi driver

---

* I'm clearly not a 'Trekkie', for anyone who's up in arms about not knowing what the ship is actually called.

to stop at a museum I'd wanted to see for years. The late Zaha Hadid, my favourite architect, designed it. (The fact I just used 'favourite' is a clever tool to imply that I know other architects, and am therefore a 'cultured' person.) She also designed the Aquatics Centre for the London 2012 Olympics.

I stepped out of the cab, and there it was. A truly stupendous sight. All shimmering white, radiant against the blue sky. It looked like a melting, free-flowing cloud. Or white waves, rippling out at sea. There wasn't a straight line anywhere from what I could see, true to her style, with the whole thing emerging from the ground as if part of nature. From the inside, it got even better. It was like I'd been transported 100 years into the future. Every fitting and fixture contributed to the seamless, wave-like structure of the building. It was genuinely magnificent. On several occasions, I actually chuckled out loud, in awe of what I was seeing. I then remembered that being fascinated by architecture rarely makes you cool. Making involuntary noises at inanimate buildings? Possibly insane.

I walked around, head cricked upwards. My jaw open, looking like some zombie possessed by architecture, a few niggling thoughts did start to pop into my head. 'Must have been pretty expensive, this one.' Not many of Hadid's buildings are in any way financially viable, due to their wave-like structures being prohibitively expensive to build. And I was right. Take a cursory glance at the other buildings she's designed – which are all magnificent – and you'll see that many if not most of them are built in autocracies. As vanity projects. China, Qatar, and countries in the Middle East predominate. Spending on which wouldn't perhaps be tolerated in places where leaders are beholden to their electorates. In autocratic regimes, cost is no issue. And right now, I was enjoying the delicious fruits of this conundrum.

Then there was the actual content of the museum, made to house Azerbaijan's cultural artefacts. Azerbaijan's impact on global affairs has been muted. The modern-day republic was only founded upon the collapse of the USSR in 1991. Its most famous historical achievement to date has probably been winning the Eurovision Song Contest in 2011. (With, to be fair, a great ballad.) Azerbaijan is just over 30 years old. And any cultural artefacts that existed before then were most likely destroyed under Soviet rule. As a result, the museum is almost completely empty. Save for a supposedly classic car exhibition. This was comprised of three of ex-president Heydar Aliyev's old Mercedes. The use of the world 'classic' was also pretty generous; the oldest car was from the late 1990s.

Finally, there was the name of the museum. The – you guessed it – Heydar Aliyev Cultural Centre. This white elephant, this beautiful, stunning white elephant, had taken my breath away. But there'd been a few red flags about Azerbaijan already too. And none bigger than the giant (mainly) red flag I hopped back in my cab to go and see next.

After around 10 minutes, I reached my next destination and exited the taxi. There it was. The third tallest flagpole in the world. It stood in a prime position overlooking the Bay of Baku, in a much more majestic location than its slightly larger counterpart in Saudi Arabia. Azerbaijan's green, red, and blue flag is pretty, and brightened up the bay. A bay that was crowded with new skyscrapers, impressive but often on the cusp of looking garish. One looked like a giant disc with a large hole punched out of the middle. I strolled down the city's leafy and stately-seeming seafront, Baku Boulevard, which was quite delightfully done. All the while, the flag fluttered away in the distance.

My mind churned. 'Okay, a few things are slightly off; everything being named after a previous leader is rarely a good sign. But Baku seems pretty nice on the whole. Saudi was too, in many ways. Good infrastructure, modern buildings. Maybe benevolent autocracy isn't so bad? After all, democracy back in the West is a mess at the moment.'

Is Democracy Really So Great Anyway?

When I was visiting Azerbaijan in 2019, I was still lamenting the 'failures' of democracy in my country and across the Western world. (And by failures, I mean things I wanted to happen didn't happen in elections and referendums). I, like many, had been whipped up into a belief that democracy had in recent years delivered some sub-optimal outcomes. In 2016, there was Brexit and Trump, and populists all over Europe and Latin America were thriving.[8]

After the Brexit vote, I heard friends saying that we shouldn't hold referendums. I heard similar things coming out of my own mouth too. Voters don't have access to enough information to make informed decisions, or so it seemed. Winston Churchill famously said that 'the best argument against democracy is a five-minute conversation with the average voter.'⁹ And I felt, at the time, he maybe had a point. Referendums and democratic elections had caused some of the world's biggest problems in recent years.

Just months after the British EU referendum, millions of Americans exercised their democratic right to elect a man-child as president. I was in the US in the run-up to the vote. Having seen Brexit happen, to the utter surprise of lentil-eating millennials like me, I warned Americans that Trump would win. In New York, people literally laughed in my face. 'I don't know anyone who's gonna vote for that idiot,' they said. I'd just driven through the Deep South and had met many people who felt very differently indeed.

In the same year, Colombians voted against ending a brutal and decades-long conflict between the Colombian government and FARC guerrillas. I was there too in the run-up to the poll, after having followed the political developments at work. I assumed locals would support a deal to end a brutal conflict that had killed an estimated 220,000 in recent decades.¹⁰ 'It'll be good when all the murders and kidnappings stop, right?' But people I spoke to in Medellín and Bogotá were split down the middle. They didn't see it that way. In the end, 52.2 percent of Colombians voted *against* the peace deal – as they were entitled to – and, in effect, voted for the continuance of war.

Turkey had been a model democracy for the Middle East until around 2014, when Recep Tayyip Erdoğan became president. When I visited in 2017, things appeared to be going in the wrong direction. I'd heard Istanbul was secular and liberal, very European. But when I visited, many of the bars had been forced to close, press freedom was declining. A few months later, Turkish voters decided to exercise *their* democratic right to vote for precisely less democracy, in a referendum that gave sweeping new powers to nationalist and religious conservative Erdoğan. Before becoming president and when he was prime minister, Erdoğan commissioned the construction of a new US$1.2 billion palace for the president. He then swiftly moved into this palace after becoming president, seemingly to the outrage of no one.

'The voter knows best' and the 'will of the people' are slogans held up as unquestionable truths in democracies. But in recent years, I'd seen that people could elect tyrants. Our social media echo chambers had divided right and left like never before. Politicians on both the far left and far right appeared happy to say anything to get in power. Their unfulfilled desire for love or acceptance manifesting itself in a craving for wielding power over others. As if each vote they received was filling some gaping hole in their lives.[*] Given what was happening in democracies, perhaps the ideology itself wasn't all it was cracked up to be?

Might Benevolent Autocracies Be the Answer?

Maybe Plato was right when he said in *The Republic* that we should be ruled by 'philosopher kings'? Particularly as I'd noticed an uncomfortable truth about benevolent autocracies.

---

[*] This is my take, at least. I'm sure some politicians have good intentions. But for the majority, it's power they seek.

Democracy: Flawed, but Dismiss it at Your Peril

These are countries led by competent, (notionally) well-meaning leaders with absolute authority. Many had been very successful in driving economic development in recent decades, more so than in democracies.

Compare the rapid development of autocratic China with the world's largest democracy, India. China's economic growth has been astonishing, leaving India trailing in its wake. While both countries had roughly equal average incomes in 1950,[11] today, average incomes in China are around *six times* higher than in India.[12] This partially reflects the fact that China's economy is supported by a government that can plan for the long term. When I visited India, it was like stepping into a different world. Infrastructure was crumbling and poverty was never far away. With over a billion people to represent and huge ethnic, religious, and cultural divisions, remedial policymaking hasn't been straightforward. Whereas in China, with an unquestioned authority that could plan for the future, the country's been able to pull decades ahead of India in the development stakes. Just as the 'Tiger Economies' of South Korea, Taiwan, and Singapore did before it. India's economy has picked up of late under Prime Minister Narendra Modi who, coincidentally, has also started pulling the country in a more authoritarian direction.[13]

Maybe this could be true for Saudi Arabia and Azerbaijan, too? These places were growing fast in economic terms. Were clean, well run. Ordered. No politics to divide people. Effectively no real elections to stop politicians planning for the long term. As these thoughts swirled around my head, I continued walking around Baku's Old Town. It'd actually been built to look old, having been destroyed in earthquakes. But they'd done a good job. There were cobbled streets and beige city walls. Crumbling sandstone houses with ornate wooden balconies. Winding alleys. And, every now and then, a glimpse of modern Baku above me: the Baku Flame Towers peeking through tiny cracks between the closely packed buildings.

As I meandered, I soon noticed that many of the capital's streets were closed to traffic. Motor racing was coming to town in a couple of weeks and Baku's Formula 1 race is popular (annoyed I've already used my 'pole position' pun). While I was having a nice time in the city, deep down I knew I was ignoring some truths about the place. Things just weren't quite right here. Why is former president Heydar Aliyev's name on literally everything? Why is his son now in charge? Could it be that Azerbaijan was using big flags, sporting events, and shiny new buildings to compensate for its shortcomings elsewhere?

As noted above, according to the Democracy Index, Azerbaijan was the 134th least free country in the world in 2022.[14] Non-profit Freedom House ranks Azerbaijan as 'Not Free', and as the tenth least free country in the world.[15] It says power remains in the hands of the Aliyev family, corruption is rampant, political opposition is weakened, and journalists are often jailed. Beyond the 'look how great this country is' vanity projects, there were many problems in Azerbaijan. It seemed like a poor country.* Housing

---

*   Average earnings here are less than half the world average. Sorry, no quippy joke in the footnotes this time.

looked very basic for most, particularly outside the city centre. As in Saudi, Azerbaijan could afford all of these glitzy projects due to it having plentiful oil and gas. In both countries, but particularly in poorer Azerbaijan, I felt they might do better spending that income on improving the lives of their people. But why bother when answering to their people is not something the government has to do?

My Personality Cult is Better than Yours

A short flight was all it took to get me to my next destination. And it was a memorable one. The gate was fairly empty before I boarded but, I reasoned, I was early. I was the first person to enter the Boeing 737, which had over 100 seats. I settled in and watched two more people board. And I waited. But after about a minute or so, the doors closed. There were *three* of us, on this massive passenger jet. Feeling quite a bit of guilt over how bad such a flight must have been for the environment, we set off. It's sometimes claimed that Turkmenistan is one of the top ten least visited countries in the world. This flight certainly seemed to corroborate that.

Everything about Turkmenistan felt weird and wrong from the moment I touched down at its brand-new international airport and stepped off the plane. A beautiful white structure, built to look like an eagle. The swooping airport roof spread out across the terminal like the bird's wings, either side of its head. But inside, it'd been finished with lurid green and gold trimming. It was modern, but already dated. A '60s attempt to be futuristic. It was cavernous and, like my plane, almost completely empty. I chatted with *every single passenger* from my flight while walking through the airport, all two of them. I wasn't surprised to learn that they were here for the same overlanding trip through Central Asia as I was.

We arrived at the passport gates, after spending an inordinate amount of time on lengthy travellators, and were greeted by about 20 border officials. And queue ropes that snaked and turned in on themselves, like for a theme park ride. As if they'd ever need to cope with thousands of arrivals at a time. The board showed there were *three* other flights arriving that day, and they'd landed hours ago.

In these sorts of countries – those viewed as unfree by international observers – 'getting a passport checked' is made deliberately difficult and ceremonial. As if it's a special privilege to be allowed into the truly magical land of Turkmenistan. Go and get a stamp from one person, dressed as if they're literally about to fight in a war. Get another person to check it. Get someone else to check that. Go and pay the entry free over there. Get scowled at again. Come back and fill in an entry form. Hand over the passport for the hundredth time. Get 15 stamps. Get bag checked. Get bag checked again. And then finally, be allowed into the country. An honour.

We were met at the airport by our guide, ostensibly called 'Matt'. He was a short man, with a neat haircut, and dark features. He wore a black T-shirt and old black jeans. He always had a wry smile on his lips, as if he knew how silly much of what he was about to show us was. Like he was in on the big joke. We knew, and had been warned by our tour operator, that he'd be as much our guide as our government minder. So we should be careful with our words. You can't travel in Turkmenistan on your own, or leave the tour group at any stage. A sign, I'd learnt on previous expeditions, that a government has a hell of a lot of stuff they don't want you to see. And that they'd instead show you what they consider to be the 'best' parts of the country.

Oh boy, were we in for a treat. Turkmenistan's capital Ashgabat was, upon first appearances, the weirdest city I'd ever seen. Hands down. We were driven into town by Matt on ten-lane roads, flanked with ornate gold-leaf streetlights and impeccably manicured trees with colourful flowers beneath them. It was pristine, all of it. The one thing missing, however, was any other cars. We didn't see a single one as we drove through the city centre, which dripped with opulence. We passed block after block of grand-looking apartment buildings, all made of white marble. The city's nickname – given to itself – is the City of White Marble. And this made sense. But was there anyone living here? I wasn't so sure. There were literally no people walking its eerie, perfectly presented streets.

The architectural vernacular was all just slightly off. We passed a quite staggering number of ridiculous, gold-plated monuments. Garish in the extreme, lacking any kind of subtlety. Their attempted lavishness came off a bit like those massive hotels in Las Vegas that try to convince Americans they don't need to actually visit Venice or Paris in person. Ashgabat felt like the mutant, autocratic love child of Las Vegas and Pyongyang. It was stonkingly odd. Looking out the minibus's window, it was like peering into an alternate reality. While the world and its people are mostly the same, Turkmenistan was one of the very few destinations in some time where I'd been taken aback by a place's strangeness.

Matt spoke, speaking as if reading from an autocue, with a Russian-sounding accent. 'You can see how excellent this city is, no? Look at the amazing monuments and beautiful structures. We have very good roads here. We have our leader to thank for this.' He delivered this with all the conviction of someone with a gun being held to their head. From what I'd heard about this nation, perhaps he did. I wouldn't have been surprised to see a red dot appear between his eyebrows if he dared to go off script.

'The leader must really be doing a quite fantastic job,' I said sarcastically to a member of our group, aware that our government minder was never far out of earshot. Although to be honest, I felt like Matt would be on our side here. At least in private.

Turkmenistan is the lesser known of the world's two main 'personality cult' countries, the other being North Korea. The all-powerful Turkmen leader had been in power since 2007 when I visited. He goes by the name of Gurbanguly Berdimuhamedow. Let's hope he lets his friends shorten it to something like 'Gurby'. Although doing so without his permission would probably result in your swift execution in Turkmenistan.

In the coming days, I'd see Gurby's face just about everywhere, with his prominent black eyebrows and Legohair side parting. Above the hotel check-in desk. Above the bed in my hotel room. On the sides of buildings. *Inside* every single building we entered. It was as if he always had his eyes on me, wherever I was. And perhaps this is the impression the authorities here want to give. In some of the images, I noticed Gurby was doing normal presidential things. Like signing documents. Opening new industrial centres. Making children laugh. Playing ancient Turkmen musical instruments. Riding horses while brandishing giant swords. Shooting machine guns. Wearing lavish robes. You know, all of the things generally required by a national leader in the modern world.

On the first day of our trip, we were taken on a sightseeing tour of Ashgabat. The authorities had planned our route, thinking it would show us Western tourists just how great Turkmenistan is. But the reality, of course, was that it left me feeling completely the opposite. Again, the lack of any human beings was curious in what was allegedly a thriving, successful city. It was also a crying shame, because there were fewer people to marvel at some of what Matt described as the city's 'very excellent' monuments.

These included the largest indoor Ferris wheel in the world. It did look impressive. A bit like one of those portals in *Stargate SG-1*. But perhaps its designers never stopped to think that the whole point of Ferris wheels is to give riders nice views. We couldn't see out of this one, which is probably why indoor Ferris wheels never took off.

Later, we visited the Arch of Neutrality. A 250-feet-high tripod. It looked like a cross between a spaceship and a Bunsen burner, all white with golden design flourishes. We also saw the blandly named Independence Monument of Turkmenistan. A ridiculously lavish gold-plated plinth. It was surrounded by tens of statues in black stone of soldiers, guarding it. In pride of place, just in front of the plinth, was an entirely gold statue of the country's first president (aka dictator), Saparmurat Niyazov, who ruled Turkmenistan for a 'mere' 16 years between 1990 and 2006. We also drove past what Matt described as the 'very famous' Ministry of Horses and the Ministry of Carpets. Which while not at all famous, were at least *actual* government ministries.

Matt continued to narrate our coach ride around the city. He still delivered all of his lines as if he himself knew he was lying, that this was some sort of joke. It was hard to tell.

'Now we come to the fantastic Olympic Park. The best one in the world.' Deadpan.

'Matt, has Turkmenistan ever hosted the Olympics?' I questioned. 'I'm pretty sure it's never been held here, no?' I said, already knowing the answer but asking in a faux-naive sort of way. In places like this, I always thought carefully as I spoke,* making sure whatever I said couldn't be deemed too controversial. I wasn't keen to spend the rest of my life in a Turkmen jail. Nor, frankly, more than a few more days in the country itself, even on holiday.

'We haven't hosted the event but one day I'm sure it will come. Perhaps the next one.'

'Yeah, um, perhaps,' I said, doubting that Matt had a complete knowledge of the International Olympic

---

* Top life hack: actually thinking about what you say is good practice, wherever you are in the world.

Democracy: Flawed, but Dismiss it at Your Peril

Committee's selection criteria for hosting the event.* The Olympic Park, we learnt, was one of the most expensive ever constructed. And, as far as I knew, the only one built in a country with no plans to host the event.[16] The marble, highly futuristic-looking stadium had a 600-ton horse on the roof. It was surrounded by other white marble arenas, connected by a monorail and tree-lined, grand boulevards. Which most probably would never be used. All of Ashgabat's underused monuments were located a short drive away from each other. Between them, there was just a weird, empty city. If it could even be called that. Filled with grand boulevards, well-manicured trees, beautifully presented benches, and no signs of human life.

Eventually, we pulled over at one of our final stops. Fluttering above us, on the outskirts of the city, was Turkmenistan's big old flag. And it was a goodie. Largely green but with a vertical red stripe on the left-hand side that was a nod to the symbolic importance of carpets to Turkmenistan's national identity. The flagpole was impressive too, it towered over the capital. It created a pleasing contrast between its colours and the rugged, dark mountains which lay on the hazy horizon. Matt told us the flagpole was the fifth tallest in the world. Turkmenistan is the seventh least democratic nation on Earth.[17]

At this stage, some of you might be wondering what

---

* To be fair, as with the equally grotesque organisation FIFA, it's quite simple to understand. Whoever bribes them the most money wins, allegedly. Maybe Turkmenistan does actually have a chance of hosting it.

the big deal is? So Turkmenistan has lots of monuments. Is that really the worst thing in the world? Well, actually, this trend can flag (ahem) larger problems in societies. Turkmenistan is an incredibly poor country, which in recent years has struggled with food shortages and famine (albeit denied by the authorities).[18] Although it amazingly was one of the only countries in the world to not have a COVID-19 outbreak (according, of course, to the government). Turkmenistan has lots of natural gas and resources. It should be wealthy. But it's the opposite.

During our tour, we got a few glimpses of the 'real' Turkmenistan. We grabbed lunch at an old, grey, covered food market. There wasn't a great deal on offer – mainly local bread and *plov* (which I mentioned earlier and which we'd sadly eat much of on our trip through Central Asia). But there were actually people here. I guessed that this was a district in which they actually lived. Not in the bizarre, patriotic theme park we'd been shown. People were skinny in a way that I'd realised was often only tolerated in non-democracies. There were few smiles. A sombre atmosphere. In autocracies, people seem like they've had the life sucked out of them. It's as if the constant propaganda, watching what you say, government untruths, eventually take a physical as much as mental toll.

I felt incredibly sorry for many who live here. I've since been heartened to learn that an estimated three million people have managed to escape Turkmenistan in recent years. The government maintains its population is six million. In reality, it's estimated to be less than half that.[19] Perhaps this was why the place seemed so empty?

Democracy: Flawed, but Dismiss it at Your Peril

Turkmenistan's autocratic leaders have no reason to think about the well-being of their people. They will never face them at the ballot box. At least not a real one. Gurby romped to victory with a totally believable 97.7 percent of the vote in the definitely free and fair 2017 elections.[20] Since I visited, he has actually stepped down. But only to be replaced by the winner of the 2022 'vote' – drum roll please – his son, Serdar Berdimuhamedow. That autocracies so frequently turn into rule by one family is another of their many failings.

Instead of using their concentrated power to improve lives, autocrats often prefer to use propaganda, stifle press freedoms, and chuck all their opponents in jail to remain in power. And then be free to give billions of dollars to themselves and their family. Or in some cases, spend billions on utterly stupid monuments, rather than feeding the population. You can't kick out leaders in autocracies, even when they're terrible leaders (which they almost always are). While politicians in democracies are still mostly awful, on both the right and left, at least we can kick out the ones who are doing the worst job. We all know that power is corrosive to humans. We only need to look at our collective history. Which is mainly one of deranged monarchs or dictators waging war on each other while stuffing their faces and pockets.

The Perils of Philosopher Kings

Truly benevolent dictators are a rare thing. Those who might at one stage have been well-meaning, soon enough, and as reliably as clockwork, become terrible once they've tasted power. Plato's philosopher king would be no different. Democracy – at least – is one attempt to rein in this fundamentally damaging human instinct for control. Our evolutionary hardwiring leads men to seek status.[21] This would've been the surest way to get a mate in prehistory (and might still be, dare we admit it to ourselves).

Back to Churchill for another reliably insightful quote:

> Many forms of Government have been tried, and will be tried in this world of sin and woe. No one pretends that democracy is perfect or all-wise. Indeed it has been said that democracy is the worst form of Government except for all those other forms that have been tried from time to time …[22]

My journey through Turkmenistan, and indeed around the world, had vindicated Churchill. Different models of governance – like fascism or communism – produced the worst horrors of human history in the 20th century. Democracy isn't perfect, but rule by the masses *has to be* the only legitimate way for a society to function. And this is something that had also been made clear to me when I visited the tiny landlocked nation of Eswatini, a few years previously.

I'd heard a few strange things about Eswatini before my visit. First, the country had changed its named from Swaziland to Eswatini in 2018. Purportedly, this was to avoid it being confused with Switzerland. (Personally, I doubt many confused skiers arrived in Swaziland only to realise their grave mistake when hit by blistering heat). Second, that it was one of the few remaining absolute monarchies in the world.

I'd travelled from Mozambique. Along potholed roads that led from the urban sprawl of Maputo through shanty towns and bush to, after a few hours, the border with Eswatini. I switched cars and got picked up by a local guide called Sambulo. He was a smiley chap who spoke impeccable English. He was wearing black jeans, a bright red T-shirt, and a black leather jacket (or, 'An insane combination of clothes in this heat,' as I mentally labelled his outfit).

As we drove further into Eswatini and away from the sea, the scenery became wilder and more mountainous. Sweeping hills lay on the horizon. There was a stillness in the air, and I saw glimpses of the country's lively and colourful culture. We visited a local village where houses were constructed with wonky bits of wood. Where goats and cows wandered its parched centre. Women strolled around, carrying large containers of water on their heads.

As Sambulo and I chatted, the conversation switched to the country's leader, King Mswati III. I'd heard a lot about him and was keen to learn more. 'Is he a good king?' I asked.

'Oh yes. He's the champion of the people and a great leader. We all look up to him,' said Sambulo, earnestly.

Fair enough. But as he told me more about the king, my doubts started to grow. Sambulo went on to tell me that one of the 'best' festivals of the year was the annual Reed Dance. At it, thousands of unmarried girls danced topless in front of the king, wearing only skirts. The festival lasts eight days. King Mswati, who when I visited had a mere 15 wives, then chooses 365 of these women to come and live with him for a year. At the end of the year, one 'lucky' participant gets to become his next wife. Think of it as a sort of dystopian and misogynist *X Factor*.

This egregious abuse of power is what happens when you have all that power in the hands of one person. Eswatini remains poor, with around 60 percent of the population living below the poverty line.[23] I could see this for myself in the country's crumbling infrastructure, and in its basic villages. 'Perhaps the country would be better run if the king didn't spend most of the year ogling topless young girls,' I thought, not wishing to crush my driver's love for him. Or if people could vote him out. It's probably good that (most) of the world's nations have since moved on from monarchical rule.

While heading through Eswatini's flatlands and pondering how such a system had survived so long in the modern world, one of the classic scenes in *Monty Python and the Holy Grail* came to mind.[24] The scene in which King Arthur declares to a peasant that he deserves to be king because he'd been given the sword Excalibur by the Lady of the Lake. To which the peasant – literally slinging mud around – retorts that supreme executive power should derive from the people, and not from a 'farcical aquatic ceremony'.

For much of human history, most systems of government were based on ceremonies and superstitions no less silly than this. Or passed from parent to child. Most people in history spent their lives as roaming hunter-gatherers. Or later, under the rule of some form of absolute monarchy, religious dynasty, or even as slaves. The concept of individual rights has usually been an afterthought, set against the primacy of the monarch, nation, or religion that dominated their society. But King Mswati III in Eswatini is now the exception and not the rule.

That we've moved towards rule by the masses in *most* countries is surely one of humanity's greatest achievements. I estimate that only around five percent of all humans who have ever lived have lived in a democracy, all within the last hundred or so years.[25] And growing. 200 years ago, everyone lacked democratic rights. Now billions of people have them. In 1900 there was only a handful of democracies, like New Zealand and France. There were 25 by 1950, 87 by 2000, and 90 in 2022 (out of the 178 countries measured by Our World in Data).[26] The majority of countries in the world are now democratic. The direction of governmental travel is still positive.

What of autocracies? There were 112 in 1900, 130 in 1950, and 88 in 2022.[27] The number will likely continue falling in the long term, even though there will be ups and downs. COVID-19 lockdowns were a boon for autocrats with the centralisation of power it allowed. It'll take years to recover from that. However, the simple truth is economic development usually brings about a rising middle class who then demand democracy. As the world gets richer, it'll become harder for autocracies to maintain their position without granting their population at least some semblance of representation. King Mswati's days might well be numbered.

The Travelling Ape

Meet Me at the Gates of Hell

Back in Turkmenistan, we had a couple more days in Ashgabat, and then we were off, overlanding deep into the country's interior. It didn't take long before we saw more of the 'real' Turkmenistan. The glitzy, marble splendour of the capital was quickly replaced by ageing roads, joyless old Soviet blocks, and poverty. Lots of it. Heading north, I stared out of the overlanding truck's window. The money Gurby had spent on large white elephants could perhaps have been put to better use elsewhere, I figured. Investing in some less flashy things like running water, electricity, and paved roads rather than an indoor Ferris wheel, for example.

After an hour or two, the scenery became utterly desolate. Miles of perfectly flat land on either side of our bus. Almost nothing growing, as if life had simply wilted away in the heat, to be replaced by greyish dirt. Every now and then we'd spot one of the country's weird quirks. A yellow, open-top truck that had been retrofitted so it could transport camels in the back. A dozen of them just sitting there helplessly, strapped in. As we overtook it, we got a closer look at the camel's unamused faces, wind making their mouths and ears flap as if a hairdryer was blowing on them.

We headed for the country's best-known landmark (at least outside Ashgabat). A giant, burning gas crater. When the Soviets were drilling for gas here 40 years ago, they rolled burning tyres into a crater to burn off excess gas. Four decades on, the Darvaza Gas Crater is still burning.

Democracy: Flawed, but Dismiss it at Your Peril

We sat on its edge for hours. A huge, gaping hole, around 250ft wide, filled with flickering flames and charred rock. At night, with the sky dark, it appeared as a giant orange inferno. Burning bright like an earth-bound sun against a black-blue background. A portal to hell (which, unlike this crater, doesn't exist). The heat generated by it was scarcely believable, wafting over us periodically like when you open an oven. Watching the flames was mesmerising. So much so, that we took the potentially unwise decision to camp next to the inferno. In our highly flammable tents.

I would have liked to get to know the Turkmen people more, but North Korean-style restrictions made this impossible. Matt was at least informative, amusing, friendly, and from what I could now see as we sat around our impromptu camp, a raging alcoholic. On hot nights like this in the middle of the desert, he assured us it was 'Turkmen custom' to drink lots of local and unrefrigerated vodka 'to help cool you down.' The idea of this being 'refreshing' was hard to square. Also, I wasn't sure whether it was 'Turkmen custom' to drink most of the bottle of vodka yourself, but judging by Matt's glugging of it, it seemed to be.

Once I'd retired to my tent, I could hear Matt stumbling around our hastily constructed fire (not sure why we bothered making one, given where we were camping), singing traditional Turkmen songs to himself. It was quite beautiful, moving even. Until he started singing *Do You Believe in Life after Love?*, the Cher song, which didn't have quite the same effect as the rest of his repertoire. Did Matt believe in life after love? I'll never know. What was his real Turkmen name? What would he have told us if he could speak freely? I still think about Matt occasionally, wondering how he's getting on. How things are going in Turkmenistan, the most peculiar of nations.

World's Third Best Leadership Cult

The next few weeks were spent travelling through Central Asia. Uzbekistan first, after leaving Turkmenistan. The trip passed in a haze. Camping in deserts. Seeing Samarkand's and Bukhara's ancient, Islamic architecture, which spoke of the country's rich history at the heart of the Silk Road trading route. Witnessing the oppressive influence of Soviet rule via menacing statues and brutalist, blocky architecture in the capital, Tashkent. And emptying my bowels much more frequently than I'd ideally have liked to. A common ailment for tourists here, apparently. In Uzbekistan, they cook using a local type of sunflower oil that our sensitive Western stomachs can't cope with. We camped next to rusting old boats on the dry seabed of the Aral Sea, which has virtually disappeared due to overuse of its water for irrigation in the past few decades.

Then we headed through Kazakhstan. Which from what I could see was escaping the spectre of Borat to become the region's most dynamic economy (which isn't saying much, but it's something). And then Kyrgyzstan, with its stunning and unspoilt mountains and pastures, crystal clear lakes, and difficult to type name. More nights spent camping in the middle of nowhere. Humanity absent. Feeling remote from the modern world. Keeping warm in our *ger* huts. Filling our lungs with clear, mountain air during treks.

I ultimately arrived at the final Central Asian country of the trip: Tajikistan. (It's easier to work out which 'stan' is which once you've visited them. Before then, I concede, they kind of blurred into one.) I had a few days to explore the capital, Dushanbe, on my own, before heading up into fabulous Pamir Mountains, where I'd end up eating with some of my new Tajik pals from a few chapters ago. I said farewell to the tour group and went for a little stroll. I was craving some time by myself. It'd been weeks of often intense socialising. Being watched by government officials. Sharing tents. And washing in rivers together. Not having to speak was a delight. It felt good to be alone.

I plodded along, my head craning and swivelling as I walked, taking it all in. My senses alert, enjoying the subtle buzz I feel when exploring somewhere new. Dushanbe, on initial impressions, was quite agreeable, at least compared to some of the other cities I'd been in recently. Many of the grand boulevards and streets were tree-lined. Offering protection from the sun and bringing a touch of softness to some of the architecture. Dushanbe seemed to have been built around parks and lakes. Tajikistan's rural hinterland of grassy hills and snow-capped mountains were just visible from downtown. I liked it a lot; it certainly seemed much more 'authentic' than Ashgabat.

I walked through the city's jewel, Rudaki Park, named after the famous Persian poet and musician.* It was verdant

---

★   Nope, I'd not heard of him, either.

and well ordered. With lovely little streams and fountains, statues and monuments, including an art deco sculpture of Ismael Somoni, the founder of the Samanid Empire. The piece consisted of a large, tall arch, flanked on either side by steel lions and a statue of the man himself (hadn't the foggiest idea who he was either). A statue of the park's namesake, Rudaki, was smaller but more pleasing to the eye – a deep blue and black arch, covered with ornate paintings of stars and the cosmos, its gold tiled stars flickering in the sunlight.

After passing the Palace of the Nation, I could finally see a flag fluttering. Horizontal red, white, and green stripes towered over the relatively low-rise city, soaring out of the romantically named Flagpole Park. 'So this is the second tallest flagpole in the world,' I thought. 'Hmmm. Compared to the other tall flagpoles, this one seems more out of place. So far, Dushanbe doesn't really seem to fit the mould of the other autocracies I've been to recently. It seems less controlled. Freer.'

But in the coming days, I'd come to see a different side of the city and indeed Tajikistan. The flag slowly started to make sense. From what I could see, Tajikistan was also upping the ante in the personality cult stakes. President Emomali Rahmon ticked many of the leadership cult boxes. He'd been president since 1994. First red flag. I saw portraits of him on most buildings. Second red flag. Newspapers were filled with him pictured pointing at various things, such as factories and sports pitches. Third red flag. I saw a stupidly big (partially) red flag fluttering over the capital. Fourth red flag. Literally.

Democracy: Flawed, but Dismiss it at Your Peril

I watched the news back in my hotel and saw that Rahmon had personally opened the largest swimming pool in Central Asia during my visit, with his son. A son who will be the country's next leader (sigh). While I would love to say that this means things are going swimmingly in Tajikistan, in economic terms at least, I could clearly see that this wasn't the case. Outside the leafy boulevards, on the outskirts of town, were residential areas not far off being shanty towns. The average Tajik earns just US$3,500 per year.[28]

The country lags behind most other Central Asian nations economically, which, as I've mentioned, are themselves already fairly poor compared to global averages. As always, these issues aren't anything that can't be glossed over with a little bit of good old-fashioned authoritarianism. No electricity? No matter! There are lots of large Tajik flags on the street outside your house. Poor sanitation? Yes, but at least the post office has a big portrait of your president on it. Governing is easier without a free press. Tajikistan ranks in 156th position in the Democracy Index.[29] Its approach to controlling its people is, sadly, par for the course for former Soviet republics that were part of the USSR from 1922 to 1991.

Lessons Learnt

So what did I learn on my quest to understand flags, their size, and what this can tell us about democracy? That it's best not to choose your holiday destination based on how insecure a country's autocratic leaders are, for starters. Where their insecurity leads to grand (and pointless) gestures like tall flags which project nationalist strength and aim to detract from everyday problems. Overt displays of state-driven patriotism are usually a good indicator that a nation is hiding something unsavoury.

Like in the other countries in which I'd seen them, the massive flag in Tajikistan fluttered with a menacing quality. Acting as a giant sentinel watching over its citizens. Reminding them: 'Don't dare question the omnipotence of our glorious leadership.' In these countries, the reasons for their leaders' insecurity is all too clear. Mostly, these are economically underdeveloped countries. And on my travels, I'd noticed before that there often seemed to be a rather strong correlation between a country's wealth and level of democracy. Put simply, the less democracy a country has, usually, the poorer they tend to be. And this hunch was actually confirmed by data.[30] I've also been to plenty of countries that are like those in Central Asia. They too aren't wealthy, but are just fundamentally better places due to their at least notional adherence to democratic ideals. India, Indonesia, Namibia, and Ecuador spring to mind.

Outside China – which we'll look at in more detail in a couple of chapters – the countries that buck the democracy-equals-wealth trend tend to be rich only due to oil. Places like Saudi Arabia and Qatar. And Brunei, ranked 144th on the Press Freedom Index (out of 180 countries). It doesn't have a big flag, but is low down on the list of places I'd suggest anyone should visit. The

Democracy: Flawed, but Dismiss it at Your Peril

Sultan of Brunei (a famously rich and famously eccentric person) hordes all the country's oil money to himself. His net worth is around US$28 billion. It's higher than the country's annual economic output.[31] If the Sultan shared just half of his wealth with the citizens of Brunei, they'd each get over US$20,000. But alas, he has more important things to spend money on. Like adding to his collection of 7,000 cars, the world's largest. Or hiring Michael Jackson to perform at his 50th birthday.[32] (When Jackson was still alive, obviously.)

Largely, the rest of Brunei is left to live in poverty. I remember walking around the capital, Bandar Seri Begawan. It was fairly depressing, dilapidated, all a bit run-down. To me, it appeared to be a city shackled by poverty. Shocking given how much wealth the country's oil reserves produce. Polluted and pungent smelling canals flowed through the city's drab streets. Many of its residents lived in unstable-looking shacks floating above the Brunei River. The problems weren't just economic. I'd learnt before my visit that the punishment for gay sex in Brunei was a mere stoning to death.

The Sultan doesn't need to address these issues, however. He can't be kicked out. Brunei's next leader will be one of the Sultan's five sons (his seven daughters are ineligible due to their lack of a penis). The *Monty Python* scene of serfs slinging mud around while the leaders live in luxury is painfully apposite in Brunei, and in many other autocracies worldwide. Indeed, if we briefly look at a list of the ten least democratic places on Earth, according to Democracy Index,[33] you'll soon realise that they're places you'd rather not live. The numbers represent their ranking out of 167 assessed nations and territories.

157. Tajikistan
158. Equatorial Guinea
159. Laos
160. Chad
161. Turkmenistan
162. Democratic Republic of Congo
163. Syria
164. Central African Republic
165. Democratic People's Republic of Korea
166. Myanmar
167. Afghanistan

Do you ever moan about how bad things are in your country? Did the result of an election ever make you think it would be better if people weren't given the chance to vote? If so, fancy switching places with anyone in the countries above? Because there, your moaning won't be tolerated. It'll take place in your mind, behind bars. Particularly in the ironically named 'Democratic' People's Republic of Korea. My flag odyssey to Azerbaijan, Tajikistan, Saudi, and Turkmenistan made me feel lucky not to have been born in these places, if truth be told. Profoundly happy to be in the fortunate position of having been born in a democracy.

I didn't doubt that even larger flags would be built all over the world in the coming years, as other insecure leaders try to cover up the shortcomings over their rule.

Democracy: Flawed, but Dismiss it at Your Peril

Indeed, after I'd completed my flag quest this exact scenario came to pass. The award for tallest flagpole passed to Egypt in 2021, which – and this won't surprise you – ranks in a dismal 166th in the Press Freedom Index and 131st in the Democracy Index.[34] How flipping flagtastic!

In Defence of Democracy

A few weeks after Tajikistan, I was back in the United States. And oh, did it feel sweet. So very sweet. Whenever I've just travelled in slightly more disordered parts of the world, the neat and ordered structure of the Western world is much more apparent and welcome. Good roads. Quiet streets. No litter on them. I was in Los Angeles. Which, while not my favourite US city, is still a nice part of the world. And one of its better cities. Beaches, good weather, great hikes nearby. Ashgabat eat your heart out. No massive flag, though. Shame.

I went for a stroll along the beachside boulevard in Santa Monica, one of the prettiest parts of LA. I could see surfers doing their thing out in the Pacific Ocean. A giant, wide, sweep of golden sand, filled with sunbathers and people playing ultimate frisbee (who I felt immediately compelled to dislike for some reason*). It was flanked by impossibly thin palm trees, which appeared as if somehow

---

★ I think it's because it has the word 'ultimate' in the name of the sport. It sounds just so much more exciting than the actual game, like Laser Quest.

stretched in a photo editing suite. Skateboarders cruised past me. Roller skaters too. There wasn't a cloud in the sky. The lovely, rugged hills of Malibu rolled off into the hazy horizon ahead of me. As cities go, this wasn't a bad location for one.

Needing to get some work done, I dropped into a coffee shop. It was all concrete bar tops and indoor plants. Big open windows looking out onto the beach, with sea air funnelling in. The floor was doused with a thin layer of sand. This being LA, this particular coffee shop sold all sorts of strange health foods. While not scientifically proven to do anything for you, they promised beauty and 'wellness'. For a large price. Ten bucks for a charcoal smoothie. A quinoa, kale, and other-bad-tasting-vegetables smoothie for a similar price. I settled for a coffee. I was surrounded by people who looked a bit like celebrities, wanted to be celebrities, but most definitely weren't.

I had my laptop out, as I had some articles to write. But I couldn't help but be much more intrigued by the prospect of eavesdropping on some of the other customers. (To be fair, the average Californian speaks so loudly and nasally that it would've been hard for me to ignore them.) From the content of most conversations I could hear, my word, didn't these wealthy locals living in paradise have a lot to get off their chests.

You would have literally thought that they were living in a failed state, like Syria, the way they were talking. A middle-aged couple dressed head-to-toe in athleisure wear discussed with conviction the 'inevitability' of civil war breaking out in the United States. Two men in their mid-thirties in their trunks, who'd just walked in with their surfboards and were now in a lovely coffee shop, talked about Trump and the upcoming 2020 election. They suggested that the average American was 'too stupid' to vote. That it would be better if there wasn't a vote at all. 'America's finished,' one said, as they both sipped their drinks in near paradise. A couple of teenage girls stated that they 'could never speak to, let alone date, a Republican voter'. They raged about the current government, America, and the terrible injustice of it all, in between three dollar per sip drinks. My heart bled for them (not really).

I'd just been in several countries where you simply weren't even allowed to have conversations like this. Let alone a skinny tall frappé oat-milk avocado chai latte. I'd just been in places where an average daily wage might not be enough to afford a single item on this coffee shop's menu. Where there was no political satire on TV, no different newspapers to get your news from. No ability to kick out the government (which the Americans did in 2020, although with some difficulty, it has to be said).

Perhaps these Californians hadn't realised how fortunate they were. That perversely, it's because people like them *can* criticise their leaders that those in democratic countries have an overly negative view of the societies they live in. In other countries, a lack of democracy and press freedom shields their rulers from criticism, and makes it harder for people to see how bad they truly have it. America has its issues, don't get me wrong. But compared to many places in the world? It really isn't the quasi-failed state some believed it to be. But many have never bothered to leave the country, so lack context about how lots of the rest of the world is run. Democracy is one of humanity's greatest inventions. We forget this at our peril.

People Vote with Their Feet

The bulk of the most cosmopolitan cities in the world – with the highest immigrant populations – are in democracies. Indeed, just looking around the coffee shop was evidence of the multicultural makeup of the US and its ability to attract people from across the world since its founding. After my coffee and a bit of work, I had an amazing Mexican burrito for lunch. Later that evening I ate Ethiopian food. LA's multiculturalism meant the variety of food available was awesome. I could eat cuisine from almost anywhere. In this city, visiting different neighbourhoods can be like entering a different part of the world. I could see why people so wanted to live here. And the numbers proved it – over 40 percent of LA's population was born abroad. Even if some Californians think they lived in a failed state, the evidence suggests a huge chunk of the world disagrees.

Indeed, the democratic Anglosphere countries – united by a robust respect of democratic ideals and individual freedoms – draw a staggering *two-thirds* of the world's skilled migrants.[35] This is despite the US, UK, Canada, Australia, and New Zealand together having only around five percent of the world's people. So while many in these countries may lament democracy not working in their favour in recent years,[*] the rest of the world would happily jump at the chance to live in countries that still value it. Brexit[36] and Trump[37] didn't lead to any significant slowdown in migrant arrivals. The US and the UK remain the first and fifth most popular destinations in the world for migrants.[38]

China may claim to be the next global hegemon, but it's not a particularly fun place to live. Life for many appears regimented, and at times, tightly controlled. Less than 1 percent of the estimated 750 million people who would like to migrate globally would choose China as their first choice.[39] It's not exactly a vote of confidence in the values of autocracy, or in China, which I have much more to say about in a couple of chapters. Staggeringly, there are more foreign-born people living in Sydney, Australia, than in the *entire Chinese nation.*[40] In fact, when I lived in Sydney, I was more likely to bump into someone from the UK, Brazil, or France than an actual Australian.

Why is this relevant to democracy? The truth is, for all their flaws, democracies remain overwhelmingly the most attractive places in the world to live. Of the 15 countries that have the largest number of migrants, only three aren't democracies.[41] Two are Saudi Arabia and the United Arab Emirates, where migrants are brought in to work on construction sites (which often have very poor labour

---

[*]   After the Brexit vote, for around a year I felt that referendums should never be held on anything ever again. And that it would just be easier for all involved if the government did exactly what I thought all the time.

conditions). The third is Russia, which still receives a lot of migration from ex-USSR countries. A case, it would seem, of some of the Central Asian countries being even less democratic than Russia. Quite a feat indeed.

Quality of life seems to be related to democratic government too. Let's take a look at a global quality of life top ten based upon 75 indicators for the year 2021:[42]

1. Sweden
2. Denmark
3. Canada
4. Switzerland
5. Norway
6. Finland
7. Germany
8. Netherlands
9. Australia
10. New Zealand

These countries are all democracies. Is it just a coincidence that the best countries to live in are democratic? Having been to each of these wonderful nations personally, I'm confident it's not. And so, if you find yourself complaining about where you live – likely in a democracy if you're reading this – perhaps go on big flag hunt. Take notes. And let's have a conversation when you are back.* You might feel a bit differently.

---

*   Hypothetically. I'm quite busy so I'll just assume you now agree with me.

Democracy: Flawed, but Dismiss it at Your Peril

Democracies are overwhelmingly the best places in the world to live or visit. They remain the best societies we've created in history. There'll be a few blips along the way, but democracy is in its infancy (remember there were only a small number of true democracies just over a century ago). We should cut ourselves some slack, then, when we occasionally vote for clowns. To me, it still beats rule by monarchies, or worse. My travels have shown me that democracies, on average, work better than one-party, one-person authoritarian states that rely on flags and propaganda to remain in power.

Just as democracy is often derided both by those enjoying its privileges and those opposed to it, another key Western concept has been a source of division. It has an impact on everything, on the way the world functions to the ways in which we live. Suffice it to say, the modern world wouldn't exist without it. And the modern world is a physical embodiment of it. I'm talking, of course, about capitalism.

10

Capitalism Isn't the Root of All Evil

Capitalism is a flawed system that causes many problems. But travelling the globe showed me that the alternatives are much, much worse.

I grabbed some noodles from a local hawker, eating them absent-mindedly. I had around 20 minutes to spare. I was tired and groggy after 24 hours spent on an overnight train from Beijing. I gazed at the muddy Yalu River, wide and brown. As with much of China, the pollution looked like a thick, wintry fog. But this fog was warm, and you could taste it. There was a large, steel suspension bridge crossing the river. It looked old, and not altogether robust. The green-grey steel slightly warped in places, and rusted to boot. Red Chinese flags hung limply at the end of the bridge nearest to me. On the other side, barely perceptible, was my next destination. As if only then truly realising what I was doing and where I was about to go, I felt a spike of adrenalin course around my body.

I met up with my tour group at Dandong Train Station. There were about 15 of us, again travelling with Lupine Travel. All experienced travellers. All slightly weird in their own way (I firmly include myself in this). Our guide arrived. He was a Chinese man in his mid-30s called Brooklyn (presumably in honour of David Beckham's son?), dressed casually in jeans and a T-shirt. He told us the ground rules before our border crossing.

'Okay, guys. No religious materials. No books of any kind about South Korea. No offensive materials allowed on your phones. Be respectful to the guards. Do what they say,' he said.

We piled on the train. It was dark green, with gold stripes running down the length of it. Topped with a grey roof. Each carriage was adorned with badges and crests on the doors, with a bright red star in the middle. It looked like the kind of thing I'd seen on government buildings in Russia. After we got on, a stern-looking group of men wearing khaki military uniforms boarded. I was still feeling nervous. But my fear did slightly ease, if only momentarily, when I noticed the hats they were wearing. They looked like giant mushrooms. Massive, flat-brimmed things, with a red star and band around the top. It made them all resemble Toad, from *Super Mario*. Or look like they were tourists wearing novelty-size sombreros. The hats were so wide they kept banging into the walls as they bent over to take people's details. 'Haha, if only they knew how silly they looked,' I thought to myself, while also feeling very scared indeed.

These border guards proceeded, in perfect silence, to spend a mere three hours searching through all of our belongings. Each of our bags was completely ransacked. Searched inside and out. They checked the photos on our phones. They almost threw someone off the train who dared to bring a 'Korea' *Lonely Planet* with them. It was the strictest search I've ever been involved in. Which is ironic. It was the equivalent of having a bouncer on the door of an exclusive nightclub making it very difficult to get in. One in, one out. Only to find that once you've made it in, it's actually the worst club in the entire world.

I'd heard the leadership was paranoid here. But this was my first taste of the sheer silliness of the country I was about to visit, the Democratic People's Republic of Korea (DPRK). Any country that feels the need to include the word 'democratic' in its title is usually not. Other countries that do the same include the Democratic Republic of Algeria (136th), the Democratic Republic of the Congo (124th), Lao People's Democratic Republic (160th), and of course, finally, the DPRK (180th, or last place).* The numbers included in brackets show where these countries rank in the Press Freedom Index.[1] Neither a true republic (the Kim dynasty is in effect their royal family), nor for the people, and perhaps the least free country in existence, I like to call it Silly Korea (not to Kim Jong-un's face). They also have their own giant flagpole, which I'd get to visit in a few days.

Border check complete, we finally set off. The train vibrating, its diesel engine struggling to pull us away from the station. I sat in an odd, kind of opulent carriage. It

---

*   I like how they mix up the words 'democratic' and 'people's' for the country names here. And why not, given how meaningless their use is in these contexts.

had a wooden table surrounded by leather seats. In my compartment were two Australians, also in their mid-20s. Jake and Jack, which wasn't in any way confusing. They were both tall. Jake was wiry, with curly dark hair. Jack had a moustache and a trendy man bun. They were both from Melbourne. A cool city. They both seemed cool. I wanted to be their friend. And so to do this, I, as we all do, worked out what things they appeared to like and said that I liked them too. Travelling to bizarre places like North Korea – dark tourism, as some people call it – clearly was a shared hobby. So it wasn't difficult.

We rolled through the countryside, mainly past rice paddy fields worked by labourers wearing clothes which would have looked more in place in Mao's China or in Stalin's Russia than the modern world. The farmers – at least those that I could see – wore grey shirts, grey trousers. And blank, joyless expressions on their faces. It was an expression I'd get used to seeing in the coming week. Their drab clothes, the drab sky – they acted as a metaphor for what life was like in the DPRK (actually, I won't call it Silly Korea any longer, out of fear of upsetting Mr Kim).

That said, the countryside itself was surprisingly lush. Gentle hills gave way to crystal clear streams and lazy meadows. It was actually quite beautiful. Notably, there were no cars, only bicycles (making the country inadvertently environmentally friendly). Each town, and seemingly every building, had portraits of the DRPK's mystical great leaders on them. The landscape was covered with communist slogans. At least I assume that's what they were, as all were written in Korean. But I doubt any of them said, 'Enjoy your life and personal freedoms, love who you want, and fulfil your personal desires.' Rusty tractors and skinny cows dotted the paddy fields. We chugged past what looked like crumbling Soviet-era steam engines.

Back in the USSR?

As I gazed out the window, I figured that visiting North Korea is the closest thing to being transported back to Soviet Russia or communist China at their peak. And it's also like being transported back into a more miserable time. Where people didn't have enough food to eat, had no personal freedoms, and lived miserable lives. To this day, some Western intellectuals and some on the hard left suggest communism's aims are noble and support it. After all, who wouldn't want a system where everyone is truly equal, where workers all have a stake in the means of production?

Others would disagree. They'd suggest that we've tried communism now. Several times. And it always ends in disaster. Perhaps it's just coincidence. But it's an interesting truth that each time it's been implemented, millions of people have died in some of the worst humanitarian catastrophes in history. Brutal suppression, mass prison and death camps for dissenters. Around 45 million people starved to death in communist China, all in the name of improving the lives of the poor.[2] This happened after Chairman Mao prohibited farm ownership and implemented radical changes to agricultural policy. Judging by pictures of him, Mao clearly had (more than) enough to eat. He and his tubby chums from the ruling Chinese Communist Party made sure they kept more than enough grain for themselves. Today, pictures of Kim Jong-un imply he struggles with portion control. How lovely.

What about communist Russia? Did the elites of the Soviet Politburo – the leadership of the Soviet Communist Party – practise what they preached and make sure society was truly equal? No. Around five million people died of starvation in the Soviet Union in 1932 and 1933.[3] Don't doubt that the Politburo was at the front of the queue for food and consumer goods, like cars.[4] Or that they lived in luxury. I saw where Stalin used to live. The stupendously lavish and opulent surroundings of the Kremlin in Moscow, presumably alongside lots of other 'men of the people'.

We know that power corrupts. And for communism to 'succeed', private property needs to be abolished and supreme authority needs to be vested in the hands of an elite. Or in other words, power-seeking, psychologically damaged, incompetent politicians. When, inevitably, communism starts failing, these elites seem to have mostly chosen to murder their opponents or, if they're feeling generous, throw them in gulags. Some would say, 'But this isn't communism done properly. It would work if properly implemented.' Others would argue that you can't have communism without suppression, it's an integral part of it. That communism demands taking away individual freedoms, in the name of a collective utopia. When of course this utopia doesn't arrive, millions of people must die, rather than anyone accepting that perhaps this economic system just doesn't work in practice.

By the time I visited North Korea, the hypocrisy of such far-left economic systems had already been shown to me when I travelled to Bucharest, Romania. The communist-era dictator and champion for equality, Nicolae Ceaușescu, thought it was a clever idea to build himself the biggest and most lavish palace in the world in 1984. It has 1,100 rooms, contains 3,400 tons of crystal, and is considered by some to be the heaviest and largest building in the world.[5]

I spent an entire day exploring the building, which mixes faded grandeur with Soviet undertones. It's luxurious, but also tacky. With aching limbs after hours of walking, the tour of the palace concluded. Our guide told us we'd seen just two percent of its rooms. I couldn't believe it.

Perhaps unsurprisingly, Ceaușescu never got to see his palace finished. Romanians had been enduring genocide and starvation under communism (as is custom in all supposedly utopian, communist societies), while neighbouring capitalist European countries went from strength to strength. Seeing a giant palace rising against this backdrop was probably the final straw (indeed, there was barely any grain around at the time). In 1989, civil unrest led to the collapse of communism and Ceaușescu was shot dead. From what I'd seen (and indeed what history emphatically tells us), communism doesn't work. All it does is ensure the masses all live in abject poverty, the only equality provided to them being equality of suffering (apart from the elites). Hooray.

The simple fact is that since time immemorial, humans have been greedy, whatever economic system has been in place.[6] From an evolutionary psychologist's point of view, greed could be viewed as nothing more than a biological drive to have enough to survive in times when resources are scarce. There would have been people eating more than their fair share of food in hunter-gatherer societies, and stealing extra grain in agrarian societies. Greed shouldn't be encouraged, but our genes incline us to be greedy when it comes to resources.[7] And so, the absolutely worst thing you can do is to give all unquestioned power and control over resources to a ruling elite who hoard it for themselves, while also benefitting from the state's monopoly on violence. Which is what you have to do in *all* communist societies. Like the one I'd strangely decided to go on holiday to.

A Super Fun Time at a Super Fun Hotel

After a few more hours on the train, chatting and putting the world to rights with Jake and Jack, we started to slowly chug through the urban sprawl and decay of the capital, Pyongyang. The city was surreal. The station itself looked fairly normal – with a concrete canopy and few trains. Emptier than normal stations, though. We got off our train. And then I was doing it. I'd stepped foot in North Korea. I was surrounded by actual North Korean people. People who'd lived here their whole lives, and would likely always live here. People who knew little of the outside world.

We piled onto a waiting bus. It was getting late and dark, so we didn't see a great deal on the journey. I did notice that Pyongyang was a lot less bright than other capital cities. Indeed, if you see pictures of North Korea at night from space it's positively black compared to its neighbours. After about ten minutes, we arrived at the innocuous sounding Yanggakdo Hotel. It was a 42-storey skyscraper, located on an island in the middle of Taedong River. A rectangular structure, with a circular revolving restaurant plonked on the top.

As well as having Brooklyn to look after us, we also had two DPRK 'guides' who would watch us like hawks for the duration of our stay. A man dressed in a short-sleeved shirt and suit trousers called Chin. And a lady, dressed in a short-sleeved shirt and skirt, called Hae-Won. They both wore small red badges with the faces of the country's two previous leaders on them.

Before we disembarked the bus, I asked them gingerly, 'Do you have to wear those red badges?'

'People in North Korea like to wear these badges, because they love and respect their dear leaders. So that's why we all wear them,' Chin said.

'Oh I see,' I said outwardly. But, 'That's a yes to having to wear them then,' I said in my head. Answers like these, speaking on behalf of the entire people of North Korea, would be common from both Chin and Hae-Won in the coming week. They spoke great English and seemed happy to answer questions from us, but they'd always regurgitate the party line.

I'd also been warned that they were as much here to keep an eye on us as to 'guide' us. We sat in the hotel lobby – a very tired, large room, which looked like it hadn't changed since the hotel was built in the 1980s – while Chin and Hae-Won laid down a few of the 'ground rules' for our stay. No photos unless at specified monuments. And only from approved angles. Don't walk away from the tour group. No leaving the hotel without guides.

'I wonder what its TripAdvisor ratings are like? Pros: revolving restaurant on the roof. Nice river views. Cons: it's a prison,' I said under my breath to Jake and Jack, trying to make light of the situation. But I wasn't going to test the limits.

A tragedy had taken place at the hotel just two weeks before I visited. This was the hotel where a 20-year-old American student, Otto Warmbier, stole a propaganda poster. He was sentenced to 15 years of hard labour. A year later he was released back to the US in a vegetative state, and died shortly afterwards. While I would say stealing propaganda was an unwise move in a police state, clearly the punishment here didn't fit the crime.

If you could put aside the fact that our rooms were bugged and getting off on the wrong floor could result in your death, the hotel itself was surprisingly fun. It was clearly designed by someone with limited knowledge of the West, but who had tried to guess what everyone likes over here. A labyrinth of bizarre corridors with low ceilings led to the following individual activity rooms:

pool (the game); pool (a pool); bowling; karaoke; darts; and a hairdresser. Jack visited the latter on the final day of the trip and asked for a 'Kim Jong-un'. The barber sadly declined.

But alas, these super fun activities would have to wait for another night. I was tired. And also scared of the very hotel I was staying in, so I instead kicked back with some of the DPRK's finest TV. Some light-hearted comedy. The comedians were dressed in military uniform. And making jokes in front of a big screen with nuclear rockets being launched. Hmmm. The next show had a rock band. 'This is more like it.' But they were also wearing the same attire, against a similarly militaristic backdrop. It was all a parody of what I was expecting.

Pyongyang: Weird and Sad

The next morning, we woke and had breakfast. There was *loads* of food, something that would be repeated throughout our trip. A mixture of rice, eggs, kimchi, mushroom pancakes, noodles – tons really. If the food could talk, my guess is the government hoped it would be saying, 'Look how much food there is in North Korea. No one is starving and everything's completely fine.' Later in the trip, we'd notice that all of the restaurants we ate at were a bit hidden, and always on the second floor, so locals couldn't see what they were missing out on.

We piled onto the bus, and began driving around Pyongyang. It was overcast. But this grey weather was juxtaposed by a few brightly coloured government buildings, which had an almost cartoonish quality to them. They attempted to be futuristic, but ended up weirdly dated. Like an outdated version of the future, where the buildings had been designed by someone watching too much of *The Jetsons.** Some roads were massively wide, leading up to grand monuments. But there were few cars, anywhere. Beyond the grand(ish) government buildings Chin and Hae-Won were trying to make us focus on, the city's dominant architectural style was evident in the distant, giant, monolithic housing blocks we spotted. Repeating again and again to the horizon. Some had at least been painted in pastel colours, to break up the monotony of it all. But the overwhelming sense was oppressive. It felt like I'd been plonked into a scene from George Orwell's *1984.*

The tour of the city also involved being strategically shown all of the Kim family's greatest monuments and achievements, under at times hilariously zealous supervision. You couldn't stray more than a few feet from the group, before Chin and Hae-Won would trot up to you. Trying to pretend they weren't herding you away from real life in Pyongyang. First was the Mansu Hill Grand Monument. Where stood two giant bronze statues of the 'Eternal President' Kim Il-sung and his son the 'Dear

---

* To be sure, the architects are unlikely to have seen this show. Even if they did have televisions, the only thing they'd have been able to watch is thousands of hours of programmes dedicated to the unsurpassable brilliance of North Korea's leaders.

Leader' Kim Jong-il. His son, Kim Jong-un, which should surprise no one, is now the 'Supreme Leader'. I'm sure he deserved the job. The two statues sat against the backdrop of a mural of Mount Paektu, considered to be the sacred mountain of the revolution.

Chin and Hae-Won told us – in a kind and friendly way – not to do silly poses in front of any statues of the country's worshipped leaders. Their advice was always delivered in a way that seemed advisory or optional, but of course, this wasn't the case. I took the bold step of doing a double thumbs up pose in front of the statues, which was like playing with fire. I'm really not sure what came over me. Judging by the photos I got there, I was also going through a phase when I chose to wear vest tops and flip-flops a lot. Breakdowns are easier to notice after the event, it seems.

We clambered back into the bus, and then continued the tour. From what I was seeing, I felt North Korea was a stranger and even more dystopian land than I'd expected it to be. I struggled to come to terms with the fact that a society like this still existed in the modern world. It was such an anomaly in the homogenous world we live in. City streets were regimented, largely colourless, and stank of oppression (and many of the streets stank in the literal sense as well). Already I got a sense of how strict and uniform the place was. I noticed that seemingly *all* citizens had to do the following (arbitrary) things:

- Wear little red badges with pictures of either the country's founder Kim Il-sung or his son Kim Jong-il on them.

Capitalism Isn't the Root of All Evil

- Wear similar clothes. Suits for men; skirts and pastel-coloured shirts for women.
- Men should all have largely the same haircut. There are strict rules on which are allowed. Spiked hair is banned due to it being considered 'rebellious'.
- Live in a society where the great leaders touch every element of daily life. I would see the 'Supreme Leader' Kim Jong-un on the front page of the newspapers on newsstands. Every day. Usually pointing at various things in factories, schools or at other functions, highlighting the great work he was doing. What a man. And he was on every radio and TV station. Literally, at all times. Advertising is prohibited, so the only banners I saw in Pyongyang were massive billboards of the Supreme Leader just being an all-round great guy.*
- Resolve to accept that even comedians and TV personalities wear military uniform.

We hopped out of the bus again for the next stop on our really fantastic tour of really amazing and brilliant North Korea.** We first were allowed to go into a bookstore. Inside, some of the titles had been translated into English. These included the unbiased sounding *Seventy Years of Brilliant Leadership*. And the page-turner *Kim Il Sung: The Great Man of the Century*.

---

*   We may lament Western, capitalist cities being covered with adverts for things we don't need. But truthfully, which would you prefer?

**   Chin and Hae-Won's enthusiasm summarised here.

The Travelling Ape

We walked through Kim Il-sung Square. A massive concrete plaza, probably a thousand feet wide. It was flanked by rectangular buildings. They each had giant North Korean flags on top of them. Mainly red, with white and blue trimmings, and a red communist star in a white circle to the left of centre. Behind the square, the Taedong River flowed lazily, unaware it was flowing through somewhere almost not of this Earth. The Juche Tower was just visible on its far bank, jutting upwards through the grey haze. It was a tall column, rising to a height of a 50-storey-building, with a red flame on top. Done in a style which you only see in communist countries. All angular, grandiose in its scale.

As we walked through the square, North Korea's central library, the Grand People's Study House, lay ahead of us. 'It must be exhausting living in a place where even building names are trying to convince you that you live in a great country,' I said quietly to Jake. The wide building had an imposing green, traditional Korean *gaewa* roof. It had, predictably, massive portraits of the eternal and dear leaders on it. So they could still watch military shows and parades which normally take place in front of the Grand People's Study House from beyond the grave. Standing there, the general feeling I had was one of awe. Awe that a place like this existed. That people would spend their entire lives here, unable to leave. That they – 25 million of them – would forever be trapped in probably the world's worst country. I felt a deep sorrow for them. The world is the best it has ever been. But places like this were a good reminder of the progress that still needs to be made in so many places.

Re-education, Re-education, Re-education

One of the worst things – and there are many – about communism (and to some degree all extreme-left economic models) is that they exist in opposition to personal freedoms. And that the only way to paper over the very evident fact that the system is awful, people are starving, and, basically, it doesn't work, is to try to brainwash people into thinking otherwise. And if that doesn't work, kill them. With this in my mind, we stepped into the Grand People's Study House, which Chin explained was a 'university'. If it was a university, it seemed an awfully fake one. Far be it from me to contradict them, but I didn't realise that a university was a place where a handful of bewildered extras wandered around empty halls and rooms pretending to do stuff. But that's what was happening here.

Some of the things we were shown were utterly bizarre. A room – intended I think to show us how modern North Korea is – was filled with about 20 tape-deck stereos, which looked like they'd been preserved from the '80s. A different, smaller room, which had lots of closed laptops on desks, was where people could 'study and use the internet'. I opened one laptop and noticed it didn't even have a screen. Some were just laptop-shaped bits of plastic. And, of course, as always, at the front of every room, giant portraits of the country's leaders. Watching over their subjects, like zealous hawks. A system like this requires the brainwashing to be utter and complete. There wouldn't be a single thing in the study house which contradicted the state's preferred narrative. From birth, everything a North Korean person learns or sees will be filtered through the narrative of 'Communism is great and North Korea is even better'.

It's tragic really. I'm sure some North Koreans know it's a hoax. But many, I felt, wouldn't. Indeed, how could they? Had I walked up to someone in Pyongyang and offered them a British passport and a ticket out of there, I'm sure 90 percent of them would have said no. If I'd been born here, I'd bloody love the supreme leader. So would you. The average person is force-fed a diet of propaganda. This propaganda implies that South Korea (and the West) is desolate and poor. North Korea is one of the most powerful nations in the world. North Korea is regularly praised by the world's media (I saw newspapers with fake quotes from Western leaders). And so on.

It sounds horrible, but I remember thinking at the time, 'Perhaps it's better that North Koreans don't know they are being lied to, and that the outside world is much better than they believe it to be. Given that the average North Korean has scant chance of escaping, ignorance might be less painful than knowing the truth.' Checkpoints all over the country make it hard to leave your city or province, let alone the country. Many books talk about how hard it is to leave, and the severe punishments dished out to those who try.[8]

Sightseeing Done Differently

The next few days passed in a blur of continued strangeness, underpinned by an almost constant feeling of unreality. Like I was in *The Matrix*, or had stepped into the past. A trip on the Pyongyang Metro was notable. Par for the course in other places where communism had taken root in the past, like in Moscow, St Petersburg, and Tashkent, the Metro was grand and opulent. Stations were cavernous. Most had elaborate murals depicting communist ideals. Some even had chandeliers hanging above the platforms. We were only allowed to ride it for two stops.* Also, one of our tour group got left behind. Brooklyn looked incredibly worried when he realised we'd lost a member of the party. Perhaps only he knew what the punishment would be. Later back in the hotel, the Spanish man who'd got lost looked quite sheepish indeed, but was at least safe. He was confined to the hotel for the remainder of his sentence (I mean holiday).

Another 'highlight' was the Pyongyang Circus. The acts and acrobatics were genuinely the best I've ever seen, the show rehearsed to perfection. There was probably a good reason for this. I worried what the consequences would be for any performer who made a mistake. The most surreal bit, apart from a sad interlude where a monkey rode a goat (to uproarious laughter), were the clown sketches. Like everything here, *even the circus* was used as propaganda. In this case, the clowns were dressed as South Korean soldiers. Who were not too surprisingly portrayed as bumbling, idiotic buffoons, again to great laughter. The crowd also always clapped perfectly in unison, which only added to the dystopian and cultish feel of the place.

The following day, the main focus was the Victory Day Mass Dance and a visit to the Fatherland Liberation

---

*   Perhaps we were only allowed to see the grand ones?

Victorious War Museum (actual names). There were huge celebrations in honour of the DPRK's alleged victory over the West (I can't recall when this actually happened). At the mass dance, tens of thousands took to the streets. The women wore bright and colourful Korean dresses. The men wore their normal clothes: suit trousers, a tie, a short-sleeved shirt, and a short back and sides haircut (did they ever wear anything different?). Together, they danced in almost perfect unison to the blaring music, which can only be described as a sort of sinister mix of Soviet and dated electronic music from the '80s. I watched the crowds twirling, forming perfect circles, spinning. The women's dresses shining bright against the greyness of the sky and the city. It was oddly moving. Were they happy? Could they be, in such a place?

We were allowed – even encouraged by Chin and Hae-Won – to join in with the dancing. I didn't. At the time, the prerequisite amount of poison I needed to consume before dancing was unfortunately unavailable. Jake and Jack, however, did get stuck in with the locals. The North Koreans looked happy to see us, kind of, but it looked a bit forced. Apparently, this was one of the main events where it's possible for North Koreans to meet a partner. So the Aussies getting involved was reducing their time to do so.

A Trip to the Border

After four days, my brain had been saturated with odd sightseeing experiences. And so I was excited for us to head for the Demilitarised Zone (DMZ), the border between North and South Korea. After three hours of driving – and our first true glimpse of what life was like outside the capital – we arrived. The DMZ is conspicuous for being the most militarised place I've ever been. The verdant landscape was gashed by barbed wire, muddy tracks, and fortified outposts. And also the fourth tallest flag in the world, the symbol of North Korea defiantly fluttering in the wind. The flag itself was quite small. But it was hoisted high up on a flagpole that looked more like an electricity pylon. In my view, it was the least impressive of the top five tallest flags. Oh well, at least North Korea came first in something (having the least free media in the world according to Reporters Without Borders).[9]

We left the bus and walked into one of the military huts. It was a single-storey building, surrounded by well cut grass and large barrier walls. Inside, we weren't exactly sure what we were supposed to do, so just stood there. After a few minutes, a man wearing khaki military garb entered. His lapels filled with red badges and stars, presumably signifying all his incredible military feats. He was in his mid-50s and looked like he hadn't laughed in all those years. His generally dour demeanour was only slightly offset by his mushroom hat, offering some light relief to the overall seriousness of his character and of where we were. He began speaking in Korean, forcefully, taking big pauses between sentences. His angry tone juxtaposed with the translation into English given by Hae-Won, who was generally smiley and softly spoken.

'It's important for tourists to know the great and glorious

303

history of this nation. Our Eternal President and founder of the nation, Kim Il-sung, gave birth to North Korea after World War II.* Korea was split into the North and South, after we in the North resisted America's imperial ambitions to destroy and to colonise us. We fought and defeated the US imperialists and the South Korean puppet army from 1950 to 1953. The world has never forgotten our glorious victory. Since then, North Korea has been making rapid and expeditious progress. Becoming the most glorious and perfect socialist society.' His eyes darted around the room, as if checking for any disagreement among our group.

To be honest, I wasn't sure whether he was discussing North Korea, or some alternate reality in his mind. Having visited the highly informative and not in any way biased Sinchon Museum of American War Atrocities a few days earlier – which was filled with lots of Madame Tussaudes-esque waxworks of maimed US soldiers (undermining the key argument of the museum) – I also felt like I'd heard this all before. He continued, getting angrier.

'One day, North Korea will *crush* the United States,' he said, doing a fist-into-open-palm motion to really drive home his argument. 'And the world will know the true glory of this nation and the might of the Supreme Leader.'

Whatever your thoughts about the US are, and even though some of the military general's points were valid, I

★   I couldn't tell whether this was a translation error, or whether part of the DPRK's national creation myth is that Kim Il-sung literally gave birth to the nation, out of his anus. Given what I'd seen, there was a good chance it could be the latter.

felt I needed to speak up. I'd heard enough. I put up my hand, took a deep breath, and went for it.

'Sorry to interject. But did you know that not many people in the world care much about the Korean War, which ended 70 years ago? It was essentially pointless, and resulted in lots of needless deaths. Most Americans probably don't know when or what the war even was. If they did, they wouldn't be too scared about the DPRK either. The US has a population 12 times the size of the DPRK and spends more on its military than the next 20 or so countries globally, combined.'

At least this is what I would have said, had I never wanted to leave North Korea. I, of course, didn't say any of these things out loud. I just thought them in my head, as I am again now, writing this book. But Christ, imagine. You wouldn't be reading this book if I had spoken to the general like that, on account of me living out my days in a gulag.

Following his lecture, we went to see the border itself. On our side, goose-stepping North Korean soldiers. On the other, just feet away, South Korean soldiers marching back and forth. In between, a series of small blue huts, one-floor high and made of concrete. Electric fences and barbed wire criss-crossed the horizon. This is where Donald Trump met Kim Jong-un in 2019. It's where negotiations take place between both sides (on the very rare occasions when they actually happen). It was so strange to see this border. It split a people who shared a common culture, language, families, and a nation until the 1950s. But who, since then, have been separated by more than just this militarised border. They are divided by vast ideological chasms.

The Travelling Ape

Eventually, it was time to head back to Pyongyang. When being driven around the country, we weren't allowed to take photos. But this is where I felt I got a look at the 'real' North Korea, where I could see how people *actually* lived. Rather than being shown the sanitised and government-approved version. We drove through towns which made Pyongyang look positively booming, space-age. They were much more rundown. Much greyer. Coal power plants belching fumes out from the centre of them. There were no shops, no visible signs of fun or joy. Just a lot of bleakness.

In the countryside, things weren't a great deal better. At least there was more greenery, rolling hills. But even here there was a hum of despair, of sadness. People looked emaciated in many cases. Nowhere did we see any overweight people (apart from the country's leadership in pictures). The government choose to centralise food distribution, contributing to an estimated two to three million deaths from hunger between 1995 and 1998.[10] Through history, why is famine always such a reliable outcome of communist or far-left economic systems? Some would argue this is just coincidence, the system being implemented incorrectly. Others would disagree, suggesting that centrally planned food-procurement systems often fail. That human nature precludes people from striving unless they'll be rewarded for their toil. They'd suggest it makes no sense for a farmer to work hard to produce extra food that they won't ever get to eat or to sell for a profit. That communism is a fundamentally demotivating system.

Capitalism Isn't the Root of All Evil

I remember thinking how sad it was that so many people have to suffer, to this day, in the name of economic ideology. Although accurate data is non-existent in North Korea, it's commonly accepted that average incomes are well below US$1,700 annually.[11] At some level, the authorities perhaps didn't even accept that communism fully works. Back on the way to Pyongyang, we stopped for a toilet break, and I wanted a bottle of water. I saw a little roadside vendor. Perfect. I asked the guides if I could go and purchase some, which seemed like a reasonable thing to request. Despite seeing a North Korean person handing money over at the stall at that exact moment, Chin, smiling, told me that, 'We do not need money in the People's Democratic Republic of Korea, so there is nowhere to buy anything. The state gives us all we need.'

'So can I get the water then?' I pushed. Chin walked off, went to the vendor and grabbed me a water. Something changed hands but he did his best to angle his body so I couldn't see. In a country where capitalism is derided and in effect banned, it was interesting to see the capitalist forces of supply and demand still operating in some form, beneath the surface. Apparently, state-supplied rations are barely adequate for most households, so many rely on informal street markets to have enough food.[12]

Time to Pay My Respects

By the final day, I was desperate to get out of North Korea. Almost a week of endless propaganda was starting to take its toll. God knows what it must be like for those who have endured it for years. But there was still time, clearly, for a final hit of North Korean greatness to be mainlined into my brain. We were due to visit the Mausoleum of Kim Il-sung and Kim Jong-il.

Unquestionably, this ended up being the strangest experience of my life. We all had to wear suits. And to remain silent. 'Imagine you are attending a funeral,' explained Brooklyn. 'This is the most sacred place to the people here.' The palace where the leaders' bodies lie – the Kumsusan Palace of the Sun – was one of the grandest and largest I'd ever seen. A huge, grey structure. So wide it seemed to spread beyond the limits of my peripheral vision. We were told that some of its halls were half a mile long, and that this was the biggest mausoleum on Earth.

Leading up to the palace were row upon row of North Korean flags. Well-ordered fountains. Man-made water features, like streams directing your eyes up to the building. And, of course, giant portraits of the men themselves, taking pride of place at the top of the mausoleum. As in most communist countries I'd visited, the rules of equality and wealth redistribution don't appear to extend to everyone in practice. And often, building lavish monuments to dead people clearly took priority here over housing the impoverished.

On one of the many airport-style travellators through the marble interior of the palace (welcome as the place was so vast), we passed multiple framed photos of Kim Jong-un. Placed every few feet to make sure there wasn't a second you weren't being propagandised. These pictures mainly consisted of the leader pointing and smiling at something, with several men standing with clipboards behind, in a military base/science lab/factory, clapping and smiling enthusiastically.*

We spent about five minutes on the travellators, wearing suits, not saying a peep. Local people were riding behind and ahead of us. The first tomb, when we entered it, felt like a scene from *James Bond*. A cavernous room. So dark you could barely see. But in the middle of it – shining brightly – the embalmed body (read: waxwork) of Kim Il-sung. In a giant glass box. Surrounded by red flowers and a red carpet glowing like blood in the dark. We slowly shuffled around it. And then all had to lean our torsos towards the ground in a bodily movement widely accepted to signify respect and deference (a bow). In fact, we had to bow several times, both in this room and then the next, which had the body of his son in it.

Once finished 'paying our respects', we watched as local North Koreans walked into the mausoleum. And then out a few minutes later, weeping. Hearing and seeing groups of locals wailing and sobbing uncontrollably, even collapsing to the floor at the sight of the deceased leaders, was hard to fathom. Some appeared utterly inconsolable. The emotion looked real to me, but, like everything we saw, I still couldn't be sure it wasn't a set-up. It might simply be a case of self-preservation. Cry or die. I'll never know. I felt I'd leave North Korea with perhaps more questions

---

* For those who want to get a good idea of this, just google 'Kim Jong-un looking at things'.

than answers. Although one answer I had received, emphatically, was that anyone who decries capitalism and thinks we should give communism another go, should be forced to visit this weird country. And see if they change their mind.

The Consistently Dire Outcomes of Non-Capitalist Economic Systems

After seeing the dead bodies, we were lucky enough to be shown the many medals and other honours bestowed upon them. Which – surprise, surprise – filled several large rooms. One of these rooms showed all of the gifts that the leaders had received from other 'friendly countries' (or horrible despotic regimes, depending on your viewpoint). There were cars. A luxury train carriage. Paintings. Military ornaments. Vases. Metal shields. Placards denoting the wonderful comradeship between North Korea and its many allies.

'I didn't realise North Korea had so many admirers around the world,' I remember thinking. I soon realised, however, that almost all of the gifts came from just a few countries. Russia. China. Predictable. Venezuela. Cuba. Zimbabwe. Makes sense. All dictatorships to some degree, with the last three espousing anti-capitalist economic ideals. I'd been to all of these places. Some academics would suggest they are simply examples of communism being implemented imperfectly. So maybe it was just an interesting coincidence that most of these countries were also poor, repressed, and generally not very good places to live.

Venezuela was once the richest country in South America.[13] And then left-wing populist Hugo Chavez was elected president in 1998. The next year, he ripped up the country's constitution to push through what he called an 'anti-capitalist' replacement.[14] He spent the country's vast oil revenues on nationalising key industries and social security programmes.

Fair enough. As did his successor, Nicolas Maduro. When oil prices collapsed in 2014, Maduro couldn't afford to pay for many of the generous state-led programmes. So he printed money to pay for it. Simple? Well, the rapidly increasing money supply led to hyperinflation – which reached a staggering 9,585.5 percent in 2019 according to the central bank, although this is likely a huge underestimate.[15]

So what? Hyperinflation means the value of your life savings disappears overnight, basic goods and services become unaffordable, and people starve.[16] Unemployment has hovered at around almost 50 percent in Venezuela in recent years.[17] Against such a backdrop, people lose hope. And when people lose hope, bad things happen. Hyperinflation in Germany preceded the rise of the Nazis. It's not to be trifled with. And in oil-rich Venezuela's case, this outcome reflected the disastrous, communist-inspired policies of Chavez and Maduro.

My visit to Venezuela was not the most successful one, largely because it didn't quite happen. I had to change my plans at the last minute due to unrest in the country, but

The Travelling Ape

I still had to transit through Caracas.* At the airport, I exchanged around US$10 worth of bolivars to buy some food while I waited for my connection. I was handed two giant wads of cash, big enough to fill a backpack. Thanks, hyperinflation.

The tiller told me not to leave the airport with it; I was glad I wasn't planning to. Flying on to Peru, I watched Caracas's slums rising up into the foothills of the Cordillera de la Costa Mountains. Many of them in various states of disrepair. When an economic ideology fails, it's the people who bear the brunt. Over four million Venezuelans have left the country since 2015, many heading to Colombia.[18] I don't blame them.

A visit to Cuba was much more successful (in the sense that it was an actual visit). It's a charming and vibrant nation. But its continued devotion to Marxist-Leninist economic ideals clearly causes needless suffering for many.[19] The capital, Havana, was beautiful in many ways. But as I strayed from the parts of the city which have been spruced up for tourists, it was clear that Havana is crumbling. Vegetation seeped out of the growing cracks in the old Spanish colonial architecture. Potholes in roads were so large that we had to slalom down motorways to avoid them. No mean feat, given the restricted turning abilities of the decades-old American cars which are everywhere in Cuba.[20] Or worse, Russian-made Ladas, which emit so much pollution I felt as if the car's exhaust pipe was in my mouth whenever riding in one. I found it

---

* No, I obviously don't count this as a 'visit' to Venezuela.

312

almost impossible to access the internet, anywhere. While nice for holidaymakers trying to 'unplug' for a week or two, the reality for Cubans is more sinister. It makes it much easier for the government to hide its dire performance to its population. And there is much to hide.

Average incomes in Cuba are low,[21] infrastructure is terrible, and the country's human rights record leaves much to be desired.[22] While its healthcare and education programmes are better than some, it's not like a good Cuban education sets you up to excel in life. I spoke to a retired doctor who ran our homestay in Trinidad, a lovely town made up of a sea of pastel-coloured colonial buildings. He made US$40 per month when he was practising. He gave up medicine as a result. Instead, he made a better living selling (to chumps like me) probably fake Cuban cigars, while his wife taught guests how to dance. She was a poor teacher, at least judging by my lack of improvement.

No wonder so many Cubans try to escape – and succeed, seemingly. In Miami, I heard Spanish spoken across much of the city. Over a quarter of Miami's residents were born in Cuba, with many more of Cuban descent.[23] It's hardly a vote of confidence in the communist economic experiment playing out on an island 90 miles from the US.

Gross National Happiness?

I was becoming increasingly keen for our tour of North Korea to finish. I'd eaten more than enough kimchi. I'd been told of the DPRK's amazing achievements for the ten thousandth time. I was tired of it all.* So I was pleased when the endless slabs of Soviet-style housing blocks slipped mercifully away behind us as we took the train back to Dandong. I was starting to get nervous again, with a final border check separating us from sweet, sweet (if relative) freedom in China. The inspection on the way out was even more thorough than the one on the way in. All the photographs we'd taken were closely scrutinised. Ones that were deemed unacceptable were deleted, mainly any giving glimpses of real North Korean daily life. After the three-hour check was complete, a guard chillingly called my name.

He asked for the 'leaflet'. On the way into North Korea, a guard found a leaflet on Buddhism in my bag. It was given to me by a monk I'd meditated with in Bhutan (I realise this sentence is one of the most pretentious travelling things I've ever said, by the way). Religion is banned in the DPRK. He let me keep it, but scribbled something down in a logbook after he'd done so. I was going to chuck the leaflet away at the first opportunity when we arrived in Pyongyang, but a group member said I should hold onto it. And he was right. On the way out of the country, the guards wanted to check I hadn't distributed the leaflet to any North Koreans, lest it corrupt them. I handed over the crumpled pieces of paper, and held my breath.

All this fuss, over a small leaflet, with a few words typed on it in Comic Sans. It was hardly the Bible. But here, any evidence of other countries doing things differently

---

* The endless propaganda. Kimchi I still very much enjoy.

was simply destroyed. Interestingly, like North Korea, the country where I'd picked up the leaflet was one of the few places globally that had also opted against capitalism. Bhutan is a magical, mystical-feeling place. And certainly so in comparison to North Korea. Landing in Paro was one of the most exciting events of my life. In the sense that almost dying is really exciting. It's the most dangerous airport approach in the world, tucked away in the middle of the mighty Himalayas. The plane nose tilted downwards, we violently swerved to avoid a hill situated right at the start of the runway, and clattered and bumped to a stop. Most passengers looked shell-shocked, and none more than me.

I was keen to get a sense of the country. It had only opened up its beauty to tourists in the last couple of decades, after years of economic and political isolation. I was intrigued by the fact that Bhutan is the only country in the world to use Gross National Happiness (GNH) as its main measure of national development, rather than the Gross Domestic Product (GDP) used commonly elsewhere in capitalist societies. When I discovered this, I was immediately torn. The economist in me was sceptical of a non-quantifiable development measure, while the pretentious millennial in me loved the concept. Like all things in life (and particularly in economics), there are no simple answers.

Clearly, parts of this focus on GNH, as opposed to a capitalist focus on economic growth, were working. On the positive side, Bhutan's use of GNH means it was one of the few countries in the world where the preservation of the environment, sustainable societal development, and the promotion of culture are main aims of the government. These are clearly good things. Driving around with my guides, I noticed the roads, streets, and countryside were immaculate (particularly compared to Bangladesh, where I'd just flown in from). The pace of life was slow. People weren't rushing around going to meetings or after-work drinks or other tedious things Western capitalists have to do. It felt like an enchanting Himalayan kingdom. Its non-capitalist serenity helped me fall in love with it.

But. On the downside, a lack of focus on GDP growth means meagre government revenues. In turn, this meant poor healthcare, public services, and schools. I saw much poverty when I was in Bhutan. My guides told me they'd grown up living basic lives as subsistence farmers, and didn't enjoy lots of it. They wanted to leave the country. Female literacy is only just above 50 percent and poverty is still a massive problem.[24] Life expectancy at birth is just 73, ranking it in a lowly 116th position globally (just behind North Korea and Russia).[25] Perhaps this is a price worth paying for its novel approach to development? It's hard to say. But for all Bhutan's loveliness, I wasn't convinced their system, any more than communism, was a perfect alternative to capitalism. It's easy to criticise something without suggesting a viable alternative. And from my travels, I've been left feeling the alternatives we've tried so far are profoundly worse than capitalism itself.

Capitalism Isn't the Root of All Evil

South of the Border

Days after I'd left North Korea, I was hot, in a crowded and sweaty place. I could barely move it was so busy. It felt like I'd be crushed. The noise was deafening. The floor slippery. Practically gasping for air among the sea of people, a strange thing started to happen. I looked around. Hordes of those people had started to prance around like horses. Was it real? Had I lost my mind? Was I dreaming?

I was in Seoul. I'd drunk too much *soju*. And people were dancing to PSY's massive hit 'Gangnam Style', which was at one point the most watched YouTube video in history. (If you want to be concerned about the direction humanity's headed in, google the current rankings.) I was on a night out. This, like most other ones, involved lots of great apes, who mostly don't know each other, crushing into small underground places and drinking harmful chemicals together. Korea's favourite poison, *soju*, is a famously potent potato-based spirit. It got the better of me.

Koreans really like a drink. And most speak English. So I spent much of the remainder of my night doing what many tourists do when trying to fit in: shouting the name of a famous person you know from that country at locals. This time, it was Park Ji-sung, a South Korean footballer who played for Manchester United a few years ago. To those I bothered that night, I apologise.

Responses to my inane ramblings were mainly a shrug of the shoulders or a vague nod of acceptance. It must be annoying. The equivalent would be if every Italian tourist in London kept smiling and shouting, 'David Beckham!'

at me, expecting some sort of pat on the back in response. (I would actually pat them on the back, to be fair. I love him.)

Here I was in South Korea. Wealthy. Modern. Free. Liberal. I was surrounded by people having an absolute blast. They were free to do as they pleased. And 'as they pleased' appeared to be 'get smashed', and that's fine. I stumbled out of the club, and onto the streets of Seoul. All gadgets, neon lights, and glittering skyscrapers. I found it hard to believe I'd not arrived in the future. Perhaps less philosophically, I realised I'd also lost my room key. (There were spares at the hostel, luckily.).

I woke the next day with a sore head. I downed a massive iced coffee, and then another, and set off for a stroll around the capital. My first impressions were that this was quite possibly one of the most space-age places I'd ever been. Incredibly forward-thinking and modern. The transport was well run. Trains had air conditioning, and were large enough for actual human adults (a novelty coming from London with its tiny Victorian-era tunnels). Many people appeared to spend more of their lives looking at their smartphones than the real world. On this point, I agree with eccentric tech overlord Elon Musk. He posits that we're already cyborgs with two brains. One, real and existing, in our heads. The other also real but in our pockets (or a few centimetres away from our faces when we sleep).

Seoul is vast. The greater Seoul area has around 26 million people, more than all of North Korea. Many buildings scrape the sky. Concrete extends in all directions, punctuated by flashing neon lights. The sombre darkness of the other Korean capital, Pyongyang, couldn't have been more different. I got used to crossing roads which were often over ten lanes wide. Except this time, there were *actual* cars everywhere. And people, happy-looking people. Who I was free to talk to, if I so pleased (not that I would, particularly with a hangover).

There are pockets of Seoul's past that still remained. Most notably the Changdeokgung and Gyeongbokgung palaces, which are as pretty as they are hard to spell: very. But the rest of the city was as if apparently imported from the future. Seoul seemed an impossibly large metropolis. An extremely interesting place to visit, but too big. Slightly soulless, dare I say it.*

I went for a walk down Cheonggyecheon sunken park. The sky was cloudy, but it was summer, so achingly humid. The 'park' used to be a sunken highway, which they'd removed to unearth the gently flowing stream that lay beneath it. It was lined on both sides by inviting footpaths, with pretty little shrubs, trees, and benches for people to sit. It was an oasis of calm in this most metropolitan of cities. Glass tower blocks were just visible, reflected in the gently rippling water of the stream beside me.

I took my shoes off and started padding down the path.

---

* I was going to spell soulless as 'Seoulless', in case anyone missed the pun, which was intended. In fact, I thought of it while walking around the city. I was so pleased with it that I wrote it down on my phone. But by the time I had taken my phone out of my bag it became less and less funny, and actually started to annoy me a few steps later down the street. To the point I now regret mentioning it at all.

The Travelling Ape

I occasionally stopped to dunk my feet in the stream.[*] Eventually, I decided to sit on the side of the river and dangle my legs in for a bit. I would've liked to dangle my foggy head in too, but I felt this would probably look too weird. I could hear the birds chirping. The sounds of the stream sloshing and trickling over cleverly positioned pebbles and stones. And also the thudding of my temples, owing to the night before.

Seoul was so, well, nice. Developed. The events of the week before still weighed heavily on me. I thought of Hae-Won and Chin, and a sense of sadness rose up inside me. They were nice people, like most average North Koreans were, I'm sure. And unfortunately, they must have known 'the truth'. We showed them pictures of our lives back in the West on our smartphones and iPads. We told them we didn't hate the North Korean people, as state propaganda tried to make them believe. Like Matt in Turkmenistan, deep down they must have known they needed to continue espousing lies to keep themselves safe. The main lie being that their country's treasured economic system hadn't been an utter disaster.

I sat there in this little oasis, in this thriving and modern city. Less than a week earlier, I'd been north of the border. In the grim, oppressive, and largely smile-free nightmare of North Korea. Where cityscapes resembled brutalist, bleak, communist-town dystopias. It felt a world away.

---

[*] As far as annoying traveller stereotypes go, I concede that walking around shoeless is bad. As bad as hanging out with monks in Bhutan? That's for you to decide.

Capitalism Isn't the Root of All Evil

And yet the border was only around 30 miles from where I was sitting. That these two now vastly dissimilar nations had been united as one, poor country just 75 years or so ago was hard for me to comprehend. But since partition in 1945, they'd experimented with different economic systems.

One country now has an average income of around US$40,000 per year, the other just US$1,700.[26] One has citizens who are on average between one and three inches taller than their genetic cousins across the border.[27] One is among the most liberal countries in Asia; and one offers its citizens perhaps less personal freedom than any country in the world. One has among the highest living standards in the world; one the lowest. In 1957, both countries had average incomes lower than Ghana's.[28] Today, one has an average income 15 times higher than Ghana's; the other's remains below it.[29] Can you guess which is which?

Many people in the media and in the West like to moan about capitalism. But truthfully, would they rather live in capitalist South Korea or communist North Korea? I'd always been a bit wary of capitalism. After all, trendy hipsters and rich celebrities are always harping on about how 'evil' it is (despite so clearly benefitting from it personally). So to fit in, and without any reason not to, I unquestioningly took these criticisms as a given. But the problem was, my experiences travelling almost everywhere contradicted what I'd been told to think at university and had read in the media, that capitalism is a flawed and immoral system.

Comparing South Korea with communist North Korea

left me thinking that capitalism really can't be as bad as so many make it out to be. And indeed, when I reflect on my journeys around the world, the same trends held mostly true. Most of the countries with the highest average living standards tended to be avowedly capitalist, and many with the lowest living standards had implemented alternative economic systems, as in North Korea, Cuba, Venezuela, and Bhutan. Could these examples all simply be flukes?

The Positives of Capitalism

Capitalism is a system where private firms or people (rather than governments) control the means of production. Goods and services are sold on free markets, with the aim of generating profits.[30] The adoption of this system across much of the world has been followed by the largest and fastest decline in the rates of poverty ever seen, and the biggest improvements in global living conditions. Capitalism emerged around the 17th century. Prior to its emergence, practically every person on Earth lived a grim life of subsistence, suffering extreme poverty and ill health. Indeed, roughly 94 percent of the world's population lived in poverty even in the 1820s. This figure has since dropped to under 10 percent.[31] Literally billions of people have been lifted out of poverty, strangely, in step with capitalism spreading around the world. Average earnings globally per person in the year 1500 (before capitalism) are estimated to have been around US$675, compared to over US$12,200 in 2021.[32] And this accounts for inflation.

Capitalism Isn't the Root of All Evil

This is one of the greatest achievements in history. In many countries, the decision to adopt capitalist economic principles marked the turning point in their nation's battle against poverty. None more so than in China. Up until 1978, communist China was poor and a shadow of its former self. But then, even while refusing to budge on democracy, the country plugged into the global market economy, established economic zones, and allowed private sectors to open up again. It embraced a state-led version of capitalism.

Guess what happened? The economy has since exploded. It's now around *90 times* its 1978 size. Average incomes have risen from around just US$200 to over US$10,000.[33] This has allowed almost a billion Chinese people to escape poverty in the last four decades, accounting for around 70 percent of global poverty reduction in this period.[34] I hate to say I told you so.* (More on China in the next chapter.)

The story is similar in Singapore. Visiting its National Museum, I looked at old grainy pictures of the city-state. When Singapore became independent from Britain in 1965, I learnt it was a small, poor, fishing settlement, with few natural resources. Average annual incomes were around US$500.[35] Today, Singapore is one of the most advanced countries on Earth, a city of the future.

Average incomes have risen by a factor of over 125, to around US$60,000. How? By positioning itself as a centre for finance, and by adopting capitalist economic principles. Allowing the free market to allocate resources, generally

---

★   I really don't. It feels great!

speaking. Most Singaporeans have nothing bad to say about capitalism as a result, at least in conversations I've had with locals while spending several weeks there for work.

In the 20th century, the so-called 'Tiger Economies' of South Korea, Singapore, and Taiwan transformed into some of the richest in the world, all from humble beginnings. In each case, they mixed capitalism with centralised, long-term economic planning. Rapid economic development emboldened the middle classes, who then demanded true democracy in South Korea and Taiwan. It didn't happen the other way around.

Economic development means better healthcare, sanitation, education, and ultimately, better lives. People often decry 'economic growth' as an abstract, meaningless thing. But they fail to see how growth is a proxy for people living better lives. More growth equals more resources to go around, more opportunities, and often, less suffering. Growth and GDP have real-life health consequences. And so South Koreans are taller and heavier than their brothers and sisters to the north, despite being literally the same people.

I'd noticed a theme on my travels. Almost all the world's most developed countries had at some stage adopted overwhelmingly capitalist economic systems, with only a few exceptions.[36] This appears to be supported by data. In a sample of 127 countries, the 63 with the highest degree of economic freedom had more than four times the average income and nearly twice the growth of the countries that didn't.[37] Some would argue capitalism succeeds because it aligns more closely with human nature. That we need to be rewarded for our work, that we are inclined to build up resources for ourselves and our families. That a capitalist framework allows supply and demand to respond to what people want, rather than what they *should* want. They might be right.

Apart from widespread poverty reduction (which alone really would be enough to justify its implementation), there are other benefits of capitalism. A free economic system usually leads to more political freedom and innovation. Governments are cumbersome and inefficient. Services provided by them have no incentive to be cost-efficient, nor to provide a positive experience for users. They are backed by taxes and in effect cannot go bust, unlike firms in the private sector. The profit incentive drives innovation and efficiency. The spread of global trade has coincided with a collapse in global conflicts. Increased consumer choice means our lives are much less dull and full of less suffering than they used to be.

Am I a Capitalist Pig?

Later on that day, I rode the subway to the district of Gangnam. Walking out from the subway station, I stopped. I did a full body turn to take it all in. I was immediately enchanted by the shiny glass and shimmering neon lights of the place. It was starting to get dark. The sky pinkening. The time of the day when cities always look their best. When glass panels on buildings reflect the hues of the setting sun, and they start to twinkle and glisten from the lights within them.

The Travelling Ape

It seemed fancy, and I had indeed heard that Gangnam was one of the wealthiest parts of Seoul. I could see new luxury high-rises, bisected by broad and busy roads. The pavements were filled with shoppers busily scurrying around, many with multiple shopping bags; revellers heading out for a night on the town. I'd not be one of them this time, not after the previous night. I instead took shelter at a Korean barbecue place, which had almost zero veggie options. But I at least had the novelty of watching other people cut their meat with scissors (a thing in South Korea, which works much better than knives, as it turns out).

To me, Gangnam seemed like a privileged place. I grabbed my phone, and went into a rabbit hole. A much-warranted look into the etymology of the name 'Gangnam Style' ensued. The phrase is a Korean neologism that refers to the upper-class district I was in. The horse dance? A satirical reference to wealthy girls being given horses by their fathers. Was this seemingly fun-filled smash hit actually a hard-hitting critique of the growing social and economic inequalities in modern Seoul? Probably not. Most of PSY's song lyrics appear to make only limited sense. And the song reportedly made him over US$8 million from YouTube streams alone, so I'm sure he won't mind my criticism of his lyrics. He could also now live in Gangnam if he wanted.

But perhaps the song's possible criticism of capitalism – accidental or not – did point to some of the larger issues which exist within it. I was joined at dinner by an American from my hotel. His name was Justin, and he was around

30. He had blond spiky hair, was tall, and liked a good meal, it seemed. And, like many Americans do, within a short space of time after meeting him at the hotel, he'd managed to tell me that he earned, 'About 100,000 dollars a year. Before bonuses.' Before I even knew what his name was. But I was travelling, and he'd have to do.

The barbecue restaurant was sleek, modern. It had shiny granite surfaces, dimmed lights, polished concrete floors, and houseplants. A cool ambience. Justin talked of what seemed to be his rather charmed life in 'the city'.

'Which city?' I asked, reasonably. He was shocked that I didn't realise 'the city' is what people who live in San Francisco call San Francisco (this was his first trip to Asia, and he hadn't left the States much). Despite clearly benefitting from capitalism, like many in California, Justin described himself as a 'Bernie Bro' – one of leftist senator Bernie Sanders's fans. Sanders ran for president in 2016 and 2020, and has a fairly robust dislike of capitalism.[*38] Justin started talking vaguely about 'bringing down the capitalist system'. Without, I think, really analysing what he was saying.

'Do you *really* believe the world would be better if this happened? Do you think America would be better if it ditched capitalism, for socialism or communism?' I asked, genuinely keen to hear what he had to say.

---

[*] So much so that he used the evil capitalist precepts of supply and demand to charge guests a mere US$95 for tickets to attend a talk of his, where he promoted his book *It's Okay to be Angry About Capitalism* in 2023.

The Travelling Ape

'Yeah man, you know, it's just that the capitalist machine destroys everything and everyone, you know?'

'In America? Or here in South Korea? They are both better than a lot of places, at least from what I've seen.'

I went on to tell Justin about my experiences in North Korea the past week, and across the world (he hadn't asked). And how they and other travel experiences had changed my views on things a bit. He didn't seem to be getting angry in any way. But as with any conversations about politics, and particularly with Americans, I knew that expressing anything other than devotion to the churches of left or right could lead to me being labelled evil (depending on their preference).

'I think I'm just somewhere in the middle. I'd call myself a centrist, I guess. I prefer incremental progress rather than revolution. I think capitalism's been good for the world on balance, but it's by no means perfect,' I said tentatively. Trying not to poke the bear.

I could see I was losing him, though. And given that we'd not yet got our mains, felt it would be useful to get him back on side so that the next hour or two would be a little more enjoyable. Fortunately, the ensuing conversation crystallised what I already knew about capitalism and its downsides – that it solves many problems but causes others.

While you might have realised by now that I think capitalism is the best economic system we have, especially compared to other options, this doesn't mean that I love it. Or that I don't see its downsides, too. I'm not some megalomaniacal free market fanboy. I don't love the views of Austrian economic theory (look it up) and Milton Friedman (look him up, too), views that are as compassionate as they are famous outside economists' circles: not very. I don't think capitalism has all the answers to the world's problems, and it is indeed deeply flawed. It's just the best system we have, out of an imperfect bunch.

There's a number of good reasons why capitalism is a naughty word for so many people, a couple of which were on show here in Gangnam. While capitalism is driving progress and helps explain why the world is the best it's ever been, my travels had also exposed a few key issues with it.

The first is that capitalism's profit motive has allowed inequality to flourish.[39] The spread of capitalism has led to huge levels of inequality both within and between nations. According to some estimates, the richest 1 percent of the world's population owns 44 percent of the world's wealth.[40]

I've seen for myself some of the most grotesque inequality. First, between nations. To do this, I simply get on a plane in London, and get off in any country in Africa, Latin America, and most of Asia. For all of the UK's ills, whenever I land back in this green and pleasant land from these regions, I'm always struck by how overwhelmingly developed it is. Clean, modern, and efficient. Things people in the UK never talk about, having not had the context of seeing how most people in the world live.

Inequality isn't hard to see when you travel. In the same year, I went to both Monaco and Malawi. In the tiny, tax-haven state of Monaco in southern France, there isn't much to do apart from gawp at Ferraris and luxury yachts.

That, and drive very slowly around the Formula 1 track, which goes right through the heart of the city. When I visited, I was driving my mum's car – a people carrier – which appeared to anger everyone else following the same route in sports cars and convertibles.

Compare this to Malawi. I stayed in a small village on the shores of Lake Malawi. There wasn't any electricity, and structures made of concrete were rare. Most 'buildings' were hastily constructed out of any spare bits of material lying about. There was one running water tap for the whole village. That the average citizen of Monaco earns almost 100 times that of a citizen of Malawi was abundantly evident.[41] It's not right that such wide disparities can exist in the modern world. Saying that, it's worth noting that inequality between nations, as measured by the global Gini coeffect, has declined significantly since the late '80s.[42]

Then there's inequality within nations. One of the largest slums on Earth is the Dharavi slum, in Mumbai. On my visit, I snaked my way around its claustrophobic, smelly, and dirty alleys. It was damp, dark, and oppressive. Youngsters' laughs could be heard, but they made me feel melancholic, given the surroundings. The sheer number of people living in these conditions – one million – was hard to comprehend. Even more difficult to understand was the fact that this slum was ringed by gleaming skyscrapers, a testament to India's increasing wealth – and inequality.[43] One of the skyscrapers was Indian billionaire Mukesh Ambani's *house*. It's 27 storeys tall.

I once visited beautiful Camps Bay, in Cape Town. I could have been forgiven for thinking I was in Malibu,

Capitalism Isn't the Root of All Evil

California. Boutique coffee shops selling pretentious drinks (that I really like) dotted the stunning coastline. Drop-top convertibles cruising by. Very much out of sight (and out of mind), though, on the other side of Table Mountain, were the Cape Flats townships, which I drove past on the way from the airport. Around 500,000 people live in shanty towns here, in varying degrees of poverty. That's more people than live in Cape Town proper. It was shocking.

Similarly galling are some of the displays of inequality I saw in Rio de Janeiro. Paddling in the sea on the iconic Copacabana Beach, I looked back over the bright-white splash of sand, backed by tall luxury five-star hotels and fancy restaurants. But looming over the horizon, I could see favelas extending into the distance. The hastily constructed shacks clinging perilously to Rio's vertiginous hills.

I stayed in one, unwittingly.* To get there, I passed bright but rickety houses. Narrow streets zig-zagged chaotically into the hillside, with vegetation growing wherever there was space between buildings. Step after step, I found myself heading deeper into the favela. A teenager walked past, cheerily, and said 'olá'. Years of travel and impeccable language skills led me to believe he was saying 'hello'. Fairly normal. What was less normal was that he was holding an AK-47.

The owner of the favela hostel said it was nothing to worry about. Many of the favelas here have their own

---

★ The hostel owners said it had a view of the beach, which was true. But failed to say it was located in a favela.

unofficial police forces and criminal punishment systems. It didn't fill me with confidence. It was also a stark reminder of how people can find themselves existing in different universes – despite living just a matter of miles apart – in part due to capitalism.

But those who blame inequality solely on capitalism would do well to take a cursory glance at history. In doing so, they might realise that the world was *more unequal* before capitalism spread. History is essentially a long story of kings and sultans and the like living lives of opulence, while almost everyone else lived in abject despair. Up until the 14th century, serfdom existed in Europe (and well beyond in some parts of the continent). This meant peasants were literally the property of their rulers, with rights for common people remaining almost non-existent until the 18th century.[44] Just when capitalism was gaining momentum globally. The share of wealth owned by the richest 1 percent in Europe was almost 55 percent in 1810, and has more than halved in Europe since then, curiously as capitalism and industrialisation spread.[45] This represents progress, but is still a high level of inequality. Implementing policies to promote economic growth, while preventing inequality from driving social unrest or divisions in society, remains policymakers' most difficult challenge in capitalist countries.

That said, travelling showed me a few more criticisms of capitalism. That it turns humans into commodified machines.[46] That it relies on the relentless consumption of stuff, which I've seen in the eyes of deranged shoppers in the malls of Dubai or on Fifth Avenue in New York.

Capitalism Isn't the Root of All Evil

Meanwhile, this rampant consumption of needless stuff is leading to the destruction of our only home, this planet, and making climate change and environmental challenges more acute.

Deregulation since the Thatcher and Reagan eras, coupled with a religious belief in the wisdom of free markets, has led to an explosion in the finance industry since the 1980s.[47] When surveying the cityscapes of Manhattan, Singapore, or London's Canary Wharf, it always strikes me as odd that we need buildings as tall as mountains just so banks can lend some money to people. But of course, that isn't all that they're doing. Financial markets are supposed to exist to allocate resources effectively in society. But banks have allowed markets to morph into a monster, by offering huge salaries to those working for them and almost nothing useful to society.[48] And yet, when it goes wrong, as it did in 2008,[49] the taxpayer is forced to bail banks out, banks that have become rich by gambling other people's money.[50] If you want to try to understand the populist resurgence throughout the Western world in recent years, look no further than anger at bankers. And this is something that capitalism will have to answer to, if it's to survive and flourish.

Despite these important issues, my experiences in the Korean peninsula and across the world in general fundamentally changed my view on capitalism – to a more positive one. While it still leads to much suffering and is nowhere near perfect, I'm convinced it's the best economic system we have at our disposal. It has been the best thing for poverty reduction, bar nothing. I've yet to visit anywhere that's tried an alternative economic system that's worked. In fact, I found that the most ideological and anti-capitalist societies were some of the worst places on this Earth. Coincidence? Unlikely.

We should aim to fix capitalism's flaws, rather than hoping the whole system will fail one day. It is unlikely to. We'd do well follow the example set by the Nordics. The most advanced societies on the planet. They've not abandoned capitalism, but have instead focused on producing superior societal outcomes within a capitalist framework.

It's possible for us to rein in the parts of capitalism that sometimes don't work. In some ways, there's already one nation that's been doing this for decades. Cherry-picking some aspects of capitalism, while at the same time steering clear of any of the 'hassles' that might be caused by granting their citizens a vote or democracy. While we in the West have been tearing ourselves apart over financial crises, populism, and pandemics, one nation has been quietly, but inexorably, focusing on getting itself a seat at the top table of world affairs. In fact, this nation has its eyes set on the throne at the head of this table. I'm talking, of course, about China.

11

China's Staggering, Slightly Scary Rise

China's already risen to the top. Does a
non-democratic hegemon await?

I hung there for a few minutes. The bubble-like plastic capsule surrounding me bounced and swayed. The gondola had come to a sudden, grinding halt. It was a bright spring day, which, while not overly hot, was starting to feel a little uncomfortable in this ventless little cabin. Especially given that at the time it was filled with four other rather large men, my friends. All in our mid-twenties.

'There'll be people on the wall selling beers, I can guarantee it,' my skinny and blond friend Reesey said, answering a question that no one had asked.

'What makes you so sure?' replied Andrew, tall and with a sceptical look on his face.

'You know, in these sorts of places, there just will be,' Reesey countered. Offering no evidence, but delivered so confidently I felt he might have a point.

The 'these sorts of places' that Reesey was referring to was, in fact, one of the New Seven Wonders of the World. I was visiting China with Andrew and Reesey, as well as two other pals, Matt and James. The latter two wore black jeans, black T-shirts, and black jackets (believing at this stage that they were international deejays or something). We were young and much more full of life than today. And evidently, our interest in drinking beer was at least more than equal to our desire to soak up and engage fully with local culture. But still, we'd made it to China. We were at the Great Wall. So we were doing more than most.

The gondola lurched forward for a moment. And then continued being winched up the parched and brown hill we were ascending, just a couple of hours north of the capital, Beijing. Out of the scratched and slightly foggy plastic windows, I could see what looked like more brown hills, stretching as far as the eye could see. And up in the distance, our destination. A bloody great big wall.

For some reason, I didn't have the highest hopes when going to see the Great Wall of China. I couldn't imagine a long wall being as structurally impressive as some of the other New Seven Wonders I'd already been to, like the Taj Mahal. But this opinion quickly changed once we disembarked the gondola. Taking our first steps onto the Great Wall's potholed, wonky, and ancient granite blocks. Before I'd even had the time to get my bearings, Reesey ran back over to us, having just done a recce. He looked overawed by the experience, elated even. For a second, I'd (naively) thought that this was a man who'd just been overcome with the profundity of setting eyes upon one of humanity's ancient engineering marvels.

'See! Told you there'd be people selling beers up here,' he said, clutching a few cans of Tsingtao in his hands and looking like the cat who'd got the cream. The wall's majestic turrets looked like miniature castles with their thin windows and stone battlements atop them. Inside were hawkers selling refreshments. And clearly, they were answering to the forces of supply and demand. The demand being beer for stupid tourists.

We sipped on our Tsingtaos, which, heavens alive, were even cold. Perhaps the hawker had taken a mini fridge up to the wall with him. We strolled leisurely along the ancient structure, enjoying the sunshine on our skin, the cloudless sky. The crisp spring air here was far less polluted than what we'd just been inhaling in Beijing. Where at times it felt like I always had a cigarette in my mouth and our clothes smelled like they'd been drying next to a campfire after just one wear.

The Great Wall looked truly stunning. My initially low expectations were surpassed, and then some. Having now seen each of the New Seven Wonders, I felt it would definitely be in the top three, narrowly pipped by the Great Pyramids and the Taj Mahal. The wall appeared as if one with nature. Rippling and dancing with the hills and mountains. Inextricably linked to the scenery. Winding its way towards the distant, hazy horizons, as if always part of these ancient landscapes. But the wall most definitely hadn't always been here. Some 300,000 soldiers and peasants are estimated to have built it over a period covering almost 2,000 years.[1] Which can't have been very much fun at all.

Parts of it were crumbling. But most had stood the test of time. Stunning, really, given that its construction started in the 7th century BCE. Sections of it wriggled haphazardly one way, before almost turning back on themselves. As if a winding river, trying to cut the easiest route through some mountains. Other parts of it were truly vertiginous, sometimes seemingly angled at near to 45 degrees. And as if sipping our beers and gazing at this wonder of humanity wasn't enough, we had the pleasure of watching marathon runners, haplessly scrambling up the steepest parts of the wall and its ramparts. Seemingly about to take their last breaths. I can't think of many harder places to go for a short jog, let alone a marathon. But it made our visit even more special.

Seeing the Great Wall was awe-inspiring. It can't be seen from space, as is commonly claimed, but it does stand as a monument to China's long and rich history. It spans a not inconsequential 13,000 miles. Built to protect the country from nomadic tribes and invasions from the north. It was also built to demonstrate the power and control of its various ruling dynasties.[2]

The next day, we toured Beijing. The scale and grandeur of the Forbidden City was magnificent to witness. Its 900 rooms, beautifully crafted terracotta roofs, and ornate red wooden supports and walls speaking to China's historic core (even though our visit was somewhat spoilt by several parents letting their children defecate on the floor of this most sacred national monument. Yes, really). We also ambled around Beijing's *hutongs*. Narrow and ramshackle alleys. Claustrophobic and wonky. Surrounded by rustic one- and two-storey houses with courtyards, many of which were hundreds of years old. The depth of China's history was evident everywhere. Rather surprisingly, I learnt that China was the largest economy in the world for *almost two thousand years*, spanning from the 1st century

China's Staggering, Slightly Scary Rise

CE to around the 19th century.[3] People abroad often talk of China's rise. But in China, they merely talk about the country returning to where they rightly belong: the top of the global power pyramid.

Later that day on our tour around the capital, there were also clear signs of where things had started to go sour for China in the 19th and then 20th centuries. Economic power started to shift to Europe and the US during the industrial revolution in the 19th century, with foreign capitalists increasingly taking control of China economically.[4] The Xinhai Revolution saw the end of the Manchu-led Qing dynasty and the creation of a republic in 1912. And then, after a civil war, the Chinese Communist Party (CCP) rose to power in 1949.[5] Notable, monolithic monuments to its communist experiment still exist in Beijing to this day. The CCP transformed the Chinese state, collectivised agriculture, and purged all political dissent. I've spoken quite enough already about communism (I imagine you'd agree) but I'll merely add here that shortly after the CCP took power, China fast became one of the poorest countries on Earth. Some estimates suggest that between 40 and 80 million died as a result of political purges and famine under Chairman Mao's rule from 1949 to 1976,[6] deaths tolls that are usually hallmarks reserved only for supposedly utopian, socialist civilisations. Far from being the most economically powerful nation on Earth, by 1960, China's GDP per capita was just US$90.[7]

We went for a stroll around Tiananmen Square, just outside the Forbidden City. It was a truly immense void of concrete.

The Travelling Ape

'Not exactly St Mark's Square, is it?' I said, to nods of agreement from the others.

It had a slightly bleak, but at the same time very impactful feeling. Redolent of power. Authority.

Tiananmen Square's giant footprint was flanked by buildings that looked like they'd been flown in from Soviet Russia. Giant, triumphalist constructions lay on either side of the giant expanse, devoid of any vegetation. Most buildings were covered in tens of red Chinese flags, understandably so as they were government offices and China's legislature buildings. The red flags, of course, were not the only bloody things about the place. The stains may be gone, but we – but not the locals – all knew that this was where several thousand pro-democracy protesters were allegedly killed by the government in the 1989 Tiananmen Square Massacre.

We continued our sightseeing. Beijing, it has to be said, felt like an alien place; the customs were shockingly different to back home. The poo incident in the Forbidden City sadly turned out not to be an isolated one. Spitting was much more common than we were used to. Our attempts to flag down cabs were almost always unsuccessful. They'd slow down, realise we were tourists, and speed off, refusing to take us.

In Beijing, I felt very far from home indeed. We ate at food markets where you could chew on chicken feet, or chow down on snakes and cockroaches. We found it hard to eat at restaurants too (even though their menus were much less strange). We walked into a bustling place, only to be frantically shooed out of it by the restaurant owner.

He kept insisting, 'No food, it's closed, it's closed,' despite the quite obvious evidence to the contrary. The language, food, and, at times, poor queuing etiquette (a big no-no for British people) were hard to get my head around. But people were still friendly, in their own way. The people of China are really no different to those in the rest of the world. Generally good, and kind. It's just that with over 1.4 billion of them, conventions relating to crowds and a few other things are a little bit different to back home.

While Beijing was not my favourite place in the world, it has to be said that it was fascinating to spend time there. To witness these cultural differences between here and the West and to gain a glimpse of China's past. And also, perhaps get a snapshot of its future. Beijing's long history was starting to take a back seat to its pulsating present. The city had a network of unfeasibly large, frenetically busy highways. There were cranes everywhere. The sounds of construction were never out of earshot. Skyscrapers were being erected all over the city. There were fancy shopping districts selling luxury goods from Europe. With massive billboards suggesting buying stuff would make you happy, odd in a country led by the CCP. Something, it was clear, was changing in China.

China Begins to Take Off (Again)

After a few more days in the capital, it was time to move on. The boys and I took a high-speed train to Shanghai and settled in for the ride (is there a better way to see a country than by train?). At times, the two sides of China – old and modern – seemed to press uncomfortably against each other as the country zoomed past us in a blur. Green paddy fields ended abruptly, replaced by towering, grey, new skyscrapers. Partially finished and empty motorways appeared in what seemed to be a few of China's many planned cities. At the time, some of these looked like ghost towns. But the authorities still expect millions more rural workers to move to urban areas in coming years, following the half a billion or so who've made the journey already since the '80s.[8] And they'll have plenty of cities to choose from, clearly.

'They aren't really messing about here, are they?' Andrew said, as another of these planned cities zipped past us.

'Kind of looks like they're building a city from scratch, *SimCity* style,' I added. I quickly remembered that most 'normal' people didn't waste months of their youth playing city planning simulator games, and so the reference wouldn't make any sense to them.

'I remember hearing somewhere,'* I said, matter-of-factly, 'that China now has more miles of high-speed rail than any other country in the world. It's insane.'

'Oh, that's cool,' said James neutrally, before the conversation swiftly moved on to things that the rest of my friends didn't find boring.

Realising that my obsession with infrastructure,

---

*   On an infrastructure enthusiast forum that I visited intentionally, and a lot.

skyscrapers, and such, was best left to internet forums, I grabbed my phone and fact checked myself. It confirmed what I'd learnt. In 2008, China hadn't connected any of its major cities by high-speed rail. Less than a decade later, most of its major cities were connected in this way. And in fact, it had more miles of high-speed rail than the rest of the world, combined.[9]

'I guess it's much easier to plan infrastructure projects when you don't need to properly compensate those who are "in the way" of your railways, which makes similar projects in the West painfully slow and expensive. But still, what a feat,' I said, not able to keep it to myself. I have very tolerant friends.

More of China slipped by. Overcast skies. Huge apartment blocks emerging out of the haze. Cranes, so many cranes. Something about the scenes felt ominous. What I thought was most shocking was the *sheer size* of some of the cities that we were speeding through. Tianjin: 14 million people. Weifang: 2.6 million. Lianyungang: 2 million. Yancheng: 1.6 million. Nantong: 2.3 million.[10] And all in just four hours on the train. I like to think of myself as relatively clued up on geography, but I'll be honest, I'd not heard of many of these cities apart from Tianjin. And yet, if any of these cities were in the UK, they'd be the largest city after London, by a country mile. It was eye-opening.

China has a *lot* of big cities. Of the 50 largest in the world, an incredible 15 are in China.[11] But how many can you name? I bet most people would probably get three, maybe four. Beijing, Shanghai, Hong Kong being the obvious ones. I was also able to name Xi'an, Shenzhen, Guangzhou, and Tianjin – but only because I'd done some research before the trip.

But what of Chongqing, Chengdu, Nanjing, Wuhan, Dongguan, Hangzhou, Foshan, and Shenyang? These are some of the largest conurbations on the planet, but many of us don't even know they exist. They've exploded in size only in the last few decades, much like China on the global stage. So perhaps we could be forgiven for our ignorance? From what I could see, most of these Chinese cities were filled with huge, rectangular housing blocks, which seeped towards the horizon as if they'd been cloned. Neon lights and pedestrians thronged wide, busy streets, almost all ordered in a perfectly symmetrical grid system. Green space of any kind was relatively rare. The rapid pace of urbanisation seemingly meant city planners couldn't spare much space for trees and grass. Just 2.8 percent of Shanghai is open green space, compared to around 46 percent in both Sydney and Singapore.[12]

The train ride showed me in the most visceral way just how rapidly China's been growing. The CCP swapped their spectacularly unsuccessful dalliance with communism for a 'socialist market economy' romance – effectively capitalism without democracy. This new affair has been going on since the early 1990s. Using elements of trade-based capitalism (without democracy) has been staggeringly successful for them, although China still remains much poorer in average income terms than most Western liberal democracies.

Indeed, by the time I visited, these changes had

propelled China into a pre-eminent global power, with many believing it will one day be *the* pre-eminent global power. In 1990, the US economy was around 15 times the size of China's. By 2021, China's economy had reached three-quarters of the size of the US, and was the second largest in the world.[13] Hundreds of millions of Chinese people have been pulled out of poverty in this period. Some expect China's economy to overtake the US as the world's largest as soon as 2025, although I think this now looks very optimistic.[14] The scale of development I saw in China was jaw-dropping. And statistics back up what I'd seen. China used more concrete between 2011 and 2013 than the US did in the entire 20th century.[15] It's no wonder US infrastructure seems to be crumbling in comparison.

The train started to slow as we reached the outskirts of Shanghai. A sprawling, gigantic urban monster of a city. Seeing this city, which had grown in size from 6 million in 1980 to over 25 million when I visited, I couldn't help but think that the United States seemed so 'last century'. That it had had its time in the sun. And I wasn't sure this was a good thing.

For good or for bad, having a dominant global hegemon is positive for global political stability. If you have a world policeman who's pretty much as powerful as the rest of the world combined, it's hard for countries to step out of line.[16] It's when there are multiple powers sizing up each other that bad things happen. Think both World Wars, the Cold War, and the fact that historical great powers like England and France were fighting each other for centuries.

In other times, much of the world's been run by a

global hegemon. Think of the Romans, the British up until World War I, and largely the United States thereafter (with the USSR trying to put a few spanners in the works). Indeed, we'll look back at the period 1991 to 2016 as one of complete American dominance over the world. And as an unprecedented period of global peace and strong global economic growth,[17] even considering the 2003 war in Iraq and other wars in Bosnia, Afghanistan, Syria, among others.

When the Soviet Union collapsed in 1991, American military spending accounted for 42.2 percent of the global total.[18] Put simply, it could have declared war on the rest of the world and would have had a good chance of winning. And that included puny China, which at the time accounted for less than two percent of global military spending. But the days of unipolarity are now behind us. We're now living in a multipolar world. There's a new cold war, this time between the US and China. America's share of global military spending had fallen to (a still not insignificant) 38 percent by 2021.[19] China now comprises 15 percent of the total. And is still rising. Chinese military spending now exceeds that of France, Germany, India, Japan, and South Korea. Combined. This is a massive shift in global power dynamics.

China's rise should have been the most important topic in every Western election over the past decade. But it wasn't. In the West, we've all been tearing ourselves apart internally over petty nationalism and left-right name calling. We've been too busy trolling each other on social media to care that China has been strengthening its economy and its military, and preparing to take what it sees as its rightful place back on top of the global power pyramid.

Welcome to the Future?

Having arrived in Shanghai, exhausted from the journey, we decided to get an early night. The next day, we made a beeline for the Bund, Shanghai's historic riverfront promenade. The sun was shining; it was hot but not overwhelmingly so. And Shanghai didn't seem as polluted as Beijing. As we strolled down the famous promenade, we all agreed that early impressions of the place were that it felt slightly less 'alien' than Beijing did. For starters, the Bund was lined with grand European colonial architecture. And for dessert, no children were emptying their bowels on the street.

The Bund reminded me of Madrid, Paris, or Buenos Aries. The buildings were made up of Art Deco, Baroque, Gothic, and Neoclassical styles. Most were made with sandstone. Some had towering columns, others had large clock towers or impressive domes, reminding me of London or Budapest. Most of these buildings were in fact built by the UK, US, France, Italy, and other European powers in the 19th century. The Bund was effectively a foreign city when it was built, and was simply called the International Settlement for many decades.

We continued ambling along. These old buildings seemed like a reminder of China's former weakness. A different China, beholden to European imperial interests decades ago. Just over the mighty Huangpu River, however, the skyscrapers of Pudong stood proudly as the vanguard of the new, self-confident China. One curved and writhed as it reached for the sky. It had a staggering 128 floors (I counted them). Another looked like a series of pearls levitating on stilts, in a highly futuristic-looking TV tower. Pudong contained some of the tallest buildings in the world.[20] And looked like a scene from the 22nd century. The skyline had a 'wow' factor. But just 25 years ago, the land where these skyscrapers stood was made up of mainly old, crumbling, low-rise factories and warehouses. This was the new China. And it meant business.

It took around half an hour to walk the length of the Bund. There weren't any obvious river crossing points. But we'd heard there was this kind of tourist tunnel that had been built a few years ago, so we headed for it. After descending deep underground, we arrived at some little glass pods that would take us to the other side of the river. There was no driver, and the pods were just big enough to fit the five of us. Off we went. Despite our initial cynicism, it was actually pretty impressive. Bright, psychedelic lights covered the tunnel walls, surrounding us on each side as we glided onwards. We headed past stars and galaxies. A corkscrew kind of constellation spun around us, disorientating us, and upsetting our balance. The pod slowed to a halt. We stepped out.

'That was fun,' I said, 'but over time that'd probably be quite an emotionally exhausting way to commute to work each day.'

China's Staggering, Slightly Scary Rise

'Yeah, beats the Northern Line in London, though,' said Matt, 'where we have to endure our faces being jammed into smelly commuters' armpits.' We laughed heartily. Until it dawned on us that he'd just mocked our daily commute, and in effect, mocked the reality of our lives back home.

We emerged into bright, crisp sunshine. The Pudong district is connected by a series of skybridges that allow you to serenely float above the traffic below. We all agreed that it felt like the kind of city you'd see in sci-fi movies, all clean and sanitised. We wondered aloud about how modern, how well ordered the place seemed. (And also laughed childishly at the phonetic pronunciation of Pudong.)

We spent the next few hours exploring, eventually deciding we wanted to get a bird's eye view of the place. So we surveyed Shanghai from the top of the Shanghai World Financial Center. Aside from the incredibly generic name, the building was a marvel. It looked like a kind of elongated bottle opener* with a large hole in the top of it. The observation deck was located on top of this hole, on a cantilevered viewing deck with a glass floor. The city spread as far as my eyes could see. Cranes and newly finished buildings in all directions. And no sign of the countryside that surrounded the city. Even on the most distant horizon, more tower blocks disappeared into a grey urban abyss.

Cognisant that the boys most likely didn't fancy another of my lectures about urban planning, I gazed out of the window silently and took a few moments to myself.

---

*   At least it did in our collective eyes, given our hobby at that time.

The Travelling Ape

The Chinese had built one of the largest cities in the world in the blink of an eye, and, by the look of things, were only just getting started. I was awed. I felt like this when I was in New York as a boy, like I'd arrived in the centre of the world. And now Shanghai was the new kid on the block, shiny and new.

When I was visiting China back in 2014, I'd heard stories about China's rise. I'd even written my International Relations MSc dissertation on it. But as is so often the case with travel, no amount of reading or learning compares to seeing things for yourself. I'd already forecast the US stepping back from its world leadership role, and argued China would attempt to step into the vacuum in the dissertation. My tutor was so alarmed by what he read that he spoke to some of his contacts at the Foreign Office, where it was then distributed widely and escalated to the highest levels of government. He also printed out thousands of copies of the dissertation and spent the rest of his career thrusting copies of it into the hands of alarmed bystanders, warning them of the impending peril the global political order was about to find itself in. The world was set for a radical change. That much was true. Even if the bit about my tutor definitely wasn't (pretty sure it was a dream I had while writing it).

Everywhere You Go, Here Comes China

After Shanghai, we were heading for Tokyo. I remember being quite excited about the train journey, despite it only being a relatively short one to the airport. I'd read about this particular train ride before.* I stepped off the platform and onto the train. The interior was immaculate, all smooth lines and sleek, contemporary finishes. I sat down and got comfortable. And then it happened.

The carriage started to float, ever so slightly, off the ground. There was a perceptible sensation of it levitating, slightly vibrating. Because – incredibly – it was. I'd boarded the Shanghai maglev. A train that floats on magnets. It has no wheels. And if that wasn't impressive enough, it's also one of the fastest trains in the world. As we accelerated, I got pressed forcefully back into my chair. I watched as the speedometer rose to over 260 miles per hour (there were speedometers in the carriages, I hadn't barged my way into the driver's cabin). A fittingly futuristic way to leave this future-facing city and round off a most enlightening trip.

Departing China, I felt like I'd barely scratched the surface of this nation. And that the rest of its surface might remain largely unexplored for me (I'm not sure the Chinese authorities will grant me a visa after reading this chapter). Fortunately, in the following years, I still learnt much about the country and where it was going through global travel. Oddly, it was often easier to understand where China was heading when I travelled *outside* it.

Backpacking outside China showed me it already wields huge influence across the world. It has been spending staggering sums of money building most of the world's infrastructure, and in Africa in particular.[21] The business

---

*   Trainspotters are cool, right?

model is thus: China grants a loan for the construction of an infrastructure project and then sends its own workers to the country to construct it. This establishes goodwill with the benefactor nation. But there's also scope for these countries to be 'on the hook' to China in the future, in the not too unlikely scenario where the benefactor can't repay its loans. I'd seen this sort of thing, many times, for myself.

In tiny Montenegro, in the Balkans, I drove underneath a gigantic new raised motorway. It cut straight through the country's famous black mountains in tunnels, and crossed deep valleys with huge bridges. For a relatively poor country by European standards, with fewer than a million people, I felt Montenegro perhaps had bitten off more than it could chew with such a huge project. And it had, as it turned out. I squinted, and could see Chinese script adorning the highway's soaring pillars. I learnt that Montenegro had offered *part of its land* as collateral for the Chinese-backed construction project. Given that it has less land than almost any other country on Earth, this was probably an unwise move.[22] As I write this, Montenegro was struggling to pay back the loan used to fund the project. Will it one day have to offer some if its land to China as penance?

Similarly, the Chinese have helped build 35 ports all over the world in the past decade.[23] I remember once driving along Sri Lanka's southern coast, where the Hambantota Port's huge cranes and boats sidled into view. They sat incongruously against the surrounding dilapidated villages, lush palm trees, and tropical vegetation. It seemed unnecessary. Like many of these developments, it turns out the Sri Lankan government couldn't afford it. So the land the port is on has been leased back to the Chinese, making it in effect Chinese territory.[24] Many of the other ports China has built are likely to follow suit.

I've also seen how ambitious China's 'Belt and Road' infrastructure initiative is firsthand, an initiative that hopes to improve trade links across the old Silk Road trading route. I saw Chinese workers and construction sites all over Central Asia. In Tajikistan, Chinese workers had even made it right up into the remote Pamir Mountains, where they were installing electricity pylons. My guide complained, 'We need their help, but the Chinese now own everything in Tajikistan. We're powerless.' This wasn't true colonialism, but it felt a lot like it.

It's the same story in Africa. And nowhere more so than in Addis Ababa, the capital of Ethiopia. When I was there, at times I felt like I was in a Chinese city. I landed in the giant, new Chinese-built airport terminal; I saw commuters riding Chinese trains to work; mainly Chinese cars ran on smooth Chinese-built roads; Chinese cranes dotted the city's growing skyline. I saw the African Union's headquarters – Africa's equivalent to the EU. It was a shiny new building, built by guess who?

In a visit to Algeria in the same year, I saw China-funded projects taking place all over the country. China has built over 250,000 new homes in Algeria since 2000, many of them low-cost social housing that have acted as upgrades for those living in slums. When I drove into Algiers, I was greeted by the minaret of the Great Mosque of Algiers, some 70 storeys tall. It was recently finished, and paid for by you know who.[25] (China, not Voldemort.) Similar scenes crop up across the continent, with Chinese script reminding everyone who to thank for the improvements. Was history repeating itself with a strident China replacing the European countries a century earlier?

The Scramble for Africa (Part Two)

In the biggest colonial expansion of the 19th century, European powers met up and signed the Treaty of Berlin in 1884-85,[26] redrawing and implementing arbitrary borders all over Africa. Take the kink in the border between Tanzania and Kenya. It exists because Queen Victoria wanted to give Mount Kilimanjaro as a 'present' to her grandson Kaiser Wilhelm of Germany, whose country governed the region that became Tanzania. Most of the other borders in Africa are no less indiscriminate, ignoring ingrained tribal, cultural, and geographical divisions. Some of this European nation-building via the tip of a pen – known as the Scramble for Africa – can explain ethnic and political conflict in Africa to this day.

China's now currently engaged in a new scramble of its own in the continent. It's a less violent one, it must be added, than the European effort. And provides vital infrastructure that many African nations badly need. But equally, it could be argued that the way the system works, saddling African countries with unsustainable debt, will cause problems down the line, and means China will have leverage for decades.

While some resent the impact China is having in Africa,

most don't, from what I could see and from the people I spoke to. Most locals appear deeply thankful for the improvements the schemes produce. Africa's population is set to double by 2050, and its economy to boom.[27] If the West and China get into a large dispute in the years ahead, it doesn't take a genius to see which side Africa will be on. With support from much of the world and a huge military to boot, China will be in a very strong position indeed.

You might rightly ask, what's the big deal? It's not as if European powers and the US were much more benevolent world leaders. In fact, China's rise to the top has (at least so far) been one of the most peaceful in history. It hasn't really fought in any wars. 'China's peaceful rise' was an official policy under leader Hu Jintao, who led between 2003 and 2013. He tried to ensure that the country's economic and political rise wouldn't threaten international peace and security.[28] And to all intents and purposes, it's worked. While the West gets very upset about China building artificial islands in the South China Sea for military bases, the US *already has* military bases in every single corner of the globe. Is this really so different?

China expanded its territory to the west by invading Tibet in 1950. And is now eroding democracy in Hong Kong faster than you can say 'repression'. But how different was this to the behaviour of any dominant nation in history? European powers travelled literally thousands of miles from home to bring vast swathes of the world's population under their control. China's risen peacefully so far, who says it wouldn't be a peaceful hegemonic leader?

Further, China's rapid GDP growth has had real-life,

positive tangible impacts. Most (around 75 percent) of global poverty reduction in recent decades has been done by China. Over the past 40 years, nearly 750 million people there have been brought out of poverty as its economy has developed, a feat unprecedented in human history.[29] On this metric alone, one has to stand back and appreciate the real-life positive change which has taken place in this country, even if we don't like how the authorities have got the country to this point.

So Should We be Afraid?

The story, however, isn't all positive. China scares me. A lot. For one thing, you know you're dealing with a 'scary' state when you feel concerned about publishing your opinions about the country anywhere (as I do right now). You know a state has slightly sinister underpinnings when they feel they know 'better' than their populations. That their people don't have the right to say how the country is governed. When travelling, the places I fear the most aren't those which have high levels of crime. They're places like China. Countries where the state has unquestioned, absolute authority. Over everything. And where if they so decided, they could chuck you in a prison cell forever, for merely not agreeing with their warped world view.

Many non-government organisations say China is one of the least free nations on the planet, with non-existent press freedom and a media that's just a mouthpiece for the government.[30] Reporters Without Borders suggest China has more jailed journalists than any other country. China is a unitary one-party socialist republic. Any elections that do take place are between candidates carefully selected by the Chinese Communist Party. There's also an almost religious devotion to the state and to the idea that China reigns supreme.

Freedom House argues that everything children and university students are taught will have been heavily censored to support the state's narrative.[31] In simplified terms, I expect this narrative would read something like, 'How amazingly great is everything about China and how very bad is everything about the West.' And, 'Amazing how scientists were researching coronaviruses in a lab in Wuhan, but this definitely had nothing to do with the pandemic that spread from the city and killed millions across the world.'[32] People are effectively brainwashed from birth. And now with the use of artificial intelligence and machine learning, some argue they'll more easily be able to crack down on dissent.[33] If you live in a country where the media openly criticise its leaders, be grateful, because this is a very good thing. And something you most definitely won't see in China.

China's dislike of democracy is unsettling, and this makes it a much worse place to live in than it needs to be. The Council on Foreign Relations (among many other NGOs) believes that the state has sent more than a million Muslim Uyghurs to re-education camps, condemning them to detention, forced labour, and sometimes even sterilisation.[34] China likes to cosy up to other autocratic regimes to justify their model of government. Its backing of Russia in Ukraine is disgraceful. Its cosy ties with North Korea are all too predictable. Its support of African dictatorships effectively reduces their need to transition to democracy, to the detriment of people all over the continent. It aims to make Taiwan part of Mainland China, even though Taiwan is a thriving democracy. A 2022 poll showed that only six percent of Taiwanese population favoured unification with China.[35]

As in all centralised, totalitarian regimes, when people don't think the 'right' way (in other words the state's way) force is the inevitable reaction. Like when China cracked down on pro-democracy protests in Hong Kong in 2019. Like when Russia invaded Ukraine in 2022. And, probably, when China invades Taiwan to dominate millions against their wishes. Using force to impose the will of the 'red dragon' onto a peaceful, thriving democracy. For all of the US's ills, having a global policeman committed to democratic norms has been a good thing for the world. The spectre of a world run by China should worry us.

Reasons To Be Less Fearful

Despite what I'd seen and learnt about China, a few things gave me reason to hope. To believe that China's ascent won't be straightforward. To begin with, I saw a hell of a lot of old people when I was there. Working in markets, walking the streets. Everywhere, really. Children? Not so much. While this might not seem like a big deal, a realisation hit home when I was in Japan just afterwards.

China's Staggering, Slightly Scary Rise

Japan has one of the oldest populations in the world – the median age is 49 – and its population is set to rapidly decline in the coming decades.[36] Like China now, in the 1980s many people assumed Japan would overtake the US to be the next global superpower. Its economy boomed, it was at the forefront of technological progress. And then, suddenly, things collapsed. Japan has barely grown in decades. And above all, the main reason for this is its greying, shrinking population. And China is about to witness a similar population collapse but on a staggering scale never yet seen in the world.[37]

Thanks to the One Child Policy, which ran between 1980 and 2016, China's population has already started to decline.[38] It shrank for the first time on record in 2022. The authorities have relaxed the policy, but a generation of single-child households sees no reason to have more than one. The UN forecasts that the Chinese population will decline from around 1.4 billion in 2022 to just 800 million by 2100, a fall of over 40 percent.[39] This trend alone will ensure the economy slows and then likely stagnates, given that the increase in the labour force is one of the inputs for long-term GDP growth.

Some would argue that the policy, by reducing future population growth, is one of the greatest environmental acts ever.[40] Others, like this writer, view it as perhaps the most profound impingement on personal liberty the world has ever seen.

This trend will be made worse by the fact that 'old countries' are less dynamic, with older people innovating less and working less than younger populations. Barring some sort of fertility miracle, some commentators now think that the size of the Chinese economy will never catch up to the US. Or that if China overtakes the US, it will be only temporary, with the US (and one day India) catching up with China again from the middle of the century onwards.[41]

China's lack of personal freedoms undermines its appeal as a place to live. This means it won't be able to replace its population with immigrants. All of the world's most skilled workers would still prefer to go to the United States, ensuring that its population and economy continue to thrive. In 100 years, we might see a world split between three or four power blocs. And I'll cheer the fact that democracies like the US and India will still exert massive influence in the world. (Well at least notionally; I'll be decomposing and getting eaten by worms by then.)

The average Chinese person will still have much less wealth per head than their American counterparts for the foreseeable future (China's population is four times bigger). But on average, Chinese people should still continue to get richer in the coming decades. One of the strangest things about being in China is seeing the glitzy new skyscrapers and shopping malls, which were once representative of life in the US, but now exist in a place where freedom is the lowest priority for those in power. My hope is that in the decades to come, its growing middle class ends up demanding a more liberal society, something that's happened many times in history. So there's hope that as China gets richer, it will have to cede ground on personal freedoms and democracy, too.

China's Staggering, Slightly Scary Rise

Travelling both inside and outside of China has shown me it's destined to play a much greater role in the geopolitical sphere for decades to come, for better or for worse (for worse). But we shouldn't panic. Its rise will not be straightforward, and you should discount the US at your peril. In any case, the world's geopolitical drama will always be there.

The Roman and Greek Stoic philosophers argued that history repeats itself. That the same thing happens again and again in endless and (ultimately futile) cycles.[42] And this will be the same going forward, regardless of whether China or the US is notionally in charge of the world. It'll never end. It's a world in constant flux, and this is life on Earth from what I've seen.

The grand stage of history is one of battles, epic conquests, empires, and kings. Of competing ideologies, as in autocratic China and the democratic West. These systems, at least notionally, claim that they'll lead to the maximal happiness of those living within them. But happiness is often a low priority for governments who are focused on self-preservation and geopolitical concerns.

The search for happiness is everyone's mission in life. We all run around, doing various things, often with incredible purpose, to try to reach the point of happiness and satisfaction. But it rarely comes. And when it does, it's often slippery and elusive. For all the staggering progress we've made as a species, my travels have left me thinking we still seem to be stuck in first gear when it comes to happiness. Why is this happening? And what can be done about it?

PART IV

Happiness: Wealth is a
Poor Predictor of Happiness

12

Why Aren't We in the West Happier?

We live in the best societies ever.
So why aren't we happier about it?

We'd been driving for hours. At first down tarmacked roads, allowing us to smoothly slice through the thick and verdant rainforest, with mist clinging to the canopy. We passed the jagged peaks of Mount Kinabalu, a sharp granite pyramid bursting through the green, before heading deeper into the jungle. Heading further from humanity and, in some ways, back into a way of life largely consigned to history in much of the West. Eventually, we pulled over at an unremarkable roadside market. It was filled with people. There was a number of orange and blue tarpaulins, held up by wonky, wooden sticks, with vendors selling their goods beneath them. As we stepped off the bus, the ground beneath us was damp under the grey and humid skies.

Our tour leader told us that this would be our 'last chance' to purchase 'anything' for the next month or so. And while this made me want to stock up, there was only so much roti bread I could eat in one sitting. So, sort of as a novelty, I picked up some durian, a speciality in this part of the world. A spiky green fruit that looked like a cross between a melon and a hedgehog. The stench of it – rotting flesh – is quite something. It made me want to gag. And I wasn't alone. There are signs all over Malaysia that tell you where you can't eat durian, such is its pungency. In this part of the country, in the ancient rainforests of Borneo, the authorities had been laxer with their signage. So I tucked in, to see what all the fuss was about.

'You're not bringing that thing in the Land Cruiser with us. Seriously, eat it now or chuck it,' said Harry, also from London, putting a scarf round his mouth and nose. We were both on gap years between school and university, and in our late teens.

I'd bought a not insubstantial amount of durian. And didn't want to waste it. So I forced the fruit down my throat, grimacing and retching. But it actually tasted okay. At least when I held my nose as I ate. I wasn't sure whether this was something you should have to do to enjoy a meal, though. I tried to convince everyone it was 'nicer than it smells', without much success, and hopped into the Land Cruiser. We set off again. We were travelling in a convoy of three 4x4s, whose open-top boots were laden with the food and supplies we'd need for the next few weeks, contained in big blue barrels. I was in Borneo on a charity expedition with Raleigh International. It's a British youth charity that runs expeditions to less economically developed countries, with the aim of helping local communities. Some like to jokingly call it 'Rah'-leigh, given that both Prince William and Kate Middleton went on an expedition with Raleigh once. And because some, but not all (and most definitely not me), of the attendees come from privileged backgrounds. However, a proportion of attendees come to overcome alcoholism or other issues they may be facing in their lives.

After about five minutes, we turned off the tarmac and were told that this was the last bit of 'proper' road until we reached our destination. 'Do you think we're going to get warned about 'the last' everything on this drive,' I said sarcastically to Harry.

The tracks we were now driving on were bright orange. Deep tyre tracks that had been gouged out of them were filled with muddy puddles, the result of the frequent showers you get in this part of the world. We were in a rainforest, so I should've figured. The pace of progress became glacial. We slipped, and then jerked forwards. The wheels spinning and struggling to grip. Every half hour or so, one of the Land Cruisers would get stuck. We'd all get out to help push. Which essentially meant getting mud flung over you without making much of an impact on a two-ton vehicle. We'd get in, drive for a depressingly small amount of time, and repeat this process. And this process, as it turned out, lasted nearly eight hours. Eight hours to travel around 60 miles off road.

On either side of the track, the rainforests that we'd enjoyed for the first part of our trip were notably absent. Instead, we passed mile after mile of palm oil plantations, where the beautiful and overwhelming chaos of the jungle had been replaced by the regimented sight of thousands of palm trees stretching into the distance. In perfect rows, so clearly of human doing. Nature in some ways, but distinctly not so in others.

After what seemed like an eternity of bumping and sliding, we reached the top of a large hill. We climbed out of the 4x4 (again) and were greeted with quite a sight. There was perhaps a mile or two of palm oil plantations, which then gave way to rainforest. Rolling hills covered in tall trees in hundreds of shades of green, heading out onto the horizon as far as my eyes could see, repeating endlessly into the mist. The noises of the rainforest hummed in the background.

The skies here were filled with menacing clouds, some ready to burst by the looks of things. Below us, almost in a punch bowl, was a village – really just a collection of small and ramshackle buildings. They were mainly wooden structures, slightly uneven, and were raised up on stilts. They had rusting corrugated roofs, the rust appearing from this distance as pleasantly pink hues. There was an open, rectangular patch of grass in the middle of the village, which looked like it was being used as a football pitch. A couple of water towers, with big black plastic barrels sitting on top of metal stilts. And then the dense rainforest, almost engulfing the village from all sides. This was Tampa Sak. My home for the next six weeks.

A Warm Welcome

We rumbled down the final bit of track and emerged into the clearing where the village lay. Seemingly the entire village was there to greet us. Around 100 people. Of them, probably 40 were children, who were predictably the ones who greeted us most enthusiastically. Running up to our vehicles and screaming, 'Hello! You're Welcome!' while we were still moving in some cases. Fortunately, nobody was hurt.

The children all wore a colourful array of clothes, with flip-flops or just bare feet. There were lots of football shirts. Splashes of orange, and green, and blue, bright against the white skies and green canopy. Their clothes were often muddy and shabby, with slightly frayed edges. They jumped and screamed as we disembarked, with many wanting to shake our hands. It was a lovely way to be welcomed into their community.

Our local Malay guide was called Hanri. He was a fairly wiry man, clean-shaven, with thick, black hair tied up into a neat bun. He looked much younger than his 50 years. He was delighted to show us his village, and like many of the local Tampa Sakers, he had large smile lines at the edge of his kind eyes. As enthusiastically as the children, Hanri proceeded to introduce us, one by one, to literally every person in the village. He made sure to say each name several times, optimistically thinking this would help us remember them in the first instance (by the end of the stay, we probably weren't far off).

A church was the focal point of the village. It was a Catholic one (remember that chapter on religion you just read?). Clearly, missionaries had managed to make it hundreds of miles into the rainforests of Borneo, as they had in so many other places. The building was covered in light blue wooden panels. It had a porch and a small steeple. Inside, food had been laid out on large tables, on patterned plastic covers. Rice, banana, roti, *mee goreng mamak* (Malaysian-style fried noodles), and yes, durian. I needn't have bothered earlier. Also rice wine, served in small bamboo cups, which we sadly weren't able to indulge in as part of the rules of our expedition – for safety, and also as we had some recovering addicts in our group.

Before we ate, Hanri asked for us to be seated. There were about ten of us, mainly from the UK, Ireland, the Netherlands, and Canada. What seemed like a local rock band took to the floor, and everyone clapped wholeheartedly. The band used a drum kit, which had a ruptured kickdrum, making it sound more like someone was rhythmically slapping a loose plastic sheet than a kickdrum. They'd fired up the diesel generator (the only form of electricity here), so that the bass guitar amp would work. It did, but the speaker fizzed and rattled as the bass was played. And then there was a female singer, who also played a rickety old piano. They didn't have the best instruments, but they did a decent job. All of the local villagers started singing along to the upbeat anthem, which sounded a bit like a rockier form of gospel. Smiling faces and gestures from the villagers suggested that we should join in with the singing too, notwithstanding our inability to speak Malay or the fact that we'd never heard this song before.

The performance concluded. Most everyone cheered and laughed, particularly the children. We were then instructed to fill our plates – before anyone else's – and to tuck in, which we did with gusto. Hanri sat down next to me, and we had a chance to speak.

'What a welcome. Thanks so much for showing us your village. Everyone seems so friendly here,' I said earnestly.

'That's no problem. Everyone here wants to make you feel at home. We have a strong bond, a strong community here, and want to share it with you,' he replied, gesturing around the room to his friends and family.

'That's very kind. And thanks for the food too, it's delicious.' My eyes darted around the room for a moment or two. Almost my entire visual field was filled with happy faces. Laughing, energetic children. Adults belly laughing and telling jokes.

'It seems like a really happy community you have here. Do you enjoy living here?' I asked.

Hanri said, 'Oh yes, very much. We're very happy here, very content. We don't have much. But we have each other, and the support of our families and the community.' He paused for a second and looked thoughtful. 'I tried to live in Kuala Lumpur when I became an adult. It was too busy, and I was lonely, even though there were millions of people around me. I came back after only a month, like many do in this village. The experience showed me that Tampa Sak will always be my home, it's always where I'll be happiest. And I think many others agree with me too,' he said, with his impressive grasp of English.

'Well I can see that it does seem that way,' I concluded, as I looked around the room again and smiled. Hanri raised a bamboo cup of rice wine for me to cheers, which again I had to decline, despite his protestations.

In the next few days, we got acquainted with life in the village. It was simple living; services were basic. There was no running water or electricity. Most villagers were subsistence farmers, or worked on nearby palm oil plantations. Almost no houses had beds. Families slept on the floor together, often practically on top of each other. I'd presumed that the smiles we saw on the first night might have just been something to do with it being a party atmosphere. But this didn't appear to be the case. I'd never been *anywhere* where people laughed and smiled so much. Almost every interaction was a chance to play practical jokes or laugh. Even children's laughs and shrieks here seemed louder than at home, a sign of the freedom they enjoyed in the village. They had almost complete run of the place. Playing as they pleased, without even a hint of parental regulation from about the age of three upwards.

I was only 19 at the time. I'd naively expected this village to be a sad place. Indeed, that's why I assumed we'd been sent here to help. But my early impressions completely confounded my assumptions. Tampa Sak might well have been the happiest place I'd ever been.

A Trip to the Actual Happiest Places on Earth?

A decade later, I still found myself on the road often. Or in this case, a bridge. As I gazed out the train window, I knew I didn't want to be anywhere else. The sun was shining. The sea was a rich shade of blue, and I was gliding high above it. The vast Øresund Strait stretched out around me. I was crossing one of the longest bridges on Earth, connecting Sweden to Denmark.

I love travelling by train. For me, it captures much of what's so enthralling about travel, watching strange and unfamiliar lands gliding past you. As is often the case when I travel, my senses felt sharper. Colours were slightly brighter, and hours ticked by more slowly. People who like trains are not famous for being 'cool', but as I reached the shores of Denmark, I didn't care. I was almost always happy riding on scenic trains. And for that matter, most happy when travelling.

Arriving in the charming Danish capital of Copenhagen, with its beautiful architecture and people, I was buoyant. Picturesque spires loomed over the skyline, with chocolate-box style houses sitting next to pretty little canals. Copenhagen was immaculate. Almost everyone cycled rather than drove, and there is something about Nordic design which makes cities such as Copenhagen just 'work'. According to most measures, I was now in one of the happiest countries on Earth. 'Surely it'd be hard *not* to be happy living in a place like this,' I thought.

After dropping my bags at a hostel, I went to a bar in Christiania, the hipster part of town. It's where people like me pretend to be 'alternative' while surrounded by others who dress the same and have almost identical views on everything. I started gushing about how much I loved Denmark and Copenhagen to anyone who'd listen. To my surprise, none of the Danes agreed. All I got was shrugged shoulders, shakes of the head, and then lengthy rants about all the terrible things about the country, its politics, and its people.

The Travelling Ape

'You know this is one of the best places in the world, right? According to almost all human development indexes and alike. Doesn't that count for something?' Evidently not. The Danes didn't seem happy about much from what I could see. And while it would have been easy for me to dismiss this standoffishness as a 'Danish thing' – the Danes tend not to mince their words and can have a slightly dour demeanour – it's a trend I'd seen in all of the allegedly happiest societies on Earth. In the years leading up to my Denmark trip, I'd travelled for leisure and work to every country in Western Europe. From what I'd seen and from the hundreds of conversations I'd had with locals, people didn't seem particularly happy, or at least as happy as I'd expected them to be. And certainly not compared to the villagers of Tampa Sak.

My experience in Copenhagen and other Western countries had got me thinking about the strange and elusive concept of happiness. In my travels to almost everywhere, I'd seen the full range of human emotions in the full range of human societies. And what struck me was that wealth seemed to be a poor predictor of human happiness. In some of the poorer places I'd been, people smiled and laughed more. And certainly seemed happier with their lot. Could it be true that the richest countries in the world aren't as happy as one might expect? And if not, why?

The Confusing Story of Happiness in the Rich World

My experiences travelling in the West showed me we probably aren't as happy as we could or should be. Especially

Why Aren't We in the West Happier?

when you consider the minor advantage of growing up in the wealthiest and most economically developed societies in human history. Perhaps our levels of happiness simply haven't kept pace with the medical, technological, and economic quantum leaps we've experienced in recent centuries.

I'm not being naive enough to suggest that economic security doesn't play an import role in one's happiness. Indeed, the people I'd seen in Copenhagen, despite outward grumpiness, were most likely much happier than the average person living in conflict and poverty-ridden places. But I've seen so much joy in places I'd presumed would be comparatively more joyless. From kids giggling and playing rough in the remote villages of Laos and the happy laughter of adults and children in the slums of Mumbai, to the simple joy of communal singing in the villages of Botswana, I've seen firsthand how wealth might not be the best predictor we have of happiness.

Was it true that the mopey hipsters I'd seen in Denmark (and glum Westerners generally) weren't happy? Well to begin with, it's important to note that happiness – an abstract concept – is notoriously hard to measure. Personally, accosting every passer-by I saw to ask, 'Are you happy?' didn't really seem like a realistic prospect on my travels. So I had to make do with observing things from afar, in a completely normal and non-creepy way. And also relying on statistics. But the problem is, statistics about happiness and mental health are patchy, as they often rely on people self-assessing themselves. But some studies suggest that just over 10 percent of the global population suffers from some form of mental health issue,[1] with around 300 million suffering from anxiety and 160 million from depression.[2]

Tellingly, most global happiness indices still put the world's richest countries near the top. The United Nation's 2022 *World Happiness Report* has Finland, Denmark, and Iceland making up the top three.[3] On the surface, this seemed to make sense. Each country has friendly, educated people, and fantastic public services. I was loving my experience so far in Denmark, had thoroughly enjoyed several trips to beautiful Iceland, and Finland also seemed like a great society (but also a slightly odd place – see below). But truth be told, the happiness rankings didn't match up with how happy people actually *seemed* in my visits there.

A sidebar on Finland. I don't want to say that some Finns are weird, per se, so I'll say they are unique. Some friends and I went to a traditional sauna in Helsinki. Fine. What seemed unusual, though, was that most men spent almost no time in the sauna. They instead lounged around naked in the changing rooms, doing things like playing chess, flossing themselves with towels, and wearing special sauna hats that looked like they should be worn by elves (if you can wear a hat, why not wear trunks?).

The dubious joys of acting strangely in saunas aside, there wasn't much to suggest Finns were in any way happier than people I'd seen elsewhere in the world. Indeed, people in Finland didn't smile much. They looked reserved, sombre even. They were polite, but not overly friendly. I saw many of them drinking, but not in a particularly 'fun' way (like people alone in bars slowly sipping spirits and not talking to anyone). Fun-free Finland has been topping the *World Happiness Report* for the past five years. Huh?

Happiness rankings are based on self-reported surveys, so they can't easily be compared across cultures, as well as various economic indicators (such as income and inequality).[4] In effect, these rankings presume wealth equals more happiness. But this link isn't always clear. A study done in the slums of Kolkata, for example, showed that levels of life satisfaction here were higher than for those of the average American.[5] Another study found that 16 percent of Americans believed their lives to contain more suffering than happiness, compared to only 11 percent who lived in much poorer India.[6] Maybe the *World Happiness Report* methodology was too crude? Maybe wealth and economic circumstance are less important than we think?

I travelled through all the Central American countries and Mexico a couple of years after visiting Denmark and Finland. I started in Panama, working my way up through Costa Rica, Honduras, El Salvador, Nicaragua, Guatemala, and Mexico. When most people think of these countries, two things often spring to mind: ancient, awe-inspiring Maya and Aztec temples; and the propensity of people to kill each other. I was a touch nervous visiting, as these countries had some of the highest murder rates in the world.

Given the levels of violence in these places, I thought there'd be little time for people to be happy. And indeed, these countries had mixed results in the *World*

Happiness Report.* But from my experiences, people were overwhelmingly friendly and appeared happy. They spent a lot of time with family and friends, and enjoyed a slower pace of life. The weather was beautiful, as was the scenery. Many people here had low incomes, but appeared relatively happy. Interestingly, one study found that Nicaragua, Costa Rica, Honduras, Guatemala, and Mexico were all ranked in the top 10 'smiliest countries' on Earth.[7] Could ranking smiles be a better way to measure happiness?

Wealth Can't Protect You from Despair

Trips like this had shown me that wealth doesn't guarantee happiness, or at least protect against the absence of despair. A 2010 American study suggested that a lack of money can indeed cause some unhappiness.[8] At least in the USA, the lower a person's income falls below US$75,000, the unhappier they feel on average. However, no matter how much people make *above* that US$75,000 per year figure, it made no difference to their happiness. In other countries, this earning benchmark would likely be much lower depending on their state of economic development.

American Psychologist Abraham Maslow's legendary hierarchy of needs suggests that a person will struggle to be fulfilled unless they have their basic physiological and safety needs met first,[9] which usually requires a minimum

---

* Costa Rica came in 23rd place, Guatemala in 39th, Mexico in 46th, Nicaragua in 45th, El Salvador in 49th, and Honduras in 55th.

level of income. But above this minimum level, having more income is unlikely to improve your belongingness and love, esteem, and self-actualisation needs. So above a certain minimum point, being wealthy won't protect you from being unhappy.

Could this explain what's happening in the richest countries on Earth? Where some of the allegedly happiest countries in the world also have high suicide rates? In terms of suicides per capita, Finland ranked 59th, Denmark 47th, and Iceland 75th out of 183 assessed countries.[10] While data of recorded suicides in low-income countries is patchier, it seems odd that suicides would be as high in such happy countries. And indeed, these statistics perhaps cohered more closely with the levels of happiness I'd seen on my trips in the Nordics. I tend to visit these places in summer, when the days are long and everyone's out worshipping the sun. God knows how much glummer everyone would be when it's dark all day.

European citizens enjoy better healthcare, education, and social security than almost anywhere else. Life circumstances and freedoms afforded to most Europeans simply aren't available to the rest of the world's billions, aside from those living in North America, Australia, and New Zealand. However, the suicide rate in Europe (10.5 per 100,000 in 2019) is much *higher than the global average* (9.0), despite it being one of the richest regions on Earth.[11] British philosopher Alain de Botton says simply, 'Suicide rates climb exponentially once societies become modern.'[12]

Other metrics further implied mental health issues could be actually *worse* in richer, Western countries. One respected study implied that the countries most affected by mental health issues in 2017 were Greenland, Iran, Australia, the US, New Zealand, the Netherlands, France, Morocco, Sweden, and Portugal.[13] Aside from finding the erroneous inclusion of Greenland as a country grating (it is part of Denmark), I was struck by how many amazing places were near the top of this table of mental misery. It didn't paint a picture of a Western victory over happiness. Clearly, no amount of access to good education, healthcare, and the like in the external world can necessarily overcome internal mental turmoil, the causes of which are multifaceted and nuanced. And this is hard to notice when the thing you're trying to measure (happiness) is silently locked away in the skulls of strangers.

My Experiences with Perpetual Dissatisfaction

I'm lucky, as I also had one other tool at my disposal. I've also had access to the mind of a Western person to examine: my own. I've got firsthand experience of the Western happiness conundrum, something that was only partly solved by regular travel. I've lived a privileged life. I was born in the UK, a liberal democracy. I had a loving and caring family growing up. I did well in the classroom and never really had a problem making friends. I had lots of interests outside the academic spheres, like playing sport, and every opportunity to explore them. I enjoyed writing lists about the good things in my life (and still do, clearly). My childhood was as good as I could have hoped. As an adult, I've travelled a lot, something I and most people would say brings happiness. So you might be questioning how I can rightly moan about my life in any way.

But, like everyone, I've endured difficult times. When I was 21, I suffered my first real setbacks in life. My parents' marriage unexpectedly came to an end, my girlfriend of seven years ended our relationship, my grandfather passed away, and so too did our beloved family dog. These 'traumas' pale into insignificance when compared to what some other people have had to deal with in their lives. And yet, I wasn't equipped to handle them. They completely floored me.

I suffered from racing thoughts, constant and at times severe anxiety, and insomnia. I for the first time finally understood what it meant to have poor mental health. I endured a few years where I felt confused, hurt, and unhappy. I tried to be rational. '*My* problems, compared to others in the world, are embarrassingly small. Snap out of it.' Travelling had helped by showing me how lucky I was to live in the West. And yet, forcing myself to consider my lucky position in the world didn't seem to do the trick.

As the years rolled on, I came to terms with the setbacks. I gradually began to process what had happened, and life resumed its upward trajectory. I started enjoying things a bit more again. I felt more positive. And you, the reader, were spared any further paragraphs of what is undoubtedly one of the more underwhelming sob stories you've read in print. (I don't expect you to feel sorry for me, given that you're reading a book about my nice life spent travelling.)

Or were you? When things improved again, strangely,

this is when I realised something *really was wrong*. At age 25, life was going well (true to form, I'm about to list good things about my life again). I lived in a lovely apartment in London with two of my best friends. I had the financial means to do most things I wanted, including to travel. I loved my job. At age 26, I was promoted to Head of the Europe team, focusing on assessing political and economic risk across the continent.

I'd been told – or perhaps implicitly believed – that career success would result in me getting a promotion in the happiness stakes too. But it didn't. My promotion made me more stressed and reduced the amount of free time I had. It didn't give me the perpetual feeling of having 'made it' or being an 'important person' as much as I'd imagined. On a day-to-day basis, I remained constantly, ever so slightly dissatisfied. Low-level anxiety was almost always there. Was this a quarter-life crisis?* I worried – almost solely about myself – continually. It didn't matter whether there were any actual problems in my life, I'd always find something that concerned me. My 'worry of the day'. Most of them too mundane for words, and certainly too boring to repeat here. Satisfaction and happiness were always tantalisingly just out of reach, somewhere in the future.

Often, a feeling of true fulfilment would only come with drinking and partying on weekends. But it would be gone by Monday morning. I used to like drinking (as

---

★   Many of my friends have described having some form of quarter-life crisis as they approached 30. I didn't have the heart to tell them they were unlikely to live to 120.

most do) because it switched off my thoughts and helped me relax. In retrospect, I don't think excessive drinking screams, 'I'm really happy.' Of the top 20 hardest drinking countries globally, 17 are in Europe.[14]

In Europe, we strangely treat drinking like it's a badge of honour. It's embedded in almost every Western culture. Indeed, Ireland's entire national identity is based upon how much poison they like to put in their bodies. In Dublin, drinking Guinness is an act as patriotic as saluting the flag (which no one does, because they're too busy drinking Guinness). I remember being in Dingle, on the west coast of Ireland. It's a quaint town seemingly with more pubs than people. We went out on a Monday. Even then, each pub was packed, Guinness everywhere, as were jolly Irish people singing Irish songs. It was like an Irish Disneyland. At the urinals, a man with his head slumped in his hands looked over at me. 'Whaaaat day ish it!?' he slurred. I told him, and he just said, 'Oh Christ.'

It was great fun. The Irish are great drunks. But this doesn't dial down the truth about our love for the drug, particularly in the supposedly happiest parts of the world that use it the most. That alcohol is so popular reflects our desire to change how we feel, to cope with social anxiety. And how much we all yearn to dial down the inane chatter of that voice in our heads. The voice in my head always gets louder and more negative the morning after drinking. Realising this in the past few years, I've basically quit drinking. I now only drink small amounts on rare occasions. I feel much better for it.

Why was I not happier? Why couldn't I accept my good fortune and be happy because of it? What even *is* happiness? I wasn't unhappy, but I rarely felt truly satisfied (probably because I spent so much of my life asking myself questions). I had to find answers.

In the following years, travelling helped me unearth some of the tools that have ultimately allowed me to become a much happier person, and I'll outline some of these to you in the final chapter of this book. But being happy required huge sacrifice, effort, and focus. This seemed strange, given all the advantages I'd had in my life. Could this, in part, be due to the way we're approaching happiness in the West? Are we looking for happiness in all the wrong places?

The real issue, then, is why our happiness hasn't improved alongside staggering economic, societal, technological, and informational progress. My take is that the Western approach to happiness is flawed.[15] Travelling has helped me locate two main factors which explain why we in the West aren't as happy as we should be. And this is causing us much (needless) suffering.

1) We've Lost the Value of Community

Author Jared Diamond has split his life between the US and Papua New Guinea, getting to know people in the latter who live much like our ancestral hunter-gatherers (and in less grim surroundings than in the capital, Port Moresby, I may add). In his epic telling of human history, *Guns, Germs, and Steel*, he puts forward the interesting proposition that the 'blessings of civilisation are mixed'.[16] While we in the West enjoy better healthcare, longer lives, and many other advantages, he says, Westerners have much less social support from friends and extended families. From my travels, I'd agree with him.

People in the developing world tend to have more friends and family whom they spend much more time with. I remember visiting Uganda and Mozambique, where it was not uncommon for people to have well over five siblings, and even 10, in some instances.[17] And from what I could see, these family units lived and stayed together, even as the children became adults. Research highlights the importance of such close relationships for happiness. The *Harvard Study of Adult Development* found close relationships to be the most important factor in keeping people happy throughout their lives. Having close connections with others were better predictors of long and happy lives than IQ, social class, or even genes. Director of the study, Robert Waldinger, said that 'taking care of your body is important, but tending to your relationships is a form of self-care too.'[18]

My own travels corroborate the results of the study. Being with people increased the happiness and resilience of people in the poorer parts of the world. And this was made evidently clear to me in Tampa Sak. After acclimatising for a day or two after our arrival, we got to work. Ostensibly, we were there to help build a kindergarten. However, none of us actually had many building skills.* So the reality

---

★   Some newspapers (and people) describe charity expeditions like this as a 'New form of Western colonialism'. But equally, I'm sure these same people would criticise you for not doing anything to help others. So I felt it was better for me to do something than nothing at all.

was we'd be mainly used for manpower, in the absence of any machines or trucks to do the work. Hanri met us on our first morning of work, and introduced us to three local villagers, who'd be helping us with the build. Like Hanri, they wore thin shorts and T-shirts. Two were wearing flip-flops, one no shoes at all. We stood at an empty plot of land. It was quite steep and overgrown, filled with tall grass and horrible spiders (probably).

'See those wooden beams down there,' said Hanri, pointing at what must have been a hundred chunks of wood around half a mile away, down a gently inclining path. 'We need to get them up here. So that will be the job for the next few days.' And so it was.

It took around three or four of us to lift each beam. And then around 20 sweltering, uncomfortable minutes to get that beam to the building site. It was a laborious process. Spirits were high for the first day or so – after all, it was still a novelty – but after around a week of this, it started to become challenging. I found myself internally moaning. Some days, Hanri and his pals would turn up late or wouldn't turn up at all. I found it frustrating and questioned why they didn't want to get the structure up as fast as possible (again, in my head).

But Hanri and his friends weren't in a rush. They seemed to be enjoying the process. Taking their time. 'There's no rush' almost became his catchphrase. He explained that currency didn't really exist in Tampa Sak. Instead, the society functioned on a system of favours: *If I help you build your house, you can help me when I need to fix mine.* They were helping build the kindergarten now.

And after this, they'd move on to another project, perhaps someone's house. They couldn't understand why we were so obsessed with deadlines, progress, and punctuality. After all, everyone would be helped, eventually.

Some days, after work, we'd go for tea together. Hanri took us back to his house, a small structure on stilts, which was a touch dark inside. There were large gaps in the floorboards, and the whole thing creaked as we piled in. Waiting for us were Hanri's wife and four kids. All waving and saying 'Hallo!' as we entered. Also there, Hanri gestured towards them, his mother and father. From what I could see in Tampa Sak, families lived together, with children, parents, and grandparents all sharing a home. The villagers looked after their elderly, as they do in much of the developing world. This is something that I'd also noticed on trips to China and India.[19] As countries get richer, so does the belief that people don't need to look after the elderly directly.[20] By contrast, in Tampa Sak, there were always people around to spend time with. Everyone knew each other. The whole village was like one big family.

In direct comparison to this, we in the West are living increasingly isolated lives. I've seen for myself how we spend less and less time with other people. Across Europe, people often live in small apartments, in big cities where they know only a handful of people. In the United States, a country built for cars, vast distances often separate people from friends and family.

Whenever I've been in the States, it's always struck me how few people even share a car. The 'carpool' lanes on motorways are always empty, apart from the occasional person with a blow-up doll in the passenger seat. Americans often endure long, lonely commutes. And then they drive huge distances to the part of the city where they live, with mile upon mile of suburbia separating them from everyone else they know. The rise in hybrid working means fewer Americans say that they have friends at work.[21] Overall, the percentage of Americans who say they have zero friends has risen from 3 percent in 1990 to 12 percent in 2021.[22]

We have an obsession with the individual at the expense of group bonds and this might be denting our happiness. Studies show Westerners and non-Westerners see the world differently. One showed that while Americans focus on central figures in photographs, Chinese people tend to pay more attention to background figures and the picture as a whole.[23] Western philosophers emphasise freedom and independence, whereas Eastern traditions like Taoism tend to focus on unity.

In Asia, some argue the concept of happiness itself is biased towards a Western ideal, and that studying the happiness of the collective should also be considered.[24] There's no word for 'individualism' in Chinese. The closest word is 'selfishness'. This doesn't mean people in China are happier than their Western counterparts (indeed, the CCP are doing their best to make people's lives as rigid and dull as possible). But this focus on community and the collective could make them more resilient when times get tough. Historian Yuval Noah Harari argues that material conditions only explain part of happiness. That modern societies suffer greatly from alienation and meaninglessness in a way our ancestors did not, given their connection with nature, community, and their religions.[25]

Close bonds with other humans are one of the central keys to human happiness. Evolutionary and social psychologists say that our mental growth began with hunting and living in communal camps. A premium was placed on personal relationships and cooperation among members in a hunter-gatherer tribe.[26] To this day, our fear of social rejection highlights how deeply we value connection and groups. We get nervous before speeches and care so deeply about what others think of us. Why? Because being socially rejected from our hunter-gatherer group would've been a death sentence. Perhaps this explains why so many social interactions are tinged with an undercurrent of nervousness and insecurity.

We evolved to live in wandering hunter-gatherer tribes of up to 100 or so people – which, interestingly, was roughly how many people lived in Tampa Sak, even if they no longer roamed as our ancestors did. Our early ancestors likely spent thousands of generations huddling together in caves.[27] They shared every aspect of their lives. Put simply, the concept of personal space or solitude didn't exist. We've spent 99 percent of our history constantly surrounded by lots of other humans.

Compare this to today. The average global household size is four.[28] This rises to around eight in Africa. In Europe, if I now see a family with more than four children, I presume there've been some slip-ups on the contraception front. On average, two- or one-child families appear to be the norm in the West, and this is supported by data.

Average sizes are just 2.4 in Europe and 2.6 in the US. This is a rather bleak situation when you compare it to the potentially huge network of caregivers and playmates children would have had in prehistory. Psychological studies have shown a link between child-rearing practices common in hunter-gatherer societies and better mental health, greater empathy, and higher intelligence in children.[29] And these are the sort of practices we get further away from with every passing generation in the West.

The number of people living alone is exploding in the West as well. This partly reflects the fact that lots of people are getting divorced. People are also living longer, and outliving their partners. In the US, for example, the proportion of people living alone has *doubled* from around 13 percent in 1960 to 28 percent in 2018.[30] And that's just in one generation. Just wait until the year 2060, when we'll all live alone, plugged into virtual reality sets, having a terrible, or utterly sensational, time, depending on how much you like video games.

In Northern European countries – the really advanced societies – almost 40 percent of people now live alone. The figure is less than 1 percent in low-income Asian countries.[31] As our societies advance, we choose to be alone more often. Perhaps those high Nordic suicide rates start to make a bit more sense against this backdrop. Norway's a great example. It's one of the wealthiest and most developed countries in the world, and came fifth in the *World Happiness Report*. I remember being in a bar in Oslo, chatting to a friendly Norwegian chap. He was around 33, lived alone, said all his friends lived alone, and he wouldn't want it any other way. But is this really making them happy?

'You're certainly free to be alone, but loneliness is a killer,' I thought. I felt it would have been morose to tell him this in real life. We get stressed when we're lonely. Loneliness would've been a precursor to death in hunter-gatherer times. A lack of social connections can damage your health, sparking inflammation and changes in the immune system.[32] Indeed, people who sleep with a partner get around 10 percent more rapid eye movement (REM) sleep – which helps with memory consolidation and emotional regulation – than those who sleep alone.[33] It's no wonder, then, that lonely people have a 50 percent greater chance of early death compared to those who aren't lonely.[34] For all our incredible advances in the West, we might just be the loneliest people who've ever lived.

Were he alive today, Greek philosopher Epicurus would have much to say about modern Western individualism. He stated that happiness was intrinsically linked to friendships and close bonds with others.[35] He believed in his theory so much that he chose to live on a plot of rural land in Greece with his friends over 2,000 years ago. It was probably the world's first commune.

In my journeys to all the world's Western countries, I've found it striking how far we're moving away from a group-minded model of living. Increasingly, and particularly among the young, people take pride in their independence. They don't need anyone, they don't want anyone, and they're proud as hell about it. They're sceptical about marriage. But I just wonder, are we in the West storing up unhappiness for later life? More disconnection from others. More isolation. And ultimately, more loneliness, lies on our collective horizons.

We spent another few days lugging wooden beams up the hill in Tampa Sak, all the while embedding ourselves further in village life. To do this, we had to live in a more stripped-back manner than we were used to at home. We had to dig a hole in the ground that would be our toilet for the next month. We'd collect muddy water from the local river, drop some chlorine tablets into it, and then drink it (it tasted like a mix of swimming pool water and earth). We slept in damp hammocks tied between trees, with a seemingly pointless tarpaulin above our heads. Ostensibly it was supposed to keep the rain off us, but didn't seem to help much. We didn't shower, and wore the same clothes every day. We smelled, I'm sure. But as we all did, it didn't matter.

Despite these inconveniences, I was having the time of my life. By stripping away some of the modern luxuries we were so used to, we understood what it was like to live in this part of the world, and to focus more on the little things. Little things like showing some small children how much stronger and better at football I was than them. Every day, at lunchtime, Harry, a few others, and I would head to the rectangle of damp open grass in the centre of the village, which doubled as the football pitch. It was muddy, and completely uneven. Dotted with massive 'ankle-breaker' potholes, as I liked to call them.

The kids didn't seem to mind. They would meet us there each day. To them, that little sphere filled with air I was holding was literally priceless.* The children ranged in age from around four to early teens. None could take their eyes off the football. Each day, I'd kick it into the eagerly waiting young crowd and wait for an eruption of joy as it bounced in among them. The kids cheered with sheer happiness, utter delight. A sort of full contact and fairly violent game of 'football' usually followed. Laughs and screams were still audible among the scuffles, which allayed my fears that I was essentially encouraging them to fight each other.

These kids were a hardy bunch. Keen to show them my (self-perceived) footballing prowess, I hoofed the ball as hard as I could into the distance. Only for a toddler to stumble (in a way that only toddlers can) into the oncoming path of the ball. The force of it lifted him clean off his feet, into an accidental backflip.** No tears, just laughter. Rough and tumble play in Tampa Sak was the norm.

The joy that something as simple as a football game could bring to people in the village got me thinking. I chatted to Harry as we walked back from another match, dripping with sweat and panting after what felt like fairly vigorous exercise.

'Christ that was so much fun, wasn't it? Those kids are absolutely nuts. They have so much energy!' I said, breathing heavily as we made our way up the gentle incline to our accommodation (aka the nearby trees).

'Yeah, they're such a great bunch. I hope that toddler

---

*   Travelling with a football is always a wise move.
**   Again, I am keen to stress that I can kick a football *really* hard.

you steamrollered is okay, though,' Harry said, with a slightly concerned look on his face.

'Yeah, I think he's fine. I mean, he didn't even cry, he just laughed it off. It seems so different to home. If I'd lobbed a football into a crowd of children in England, I'd probably face the ire of their parents – both for endangering their precious little children and also, probably, for being an adult who takes any interest in a child other than their own. Also, the football wouldn't have had anywhere near the same effect on those kids. A spoilt Western child* might have needed a PlayStation to engender the same levels of joy and happiness.'

'That's true, but also PlayStations are pretty great,' Harry added, before we sat down to enjoy some crackers and Spam. And enjoy it we did, amazingly. When stripped of access to the wide selection of foods we normally enjoyed, and the number of calories we normally consumed, even the simplest foods could taste quite, quite wonderful. The crumbling biscuit juxtaposed with the soggy meat was genuinely enjoyable. Something that seems impossible for me to believe as I write this.

In between crunching away, crumbs spilling all over my lap, we continued our discussion.

'If happiness is a feeling in the body, a collection of sensations that feel pleasurable, maybe the joy felt by children playing football here or a PlayStation in Monaco is, neurologically speaking, exactly the same. They'll feel

---

* Not unlike me, or you, if you have the leisure time to simply read a book.

similar sensations of happiness, regardless of the financial cost involved in generating the joy?' I said, not altogether confidently, wary of veering into the realm of pop-psychology, which I most definitely was.

'Perhaps,' Harry replied, 'the threshold for joy is lower here because people don't expect as much as we do. Their joy costs less than ours. And this makes happiness and resilience more common than you might think?'

We were possibly being naive. Trying to make ourselves feel better about global inequality, and the fact that we won big in the life lottery. But we might have had a point. I've learnt since that children's brains are more neuroplastic than adult ones. A child's ability to adapt and thrive in almost any environment (within reason) reflects the ability of neural networks in the brain to be shaped by world experience.[36] In other words, children's malleable brains make them well positioned to adapt and thrive in most situations they were born into, so long as they're loved. So if a child's brain doesn't *come to expect* the luxuries children in the West are used to, it in effect adapts to deriving similar levels of joy from less.

A couple of days later, Hanri wanted to take us for a trek through the nearby rainforest for a couple of weeks. We filled our large, 50-litre backpacks. Those ones with millions of pointless clips, zips, and straps. As well as rain macs, sleeping bags, tarpaulins, and mess tins. A few books. A head torch. Our iPods (it was 2008), a towel, and a travel pillow. A few more bits and bobs. Everything we could possibly need for a jungle excursion.

When we met in the centre of the village to begin the

trek, Hanri looked at us and started chuckling. 'Are you all planning on moving house?' he remarked. He was wearing thin black shorts and a discoloured vest, his long black hair tied tightly in a bun. He had a rolled-up hammock tied to his back with a piece string, and a *parang* (a Malaysian knife). And that was it.

'Um, Hanri, are you not going to bring *anything* with you?' I joked.

He smiled, accentuating the laughter lines around his eyes. 'I have everything I need. I have some clothes to wear. And I have my credit card.'

'Huh. Your credit card?' I asked.

'Yes. My credit card gives me access to everything I need in the rainforest. Food and shelter. That's it. The best thing about my credit card, though, is that everything's free, and comes from the rainforest.'

There were about six of us from the expedition going on the trek, Harry and I included. We stood there, looking both perplexed and embarrassingly overprepared for this walk. Hanri pulled out his *parang*.

'See? My credit card,' he said, flicking it around with ease. 'This is all I need.'

I was impressed. But at the same time, still didn't really understand how he'd be able to be live comfortably on our trek. Indeed, in the coming days, I found it challenging even with everything I'd brought with me. My 'home' was a damp and stinky hammock that I had to construct every day between two trees. There were times when we were eating fewer than 1,250 calories per day, after trekking for eight hours.

Why Aren't We in the West Happier?

No electricity, no running water, no toilets. It rained constantly. While I'd been well aware I was going to spend months in a rainforest before I'd left the UK, I hadn't fully realised how mentally draining rain could be. It was so wet, in fact, that our clothes never dried and most of us got trench foot. I'd often wake up covered in blood, dramatically thinking I'd contracted some awful tropical disease. Only to find a relatively harmless leech had wiggled its way into my sodden sleeping bag at night, and had a midnight feast. All the while, the cacophony of rainforest bugs and birds acted as a constant soundtrack to our every moment. Sometimes beautiful, sometimes making sleep a challenge.

A typical day involved waking when it got light. Dismantling our temporary homes. Trudging through the thick and dense rainforests of Borneo, which, while ancient and beautiful, tended to lose their allure when I was soaked to the bone. As did thinking about food. I was hungry the whole time. And not 'it's time for my third meal of the day' hungry. Actual hunger, as in, 'My body has burned more calories than I have ingested, my fat reserves are being painfully depleted.'

In comparison to us, Hanri was completely at home. He'd stomp ahead of us, using his 'credit card' to swipe away the undergrowth, clearing a path. Each evening, as we spent an unreasonably long time fiddling around with our hammocks and tarps, Hanri would calmly stroll off into the rainforest. By the time we'd finished our set up, he would have basically constructed a little makeshift bedroom for himself in the middle of the jungle.

The Travelling Ape

Using his 'credit card', he'd build a little wooden bed, kind of like a raised stretcher (and infinitely more comfortable than the hammocks we were sleeping on). As if to show off, he'd also build himself a little side table each night with bamboo or carved from branches, where he'd put his watch. If this was done solely to impress us, it worked. He'd then wander around for about 20 minutes and come back with fruits that we could eat, or bamboo that had water we could drink. And, one time, with a deer which he'd managed to catch in a trap he had, of course, knocked up himself. One night, by the fire (which Hanri stepped in and lit in a heartbeat after we'd struggled for ages), I asked him about this way of life. And whether he enjoyed it.

'I live a good life. I've probably spent ten years living like this in the rainforest, with no belongings. It makes me feel calm. It shows me how simple life can be. That we need little to survive. Nature can provide it all for us.'

'But does it get boring?' I added.

'Maybe a bit. But I tried living in the modern world, in the big city. And it was overwhelming. Everyone moving so fast, in such a rush. Where are they rushing to? Why rush things when life is supposed to be enjoyed?' he said, matter-of-factly, as we both gazed into the roaring campfire, warming us after the almost constant damp of the rainforest.

'I now have my family and I have the rainforest. This is all I need. I saw in Kuala Lumpur that if you expect too much from life and get used to luxuries, you'll never be satisfied. You get a new thing and then it gets old, and then you want another new thing. It never stops. And it means you'll never be happy. Coming to the jungle reminds me how little I need.'

'I understand,' I said.

But did I? Sure, I'd been in the jungle for a few days. I now thought I was Ray Mears or Bear Grylls. A bit. But I'd lived a life full of stuff. Full of what I viewed as necessities, which I thoroughly enjoyed. It was a life full of food. Power. Hot water. Media. Stimulation. And as I outlined a few chapters ago, I felt these things had made my life better, as they had the lives of billions across the world in recent decades too. I wasn't going to give up the comforts I enjoyed and was used to. But did Hanri have a point? Could it be that we simply get used to comforts and then take them for granted? That as countries develop and living standards improve, the baseline of things we need in our lives to be happy increases?

2) Sky-High Expectations

My travels across the Western world since Tampa Sak have made me feel that high and rising expectations in the West means we aren't as happy as we should be. As we expect more, we set ourselves up for dissatisfaction. In his book *Solve for Happy*, Mo Gawdat says expectations are the *main* factor that determine human happiness. His Happiness Equation states that happiness equals the events of your life minus your expectations of what it should be like.[37] Put simply, if you expect more, don't be surprised if life consistently misses your expectations. And happiness is elusive.

It isn't hard to see when you travel that those living in the West expect more from life than any humans in history. As our lives have become more comfortable over the decades, collective increases in societal expectations mean our happiness hasn't increased as much as you'd expect. Electricity gets invented. Our lives are transformed. But after not too long, having electricity becomes a 'given' and you can't cope without it. The bar of expectation has risen, and you in effect need more to be happy. You're likely to be unhappy if there's a power cut and the lights go off. But someone like Hanri, who's never had reliable electricity, might not. Personally, I was happy to live somewhere I had access to basic things like electricity and running water. But I took it all completely for granted. And when they were taken away from me – like they had been trekking in the jungle – I struggled. I needed more to be happy than Hanri. My happiness had more caveats.

The so-called 'hedonic treadmill' is the tendency of humans to return to a baseline level of happiness, irrespective of positive or negative life events. Modern Stoic author Ryan Holiday, calls this trend 'comfort creep'.[38] As we get used to a certain level of comfort and luxury, it becomes inconceivable that we ever lived without it. This applies to whole nation states too. 'Hedonic adaption' theory suggests national happiness stays flat over time. The theory argues that our collective levels of happiness have remained largely flat through the sexual revolution, several economic booms and busts, the spread of therapy, and the normalisation of mental health issues.[39]

With our basic needs in the West largely taken care of, and taken for granted, we're left with an insatiable appetite for more. Today in the West, some people talk of having a nice apartment, a fulfilling career, the ability to eat out at restaurants occasionally, and to go on at least one holiday per year (or to go to every country in the world) as *prerequisites* for being happy. As a minimum. This is a much higher bar than in the developing world. And certainly, much higher than in Tampa Sak, where spending time with family and community seemed to give them so much joy. You can see how easy it is for rising Western expectations from life not to be met. If these demands *aren't* met, feelings of dissatisfaction creep back. And happiness is elusive.

Once back from our trek, the next couple of weeks in Tampa Sak passed in a blur of teaching English, helping out on the building site, sharing food with the local villagers, and becoming weirdly used to picking leeches off my body. It was a wonderful time, and we developed close bonds with the Tampa Sakers, particularly the kids. When you visit a place where children are allowed to roam free, not being constantly forced to sit exams and study from a stupidly young age, you see how carefree childhood can be. I'd come to Tampa Sak expecting to feel great pity for those living here. But, truth be told, part of me felt envious of them. Their strong community bonds showed me a way of living that had long disappeared in my part of the world.

That said, in our final week, there were reminders of the challenges faced by people living here and indeed the wider developing world. Being so remote raises several problems. Most notably, being hours away from the nearest hospital. We attended two funerals in our short time in the village. In the final week, it was for a woman who was only in her fifties; the lack of any kind of healthcare most likely played a part. Whenever someone died, the whole village came together. Unlike in the West, the funeral was a colourful affair.

We were all encouraged to pay our respects, and to step into the deceased lady's house. It was packed with people, all wailing and sobbing. It was as if displays of grief were actively encouraged as friends and family surrounded her body. There wasn't a casket. Instead, her body was on show, decorated with flowers and covered in a bright red shawl. It was incredibly moving. Would she have died if she'd lived nearer a hospital? Who knows?

It was a reminder that on a global level, we should strive to continue improving living conditions for all, via economic growth and development. Despite a tendency for societies to abandon some of the things that make them happier as they get wealthier. Those in Tampa Sak and in the wider developing world faced real struggles from what I could see, yet their closeness and connection was priceless, their happiness infectious. Put simply, the hardships of life are easier to navigate together when you have a wall of arms around you.

Why Aren't We in the West Happier?

This all hung in my mind as I sat in the back of one of our Land Cruisers, waving to the villagers as we left Tampa Sak for the final time. Their beaming smiles have stayed with me ever since. Indeed, my time in Borneo overall had given me a completely different perspective on happiness. For all the incredible advancements we've made in recent decades, my travels made me feel that Westerners don't appear to be as happy as they *should* be, given their fortunate positions in the world. Too many times to mention I've been shown how happiness isn't always based on one's economic circumstances. Having more realistic expectations and closer ties with family and community help most with the inevitable struggles that life will throw our way. And from what I'd seen in Borneo and across the developing world, this means happiness is much more common than we'd expect.

Which made me think: 'What to do about happiness in the West then? And what about my happiness? I'm not going to move to the developing world.* I can't cajole all my friends and family to live on top of each other in some form of commune. So what am I left with? Am I, a spoilt Westerner, to spend the rest of my days suffering from perpetual dissatisfaction?' Well, not quite.

Over the years, something started to change. Being exposed to so many different cultures and ways of living made me start questioning the way we do things in the West. My physical travels across the world coincided with a

---

*   A sign, perhaps, that I have also become too used to our Western comforts to consider living without them.

sort of mental travel. I was determined to approach personal development and indeed happiness like I'd approached seeing the world itself: I wanted to experience it all. This meant trying everything and anything that might help me better understand happiness, inspired by things I'd seen across the world's countries. It wasn't always easy. And I've done some frankly weird stuff along the way. But I'm glad to say my mental travels were fruitful. I'm much, much happier than I once was. Why?

13

Travels for the Mind

*Satisfaction isn't natural. But could travelling
the world show me some tools to be happier?*

I sat staring out the window, glumly. I could see a slew of palm trees and tropical plants, all encased within a 10-foot-high yellow wall. A few low-rise huts, and a large concrete patio, where a few other people mingled around, utterly aimlessly. Some walking back and forth slowly, others just sitting on the wall, staring into space. Next to each other but not making a sound.

The humidity was overwhelming. Beads of sweat dripped down my back. It was dinner time, so that was something to be excited about, I supposed. An elderly man, who had a grey beard and grey hair and dark and weathered skin, plonked down a glass of lemon water in front of me. It was day five, and at this stage I was kind of getting used to the lack of food. I'd not eaten a solid meal since 11am, and knew that lemon water would be all I was getting until breakfast tomorrow (at the rather unreasonable time of 5am). I gulped it down and my taste buds exploded with pleasure. It was as if I was drinking the nectar of the gods, the elixir of life. But I wasn't. I was drinking lemon water, for Christ's sake.

Funny things start to happen when you're denied access to the things you take for granted. Things like talking. Or solid food after 11am. Or reading. Or writing. Or TV. Or your phone. Or going on a walk. Without these distractions, I was learning, all you can do is focus on what's in front of you, in the present moment. And, if done properly, I was finding taste to be a monumentally pleasurable sense.

Feeling weirdly satisfied after my non-meal, I stood up and retired to my cell. And it was a cell. The only luxury it came with was an alleged 'mattress', which was around two inches deep. They'd even gone the whole hog and put bars in the windows, instead of glass, as if to ram home the prison theme. But when I got to the door of my cell, I was met by a man with a grave and pained look on his face. Unable to talk to me, he kept inexplicably pointing towards my feet. There was such anguish in his face. I thought he'd had some sort of breakdown, which wouldn't be surprising given my bizarre surroundings, so I tried to walk away and pretend it wasn't happening. Only to realise I'd walked off in his flip-flops earlier. He simply wanted them back. A 10-day silent meditation retreat is a strange place.

I was in Kanpur, India. It was summer, and, without air con, it was one of the hottest places I'd ever been. I'd assumed it wouldn't have been so extreme and there'd be lots of annoying 'spiritual' types from the West on the retreat. But I realised I was the only Westerner when we sat down for our first session on day one. I remember being concerned that no one could speak English, before quickly remembering I'd come here with the sole intention of not speaking to anyone.

While I was technically on a 'retreat', I felt the term was inaccurate. At times, a '10-day silent torture prison' would have been more apt. I was only halfway through the course when I was drinking my lemon water, but it'd already been the hardest physical and mental challenge of my life. I'd get up at 4am, spend around 16 hours meditating, and then go to bed. There was barely any leisure time or distractions in between meditation sits. For three of the hour-long meditation sessions per day – held in a circular hall with tiled floors and semi-open sides – I was instructed by the teacher to demonstrate 'strong determination' by not moving a muscle the entire time.

With beads of sweat dripping down my back (the teacher turned off the fans during each session) and legs in agony after days of sitting, the desire to change my posture and alleviate my suffering became unbearable.* If you want to understand what it's like to be on this retreat, sit alone and do nothing for 30 minutes. Then imagine doing that for 16 hours, for 10 days in a row, in blistering heat and humidity. It's not for the faint-hearted. French mathematician Blaise Pascal famously said in 1654 that 'all of humanity's problems stem from a man's inability to sit quietly in a room alone.'[1] On this evidence, overcoming humanity's problems wouldn't be easy.

★   The teacher's name escapes me, but I think was something like Guru Sadistic Arsehole.

The Travelling Ape

Making matters worse, while sitting in the sweltering meditation hall, questions kept circling around in my head. What the hell was I doing here? Why had I flown halfway across the world to seemingly put myself in jail? Why would any notionally sane person do this? Am I sane? Who's this voice in my head? Is this the self? Do I have a self? Will England ever win a football tournament in my lifetime?

But then, strangely, moments of suffering and pain would occasionally be replaced by moments of great happiness and peace. Indeed, some of those moments I spent on the retreat were the happiest of my life. Sheer bliss would arise during meditation. I could drop into mental states that felt so calming and euphoric. States that are ineffable, and yet, I'll plough on and try to describe them here. Where any sense that I had a body dissipated. All 'I' could feel was a stream of serene and shimmering vibrations coursing through my body. As if I was water rushing down a river, or clouds floating through the sky. I had no worries. Only presence. One day, after a particularly joyful sit, I remember thinking, 'If I can at times be this happy, living in objectively terrible conditions, maybe I should rethink my approach to happiness in the outside world.'

In reading the previous paragraph, I'm aware many of you will probably feel I've lost the plot. That I've gone full wacko, full woo-woo. Fine. But all I can do is faithfully report back on what states of consciousness are possible if you dare to explore them. By stripping away distraction, and intensely following the breath, it's possible to completely lose any idea that there's a self. And all that's left is a sublime feeling of unity with all people and all things. It's pretty amazing, really. But I concede it would be easier to sell to others if you didn't have to put yourself through hell on a retreat to get there.

In other moments, sitting on the pillow in the meditation hall, very strange things started to happen. Repressed memories would come up from down below, where they'd been pushed. They were so clear. It was as if I were reliving them, along with all the emotions I experienced at the time. I came to realise that I hadn't grieved the death of my dog ten years earlier. That I was still scarred by a couple of years of prep school, where I was bullied. That I had unresolved emotions related to my parents' marriage breaking down. In each case, these memories were accompanied by tears rolling down my cheeks. And then associated with a bodily release – a large 'crick' in my shoulder, or the feeling of muscles cramping and releasing, as the emotional imprint of the traumas were released from my body.[2] It was cathartic, and enjoyable in some ways. And I always felt lighter afterwards.

On the retreat, I also learnt how much of our suffering is optional. On about day seven, one of the attendees was really starting to piss me off. He walked around, flanked by two of his cronies. He had a perfectly groomed side parting, immaculate white clothes, and was in his mid-20s. Probably a wealthy resident of New Delhi, I figured. Perhaps this explained his arrogance? He also wore a very smug look on his face. And he kept talking to his friends. Not even trying to hide it. Not only was it really distracting, but it also clearly made me jealous. 'He gets to chat with his pals while we suffer in silence? How's this fair?' I reasoned. To myself. Silently.

For days, whenever I saw him, my blood boiled. Sensations of anger rose up in my chest, my body moving into fight or flight mode. One day at breakfast he sat down next to me, and predictably, started to mumble to his cronies. I snapped. I said, 'Shhhhhh,' accompanied by an angry face and finger over my lips. This was big. A level up from rolling my eyes, tutting, and looking expectantly at others to see if they felt the same way.* I'd lost it.

'Okay, sorry,' he said sheepishly and quietly. And we returned to our meals. Gruel. Or something that looked a bit like gruel (tasted amazing, though). At the end of the retreat, we had a few hours where we were allowed to speak to each other. Everyone was very friendly. I quickly realised that in this part of Kanpur they didn't get many Westerners. And so, one by one, almost everyone on the course asked to have a selfie with me, against the backdrop of the pinkening sky and the golden turrets of the main pagoda and meditation hell.** Eventually, my nemesis rocked up and started heading towards me. 'He daren't ask me for a selfie,' I thought. He came closer.

'Hi, sir. I'm very sorry about distracting you on the course. I came with my friends for support. I recently lost my wife, and being here was really difficult. It brought up

---

*   This is what furious British people do when someone queue jumps, rather than actually saying anything to the perpetrator.

**   Hall. Freudian slip?

a lot of pain. I know we weren't supposed to talk, but my friends were supporting me and it helped.'

'Oh. God. I'm so sorry. I didn't realise. I hope you're okay,' I managed to respond, words still feeling strange in my mouth having not spoken for so long. I never caught his name. But we continued to chat. He wasn't a wealthy man from New Delhi, he lived a quiet rural life in the foothills of the Himalayas. He had a child, and had lost his wife in tragic circumstances. And he was a nice person, who offered to give me a lift if I needed one after the retreat.

I was heading in the opposite direction, towards Lucknow, so declined his kind offer. I packed my things, and hopped in a yellow and green tuk tuk. We sped around narrow and winding country lanes, where palm trees occasionally encroached onto the sides of the crumbling, potholed asphalt. Miles of flat paddy fields stretched into the distance. The horizon broken up by the occasional plume of smoke from a fire, or the silhouette of someone harvesting the rice. The visual stimulation was such a welcome change after the previous ten days.

I reflected on the retreat, and how wrong my preconceptions had been about my nemesis. On how my anger towards him was both baseless, and futile. It was *optional* suffering. And I had had some of the happiest and most blissful moments of my life, despite the incredibly basic and simple lifestyle on the retreat. I felt I'd learnt a lot about how the human mind works, from the inside. Seeing so much happiness in the developing world, I already understood that economic privilege doesn't guarantee contentment. Here in India, on a meditation retreat, I had learnt that happiness has much more to do with the *quality of your mind* than anything else. It was eye-opening. The meditation retreat felt like a form of mental travel. I was hooked.

Since that experience, I've become obsessed with what different cultures do to be happy. Trying to answer questions like: How do people live? What do they do to unwind? When do they go to sleep? What do they eat? How do they approach socialising? And, most importantly, are any of these efforts working? Are people happy *there*? Over the years, I've adopted or adapted, from across the world, the best tools I've seen to boost my happiness. And by integrating them into my life, I've become a profoundly happier ape. This chapter will outline how I got here.

A Mediocre Starting Point

From what I've seen in my travels, it appears most of us spend our lives hectically engaging in an impossibly vast array of jobs, tasks, and hobbies, all in the hope they'll somehow lead to happiness. It's what we all want.

So isn't it strange we aren't taught how to be happy? We arrive on the planet. We find ourselves in control of the most complex and advanced piece of machinery in the known universe. Our brains. Which have 100 billion neurons. Some quantum physicists believe our brains are more powerful than computers. And not just one computer, more powerful than *every single computer on Earth combined*. It's a universe in itself. You'd think it should come with an instruction manual or something. Or that adults should teach kids how it works.

But of course we don't do this. You go to school, and your brain gets filled with sometimes interesting but mostly useless facts about the world. 'A thousand years ago, this king killed that king ... The Latin word for toilet is *latrina* ... The capital of Liberia is Monrovia ... I only became a teacher for the long holidays; I despise children.' All interesting, sure. But you'd think that out of those thousands of hours in which we fill our children's minds with facts, a few of them could be set aside for teaching them about life. What does it mean to be a human being? What do I need to do to be happy? What is the fundamental nature of consciousness and indeed life itself?

But we don't. And I had to work this out for myself, on my travels. One of the first major lessons that started my global happiness quest came in Sri Lanka, a few years before my Indian retreat. It was humid and drizzly. I plodded up and up the seemingly endless steps, taking me to the top of a giant rock with stunning views of the canopy below. It was thick, with shades of dark and bright green. The tree line perforated by the occasional steep hill, the kind a child would draw. The Dambulla Cave Temple towered 525 feet (or around 50 storeys) above the surrounding rainforest. When I reached the summit, I was guided into the cave. Inside were 153 statues of the Buddha. Having seen statues of this fella in India, Nepal, Thailand, Myanmar, Laos, Cambodia, and a few other places, I was nonplussed. Also, my legs hurt after walking up thousands of steps. And I was soaking wet.

The Travelling Ape

I was grumpy as hell. 'Maybe the Buddha has a point? Maybe life *is* suffering?'

After all, I was travelling in an awesome country, but was still focusing mostly on the negative things happening in my life. So, while I had precisely zero time for the supernatural side of Buddhism, I started reading about the more practical teachings of Buddhism after my li'l tantrum in the cave. For the remainder of the stay in Sri Lanka, and for many more months after, I started learning about Buddhism. And most of it seemed to be true (save for the mystical stuff).

One of the main truths of Buddhism is, as mentioned above, that life is suffering. This might sound depressing, but it's true. Even if you had the perfect childhood, with the perfect family, with all the money in the world, lived in the best country on Earth, this doesn't preclude you from suffering. You suffer from the moment of birth. The process of being born is deeply distressing. The process of being a baby – unable to understand the sensory stimuli 'you' are experiencing – is suffering.

Gradually noticing you aren't the same person as your mother and being ripped away from her is suffering. Almost every stage of childhood is about learning to behave differently than how you'd choose to if left to your own devices (use the toilet rather than the floor; wear clothes rather than charge around naked). This can't be easy. Being a parent is agreeing to manage the suffering of your child, and failing mostly. Whether we realise it or not, the simple fact of being a human is traumatic in a vast array of ways. And this is true whether you live in Harare or the Hamptons. This is what unites us.

Travels for the Mind

When I applied the Buddhist principles I was learning to adult life, they still seemed to hold. If I delved into the minutiae of my daily existence, I realised that 'life' is just endless problem solving. In a normal day, there were hundreds of little problems to solve, like emptying my bladder or feeding myself. And then bigger ones, like worrying about my future or the well-being of my family. The 14th and current Dalai Lama argues that we face daily problems, on top of the much bigger problems we'll 'inevitably have to face, like old age, illness, and death.'[3] Even if you solve all your smaller problems (temporarily), there remains the rather trifling problem that you and everyone you know and love will one day die.

A year later, in Myanmar, I'd been using an app to learn to meditate. And was loving it. So I took the next logical step that any clichéd backpacker would take – I went to see a monk. I hopped on my electric moped and made my way past the hundreds of orange temples that cover the dry and dusty landscape of Bagan. The temples looked a bit like ant hills – triangular in shape, leading to a pointy top. There were small ones in every direction. And the occasional giant one, jutting elegantly above the green canopy and into the sky, merging with the backdrop of the surrounding parched hills and mountains. There were red and orange hot air balloons drifting above me. Bagan is one of those locations where you can't help but be absorbed by your surroundings, where you think: 'This place we call Earth is so very strange and wonderful.'

Eventually, I pulled over and ditched my bike. I took off my shoes and approached the pagoda, which had open

415

sides and a shiny wooden floor. There were two little meditation cushions on top of it, and my teacher for the day was sitting on one of them. He had a shaved head and was wearing burgundy robes, exposing his left shoulder. He wasn't wearing any shoes. He looked quite serious. As a relatively novice meditator at this stage, it was all a bit intimidating.

I stepped towards him, and sat down. He was doing a double lotus posture, which I automatically tried to copy, before realising I was nowhere near flexible enough. So I just tried to style it out as an odd kind of stretch. His eyes were still closed. I assumed he must have heard me so waited. But after a minute or so, I needed to break the silence.

'Hi, my name's Mike, nice to meet you.' Voice trembling a little.

The monk's eyes opened slowly. He stared at me, with a rather serious look on his face. But this all changed, as soon as he spoke. 'Hello, Mr Richards, I've been expecting you,' he said, delivered, despite the wording, in a manner as far from a James Bond villain as it's possible to speak. He shook my hand vigorously, with his other hand over his heart.* His face lit up with a bright smile.

As I explained why I was here and what I knew about meditation, I kept my eyes on him. He might just have been the happiest man I'd ever seen, it simply radiated out of him. He had huge crow's feet – which made perfect

---

*   A bit cringey. But this guy was literally a monk, so I think I can forgive him.

sense given how much he smiled. I found myself wanting to laugh, simply because I was near him. We chatted about meditation. He seemed utterly engrossed and engaged in what I had to say. Perhaps I was saying some incredibly interesting things. More likely, this was how he was with everyone.

'How come you're so happy?' I asked.

'I didn't used to be,' he said chuckling. 'I was a successful businessman in Yangon and very wealthy. And miserable, oh so miserable. I suffered constantly. But then I found meditation.'

'Oh okay. Seems to be a common theme among people who find meditation. Do you think I could be this happy, if I meditated all of the time, like you?' I continued.

'Well, it's not that simple. But for me, meditation has given me lasting happiness, much more so than any material or career success.' Each sentence was punctuated with a long pause. As if he was picking each word as precisely as possible.

'We're all predisposed to have a baseline happiness level. Some people might be lucky enough to have a 7 out of 10. Some will be less lucky and be down at a 3. My natural score was probably a 4. After positive or negative life events, we all (usually) revert back to our happiness baseline after a certain amount of time. But meditation is one way to raise your baseline happiness score, and to permanently boost your day-to-day level of happiness, regardless of what happens in your life.'

'I see,' I said, trying to take it all in. 'I reckon my baseline happiness score would probably be a 5,' I said.

The Travelling Ape

'I'm naturally quite anxious and worry a lot. What's your score now, if you could place it?'

The monk said, 'It's hard to say. Maybe a 9? But I don't know. I just try to live my life right now, in the present moment. And when I do this, I notice there's something enriching about simply existing, simply being alive.'

He then led me in meditation for an hour. And during the practice, incredibly, he began levitating a few inches off the ground. Before his face wrinkled in concentration, and he flew off into the sky, with his burgundy robes bellowing behind him like a cape. Or at least he would have, if any of those who believe in the New Age superstitious powers of meditation had anything to say about it. (Meditation is powerful, but the supernatural stuff is obviously guff.)

After the session, as I hopped back on my electric bike, I was so preoccupied with what had just happened (seeing the monk, not the flying bit), that I barely noticed the beautiful surrounds of Bagan slipping past me again. The bike riding as if by itself, with me periodically awaking from thoughts to remember I should probably pay attention to what I was doing. How the monk felt and appeared was so far removed from my way of living. I thought, if enlightenment exists – and I was sceptical that it did – this man might be close to it.

Years later – after thousands of hours of meditation and cumulatively many weeks spent on silent retreats – I still feel enlightenment will be forever out of reach. But I now know that what much of the monk told me was true. That it is possible to raise your baseline happiness level. I'm now running on a 7 or 8. I'm much less anxious. I'm able to enjoy the good bits of life more, and ride out the bad. I'm not cured. I still have bad days, but these happen much less frequently than they used to. Why? Because travelling nearly everywhere revealed seven key precepts which helped me become happier. They could work for others too, who knows?

1) Calm the Voice in Your Head

At the silent meditation retreat in India, the most important truth about happiness became clear to me. I was suffering on my meditation cushion, sweaty as hell, and miserable as hell. 'This is rubbish. Why don't you just go home? You're going to quit eventually anyway, so you may as well leave now. Meditation is stupid. My knee hurts. My back hurts. I'm bored.' It was a light-bulb moment. Without distractions, I realised my life was narrated by a narcissistic pain-in-the-backside voice in my head. Which never shuts up. On the retreat, I realised that shutting this voice up would probably make life much more enjoyable. After all, all it seemed to do on the retreat was worry and complain.

Before going to India, I'd never truly understood this truth. But the fact that around 80 percent of our thoughts are negative and 95 percent are repetitive suddenly made perfect sense to me.[4] As did our negativity bias. Those in prehistory who were constantly worried and anxious about any threats – real or perceived – were much more likely to pass on their genes, while those less worried often ended up inside the stomachs of predators.[5] And so, today, the worriers' genes survive in us. Leaving us with highly sophisticated, complex brains, skewed inexorably towards negativity.

Brains that just won't keep their gobs shut while you're trying to follow your breath in a meditation hall in India. In a world with few real threats to our lives, our brains do their best to find threats where there are none. And we all remain stuck in perpetual and frankly exhausting self-referential thought patterns. Which makes it very hard indeed to simply enjoy what's happening in the present moment. Or to be happy.

My time in India showed me that the relentlessly chattering voice in all our heads is the biggest barrier to human happiness that exists. I'd go as far as to say that if you don't at least start to gain a handle on that arsehole rattling around in the depths of your skull, true happiness will elude you. Following the breath – meditation – is a form of mind training that helps you do this.

Quietening the voice in my head became a goal. And my backpacking confirmed to me how important and difficult this task would be. I remember being in the beautiful and leafy town of Luang Prabang in Laos. The Mekong River rolled slowly through town, while the horizon was peppered with rounded, rolling hills and gilded *wats* (a Buddhist temple). Saffron-robed monks, young and old, padded lazily around town. They had an air of serenity, hard to put your finger on. But after my experience in Kanpur, I knew this serenity was hard won. They had made quietening their minds a 24/7 pursuit, their life's work.

Travels for the Mind

I wasn't willing to go that far. But I've made it a big part of my life. I meditate each morning for 45 minutes to an hour, and again in the afternoon, for a shorter time. Since India, I've attended further silent retreats in Australia, Bali, Myanmar, and the UK, among others. I now teach meditation to others. All of this effort has had the desired results. Before I learnt to meditate, my mind was like an untrained puppy. It did what it wanted, and I was almost powerless to control it. Whereas today, after years of studious practice, I feel like I'm now in control of a well-trained dog most of the time, even though the dog occasionally misbehaves and ignores my commands. The voice is quieter than it used to be, but still there.

Fortunately, telling people I meditate causes less of a negative reaction now than it would have a few years ago. And I'm heartened by the fact that so many successful (and non-weird) people these days choose to meditate. American author Tim Ferris interviewed 200 world-class performers from a variety of different fields to find out what makes people thrive in their field. He said that more than 80 percent of the world-class performers he interviewed 'have a regular mindfulness or meditation practice.'[6] If it's good enough for them, I figured, it's surely good enough for me.

The scientific community has also proven unequivocally just how good meditation is for your mental and physical well-being (if someone thinks I'm weird because I meditate, I just shout science facts at them until they lose interest). In 2008, there were 82 academic publications written on mindfulness and meditation. By

2020, this number had increased by a factor of almost thirty-five to 2,808.[7*]

Many of these journals point to long-term sustained meditation practice improving sleep, attention span, and kindness, while also lowering blood pressure, stress, and slowing age-related memory loss.[8] The most exhaustive summary of recent scientific material was put together by Daniel Goleman and Richard Davidson in their book *Altered Traits*. It shows that long-term meditation can also cultivate qualities such as selflessness, equanimity, love, and compassion, while redesigning our neural circuitry.[9] Indeed, meditation even changes your brain structure and your brainwaves.[10]

The spread of apps has been a game changer as far as meditation goes. I'm now just as likely to see someone meditating in the West as I am when in a Buddhist country. It's in places like Los Angeles, New York, London, and other urban areas that having a conversation about meditation is least likely to go down like a lead balloon. I teach it to businesspeople in the corporate world, when not working as an economic and political risk analyst. If even those working in financial corporations are now open to the idea, the tide is changing. And this has to be a good thing in our quest for collective global happiness.

★ I've included these statistics as an attempt to say, 'See, I'm not crazy!' to all of those who clearly felt my desire to go on retreats was bizarre. Like you do, perhaps.

2) Prepare Yourself for Struggles

Seeing so much suffering in the developed world had a big impact on me. It showed me our sky-high and ever-increasing expectations from life are killing our chances of being happy. I could see this happening for myself. And it was when in Rome (literally) that I came across a belief system that changed my approach to happiness forever.

Strolling the streets of the Italian capital, flanked by pastel-coloured architectural gems, I reached the top of a long staircase and saw a bronze statue of a man on a horse. Which for Rome (and indeed the world), wasn't a particularly strange thing to see. This particular man was called Marcus Aurelius. He was emperor of the Roman Empire around 1,900 years ago, a ruler of millions. So what? History tells us most of these dudes were complete jerks, right? But I listened in on a walking tour taking place next to the statue. And the guide kept talking about how Marcus Aurelius was different, he was a 'philosopher king'. 'That's how all emperors refer to themselves,' I thought. But my interest was piqued, nonetheless.

I bought one of his books in a local English bookstore, *Meditations*, and devoured it in about two days. Dipping in and out of it when pausing in one of the city's many cafes, I imagined what life would have been like in the Roman Empire. But I needn't have. The advice held within *Meditations* was strikingly practical, strikingly relevant to the modern world, and even more strikingly, said nothing about religion. It could've been written last week. I'd inadvertently stumbled across Stoicism. And I was hooked. In the simplest terms, Stoicism says life will be hard and difficult, and people will disappoint you. The only thing you have true control over is your reaction to these difficult life events.

In other words, Stoics believe our perception of things, rather than the things themselves, cause most of life's problems.[11] This approach isn't incompatible with being extremely motivated and driven, underpinned by deep gratitude for the many joys (and aware of the challenges) that life has to offer. It's simply a more realistic view on life, which is severely lacking in the West.

I learnt more about the philosopher king. As a child, and sporadically through the rest of his life, it's said that despite being a Roman emperor, Marcus thought there was significant utility in voluntary discomfort, like many of the Stoics did. He'd sleep on the floor and live on a restricted diet for a limited time, to remind himself that humans can survive and cope in difficult situations. And that happiness comes from a quiet, disciplined, and examined mind:

Men seek retreats for themselves – in the country, by the sea, in the hills – and you yourself are particularly prone to this yearning. But all this is quite unphilosophic, when it is open to you, at any time you want, to retreat into yourself. No retreat offers someone more quiet and relaxation than that into his own mind, especially if he can dip into thoughts there which put him at immediate and complete ease.[12]

Travels for the Mind

Far be it from me to say whether my decision to go on silent retreats makes me as wise as Marcus. But it was comforting to know that the Stoics saw utility in strengthening the resolve of the mind. Learning to prepare for the worst, to be pessimistic, has, perversely, made me a happier person in daily life. And I noticed there were crossovers with what I'd learnt meditating. Vietnamese Buddhist Monk Thich Nhat Hanh, viewed by some as the father of mindfulness, sums up the predicament of pessimism perfectly. He says that you can be viewed as pessimistic if you look at the world through a Buddhist perspective, but this 'oversimplifies the truth. The problem is to see reality as it is.'[13]

Thich Nhat Hanh is basically saying we need to acknowledge the reality that life is difficult. In this sense, learning about Stoicism in Rome made me believe *measured pessimism* offers a much more positive way to live your life. Expect the worst, be prepared for struggles, and accept that life will be hard. You'll then be ready when it is. In the moments when it's easy, you'll be pleasantly surprised – and genuinely happy.

Stoics say situations in your life aren't problems, they're only problems because you think they are. As Shakespeare famously said, 'There is nothing either good or bad, but thinking makes it so.' Or as Stoic philosopher Epictetus put it neatly, 'Men are disturbed not by things, but by their opinions on them.'[14] Or as I said much less eloquently about three sentences ago, 'Situations in your life aren't problems, they're only problems because you think they are.'

Around the globe I've seen people who are already

reaping the benefits of Stoicism, even if they didn't realise it themselves. People across much of the developing world, in places like Tampa Sak, who were often so much happier and certainly more resilient than I thought they'd be. They'd prepared for hardship and struggles. They expected less. And they became much more hardy human beings as a direct result.

3) Speak to the Dead

In a trip to Porto, Portugal, I visited the Livraria Lello. It's one of the city's best-known sights. And it's one of those places where you have an amazing opportunity to communicate with the dead. Where you can hear from the greatest minds the world has ever produced. I'm not talking about wasting your time and money consulting a medium or attending a séance (which, given the last chapter, is advice you might have expected from someone who enjoys stuff like meditation). In this corner of the city you can read. Books. Thousands of them.

The Livraria Lello is a bookshop and a monument to our love of the written word. I couldn't see the walls; only books rising high into the vaulted ceilings. A stunning wooden staircase plunged into the middle of the room. All over this elegant and opulent store were detailed and beautiful carvings cut into the building's ancient, wooden frame. It felt like a church for books. I'd visited the Livraria Lello partially because JK Rowling used it as the inspiration for the Hogwarts library. Which makes my trip seem a tad juvenile. But I remembered that *Harry Potter* was a series of books that made me passionate about reading at a young age. So being a tad juvenile was just fine.

Being surrounded by all these books hammered home something that'd become increasingly clear to me as the years rolled by. We live in such a privileged time. Over the course of human history, almost all the world's greatest thinkers have studiously jotted down their thoughts. And today you can still have a conversation with them (albeit a one-sided one). Reading books like *Meditations* or the writings of Seneca is a truly enlightening experience, as is perusing the diaries of people like Charles Darwin. Famous figures who've in some cases been dead for millennia.

Reading books – even in tablet or audiobook form* – is amazing not just because the wisdom held within them is so prescient (wink wink), but because you realise that even hundreds of years ago, we were struggling with the same problems we have today. French philosopher Descartes said the 'reading of all good books is like conversation with the finest (people) of the past centuries.'[15] Astronomer of the people Carl Sagan talked about how through reading you can hear the voice of someone who's been dead for a thousand years, and 'to read is to voyage through time.'[16] And I say, 'Read lots of books, damnit! You'll be all the better for it.'

Thanks to books, you have all the world's wisdom

---

*   As a Luddite, I continue to fill half of my backpack with real books when I travel, rather than use an e-reader. I resisted smartphones too when they first came out.

available to you at any time. Thousands of years of life experience concisely summarised into something that fits in your pocket (if you have massive pockets, depending on the book you're reading). You only have 90 years, if you are lucky, to understand life, which isn't really enough time in the grand scheme of things. But if you consult with the greatest philosophers, thinkers, and sages in our planet's history, maybe you'll have a better chance of understanding things? But most of us don't fancy doing that. Instead, we endlessly scroll Instagram, repetitively check news websites, or watch some of the world's stupidest people cavorting around on reality TV.*

Having been inspired to read more by my experience in Porto and in libraries across the world, I now do so as much as I possibly can. It's revolutionised my understanding of being a human. And ultimately helped me be happy. While I have a general rule with reading – non-fiction only unless the book has wizards – it's true to say there are few activities on Earth as rewarding and wholesome as diving into a good book (bar reading books like *Mein Kampf* and a few other notable outliers). And if you're travelling, is there any greater way to spend your time on long journeys than learning about the place you're in from reading a book, while the countryside slides by out of a train or bus window? Surely not.

---

* Shamefully, this is something I do occasionally. And more shamefully, I sometimes thoroughly enjoy it.

4) Nail the Basics

Visiting so many countries has shown me that some places are healthier than others. In some I've been struck by how happy and old so many people were. Take Italy. Why are there so many old, happy people there? Hugging and chatting and just having the nourishing sort of time mostly limited to Dolmio adverts back at home. Or Japan, where the elderly resolutely continue to live, year after year, with their health seemingly failing to deteriorate, unlike the rest of us.

Saying 'be healthy' might on the surface seem as condensing as saying 'be rich' or 'just be happier'. But given that health outcomes vary so much between societies, being healthy has to be much more of a choice than some think it is. And if you feel healthy, don't be surprised if you start to feel happier too. For this principle, I was inspired by places where people seemed healthy and long-lived. The countries with the longest life expectancies in the world are Japan, Spain, and Singapore, all of which I've visited many times.[17]

These countries confirmed what I believe to be the three main essentials for being healthy: eating well, sleeping lots, and exercising. Think of it as an incredibly dull and obvious equation. Eating well + enough sleep + daily exercise = better health. I'd defy anyone to follow these basic precepts and not feel slightly better on a day-to-day basis than they did beforehand. In fact, if you ignore all of the advice in this chapter and just focus on these three things, they'll be enough to hugely boost your happiness and well-being.

The Travelling Ape

So first, diet. My experiences show me that on this subject we should look to Japan. The Japanese eat incredibly well. The food there is the best in the world, hands down. You can grab ramen from unappealing underground train stations and it'll still be unbelievably tasty. As a Westerner, I always felt compelled to stuff as much of it as I could down my throat. But in Japan, portion control reigns supreme. The Japanese adhere to a concept called *hara hachi bu*, where they aim to eat until they are only 80 percent full, stopping when there's still room for a bit more.[18]

Residents on the Japanese island of Okinawa have the longest life expectancy of anywhere on Earth and the highest proportion of centenarians. Along with portion control, they eat lots of fruit, vegetables, and grains, and eat much less meat and sugar than in other high-income countries.[19] Anyone who visits Japan will notice there are few overweight people, aside from the slightly obvious aberration of sumo wrestlers. Life expectancy in Japan is around 84 (on average between men and women). For male sumo wrestlers, it is between 60 and 65.[20] Which, if anything, is a great example of why diet is so important.

It was a trip to Japan several years ago that made me take my diet more seriously. While there, I paid close attention to portion control and was eating mainly healthy foods. I didn't get it right all of the time, but sometimes got the 80 percent full ratio just about. I felt great, and probably lost a few pounds too. So what's not to like? Even though the phrase is overused and annoying, you really are what you eat. At cellular level. The food and drink you consume contains the building blocks of your cells, skin, blood transportation systems, muscle, fat, and more. The diets of humans can even have an impact on the composition of their genes.[21] That said, it's perhaps fortunate we don't literally turn into what we eat. Otherwise the West would be filled with people who look like Pop-Tarts waddling around.

Basically (and sadly), diets high in processed food, sugars, and carbohydrates taste great. They would have been a boon to hunter-gatherers surviving on seeds, nuts, and occasionally, meat. But there's evidence our modern meat-heavy diets increase the risk of cancer[22] and heart disease.[23] In effect, our Western diets are killing us. If you eat meat, try to eat less, like the Japanese do. If you eat chocolate and cake, try to eat less, like I mostly fail to do past 8pm. If you don't feel hungry at least *some* of the time, you're probably eating too much food. Remember *hara hachi bu*.

Second, sleep. For guidance on this topic we should look to the Mediterranean. Whenever I'm in Spain, or France, or Italy, one thing I love is the concept of a siesta. Having a sleep in the middle of the day is just lovely. In Britain, we like to assume people in the Mediterranean are 'lazy', mocking the concept of economically inefficient siestas. But when you go to Spain – which has the second highest average life expectancy on Earth – you'll notice the Spanish aren't complaining. They certainly aren't envious of our Northern European and North American work ethics, where we all routinely work ourselves to early graves.

In *Why We Sleep*, neuroscientist Matthew Walker talks about how our lack of sleep is an epidemic.[24] It's shortening our lives, driving up rates of cancer, destroying our productivity, weakening our immune systems, damaging coronary arteries, and increasing the likelihood of Alzheimer's, among many other downsides. There are few worse things you can do for your health and happiness than not sleeping.

Try to get eight or nine hours a night. Or put simply: if you need to set an alarm to wake up, you might not be getting enough sleep.[25] To be sure, I was getting close to this per night, before having a baby and it all went out the window. And my caffeine addiction – already strong prior to being a father – got even worse; 85 percent of Americans also take caffeine every day.[26] Sleeping more and drinking less coffee would be helpful for us all, however hard it is to do.

Third, exercise. For which we should look to Singapore. If you walk around the city's beautifully manicured streets, you'll constantly be seeing people exercising in public parks, particularly the elderly. Coupled with extortionate taxes on cigarettes and alcohol, it's no wonder that Singaporeans are a healthy bunch. This is a big city, with limited outdoor space, and it's humid as hell. And yet people take exercise very seriously here. What excuse do you have?

Do some exercise. Every day preferably. Even if it's just a walk. For me, if I'm feeling down, sluggish, or lacking motivation, going for a run or lifting weights never fails to make me feel better.* I've never done a workout and then

---

* Grip strength correlates strongly to life expectancy, with some studies suggesting two lifting sessions a week can lower mortality risk by 40%.

thought, 'Shouldn't have done that, I feel terrible now.' No, you get high off endorphins, which feels great. And if you exercise, you'll have the added bonus of looking less like a Pop-Tart. Just as the healthy and long-lived residents of Singapore don't.

Living a long time or being healthy won't guarantee lifelong happiness. But I'd argue that *everyone* would feel at least slightly better if they felt good, looked better, and their body was in balance. Seeing healthy societies on my travels has revolutionised my approach to health. Even if my early nights, largely quitting alcohol, being a vegetarian, and exercising has left me open to cries of being 'boring' in the eyes of many. When you feel happy, these criticisms roll right off your back (notwithstanding my desire to include this chapter and prove all those critics wrong).

5) The Importance of a Morning Routine

I lived in Sydney for around six months. And one of the things that struck me was just how busy it was at seemingly crazy times in the morning. At 6am, I'd jog to Manly Beach to meditate (though the beach is called 'Manly' there isn't an admissions policy based on how masculine you are). There'd be surfers, dog walkers, people doing exercise classes, and other joggers wherever I looked. While most people across the world would rather be asleep or scrolling Instagram through a half-open eye at that time of day, from what I could see, the citizens of Sydney recognised the importance of a morning routine, even if starting it so early is not a prerequisite for a morning routine to help you. Indeed, in Sydney, some people were out before the sun had even risen, jogging in the dark as if to win the 'who was up earliest today' competition.

It was Aristotle who famously said, 'We are what we repeatedly do.'[27] (With the book about to end, I thought I'd squeeze in a final philosophical quote or two, hoping to cement this book's scholarly credentials in your minds.) Rising early and morning routine is crucial, if a tad dull to implement, like most of the other happiness nuggets I learnt travelling.

Personally, I wake up at around 5am to 6am on average, which means going to bed at 9pm at the latest. I have a busy mind (as we all do). So I need to take several steps to quiet it when I wake, lest I allow its inane chatter to ruin my day. This first involves me having a warm shower – which, if I'm feeling brave enough, I'll gradually turn to freezing by the end. It's not nice, but it has multiple health benefits.[28] I then meditate for around 45 minutes to an hour, which really kicks the voice in my head out the door (for a few hours at least).

After doing this, I feel set up for the day. Calmer, happier, and ready to work. I'm always amazed at how productive I am directly after this routine. Without neurotic mental distraction, my ability to enter a 'flow state' during writing is increased exponentially. When you're deeply focused on a task at hand, all that matters is the present, you're completely immersed in the experience, and not side-tracked by anything else.[29] We've all had experiences like this. It's in these flow states that we are happiest. So perhaps we should listen to the advice of the Aussies who all religiously boast about how early they get up, even if their boasting is preachy and annoying (much like the content of this chapter, some of you might be feeling).

6) Let Go of the Past

It took a trip to the Netherlands (and a trip in the Netherlands) for me to realise the importance of letting go of the past if you're going to be happy. I was there to take drugs. But these drugs, I was told, were the opposite of recreational. And they were legal. Having previously believed most psychedelic users were likely to be hippie dropouts, I'd read of an increasing number of Silicon Valley types going to Peru for things like ayahuasca retreats, or using psilocybin to support their personal growth. Even *The Financial Times* (of all newspapers) had cottoned on to this trend. It said: 'Curious and rigorous minds from business and finance are now turning to the 'medicine' to find answers about their goals in life and evolve ideas about their work and careers.'[30]

I read more articles, and heard from friends who said that while their experiences were all difficult (psilocybin is not fun), many reported the results as being profound. They helped them let go of past traumas, and often boosted their creativity at work. Many people have said that using psychedelics was among the top three most meaningful experiences of their lives, alongside getting married and having children. My intrigue got the better of me. So there

The Travelling Ape

I was in the Netherlands, where psilocybin in truffle form was completely legal.

I drank the warm tea, which tasted earthy because of the psilocybin truffles crushed in it, in a circle of around 10 other people. We had sitters to look after us, and a playlist to listen to. Any ideas of 'tripping' – the way hippies talked about it – couldn't have been less accurate. All the most distressing and painful events in my life flashed before my eyes. Many people in the room cried, including me. Many times, I questioned why I'd paid so much money and ventured so far to have such a miserable time. But the amazing thing was, in the days and weeks that followed, I felt so much happier. So much lighter; like I'd let these traumas go. I don't want to say it was an Earth-shattering change, but certainly it was a big one. So much so that I've made psychedelic therapy retreats something I do a couple of times annually.

People in the Amazon have been taking psychedelics for millennia. The US counterculture movement of the '60s did, too. And more people will in future. In 2020, the state of Oregon became the first in the United States to legalise psilocybin for use in therapy. Other states will follow, and, slowly, the world will.[31] Mark my words (or just remember what I said in a less sinister way.)

The recent explosion of scientific research will help normalise this tool helping people overcome trauma and tackling mental health disorders. After decades in the wilderness during the US government's 'war on drugs', psychedelic research has been picking up again since the turn of the millennium. There were 550 research papers featuring the keyword 'psychedelic' or 'psychedelics' in

2018.[32] Some estimates suggest the psychedelic therapy sector will be worth US$8.3 billion by 2028.[33]

Michael Pollan's book on psychedelic therapy, *How to Change Your Mind*, was such a hit that it marked a turning point for psychedelics in the mainstream when published in 2018. That same year, the US Food and Drug Administration changed its designation of psilocybin-assisted psychotherapy to 'breakthrough therapy' status for treatment-resistant depression.[34] Johns Hopkins University and Imperial College London both now have Psychedelic Research Units. I have money invested in a psychedelic therapy organisation listed on the Nasdaq stock exchange. It's a remarkable turnaround.

Dr Robin Carhart-Harris is head of the Centre for Psychedelic Research at Imperial, a job title certain to create moral panic among the 'drugs-are-bad' brigade. Since 2009, Carhart-Harris and his team have been using fMRI and magnetoencephalography (MEG) to observe changes in people's brains under the influence of psilocybin. In a 2017 paper, Carhart-Harris said there were positive 'changes in brain activity in depressed people treated with psilocybin' who had failed to respond to other treatments, and that several of the patients felt 'reset' after the treatment.[35]

Research has shown significant potential for psilocybin in combatting existential anxiety (the fear of death in the terminally ill),[36] in combatting addiction (particularly smoking), and in tackling depression (especially for treatment-resistant depression).[37] A team at Johns Hopkins found psychedelic therapy can elicit long-term positive changes in behaviours, attitudes, and values that overcome negative mental patterns.[38] There isn't a person alive who hasn't suffered trauma, heartbreak, or emotional pain. And for me, travelling helped me find the tools to overcome these ailments; meditation and structured psychedelic use,[39] and to become a happier person.

For you, what you need might be completely different. Indeed, the decision to undergo psychedelic therapy shouldn't be taken lightly. There are risks, particularly for those with pre-existing psychological conditions. It should always be done under the guidance of a trained professional.[40] Breathwork might be a more suitable entry point for some.[41] But finding out how to let go of the past, in your own way, is crucial if you don't want to let bitterness eat you up inside. Being angry at those who wronged you feels good, in some ways. It feels good to blame your unhappiness on another person, your upbringing, your family, the government, humanity, or whomever. But over the long term, it's literally toxic to your body.[42] My trips to (and in) the Netherlands proved to me that it just isn't worth it.

7) Make Death Your Best Friend

In my view, we need a healthier relationship with death to maximise our happiness. And to do so, we should look away from the Western world. In the West, we treat death like it'll never happen. Bringing up mortality is a no-go zone in most social situations. Whenever you watch the news and see the latest report of people dying somewhere, many of us simply do our best to ignore it. Or we trick ourselves into thinking this couldn't happen to *me*. Ernest Becker argues compellingly in *The Denial of Death* that everything humans do is in some way an unconscious denial of our 'grotesque fate'.[43] Does this in any way resonate with you?

I found as I travelled that some people live as if death is a fact of life (because it is, last time I checked). Especially in India. I remember visiting one of the most ancient and beautiful all of Indian cities, Varanasi, located on the mighty River Ganges. I walked the narrow and decorative alleys, full of shock as I passed people who were literally at death's door. They had come to the city to die. At sunset, the orange skies filled with thick, dark smoke as people cremated loved ones on wooden pyres along the river. Around 100 bodies are cremated here each day. Ignoring death is simply not an option.

I've been to funerals in many different countries, and would have to say that we in the West have gone down the gloomiest route of all when it comes to disposing of our dead. I remember a crowd of people in Madagascar singing and dancing in the street, in what looked like a carnival procession. It was only when I looked more closely that I saw a wrapped-up human-shaped package among the throngs of revellers. They were celebrating the end of someone's life. It's a ceremony called *famadihana* (the turning of the bones). The Malagasy dig up their dead once every five or seven years, spray the body in perfume and cover it in cloth, before having a right old-fashioned knees-up. What a celebration.

Regardless of our closing act in life, the outcome is

the same for all of us. Or as legendary traveller Ernest Hemingway put it, 'Every man's life ends the same way. It is only the details of how he lived and how he died that distinguishes one man from another.'[44] One truth holds eternal; we're all going to die. Stoics used to argue that philosophy was about learning to die, a point later picked up by Michel de Montaigne. He said, again referring to philosophy, that 'all the wisdom and reasoning boils down finally to this point: to teach us not to be afraid to die.'[45] Put simply, understanding death is a prerequisite for understanding life, and for being happy.

Seeing how death is a much more present reality for so many people across the world, I now teach meditation at a hospice and meditate on my death every day, forcing myself to think about the truth that this could be my last. Stoics called it *memento mori* (remember you have to die).[46] Early Buddhist texts talk about *maranasati*, which, again, reminds us to remember death.[47] Young Tibetan monks are sometimes told to meditate all night in graveyards.[48]

Travelling has brought me closer to death. Both in the sense that time has passed and I'm closer to *my* death, and also because I now think about it more. It's a paradox that thinking about death makes the present moment more precious. This is particularly useful if you're upset about something. Remembering that one day this'll all be gone can slightly take the sting out of so many difficult life events. When I face a problem, I ask myself the question, 'Would you rather have this problem, or be dead?' (In my mind, lest I freak out anyone I'm having an argument with.) It makes me feel *glad* to have the problem, rather than to be stuck in the problem-free oblivion of death.

If you think about death more, you can tune into the preciousness of life. One study found people facing imminent death were happier than would be commonly expected. They also got more positive as death approached. It showed the last words of inmates on death row and terminally ill patients were filled with love and meaning, rather than dread and fear.[49] At a silent meditation retreat I attended in Bali, an elderly gentleman summed this up beautifully. He had cancer. He described his diagnosis as the greatest gift life had ever given him.

Only through confronting his mortality was he able to truly value life. There was a high risk of him dying in the next few years. But he said this was a price worth paying for the way that his new appreciation of impermanence enriched his existence. (There was a group sharing at the end of the retreat in which talking was allowed, before you wonder whether he conveyed this message through interpretive dance.)

Embracing death can make you less scared of life. It's pushed me towards pursuing the things I love, like travel, and making the most of the staggering opportunity that is life. To make sure I don't have regrets at the end, like those outlined in Bronnie Ware's *Top Five Regrets of the Dying*.[50] Ware worked for years in palliative care. She said those who had regrets at the end were more fearful of death. The top five regrets were that people wished they'd lived a life true to themselves; hadn't worked so hard; had been brave enough to express their feelings; had stayed in touch with friends; and had let themselves be happier.

The Travelling Ape

How best to avoid making the same mistakes? Regularly remind yourself that you'll one day die. Your time is finite. Every hour that passes, the end draws nearer. Seize life with both hands. You have a tiny amount of time to enjoy being an ape on this small rock. If you want to be happier, embrace your death. *Ape diem*, if you will.

I didn't call this chapter 'How to be Happy' for good reason. Let's say you immediately start taking on board the happiness lessons I learnt from travelling. You begin to quiet your mind, prepare yourself for struggles, read, focus on the basics, adopt a morning routine, let go of the past, and think about death more. For most people, this could be overwhelming. And even if you followed these rules, they won't necessarily make you immediately happy (but I think for most it would help a bit, a least). After all, everyone's different.

I'm not going to pretend I'm enlightened. Or that what I've learnt travelling has made me happy all the time. It hasn't. I'm not 'cured'. Far from it. I can be moody, quick tempered, reactive, and anxious. All at the same time, unfortunately. I can also be worse things too, like greedy, judgemental, and narcissistic (which partly explains why this book exists). I make large mistakes in my personal life, and sometimes upset others. Quite regularly I'm sure I'm an utter pain in the arse. As we all are. We're human, after all.

But I'm definitely less of a pain in the arse than I used to be. And that has to mean something. Since sipping that lemon water in India, looking at statues of the Buddha in Sri Lanka, and chatting to the happiest man on the planet in Myanmar, my mental travels have significantly boosted my well-being and happiness. Author and meditation teacher Dan Harris famously claimed meditation made him 10 percent happier.[51] I'd say the figure for me is closer to 50 percent, when combined with all the other tools I've learnt across the world.

My ability to enjoy life has been transformed. My baseline happiness level has gone from a 5 to a 7 or 8 out of 10. My productivity and relationships have improved, and my life, generally, has become easier. Looking back on how I was in the world before my mental travels – mainly fine but perpetually dissatisfied and a bit anxious – I'm just so thankful I somehow found myself on a path of personal improvement. And that exploring and learning about other people and cultures allowed me to stumble across so many of the tools that have made me happier.

There's much to be said for what Socrates and other philosophers have referred to as 'living an examined life'.[52] Erich Fromm was also certainly correct when he argued there's an 'art of being'.[53] It's an art that we all have to work on relentlessly. Because for most of us, it doesn't come naturally. Carl Rogers, one of the founders of the humanistic approach to psychology, summarised the good life as 'a *process*, not a state of being. It's a direction, not a destination.'[54] Like world travel, it seems, my mental travels were another ride where the destination was less important than the journey itself. And for this, travel, I thank you.

Epilogue

Remember to Travel, Okay?

I write these words at my flat, plonked right in the middle of London. I can see the Shard, Tower Bridge, and the City skyline, visible in the distance in all their majesty just above the screen of my laptop. It's sunny today, a rarity in recent weeks. The skies are shining a rich shade of blue, with the sun glistening and twinkling on the glass of the City's skyscrapers. It's a lovely view. And one I've certainly got very well acquainted with over the past couple of years.

It's March 2023, almost three years since my global travels were curtailed (and, no less coincidentally, a global pandemic began). Since the pandemic began, I've had my first child and got engaged to my wonderful partner Sophie, things that I was keenly aware might make holidaying in war zones a bit trickier. At times, friends and family have trodden lightly around me. To them it appeared like my inability to travel during the pandemic was some sort of terrible diagnosis.

People would ask me, 'How are you holding up?', 'Are you coping okay?', and, less kindly, 'You must seriously lack direction now that you can't travel?' I had to remind them that in the grand scheme of things I was absolutely fine. During the pandemic I'd kept my job and so had nothing to complain about (I *did* complain, though, but mainly in my head so I'd seem noble in my suffering). And of all the wonders I've experienced in this world, I found becoming a father to be the most special of them.

I've just come back from meeting a friend, Paddy, in Borough Market. To get there, I walked down Shad Thames, a historic street full of former warehouses, now turned into flats. It's criss-crossed with ornate wrought iron bridges, which create pleasing shadows on the cobbled streets below. I popped out at Tower Bridge, looking regal and resplendent in the summer sun (Tower Bridge looked lovely too). I could see the Tower of London, the Gherkin, and countless other world-famous landmarks. The chatter of happy people drinking and socialising in the sun was audible in the background.

I chatted with Paddy over a veggie burrito and coffee (and a massive chocolate doughnut I'm less happy to mention given the preachy last chapter). The conversation moved on to the past few years and the lockdowns. My friend said there were elements he'd enjoyed, like doing less and working from home. He asked how I'd found not travelling. I was kind of surprised by the words that came out of my mouth.

'To be honest, this has been one of the best times of my life. I've missed travel. But I think I needed this time to sit back and reflect on everything I'd done, seen, and experienced across the world. Without taking the time to get my thoughts in order, I hadn't given myself the space to process all I'd learnt from so many trips. Without this time spent at home, I'm sure some of this would've been lost to me. And frankly, I'd never have got round to writing my book.'

Writing this book has been a form of travel in itself. In reflecting on my trips and my experiences, I had to look through pictures, dig into my diaries, and think deeply about some of those most memorable experiences I'd had on the road. Truth be told, it wasn't that hard. In fact, it was thoroughly enjoyable.

More than anything, reflecting on my travels made something abundantly clear. Seeing the world has been among the greatest privileges of my life. Travel has changed me and the way I see our planet. I'm frankly a different person than the one who set off on his first solo travel adventure to Southeast Asia in my late teens. Many years have since passed, but in the interim, I feel I've had several lifetimes' worth of adventures. If I got some terminal diagnosis tomorrow, I'm sure I'd be terrified. But thanks to travel, I'd at least die knowing I lived well. That I, an insignificant ape, made the most of my time on Earth by spending it travelling. I know I've taken in more than my fair share of what this incredible place has to offer.

Travel has fundamentally changed the way I think about humanity. I've seen firsthand how good the modern world is. How much better it's getting. How people are mostly decent. How we're so much more *similar* than we think. Travel has left me with the overwhelming belief that humanity is more benevolent than we're led to believe in the media. There's no substitute for seeing this for yourself.

The Travelling Ape

My global experiences have also unearthed lessons about geopolitics, which wouldn't have become clear if I'd stayed at home reading rubbish national newspapers. For all their flaws, travel proved that democracies are still easily the best places to live. I was left feeling capitalism has probably had a better impact on the world than we sometimes suppose. And although China's role in global affairs will increase, its rise won't be straightforward, and we in the West perhaps have less to fear than we commonly think.

Travel revolutionised my understanding of human happiness, and, in doing so, my personal happiness too. Seeing so much joy and resilience in the developing world, and so much continued suffering in the richest societies, allowed me to see that economic privilege is a poor predictor of human happiness. Travelling revealed the tools that've allowed me to enjoy life more.

Suffice it to say, backpacking has given my life a depth and richness I wouldn't switch for anything. My hope is that in reading this book, you'll be left feeling travel really is a worthwhile pursuit.

The aim of this book has been to make you curious about the world and yourself, supporting you in your outer and inner journey through life. Thanks for joining me for the ride. Ultimately, I hope reading this has made you want to travel. I hope it's made you keen to see the world for yourself. So if reading this book has pushed even a handful of you towards booking your tickets and setting off, that for me would be a success.

I hope it's reminded you of our collective predicament

Epilogue

too. We're all stuck on the good ship Earth together. Billions of bewildered, confused apes, here for the blink of an eye in the history of the cosmos. We share this rock, careering through a universe with more planets than grains of sand on all the world's beaches. And we don't know why. If this seems improbable, it's because your existence is.

Statistically speaking, the odds of you existing are basically zero. Your existence is a function of the odds of your parents meeting, having sex, and the sperm which became 'you' fertilising the egg in your mother's womb. To exist, every single one of your ancestors had to successfully reproduce. Not just back to the first *Homo sapiens* and *Homo erectus*, but back to the first single-celled organism, in an unbroken line stretching back four billion years.

One study estimates that as a function of these variables, the chances of you existing are 1 in 10 to the power of 2,685,000.[1] That's a 10, followed by 2,685,000 zeroes. And you exist during the only time in the history of the world (100 years out of the last few billion), that exploring the world is even possible thanks to air travel. You've won billions of lotteries in a row, statistically speaking.

In being born, you were given the staggering opportunity of (briefly) living on this planet. Don't spend your life vegetating in a little corner of it.

Notes

INTRODUCTION

1 **NomadMania is a hub for global explorers, with over 20,000 members**. 'NomadMania', https://nomadmania.com/, as accessed August 14, 2023

CHAPTER 1: WHY DO WE TRAVEL?

1 Tessa Wong, 'Prince Phillip: The Vanuatu tribes mourning the death of their god', *BBC News*, April 12, 2021, https://www.bbc.co.uk/news/world-asia-56713953, as accessed February 28, 2022.

2 **Baia has been described as the 'Las Vegas' of the Roman Empire**. Adrienne Bernhard, 'Ancient Rome's sinful city at the bottom of the sea', *BBC Travel*, January 5, 2018, https://www.bbc.com/travel/article/20180104-ancient-romes-sinful-city-at-the-bottom-of-the-sea#:~:text=Baia%20was%20the%20Las%20Vegas,carry%20out%20their%20illicit%20affairs, as accessed May 7, 2021.

3 'The Spanish quest for Terra Australis', *State Library New South Wales*, https://www.sl.nsw.gov.au/stories/spanish-quest-terra-australis, as accessed February 28, 2022.

4 Briony Leyland, 'Island holds reconciliation over cannibalism', *BBC News*, December 7, 2009, http://news.bbc.co.uk/1/hi/england/hampshire/8398126.stm, as accessed February 28, 2022.

5 Tamara Hardingham-Gill, 'Backpacking is a rite of passage for many travellers. Covid could end it forever', *CNN*, December 31, 2020, https://edition.cnn.com/travel/article/will-covid-end-backpacking-travel/index.html, as accessed April 7, 2023.

6 'In search of the ageing backpacker', *WYSE Travel Confederation*, December 9, 2019, https://www.wysetc.org/2019/12/in-search-of-the-aging-backpacker/, as accessed July 15, 2020.

7 **The benefits of travel on creativity**. Brent Crane, 'For a More Creative Brain, Travel', *The Atlantic*, March 31, 2015, https://www.theatlantic.com/health/archive/2015/03/for-a-more-creative-brain-travel/388135/, as accessed July 13, 2020.

8   **Time moves faster as we age**. James Broadway and Brittany Sandoval, 'Why Does Time Seem to Speed Up with Age?', *Scientific American*, July 1, 2016, https://www.scientificamerican.com/article/why-does-time-seem-to-speed-up-with-age/#:~:text=Our%20brain%20encodes%20new%20experiences,create%20over%20a%20certain%20period.&text=As%20adults%2C%20though%2C%20our%20lives,we%20experience%20fewer%20unfamiliar%20moments, as accessed September 11, 2020.

9   **One study found that mid-brain regions preferentially respond to novelty with dopamine**. Researchers showed participants a series of images of common scenes such as landscapes and faces. They then randomly threw in an 'oddball' image, something that was unexpected and out of the ordinary. Brian Knutson and Jeffrey Cooper, 'The Lure of the Unknown', *Neuron*, vol. 51: no. 3 (August 2006), p280-282, https://www.sciencedirect.com/science/article/pii/S0896627306005575, as accessed July 13, 2020.

10 'Dromomania', *Merriam-Webster Dictionary*, https://www.merriam-webster.com/medical/dromomania, as accessed September 10, 2020.

11 **As seen in** Peter Walbrook, 'Travellers checks', *South China Morning Post*, March 19, 2006, https://www.scmp.com/article/540963/travellers-checks, as accessed September 10, 2020.

12 **Several of these apps exist, including Been and Countries Been**. Or if you feel like laughing at the primitive technology of people who lived a decade or so ago, you can buy an actual scratch map.

13 **One 2013 study surveyed 1,500 Americans**. Of the respondents, 86% said travel improved their mood, 78% said it lowered their stress levels, 77% argued it improved their physical health, and 71% suggested it helped them enjoy the current period in their life more. 'Journey To Healthy Aging: Planning For Travel In Retirement', Transamerica Center For Retirement Studies, December 2013, p8, https://www.transamericacenter.org/docs/default-source/resources/travel-survey/tcrs2013_sr_travel_and_aging.pdf, as accessed August 24, 2020.

14 **Port Moresby has been hovering near the bottom of the rankings for years.** *The Global Liveability Index 2023: A free overview*, The Economist Intelligence Unit, 2023, p3.

15 Jo Chandler, 'Papua New Guinea Is Rich in Resources but Poor in Health', *The New York Times*, November 13, 2018, https://www.nytimes.com/2018/11/13/world/asia/papua-new-guinea-apec-polio-health-crisis.html, as accessed April 6, 2022.

Notes

CHAPTER 2: A BRIEF GUIDE TO THE PLANET

1   As quoted in Carl Gaither and Alma Cavazos-Gaither, *Astronomically Speaking: A Dictionary of Quotations on Astronomy and Physics* (New York: Taylor & Francis, 2003), p262.

2   **Fascinating insights on what it takes to go into space**. Chris Hadfield, *An Astronaut's Guide to Life on Earth: Life Lessons from Space* (London: Pan Macmillan, 2013), p1.

3   Quote in Emma Brockes, 'Chris Hadfield: in space "you recognise the unanimity of our existence", *The Guardian*, October 28, 2013, https://www.theguardian.com/science/2013/oct/26/chris-hadfield-astronaut-space-interview, as accessed December 28, 2020.

4   **How space travel can be good for the soul**. Eva C. Ihle, Jennifer Boys, and Nick Kanas, 'Positive empirical outcomes of spaceflight: an empirical study', *Aviation Space and Environmental Medicine*, vol. 77: no. 2, (March 2006), p93-101, March 2006. https://www.researchgate.net/publication/7284843_Positive_psychological_outcomes_of_spaceflight_An_empirical_study, as accessed August 26, 2020.

5   **Most astronauts feel increasingly connected to humanity and become more appalled by violence and wars after going into space**. Frank White, *The Overview Effect: Space Exploration and Human Evolution* (Boston: Houghton Mifflin, 1987).

6   **Richard Branson will take you up to space for US$250,000 while Jeff Bezos will do it for US$28 million**. Gwyn Topham and Julia Kollewe, 'Richard Branson's Virgin Galactic prepares to go public', *The Guardian*, July 9, 2019, https://www.theguardian.com/science/2019/jul/09/richard-branson-virgin-galactic-go-public, as accessed August 26, 2020 and Kenneth Chang, 'What will it cost to fly on New Shepard?', *The New York Times*, July 20, 2021, https://www.nytimes.com/2021/07/20/science/cost-to-fly-blue-origin-bezos.html, as accessed July 23, 2021.

7   **For a stranger than fiction account of how weird the universe is**. Neil deGrasse Tyson, *Astrophysics for People in a Hurry* (London: W. W. Norton, 2017), p63.

8   All population data in chapter from 'Population Dynamics', United Nations Department of Economic and Social Affairs, https://population.un.org/wup/DataQuery/, as accessed August 28, 2020.

9   **According to my own analysis**. If you plot average temperatures against GDP per capita in Western Europe, the trend is clear. Denmark, Iceland, and Norway make up the top three in terms of GDP per capita, while being three of the coldest countries.

10 **The balance of global economic power will shift dramatically in the years ahead**. PWC, *The Long View: How will the global economic order change by 2050* (London: PWC, 2017), p4, https://

www.pwc.com/gx/en/world-2050/assets/pwc-the-world-in-2050-full-report-feb-2017.pdf, as accessed December 27, 2020.

11 **The politeness of the Japanese people is legendary**. Paula Gerhold, 'The top 10 words to describe Japanese people (according to foreigners)', *Japan Today*, August 28, 2013, https://japantoday.com/category/features/lifestyle/the-top-10-words-to-describe-japanese-people-according-to-foreigners, as accessed September 21, 2020.

12 **The sacredness of nature in Japan, even in its language, is unsurpassed globally**. Marie Sugio, '11 beautiful Japanese words that don't exist in English', *Odyssey*, https://www.theodysseyonline.com/11-beautiful-untranslatable-japanese-words, as accessed September 8, 2020.

13 **Being in nature can elicit transcendent and transformative emotions**. Lisbeth Bethelmy and José Corraliza, 'Transcendence and Sublime Experience in Nature: Awe and Inspiring Energy', *Frontiers in Psychology*, vol. 10: no. 509 (March 2019), https://www.frontiersin.org/articles/10.3389/fpsyg.2019.00509/full, as accessed September 8, 2020.

14 Ibid.

15 **The data makes unhappy reading for Central American countries**. Out of 230 measured countries and territories for murders per capita, El Salvador comes in 1st, Honduras 5th, Belize 6th, Mexico 13th, Guatemala 18th, and Nicaragua 68th. 'Intentional Homicide Victims', United Nations Office on Drugs and Crime, https://dataunodc.un.org/crime/intentional-homicide-victims, as accessed on September 1, 2020.

16 **California would be an economic powerhouse in its own right**. Kieran Corcoran, 'California's economy is now the fifth biggest in the world, and has overtaken the United Kingdom', *The Independent*, May 11, 2018, https://www.independent.co.uk/news/california-economy-overtakes-uk-fifth-biggest-world-a8347291.html, as accessed September 1, 2020.

17 'The World Bank in the Pacific Islands', The World Bank, https://www.worldbank.org/en/country/pacificisland, as accessed September 3, 2020.

18 Mark Fischetti, 'Africa Is Way Bigger Than You Think', *Scientific American*, June 16, 2015, https://blogs.scientificamerican.com/observations/africa-is-way-bigger-than-you-think/, as accessed September 3, 2020.

19 **If the world feels full now, it certainly will in 100 years**. 'Population', The United Nations, https://www.un.org/en/global-issues/population#:~:text=Our%20growing%20population&text=The%20global%20human%20population%20reached,and%202%20billion%20since%201998, as accessed April 28, 2023.

Notes

CHAPTER 3: LESSONS FROM URBAN TRAVEL

1　'Quote by Christopher Morley', *Power Quotations*, https://www. powerquotations.com/quote/all-cities-are-mad-but, as accessed August 25, 2020.

2　**All urban population data from** United Nations, Department of Economic and Social Affairs, Population Division, *World Urbanization Prospects: The 2018 Revision* (New York: United Nations, 2019), https://population.un.org/wup/Publications/Files/ WUP2018-Report.pdf, as accessed December 21, 2020.

3　Brad Lendon and Emiko Jozuka, 'History's deadliest air raid happened in Tokyo during World War II and you've probably never heard of it', *CNN*, March 8, 2020, https://edition. cnn.com/2020/03/07/asia/japan-tokyo-fire-raids-operation-meetinghouse-intl-hnk/index.html, as accessed February 28, 2023.

4　**Alpha + + cities: London, New York. Alpha + cities: Beijing, Hong Kong, Shanghai, Tokyo, Dubai, Paris, Singapore.** Alpha: Amsterdam, Brussels, Chicago, Frankfurt, Jakarta, Kuala Lumpur, Los Angeles, Madrid, Mexico City, Milan, Moscow, Mumbai, São Paulo, Sydney, Toronto. Alpha – cities: Bangkok, Bangalore, Boston, Buenos Aires, Dublin, Guangzhou, Istanbul, Johannesburg, Lisbon, Luxembourg City, Manilla, Melbourne, Montreal, Munich, New Delhi, Prague, Riyadh, San Francisco, Santiago, Seoul, Shenzen, Stockholm, Taipei, Vienna, Warsaw, Zurich. 'The World According to GaWC2020', Globalization and World Cities Research Network, https://www.lboro.ac.uk/ microsites/geography/gawc/world2020.html, as accessed April 24, 2023.

5　'Index', *The Samuel Johnson Sound Bite Page*, https://www. samueljohnson.com/tiredlon.html, as accessed August 15, 2020.

6　**Having a small plant within viewing sight for office workers can reduce stress.** Masahiro Toyoda, Yuko Yokota, Marni Barnes, and Midori Kaneko, 'Potential of a Small Indoor Plant on the Desk for Reducing Office Workers' Stress', *American Society for Horticultural Science*, vol. 30: no. 1 (December 2019), p55-63, https://journals.ashs.org/horttech/view/journals/horttech/30/1/ article-p55.xml **One study suggested that having plants in hospital rooms aids patients' recoveries, by reducing stress and increasing positivity.** American Society for Horticultural Science, 'Flowering Plants Speed Post-Surgery Recovery', *Science Daily*, December 30, 2008, https://www.sciencedaily.com/ releases/2008/12/081229104700.htm, both accessed January 30, 2020.

7　**For a book that shows us how important nature is to our**

455

mental and physical health. Lucy Jones, *Losing Eden: Why our Minds need the Wild* (London: Random House, 2020), p183.

8   **The Earth's living biomass and anthropogenic mass weighed approximately 1.1 teratones in 2020**. Emily Elcham, Liad Ben-Uri, Jonothan Grozovski, Yinon M. Bar-On, and Ron Milo, 'Global human-made mass exceeds all living biomass', *Nature*, vol. 588 (2020), p442-444, https://www.nature.com/articles/s41586-020-3010-5, as accessed January 29, 2020.

CHAPTER 4: THE IMPORTANCE OF TRAVEL

1   Caroline Sherwood Bigelow, '10 Little-Known Facts About Poverty in Sierra Leone', *The Borgen Project*, July 15, 2018, https://borgenproject.org/facts-about-poverty-in-sierra-leone/, as accessed March 1, 2023.

2   Mark Twain, *The Innocents Abroad* (Hartford: American Publishing Company, 1879), p650.

3   Rutger Bregman, *Human Kind* (London: Bloomsbury, 2020), p360.

4   **Travel makes you more open**. Julia Zimmermann and Franz J. Neyer, 'Do we become a different person when hitting the road? Personality development of sojourners', *The Journal of Personality and Social Psychology*, vol. 105: no. 3 (September 2013), p515-530, https://pubmed.ncbi.nlm.nih.gov/23773042/, as accessed August 18, 2020.

5   **The more countries you visit, the more you believe in the benevolence of human nature**. The study tested the assumption across five groups that featured over 700 participants asking the question: 'Does travel make people more trusting?', with trust in this context defined to mean a generalised belief in the benevolence of human nature. The breadth (number of countries travelled) but not the depth (amount of time spent travelling) of foreign travel experiences predicted trust behaviour in a decision-making game. Jiyin Cao, Adam D. Galinsky, and William W. Maddux, 'Does Travel Broaden the Mind? Breadth of Foreign Experiences Increases Generalized Trust', *Social Psychological and Personality Science*, vol. 5: no. 5 (June 2014), p517-525, https://www.researchgate.net/publication/274063991_Does_Travel_Broaden_the_Mind_Breadth_of_Foreign_Experiences_Increases_Generalized_Trust, as accessed August 18, 2020.

6   Eric Dolan, 'New Study confirms Mark Twain's saying: Travel is fatal to prejudice', *PsyPost*, December 9, 2013, https://www.psypost.org/2013/12/new-study-confirms-mark-twains-saying-travel-is-fatal-to-prejudice-21662, as accessed August 19, 2020.

7   **The perception that Americans don't travel much is largely**

Notes

true. Lea Lane, 'Percentage of Americans Who Have Never Travelled Beyond The State Where They Were Born? A Surprise', *Forbes*, May 2, 2019, https://www.forbes.com/sites/lealane/2019/05/02/percentage-of-americans-who-never-traveled-beyond-the-state-where-they-were-born-a-surprise/#5bdac5b22898, as accessed August 17, 2020.

8   Lorenzo Ferrari, '190 million Europeans have never been abroad', *European Data Journalism Network,* June 21, 2018, https://www.europeandatajournalism.eu/eng/News/Data-news/190-million-Europeans-have-never-been-abroad, as accessed August 17, 2020.

9   **Eagleman uses the term 'livewired' to describe how our brain and personalities have the ability to change constantly throughout the course of our lives**. David Eagleman, *Livewired: The Inside Story of the Ever-Changing Brain* (Edinburgh: Canongate, 2022), p14.

10   **Outlining more of the positive benefits of travel**. Suzanne Rowan Kelleher, 'This Is Your Brain On Travel', *Forbes*, June 28, 2019, https://www.forbes.com/sites/suzannerowankelleher/2019/07/28/this-is-your-brain-on-travel/#58352b6f2bc6, as accessed August 18, 2020.

11   Brooks Gump, Karen A. Matthews, 'Are Vacations Good for Your Health? The 9-Year Mortality Experience After the Multiple Risk Factor Intervention Trial', *Psychosomatic Medicine*, vol. 62 (2000), p608-612, http://people.umass.edu/econ340/vacations_health.pdf, as accessed August 24, 2020.

12   Elaine. D. Eaker, 'Myocardial Infarction and Coronary Death among Women: Psychological Predictors from a 20-Year Follow-Up of Women in the Framingham Study', *American Journal of Epidemiology*, vol. 135: no 8 (April 1992), p854-864, https://academic.oup.com/aje/article-abstract/135/8/854/51198?redirectedFrom=fulltext, as accessed December 27, 2020.

13   Robert McMillen, 'If you think adventure is dangerous, try routine – it's lethal: Paulo Coehlo', *The Irish News*, November 7, 2016, http://www.irishnews.com/arts/thebluffer/2016/10/31/news/if-you-think-adventure-is-dangerous-try-routine---it-s-lethal-paulo-coelho-761258/, as accessed August 25 2020.

PART II: HUMANITY

CHAPTER 5: THE WORLD IS BETTER THAN WE ARE LED TO BELIEVE

1   Kate Wong, 'Tiny Genetic Differences between Humans and Other Primates Pervade the Genome', *Scientific American*, September 1,

2014, https://www.scientificamerican.com/article/tiny-genetic-differences-between-humans-and-other-primates-pervade-the-genome/, as accessed September 23, 2020.

2   Gary Strauss, 'Saving Rwanda's Endangered Species, One at a Time', *National Geographic*, September 15, 2016, https://www.nationalgeographic.com/adventure/article/olivier-nsengimana-explorer-moments-gorilla-crane, as accessed March 1, 2022.

3   Kate Wong, 'Tiny Genetic Differences between Humans and Other Primates Pervade the Genome'.

4   **If our closest relatives are this violent, perhaps humanity's history of war makes more sense?** Quote in Rami Tzabar, 'Do chimpanzee wars prove that violence is innate?', *BBC Earth*, August 11, 2015, http://www.bbc.co.uk/earth/story/20150811-do-animals-fight-wars, as accessed September 23, 2020.

5   Chelsea Whyte, 'Chimps beat up, murder and then cannibalise their former tyrant', *New Scientist*, January 30, 2017, https://www.newscientist.com/article/2119677-chimps-beat-up-murder-and-then-cannibalise-their-former-tyrant/, as accessed September 23, 2020.

6   Elaina Zachos, 'Bonobos Express Empathy and Willingly Help Strangers', *National Geographic*, November 10, 2017, https://www.nationalgeographic.com/news/2017/11/bonobo-help-stranger-behavior-animals-speed/#:~:text=Bonobos%20are%20known%20as%20the,as%20chimpanzees%2C%22%20Tan%20says, as accessed September 23, 2020.

7   **An enthralling account of why humans behave the way they do, looking at examples from our closest genetic cousins**. Frans De Waal, *Our Inner Ape: The Best and Worst of Human Nature* (London: Granta, 2005).

8   Isaac M. Marks, 'Fear and Fitness: An Evolutionary Analysis of Anxiety Disorders', *Ethology and Sociobiology*, vol. 15 (1994), p247-261.

9   Douglas J. Lisle and Alan Goldhamer, *The Pleasure Trap: Mastering the Hidden Force that Undermines Health and Happiness* (Summertown: Healthy Living Publications, 2003), p42.

10 'State of nature: how modern humans lived as nomads for 99 percent of our history', *The Independent*, February 11, 2009, https://www.independent.co.uk/news/world/world-history/state-of-nature-how-modern-humans-lived-as-nomads-for-99-per-cent-of-our-history-1604967.html, as accessed March 7, 2022.

11 Toshiko Kaneda and Car Haub, 'How Many People Have Ever Lived on Earth?', *Future World Foundation*, February 10, 2020, https://www.futureworldfoundation.org/Content/Article.aspx?ArticleID=25193#:~:text=%E2%80%9CModern%E2%80%9D%20Homo%20Sapiens%20first%20walked,species%20have%20ever%20been%20born, as accessed August 2, 2021.

Notes

12 John Noble Wilford, 'When Humans Became Human', *The New York Times*, February 26, 2020, https://www.nytimes.com/2002/02/26/science/when-humans-became-human.html, as accessed September 22, 2020.

13 **We have spread at a quite staggering pace**. Anthony Cilluffo and Neil G. Ruiz, 'World's population is projected to nearly stop growing by the end of the century', Pew Research Center, June 17, 2019, https://www.pewresearch.org/fact-tank/2019/06/17/worlds-population-is-projected-to-nearly-stop-growing-by-the-end-of-the-century/, as accessed September 22, 2020.

14 **The Aztecs were a fun bunch**. Dale Brown, *Aztecs: Reign of Blood and Splendour* (Virginia: Time-Life Books, 1992), p105.

15 **Theories differ, with some suggesting both winners and losers were sacrificed at some point during the game's history**. Andrew Evans, 'Death Ball', *National Geographic*, https://www.nationalgeographic.com/travel/article/death-ball, as accessed April 3, 2023.

16 Jens Meierhenrich, 'How Many Victims Were There in the Rwandan Genocide? A Statistical Debate', *Journal of Genocide Research*, vol. 22: no. 1 (2020), p77-82, https://doi.org/10.1080/14623528.2019.1709611, as accessed April 7, 2023.

17 'BTI 2006-2022 Scores', *Bertelsmann Transformation Index,* https://bti-project.org/en/downloads, as accessed April 7, 2023.

18 'Countries in the world by population (2020)', *Worldometer*, https://www.worldometers.info/world-population/population-by-country/, as accessed September 30, 2020.

19 **In 1950, GDP per capita ranged from US$850 in South Korea to US$2,200 in Singapore.** In each economy, it had risen more than tenfold by 2010. Paulina Restrepo Echavarria and Maria A. Arias, 'Tigers, Tiger Cubs and Economic Growth', *Federal Reserve Bank of St. Louis*, May 25, 2017, https://www.stlouisfed.org/on-the-economy/2017/may/tigers-tiger-cubs-economic-growth#:~:text=In%201950%2C%20gross%20domestic%20product,and%20%2430%2C720%20in%20Hong%20Kong., as accessed April 7, 2023.

20 'Decline of Global Extreme Poverty Continues But Has Slowed', The World Bank, September 19, 2018, https://www.worldbank.org/en/news/press-release/2018/09/19/decline-of-global-extreme-poverty-continues-but-has-slowed-world-bank, as accessed July 20, 2021.

21 Hans Rosling, *Factfulness: Ten Reasons We're Wrong About The World – And Why Things Are Better Than You Think* (London: Spectre, 2018), and Gapminder, https://www.gapminder.org/, as accessed September 25, 2022.

22   **All statistics in the following section were pulled from a combination of the following sources**: Hans Rosling, 'Factfulness', *Gapminder*, https://www.gapminder.org/downloads/; Our World in Data, https://ourworldindata.org/; The World Health Organisation, https://www.who.int/; Amnesty International, https://www.amnesty.org.uk/?utm_source=google&utm_medium=grant&utm_campaign=BRD_GEN_brand&utm_content=amnesty%20international, The World Bank Open Data, https://data.worldbank.org/, and Indur Goklany, 'Death and death rates due to extreme weather', *Journal of American Physicians and Surgeons*, vol. 14: no. 4 (2009), p102-109, https://www.jpands.org/vol14no4/goklany.pdf, all as accessed between September 30, 2020 to February 27, 2023.

CHAPTER 6: MOST PEOPLE ARE NICE

1   Megan Stewart, 'What's at stake if Turkey invades Syria, again', *Middle East Institute*, December 7, 2022, https://www.mei.edu/publications/whats-stake-if-turkey-invades-syria-again, as accessed April 7, 2023.

2   **A fantastic treatise on the merits and goodness of humans.** Rutger Bregman, *Humankind: A Hopeful History* (London: Bloomsbury, 2020), p12.

3   **We spend our lives looking at things that don't affect us or our lives**, SWNS, 'Americans check their phones 80 times a day: study', *New York Post*, November 8, 2017, https://nypost.com/2017/11/08/americans-check-their-phones-80-times-a-day-study/, as accessed October 13, 2020.

4   **The Kurds, under the protection of US forces, moved in 1992 to hold elections and distance itself from the Iraqi state**. Michael M. Gunter, 'A de facto Kurdish state in Northern Iraq', *Third World Quarterly*, vol. 14: no. 2 (1993), https://www.jstor.org/stable/3992569, as accessed April 7, 2023.

5   **Russians are much less rude than we're led to believe**. Neil Martin, 'Rude Russians and feigned politeness', *BBC*, July 27, 2015, https://www.bbc.com/russian/blogs/2015/07/150727_blog_strana_russia_pointless_politeness, as accessed October 24, 2020.

6   National Consortium for the Study of Terrorism and Responses to Terrorism, *Global Terrorism Overview: Terrorism in 2019* (Maryland: University of Maryland 2020), p10.

7   Ibid.

8   'Concern About Being Victim of a Terrorist Attack', *Gallup*, https://news.gallup.com/poll/4909/terrorism-united-states.aspx, as accessed April 7, 2023.

Notes

9 Gerely Hideg and Gianlucca Boo, 'The Calm Before the Storm: Global Violent Deaths Update 201-2020', *Small Arms Survey*, July 7, 2022, https://smallarmssurvey.medium.com/the-calm-before-the-storm-global-violent-deaths-update-2019-2020-5b56c53b6834, as accessed April 7, 2023.

10 **Human violence doesn't even make the top 10 causes of death**. Maybe we're not all awful. 'The top 10 causes of death', The World Health Organization, https://www.who.int/news-room/fact-sheets/detail/the-top-10-causes-of-death, as accessed October 23, 2020.

11 **And have killed 1.2 million people in India alone since 2020**. 'More than one million died of snake bites in India', *BBC*, July 8, 2020, https://www.bbc.co.uk/news/world-asia-india-53331803, as accessed October 23, 2020.

12 'Road Safety', World Health Organization, https://www.who.int/data/gho/data/themes/road-safety, as accessed October 26, 2020.

13 Ibid.

14 'Road Traffic Deaths and Proportion of Road Users By Country/Area – 2015', World Health Organisation, https://www.who.int/violence_injury_prevention/road_safety_status/2015/TableA2.pdf?ua=1, as accessed October 26, 2020.

15 Anne Frank, *The Diary of a Young Girl* (Amsterdam: Doubleday, 1995).

16 **An excellent reminder of the fact that we are animals**, and driven inexorably by evolution in our modern lives. Robert Wright, *The Moral Animal: Why We Are the Way We Are* (London: Abacus, 1994), p8.

CHAPTER 7: WE AREN'T SO DIFFERENT AFTER ALL

1 Aldous Huxley, *Brave New World* (New York: Harper Collins, 1932).

2 Erin Blakemore, 'Who Were the Mongols', *National Geographic*, June 21, 2019, https://www.nationalgeographic.com/culture/article/mongols#:~:text=At%20its%20peak%2C%20the%20Mongol,massive%20horde%20of%20nomadic%20warriors, as accessed March 2, 2023.

3 **The Xiongnu Empire dominated Central Asia for 500 years from the 3rd century BCE,** whose repeated incursion into northern China led to the construction of the Great Wall of China. 'Xiongnu', *Britannica*, https://www.britannica.com/topic/Xiongnu, as accessed April 7, 2023.

4 **More than 16 million men in Central Asia have the same male Y chromosome as the Mongol leader**. Robin Mckie, 'We

461

owe it all to superstud Genghis', *The Guardian*, March 2, 2003, https://www.theguardian.com/uk/2003/mar/02/science.research, as accessed March 2, 2023.

5   **We live in the future**. Jessica Brown, 'Can computer translators ever beat speaking in a foreign tongue', *BBC*, February 21, 2020, https://www.bbc.co.uk/news/business-50850239, as accessed October 28, 2020.

6   **Facebook, Instagram, and WhatsApp are banned in China.** They mostly use WeChat instead, which combines a similar service into one app. Benjamin Haas, 'China blocks WhatsApp services as censors tighten grip on internet', *The Guardian*, July 19, 2017, https://www.theguardian.com/technology/2017/jul/19/china-blocks-whatsapp-services-as-censors-tighten-grip-on-internet#:~:text=China%20has%20partially%20blocked%20the,text%20messages%20were%20not%20affected, as accessed November 2, 2020.

7   **For an entire book dedicated to the history and nuance of the English language**. Only Bill Bryson could make such a dry topic humorous and interesting. Bill Bryson, *Mother Tongue: The Story of the English Language* (London: Penguin, 1990).

8   **2017 data**. Drew DeSilver, 'Despite global concerns about democracy, more than half of countries are democratic', Pew Research Center, May 14, 2019, https://www.pewresearch.org/fact-tank/2019/05/14/more-than-half-of-countries-are-democratic/, as accessed November 2, 2020.

9   **As highlighted famously by** Albert Camus, *The Myth of Sisyphus* (London: Penguin, 2013).

10   **It's still much higher than we would like, but low if you consider the world as a whole**. Max Roser and Esteban Ortiz-Ospina, 'Primary and Secondary Education', Our World in Data, https://ourworldindata.org/primary-and-secondary-education, as accessed November 2, 2020.

11   **Even though some argue having children will actually make you less happy**. Nattavudh Powdthavee, 'Think having children will make you happy?', *The Psychologist*, vol. 22: no. 4 (April 2009), p308-311, https://www.researchgate.net/publication/292004780_Think_having_childern_will_make_you_happy, as accessed November 2, 2020.

12   **Karakorum was the capital of the empire, however, and acts as proof that the Mogolians did have some planned urban areas.** Jan Bemmann, Sven Linzen, Susanne Reichert, and LKh. Munkbayar, 'Mapping Karakorum, the capital of the Mongol Empire', *Antiquity*, vol. 96: no. 385 (February 2022), p159-178, https://www.cambridge.org/core/journals/antiquity/article/mapping-karakorum-the-capital-of-the-mongol-empire/6E86EC9

Notes

807E3354074D101D1AA15056F , as accessed April 24, 2023.

13 **Many of these groups have had regular contact with humans from the outside world, but have maintained their unique ways of life.** Sean Kane, 'More than 100 tribes across the world still live in total isolation from society', *The Independent*, March 8, 2018, https://www.independent.co.uk/news/people/100-uncontacted-tribes-amazon-rainforest-peru-indonesia-jarawa-a8245651.html, as accessed November 2, 2020.

14 Jason Palmer, 'Amondawa tribe lacks abstract idea of time, study says', *BBC*, May 20, 2011, https://www.bbc.co.uk/news/science-environment-13452711, as accessed October 29, 2020.

15 Paul Raffaele, 'Sleeping with Cannibals', *The Smithsonian Magazine*, September 2006, https://www.smithsonianmag.com/travel/sleeping-with-cannibals-128958913/, as accessed November 3, 2020.

16 '68% of the world population projected to live in urban areas by 2050, UN says', United Nations Department of Economic and Social Affairs, 16 May, 2018, https://www.un.org/development/desa/en/news/population/2018-revision-of-world-urbanization-prospects.html, as accessed November 3, 2020.

CHAPTER 8: GOD'S PLANET

1 **Lots of fables in old English, which form the basis of billions of peoples' lives.** 'Genesis 22:12', *Bible Gateway*, https://www.biblegateway.com/verse/en/Genesis%2022%3A12, as accessed November 4, 2020.

2 Dalia Fahmy, 'Americans are far more religious than adults in other wealthy nations', Pew Research Center, July 31, 2018, https://www.pewresearch.org/fact-tank/2018/07/31/americans-are-far-more-religious-than-adults-in-other-wealthy-nations/, as accessed March 6, 2023.

3 John Curtice, Elizabeth Clery, Jane Perry, Miranda Phillips, and Nilufer Rahim (eds.), *British Social Attitudes; The 36th Report* (London: The National Centre for Social Research, 2019), p21.

4 **His Labour Party worried that the population would be less amenable to a religious prime minister.** When Blair was once asked about his faith, Downing Street spin doctor Alastair Campbell bluntly interjected, 'We don't do God.' Quoted in Brian Wheeler, 'Politicians, pulpits, and God', *BBC News*, April 22, 2014, https://www.bbc.co.uk/news/uk-politics-27112774, as accessed November 4, 2020.

5 Conrad Hackett and David McClendon, 'Christians remain the world's largest religious group, but they are declining in Europe', Pew

Research Center, April 5, 2017, https://www.pewresearch.org/fact-tank/2017/04/05/christians-remain-worlds-largest-religious-group-but-they-are-declining-in-europe/, as accessed November 9, 2020.

6   Ibid.

7   **The other two are Japan, where Shintoism and Buddhism are popular. And Cuba, where Christianity has been viewed as a bit naughty, lest people forget to worship at the altar of their main religion: communism.** Stein Emil Vollset, Emily Goren, Chun-Wei Yuan, Jackie Cao, Amanda Smith, and Thomas Hsiao, 'Fertility, mortality, migration, and population scenarios for 195 countries and territories from 2017 to 2100: a forecasting analysis for the Global Burden of Disease Study', *The Lancet*, vol. 396 (October 17, 2020), p1285-1306, https://www.thelancet.com/journals/lancet/article/PIIS0140-6736(20)30677-2/fulltext#seccestitle210, as accessed November 9, 2020.

8   'From The Arab Conquests To 1830', *Britannica*, https://www.britannica.com/place/North-Africa/From-the-Arab-conquest-to-1830, as accessed November 10, 2020.

9   Farzana Shaikh, 'Pakistan's quest for identity: contesting Islam', *The Conversation*, May 6, 2020, https://theconversation.com/pakistans-quest-for-identity-contesting-islam-95571, as accessed November 10, 2020.

10   Firas Alkhateeb, 'Do you know how Islam spread in the Indian subcontinent?', *Egypt Today*, May 29, 2017, https://www.egypttoday.com/Article/4/5996/Do-you-know-how-Islam-spread-in-the-Indian-subcontinent, as accessed November 10, 2020.

11   'Hagia Sophia', *Britannica*, https://www.britannica.com/topic/Hagia-Sophia, as accessed April 14, 2023.

12   'Buddhism', *Ancient History Encyclopedia*, September 25, 2020, https://www.ancient.eu/buddhism/, as accessed November 11, 2020.

13   **Theodosius declared that Catholicism would be the empire's state religion in 380 CE.** All other religious sects lost their legal status, were deemed heretical, and had their property confiscated. Greg Forster, *The Contested Public Square: The Crisis of Christianity and Politics* (Illinois: IVP Academic, 2008), p41.

14   'Religion in Latin America: Widespread Change in a Historically Catholic Region', Pew Research Center, November 13, 2014, https://www.pewforum.org/2014/11/13/religion-in-latin-america/, as accessed November 9, 2020.

15   **After Pope Clement VII refused to grant him an annulment to Katherine of Aragon, King Henry formed his own church**. And was then free to divorce and murder as he pleased. Susan Doran, 'Henry VIII and the reformation', *British Library: Discovering Sacred*

Notes

Texts, September 23, 2019, https://www.bl.uk/sacred-texts/articles/henry-viii-and-the-reformation, as accessed November 9, 2020.

16 'Church of England', *History*, February 13, 2018, https://www.history.com/topics/british-history/church-of-england#:~:text=The%20Church%20of%20England%20is,adopted%20during%20the%20Protestant%20Reformation, as accessed November 9, 2020.

17 Estimate based on data available in 'The Global Religious Landscape: A Report on the Size and Distribution of the World's Major Religious Groups as of 2010', Pew Research Center, December 2012, https://assets.pewresearch.org/wp-content/uploads/sites/11/2014/01/global-religion-full.pdf, as accessed November 9, 2020.

18 Martin Chulov, 'I will return Saudi Arabia to moderate Islam, says crown prince', *The Guardian*, October 24, 2020, https://www.theguardian.com/world/2017/oct/24/i-will-return-saudi-arabia-moderate-islam-crown-prince, as accessed November 22, 2020.

19 **While such complex and diverse issues are hard to measure statistically, perhaps the most respected effort has been from the World Bank**. Its Global Gender Gap Index uses 14 different indicators to measure the gender gap. With one being full gender equality, the median score for the world was 0.70 in 2022, up from 0.65 in 2006, when the dataset begins. 'Overall Global Gender Gap Index', The World Bank, https://tcdata360.worldbank.org/indicators/af52ebe9?country=BRA&indicator=27959&viz=line_chart&years=2006,2018, as accessed October 20, 2020.

20 **For a slew of statistics on the persistence of gender inequality**. Esteban Ortiz-Ospina and Max Roser, 'Economic Inequality by Gender', Our World In Data, March 2018, https://ourworldindata.org/economic-inequality-by-gender, as accessed October 22, 2020.

21 Ibid.

22 **At current rates of progress the gender gap will be closed in 54 years in Western Europe**, 59 years in Latin America, 71 years in Southeast Asia, 95 years in Sub-Saharan Africa, 140 years in the Middle East and North Africa, and 163 years in East Asia and the Pacific. World Economic Forum, *Global Gender Gap Report 2020* (Geneva: World Economic Forum, 2019), p6, http://www3.weforum.org/docs/WEF_GGGR_2020.pdf, as accessed October 22, 2020.

23 Beth Kissileff, 'Women Join Talmud Celebration', *Tablet*, July 30, 2012, https://www.tabletmag.com/sections/belief/articles/women-join-talmud-celebration, as accessed November 12, 2020.

24 Lizzy Davies, 'Church of England votes against allowing women bishops', *The Guardian*, November 21, 2020, https://www.theguardian.com/world/2012/nov/20/church-of-england-no-women-bishops, as accessed November 6, 2020.

25   John Curtice et al., *British Social Attitudes, The 36th Report*, p23.

26   Patience Atuhaire, 'Uganda Anti-Homosexuality bill: Life in prison for saying you're gay', *BBC News*, March 22, 2023, https://www.bbc.com/news/world-africa-65034343, as accessed April 5, 2023.

27   'Map of Countries that Criminalise LGBT People', Human Dignity Trust, https://www.humandignitytrust.org/lgbt-the-law/map-of-criminalisation/, as accessed November 26, 2021.

28   **People define themselves in terms of which social groups they're in, in opposition to all of the other ones**. Susan Krauss Whitbourne, 'In-Groups, Out-Groups, and the Psychology of Crowds', *Psychology Today*, December 7, 2010, https://www.psychologytoday.com/gb/blog/fulfillment-any-age/201012/in-groups-out-groups-and-the-psychology-crowds, as accessed November 18, 2020.

29   **Neuroscientist David Eagleman describes how we naturally favour members of own group**. David Eagleman and Don Vaughn, 'Does your brain care about other people? It depends', *The Economist*, November 4, 2019, https://www.economist.com/open-future/2019/11/04/does-your-brain-care-about-other-people-it-depends, as accessed May 2020. For further information, look at Henri Tajfel's experiments on group bias in Henri Tajfel, M. G. Billig, R. P. Bundy, and Claude Flament, 'Social categorization and intergroup behaviour', *European Journal of Psychology*, vol. 1 (June 1971), p149-178.

30   Frans de Waal, *Our Inner Ape*, p135.

31   **Over 95,000 people are estimated to have lost their lives**. Daria Sito-Sucic and Matt Robinson, 'After years of toil, book names Bosnian war dead', *Reuters*, February 15, 2013, https://uk.reuters.com/article/us-bosnia-dead/after-years-of-toil-book-names-bosnian-war-dead-idUSBRE91E0J220130215, as accessed November 11, 2020.

32   **Around 6,700 Rohingya Muslims were killed and over 280 villages destroyed in the first month of violence**. 'Myanmar Rohingya: what you need to know about the crisis', *BBC News*, January 23, 2020, https://www.bbc.co.uk/news/world-asia-41566561, as accessed November 11, 2020.

33   **A US News and World Report poll**, featured in Andy Tix, 'When Religion Promotes Violence', *Psychology Today*, January 31, 2018, https://www.psychologytoday.com/gb/blog/the-pursuit-peace/201801/when-religion-promotes-violence, as accessed November 11, 2020.

34   **In the other study, aggression increased when the passage which called for violence even mentioned God**. Brad Bushman, Robert D Ridge, Enny Das, Colin W. Key, and Gregory L. Busath, 'When God Sanctions Killing: Effect of Scriptural

Notes

Violence on Aggression', *Psychological Science*, vol. 18: no. 3 (March 2017), p204-207, https://journals.sagepub.com/doi/abs/10.1111/j.1467-9280.2007.01873.x, as accessed November 11, 2020.

35 Daniel N. Jones, Adon L. Neria, Farzad A. Helm, Reza N, Sahlan, and Jessica R. Carre, 'Religious Overclaiming and Support for Religious Aggression', *Social Psychological and Personality Science*, vol. 11: no, 7 (April 2020), p1011-1021, https://journals.sagepub.com/doi/abs/10.1177/1948550620912880, as accessed November 6, 2020.

36 Quote in Eric W. Dolan, 'Supporters of religious violence are more likely to claim they're familiar with religious concepts that don't exist', *PsyPost*, August 4, 2020, https://www.psypost.org/2020/08/supporters-of-religious-violence-are-more-likely-to-claim-theyre-familiar-with-religious-concepts-that-dont-exist-57580, as accessed November 6, 2020.

37 'Abhinandan: Captured Indian pilot handed back by Pakistan', *BBC News*, March 1, 2019, https://www.bbc.co.uk/news/world-asia-47412884, as accessed November 12, 2020.

38 **Nationalism was also at play here**. But the nations of Pakistan and India partially exist because of religion. When the subcontinent was left by the British in 1947, it was divided into Hindu-majority India and Muslim-majority Pakistan. An estimated two million people died in communal violence when the split was implemented. William Dalrymple, 'The Great Divide', *The New Yorker*, June 22, 2015, https://www.newyorker.com/magazine/2015/06/29/the-great-divide-books-dalrymple, as accessed November 12, 2020.

39 **Sri Lankan politicians regularly endorse or espouse hate speech against Muslims**. 'Sri Lanka: Muslims Face Threats, Attacks', Human Rights Watch, July 3, 2019, https://www.hrw.org/news/2019/07/03/sri-lanka-muslims-face-threats-attacks, as accessed November 6, 2020.

40 'Israeli-Palestine Conflict', Center for Preventative Action, January 17, 2023, https://www.cfr.org/global-conflict-tracker/conflict/israeli-palestinian-conflict, as accessed April 12, 2023.

41 **An exhaustive look at the impact of religion in relation to happiness and civic engagement across the world**. 'Religion's Relationship to Happiness, Civic Engagement, and Health Around the World', Pew Research Center, January 31, 2019, https://www.pewforum.org/2019/01/31/religions-relationship-to-happiness-civic-engagement-and-health-around-the-world/, as accessed June 4, 2020.

42 Friedrich Nietzsche, *The Portable Nietzsche: Translated by Walter Kauffman* (New York: The Viking Press, 1976), p468.

The Travelling Ape

PART III: GEOPOLITICS

CHAPTER 9: DEMOCRACY: FLAWED, BUT DISMISS IT AT YOUR PERIL

1 'Quotations', Calvin Coolidge Foundation, https://www.coolidgefoundation.org/quote/quotations-f/#:~:text=We%20identify%20the%20flag%20with%20almost%20everything%20we%20hold%20dear%20on%20earth.&text=But%20when%20we%20look%20at,the%20result%20of%20duty%20done, as accessed November 18, 2020.

2 **This is the case in a number of European countries**. Emma Beswick, 'The EU countries that will punish you for disrespecting their flags', *Euronews*, November 9, 2020, https://www.euronews.com/2017/11/09/which-country-has-the-harshest-punishments-for-disrespecting-flags-and-national, as accessed November 21, 2020.

3 'Burning EU and other flags can now bring German jail term', *BBC News*, May 15, 2020, https://www.bbc.co.uk/news/world-europe-52674809, as accessed November 21, 2020.

4 Nick Ames and Sasa Ibrulj, 'Serbia v Albania abandoned after players and fans brawl on pitch', *The Guardian*, October 14, 2020, https://www.theguardian.com/football/2014/oct/14/serbia-albania-euro-2016-flag-halted, as accessed November 3, 2020.

5 **Other laws include which side of a room the flag must be on**, what kind of material it is made of, and the order in which national flags must be displayed with other national flags. Dan Nosowitz, 'Around the World in Things You Can't Do to Flags', *Atlas Obscura*, May 25, 2020, https://www.atlasobscura.com/articles/flag-desecration-laws, as accessed November 21, 2020.

6 **The index is based on the categories of electoral process and pluralism, functioning of government, political participation, political culture, and civil liberties.** 'Democracy Index 2022: Frontline democracy and the battle for Ukraine', The Economist Intelligence Unit, Democracy Index 2022 final (eiu.com), as accessed April 12, 2023.

7 **Out of 180 countries, Azerbaijan ranked in 151st, Tajikistan in 153rd, Saudi Arabia in 170th, Turkmenistan in 176th, and North Korea in 180th.** 'Press Freedom Index 2022', Reporters Without Borders, https://rsf.org/en/index, as accessed February 1, 2023.

8 **In 2017, the Front National's Marine le Pen got 33.9% of the vote in the French presidential election** and The Freedom Party's Geert Wilders came second and got 13.1% of the vote in the Dutch election. In the 2018 Italian election, the Lega party led by

Notes

nationalist firebrand Matteo Salvini came second and he became
deputy prime minister in a coalition government arrangement.

9   Quoted in Lee Pollock, 'Churchill on Trump and Clinton',
The Wall Street Journal, October 6, 2016, https://www.wsj.com/
articles/churchill-on-trump-and-clinton-1475796396, as accessed
November 29, 2020.

10   Associated Press in Bogotá, 'Colombian conflict killed 220,000 in
55 years, commission finds', *The Guardian*, July 25, 2013, https://
www.theguardian.com/world/2013/jul/25/colombia-conflict-
death-toll-commission, as accessed May 26, 2021.

11   'GDP per capita in 1950: Countries Compared', *NationMaster*,
https://www.nationmaster.com/country-info/stats/Economy/GDP-
per-capita-in-1950, as accessed April 12, 2023.

12   'GDP per capita (current US$)', The World Bank, https://data.
worldbank.org/indicator/NY.GDP.PCAP.CD, as accessed February
9, 2023.

13   **Highlighting this trend, India's rank has fallen from 80ᵗʰ
in 2002 to 150ᵗʰ in the** 'Press Freedom Index 2022', Reporters
Without Borders.

14   'Democracy Index 2022: Frontline democracy and the battle for
Ukraine', The Economist Intelligence Unit.

15   'Freedom in the World 2022: Azerbaijan', Freedom House, https://
freedomhouse.org/country/azerbaijan/freedom-world/2022,   as
accessed February 1, 2023.

16   **The Olympic Park cost an estimated US$5 billion**. The new
airport cost US$2.3 billion, despite having fewer than five flights on
some days. 'Turkmenistan: Hosting Asian Games Amid Widespread
Repression', *Human Rights Watch*, June 7, 2017, https://www.hrw.
org/news/2017/06/07/turkmenistan-hosting-asian-games-amid-
widespread-repression, as accessed November 22, 2020.

17   'Democracy Index 2022: Frontline democracy and the battle for
Ukraine', The Economist Intelligence Unit.

18   'Turkmenistan: Denial, Inaction, Worsens Food Crisis', Human
Rights Watch, September 23, 2020, https://www.hrw.org/
news/2020/09/23/turkmenistan-denial-inaction-worsen-food-
crisis, as accessed February 2, 2023.

19   Farangis Najibullah, 'Turkmenistan Faces 'Shocking Population
Decline' As Exodus Continues', *Radio Free Europe*, July 12,
2021,   https://www.rferl.org/a/turkmenistan-population-decline-
exodus/31355045.html, as accessed February 2, 2023.

20   'Gurbanguly Berdymukhamedov wins poll with 98% of the
vote', *Al Jazeera*, February 13, 2017, https://www.aljazeera.com/
news/2017/2/13/gurbanguly-berdymukhamedov-wins-poll-with-
98-of-vote, as accessed February 2, 2023.

21   von Rueden C, Gurven M, and Kaplan H. 'Why do men seek

status? Fitness payoffs to dominance and prestige', *Proceedings of the Royal Society*, vol. 278: no. 1715 (July 2022), p2223-2232, https://www.ncbi.nlm.nih.gov/pmc/articles/PMC3107626/, as accessed February 2, 2023.

22 'The Worst Form of Government', International Churchill Society, https://winstonchurchill.org/resources/quotes/the-worst-form-of-government/, as accessed November 29, 2020.

23 'The World Bank In Eswatini', The World Bank, https://www.worldbank.org/en/country/eswatini/overview, as accessed May 26, 2021.

24 *Monty Python and the Holy Grail* (1975), Online, Terry Gilliam and Terry Jones, Python Productions.

25 **I estimate that this is around five billion people, out of the roughly 100 billion people who have ever lived**.

26 Max Roser, 'Democracy', Our World in Data, June 2019, https://ourworldindata.org/democracy, as accessed November 27, 2020.

27 Ibid.

28 'GDP – Per Capita (PPP)', Central Intelligence Agency, https://www.cia.gov/the-world-factbook/about/archives/2022/field/real-gdp-per-capita/country-comparison, as accessed April 29, 2023.

29 'Democracy Index 2022: Frontline democracy and the battle for Ukraine', The Economist Intelligence Unit.

30 **Rich and undemocratic countries usually have lots of oil**. 'GDP per capita vs. electoral democracy, 2018', *Our Word in Data*, https://ourworldindata.org/grapher/gdp-per-capita-vs-electoral-democracy, as accessed February 3, 2022.

31 **Compared to GDP of around US$13 billion**. Chloe Park, 'Who Are The Richest Royals In The World And How Much Are They Worth', *Tatler*, October 14, 2019, https://sg.asiatatler.com/society/the-richest-royals-in-the-world-2019#:~:text=The%20world's%20second%20longest%2Dreigning,net%20worth%20of%20%2428%20billion, as accessed November 30, 2020.

32 Alan Yuhas, 'The Sultan of Brunei: Opulence, Power, and Hard-Line Islam', *The New York Times*, April 4, 2019, https://www.nytimes.com/2019/04/04/world/asia/who-is-sultan-brunei.html, as accessed December 28, 2020.

33 'Democracy Index 2022: Frontline democracy and the battle for Ukraine', The Economist Intelligence Unit.

34 Ibid and 'Press Freedom Index 2022', Reporters Without Borders.

35 'The Anglosphere and the Sinosphere drift apart', *The Economist: The World in 2020*, https://www.economist.com/the-world-in/2019/11/26/the-anglosphere-and-the-sinosphere-drift-apart, as accessed November 27, 2020.

36 **Immigration into the UK fell slightly after Brexit, but recovered quickly.** 'Migration Statistics: Quarterly Report:

August 2020', Office for National Statistics, August 27, 2020, https://www.ons.gov.uk/peoplepopulationandcommunity/ populationandmigration/internationalmigration/bulletins/ migrationstatisticsquarterlyreport/august2020#:~:text=As%20 such%2C%20we%20have%20made,March%202020%20 (Figure%203), as accessed November 28, 2020.

37 **For all his 'build a wall' rhetoric, the rate of immigration to the US was basically unchanged during the Trump presidency.** '2019 Yearbook of Immigration Statistics', Department of Homeland Security, Table 1, https://www.dhs.gov/immigration-statistics/yearbook/2019/table1, as accessed November 28, 2020.

38 **As of the year 2020.** 'Top 25 Destinations of International Migrants', Migration Policy Institute, https://www.migrationpolicy. org/programs/data-hub/charts/top-25-destinations-international-migrant, as accessed November 28, 2022.

39 **Compared to 21% for the US, 6% for Canada, 6% for Germany, 5% for France, 5% for Australia, and 4% for the UK.** Neli Esipova, Anita Pugliese, and Julie Ray, 'More Than 750 Million Worldwide Would Migrate if They Could', *Gallup*, December 10, 2018, https://news.gallup.com/poll/245255/750-million-worldwide-migrate.aspx, as accessed November 28, 2020.

40 'The Anglosphere and the Sinosphere drift apart', *The Economist: The World in 2020*, https://www.economist.com/the-world-ahead/2019/11/26/the-anglosphere-and-the-sinosphere-drift-apart, as accessed May 25, 2023.

41 **The top 15, in order: The US, Germany, Saudi, Russia, the UK, the UAE, France, Canada, Australia, Italy, Spain, Turkey, Ukraine, India, and Kazakhstan.** 'Top 25 Destinations of International Migrants', Migration Policy Institute.

42 **A US News annual report produced alongside the BAV group, global marketing communications company VMLY&R, and Wharton School from the University of Pennsylvania.** It's based on 75 different metrics. '2021 Best Country Rankings – Quality of Life', *US News*, https://www.usnews.com/news/best-countries/quality-of-life-rankings, as accessed May 2, 2023.

CHAPTER 10: CAPITALISM ISN'T THE ROOT OF ALL EVIL

1 'Press Freedom Index 2022', Reporters Without Borders.

2 **Although of these an estimated 2.5 million were beaten or tortured to death.** Frank Dikötter, *Mao's Great Famine: The History of China's Most Devastating Catastrophe, 1958-1962* (London: Bloomsbury, 2010), p333.

3 **Stalin managed to hide the crisis from the world.** Anne

The Travelling Ape

Applebaum, 'How Stalin Hid Ukraine's Famine From the World', *The Atlantic*, October 13, 2017, https://www.theatlantic.com/international/archive/2017/10/red-famine-anne-applebaum-ukraine-soviet-union/542610/#:~:text=The%20result%20was%20a%20catastrophe,all%20across%20the%20Soviet%20Union, as accessed November 1, 2020.

4   **For a ridiculously biased account of what things were like in Soviet Russia, check out this article (or any of the others) from state-owned news service Russia Beyond**. Tommy O'Callaghan, 'Did soviet government officials live in luxury?', *Russia Beyond*, April 30, 2018, https://www.rbth.com/history/328157-did-soviet-government-officials-live-luxuriously, as accessed December 1, 2020.

5   Shaun Walker, 'Romania comes to terms with monument to communism 30 years after Ceauşescu's death', *The Guardian*, December 22, 2019, https://www.theguardian.com/world/2019/dec/22/romania-palace-of-the-parliament-communism-30-years-after-fall-nicolae-ceausescu-christmas-day, as accessed December 17, 2020. For a highly entertaining novel on the last throws of communism in Romania read Patrick McGuinness, *The Last Hundred Days* (Bridgend, Wales: Seren, 2011).

6   **This book argues that human greed and a relentless thirst for power are the two main driving forces in the history of the world**. Philippe Deane Gigantès, *Power and Greed: A Short History of the World* (London: Constable, 2002).

7   **Everyday prehistoric life would have favoured the genes of people who hoarded food for their family, rather than share it** according to Robert Wright, *The Moral Animal,* p187.

8   **Such as in** Yeonmi Park, *In Order to Live: A North Korean Girl's Journey to Freedom* (London: Penguin, 2016)

9   'Press Freedom Index 2022', Reporters Without Borders.

10   Barbara Crossette, 'Korean Famine Toll: More Than 2 Million', *The New York Times*, August 20 1999, https://www.nytimes.com/1999/08/20/world/korean-famine-toll-more-than-2-million.html, as accessed February 8, 2023.

11   'Korea, North', *Central Intelligence Agency: The World Factbook*, https://www.cia.gov/the-world-factbook/countries/korea-north/, as accessed February 6, 2023.

12   **According to an interview with North Korea expert Benjamin Silberstien.** 'North Korea: Why doesn't it have enough food this year?', *BBC News*, June 23, 2021, https://www.bbc.co.uk/news/57524614, as accessed April 12, 2023.

13   **When it had a democratic government in 1970**. Alan Heston, Robert Summers, and Bettina Aten, 'Penn World Table Version 6', *Center for International Comparisons at the University of Pennsylvania*,

Notes

http://dc1.chass.utoronto.ca/pwt61/alphacountries.html, as accessed December 28, 2020.

14 Hannah Dreier, 'AP Explains: Venezuela's 'anti-capitalist' constitution', *Associated Press*, May 4, 2017, https://apnews.com/article/83c02039e90549819ea605e33a2b3907, as accessed November 2, 2020.

15 **The IMF estimated that inflation could be up to 10,000,000% in the same year.** 'Venezuela's inflation tumbles to 9,568% in 2019: central bank', *Reuters*, February 5, 2020, https://www.reuters.com/article/us-venezuela-economy-idUSKBN1ZY2YQ, as accessed December 28, 2020.

16 **One in three people were struggling to put enough food on the table to meet minimum nutrition requirements in 2020.** 'One in three Venezuelans not getting enough to eat, UN finds', *The Guardian*, February 24, 2020, https://www.theguardian.com/world/2020/feb/24/venezuela-hungry-food-insecure-un-world-food-program, as accessed November 24, 2020.

17 David Biller and Patricia Laya, 'Venezuela Unemployment Nears That of War-Ruined Bosnia, IMF Says', *Bloomberg*, April 9, 2020, https://www.bloomberg.com/news/articles/2019-04-09/venezuela-unemployment-nears-that-of-war-ruined-bosnia-imf-says, as accessed November 24, 2020.

18 **Colombia would have been viewed as the problem country only a few short decades ago.** 'Venezuela Refugee and Migrant Crisis', *IOM UN Migration*, March 2020, https://www.iom.int/venezuela-refugee-and-migrant-crisis, as accessed December 28, 2020.

19 **Which began in 1959 as Fidel Castro rose to power with the stated aim of moving away from a capitalist system.**

20 **This is a relic of import substitution policies aimed at limiting the inflow of American cars and mechanical parts after the Cuban revolution.**

21 'GDP – Per Capita (PPP)', *Central Intelligence Agency: The World Factbook*.

22 'Cuba: Events of 2019', Human Rights Watch, https://www.hrw.org/world-report/2020/country-chapters/cuba, as accessed November 25, 2020.

23 Rob Wile, 'Miami's new wave of immigrants looks a lot like previous ones', *Miami Herald*, August 5, 2019, https://www.miamiherald.com/news/business/article232514327.html, as accessed February 10, 2020.

24 'Sustainable Development Goals: Bhutan', UNESCO, http://uis.unesco.org/en/country/bt, as accessed December 2, 2020.

25 'Life expectancy of world population', *Worldometer*, https://www.worldometers.info/demographics/life-expectancy/, as accessed February 10, 2020.

26 'GDP – Per Capita (PPP)', Central Intelligence Agency.

27 Richard Knight, 'Are North Koreans really three inches shorter than South Koreans', *BBC News*, April 23, 2012, https://www.bbc.co.uk/news/magazine-17774210, as accessed March 3, 2023.

28 Herbert Werlin, 'Ghana and South Korea: Lessons from world bank case studies', *Public Administration and Development*, vol. 11: no. 3 (May/June 1991), p245-255, https://onlinelibrary.wiley.com/doi/10.1002/pad.4230110312, as accessed February 9, 2023.

29 'GDP per capita (current US$)', The World Bank, https://data.worldbank.org/indicator/NY.GDP.PCAP.CD, as accessed February 9, 2023.

30 **Definitions of capitalism usually differ depending on how much the person defining it hates capitalism.** But this one is fairly all-encompassing, and is close to the definition used by the IMF. Sarwat Jahan and Ahmed Saber Mahmud, 'What is Capitalism?', *Finance & Development*, vol. 52: no.2 (June 2015), p44-45, https://www.imf.org/external/pubs/ft/fandd/2015/06/basics.htm, as accessed December 1, 2020.

31 Max Roser and Esteban Ortiz-Ospina, 'Global Extreme Poverty', *Our World in Data*, March 27, 2017, https://ourworldindata.org/poverty, as accessed May 2, 2023.

32 **In Real GDP per capita terms.** The 2021 estimate comes from 'GDP per capita (current US$)', The World Bank, whereas the 1500 estimate is in 1990 international and taken from Jutta Bolt and Jan Luiten van Zanden, 'Maddison Project Database, version 2013', https://www.rug.nl/ggdc/historicaldevelopment/maddison/releases/maddison-project-database-2013, as accessed April 27, 2023.

33 'GNI (current US$) – China' and 'GNI per capita, Atlas method (current US$)', The World Bank, https://data.worldbank.org/indicator/NY.GNP.PCAP.CD?locations=CN, as accessed December 2, 2020.

34 'Consensus Reached at the International Forum on Reform and Opening Up and Poverty Reduction in China', The World Bank, November 5, 2018, https://www.worldbank.org/en/news/press-release/2018/11/05/consensus-reached-at-the-international-forum-on-reform-and-opening-up-and-poverty-reduction-in-china, as accessed December 28, 2020.

35 'GNI per capita, Atlas method', The World Bank.

36 **The few exceptions are oil rich exporters,** which while refusing to liberalise, still happily sell their black gold in the global trade marketplace (something that exists because of capitalism).

37 **This data was compellingly used to support the claim that the world is the best it's ever been**, in Matt Ridley, *The Rational Optimist* (London: Harper Collins, 2010), p117.

Notes

38 Alec Schemmel, 'Critics blast Bernie Sanders for selling $95 tickets to his 'anti-capitalism' event', *NBC Montana*, February 2, 2023, https://nbcmontana.com/news/nation-world/critics-blast-bernie-sanders-for-selling-95-tickets-to-his-anti-capitalism-event-democratic-socialist-socialism-angry-book-anthem-washington-dc, as accessed April 12, 2023.

39 **French economists are famously critical of capitalism and inequality**. So it's no surprise that the most compelling and in-depth assessment of capitalism in recent years has come in the form of French economist Thomas Piketty's lengthy and exhaustive treatise, *Capital in the Twenty-First Century* (London: Harvard University Press, 2014).

40 **For more statistics on global inequality**. 'Facts: Global Inequality', *Inequality.Org*, https://inequality.org/facts/global-inequality/, as accessed December 1, 2020.

41 **US$115,700 compared to US$1,200**. 'GDP – Per Capita (PPP)', *Central Intelligence Agency: The World Factbook*.

42 **The Gini coefficient fell from 0.70 in 1988 to 0.62 in 2013 (latest available data), where a score of 1 indicates perfect inequality.** 'Global Monitoring Report 2015/16: Development Goals In An Era of Demographic Change', The World Bank, https://www.worldbank.org/en/publication/global-monitoring-report, as accessed April 27, 2023.

43 **Wealth generation isn't being shared equally in India. Perhaps unsurprisingly, the richest 1% in India earned 73% of India's total wealth**. 'India: extreme inequality in numbers', Oxfam, https://www.oxfam.org/en/india-extreme-inequality-numbers, as accessed October 19, 2020.

44 Ray Dalio, *Principles for Dealing with the Changing World Order* (London: Simon & Schuster, 2021), p.245.

45 John Cassidy, 'Piketty's Inequality Story in Six Charts', *The New Yorker*, March 26, 2014, https://www.newyorker.com/news/john-cassidy/pikettys-inequality-story-in-six-charts, as accessed April 12, 2024.

46 **Few economists write so passionately and accessibly as Varoufakis about the problems of capitalism**, who is probably one of the few economists who has accrued a 'celebrity' status in recent years, having turned up at Downing Street wearing a biker jacket and boots while Greek Finance Minister. Yanis Varoufakis, *The Global Minotaur: America, Europe and the Future of the Global Economy* (London: Zed Books, 2015), p8.

47 **From 1970 to 2008 UK finance grew twice as fast as UK national income**. In the US, the value of the financial industry rose from around 2% of GDP in 1950 to over 8% by 2010. Stats and further background on the explosion in the power of finance

in Adair Turner, *Between Debt and the Devil: Money, Credit, and Fixing Global Finance* (Oxford: Princeton University Press, 2016), p20.

48 **For example, the value of foreign exchange trading is US$6.6 trillion. Not in a year. Every day in 2019.** That's seven times as much as it was in 1989. It's roughly the size of Japan's economy being traded every day. It's completely devoid of any need in the real economy. 'Global foreign exchange market turnover', Bank for International Settlements, https://www.bis.org/statistics/rpfx19.htm, as accessed November 1, 2020. **We now also have algorithms which trade off minute price differences thousands of times a second.** How's this useful to anybody? The lengths banks are going to to make money using this strategy are outlined by Michael Lewis. This included digging a secret fibre-optic cable between Chicago and New Jersey, with the sole aim of reducing data transmission times for high-frequency trading. Michael Lewis, *Flashboys: Cracking the Money Code* (London: Allen Lane, 2015).

49 **Excessive risk-taking by banks and the use of hedge fund trading with derivatives caused the crisis**. This led the world into a deep recession, causing real suffering for hundreds of millions of people.

50 **An excellent guide to the perils of financial excess in recent years**. John Kay, *Other People's Money: Masters of the Universe or Servants of the People?* (London: Profile Books, 2015).

CHAPTER 11: CHINA'S STAGGERING, SLIGHTY SCARY RISE

1 Kelly Pang, 'Who Built the Great Wall of China? When and Why?', *China Highlights*, December 23, 2022, https://www.chinahighlights.com/greatwall/fact/who-built.htm, as accessed February 10, 2023.

2 'Great Wall of China', *History.com*, November 5, 2019, https://www.history.com/topics/ancient-china/great-wall-of-china, as accessed February 10, 2023.

3 Derek Thompson, 'The Economic History of the Last 2,000 Years in 1 Little Graph', *The Atlantic*, June 19, 2022, https://www.theatlantic.com/business/archive/2012/06/the-economic-history-of-the-last-2-000-years-in-1-little-graph/258676/, as accessed February 10, 2023.

4 Ray Dalio, *Principles for Dealing with the Changing World Order*, p393-397.

5 Ibid.

6 Valerie Strauss and Daniel Southerl, 'The Victims of Mao Zedong's Era', *The Washington Post*, July 17, 1994, https://www.

Notes

washingtonpost.com/archive/politics/1994/07/17/how-many-died-
new-evidence-suggests-far-higher-numbers-for-the-victims-of-
mao-zedongs-era/01044df5-03dd-49f4-a453-a033c5287bcc/, as
accessed February 10, 2023.

7   'GDP per capita (current US$)', The World Bank.

8   Helen Roxburgh, 'Endless cities: will China's new urbanisation
just mean more sprawl', *The Guardian*, May 5, 2017, https://www.
theguardian.com/cities/2017/may/05/megaregions-endless-china-
urbanisation-sprawl-xiongan-jingjinji, as accessed March 3, 2023.

9   **China accounts for two-thirds of the world's high-speed
rail networks**. 'China has built the world's largest bullet-train
network: and there's a lot more to come. But is it a waste of
money?', *The Economist*, Jan 13, 2020, https://www.economist.com/
china/2017/01/13/china-has-built-the-worlds-largest-bullet-train-
network, as accessed December 6, 2020.

10 'China Population (2020)', *PopulationStat*, https://populationstat.
com/china/, as accessed March 3, 2023.

11 **According to UN data, usually focused on metropolitan
areas and urban agglomerations.**

12 **Shenzhen is one exception, which has 45% green space**.
Matt Hickman, 'Global Cities with the Most – and Least – Public
Green Space', *Treehugger*, July 23, 2019, https://www.treehugger.
com/global-cities-most-and-least-public-green-space-4868715, as
accessed December 6, 2020.

13 'GDP (current US$), The World Bank, https://data.worldbank.org/
indicator/NY.GDP.MKTP.CD?end=2021&most_recent_value_
desc=true&start=1960, as accessed April 12, 2023.

14 **According to IMF and World Bank joint GDP estimates**.
Katharina Buchholz, 'China could overtake the US as the
world's largest economy by 2024', *World Economic Forum*, July 20,
2020, https://www.weforum.org/agenda/2020/07/largest-global-
economies-1992-2008-2024/#:~:text=China%20could%20
overtake%20the%20US,largest%20economies%20from%20
1992%20%2D%202024, as accessed December 6, 2020.

15 **The US used 4.5 gigatons of cement from 1901 to 2000**,
whereas China used 6.6 gigatons between 2011 and 2013. United
States Geological Survey and Mineral Industry of China data, as see
in Bill Gates, 'Have you hugged a concrete pillar today', *GatesNotes*,
June 12, 2014, https://www.gatesnotes.com/Books/Making-
the-Modern-World?WT.mc_id=06_13_2014_smilc_tw&WT.
tsrc=Twitter, as accessed December 28, 2020.

16 **In much more eloquent terms, this is described by the
Hegemonic Stability Theory (HST)**. This posits that the
international system is more likely to remain stable when a single
nation-state is in charge.

17 **In the context of history, the US and allied operations in the Gulf are not major global conflicts**.

18 'From Cold War to War on Terror, Watch How America Outspends Everyone on the Military', *Howmuch*, May 26, 2016, https://howmuch.net/articles/military-spending-around-the-world, as accessed December 4, 2020.

19 Nan Tian, 'Military expenditure', Stockholm International Peace Research Institute (SIPRI), https://www.sipri.org/yearbook/2022/08#:~:text=Global%20military%20 expenditure%20rose%20for,equivalent%20to%20%24268%20 per%20person, as accessed April 12, 2023.

20 **Thirty-six of the 75 tallest buildings in the world are located in China**, compared to just nine in the US.

21 **In 2018, African governments accounted for 24.5% of infrastructure spending in the continent, with China just behind on 18.9%.** In the last two decades, China has financed one in five African infrastructure projects and has constructed one in three. Hannah Marais and Jean-Pierre Labuschagne, 'If you want to prosper, consider building roads: China's role in African infrastructure and capital projects', *Deloitte*, March 22, 2019, https://www2.deloitte.com/us/en/insights/industry/public-sector/china-investment-africa-infrastructure-development.html#endnote-9, as accessed December 6, 2020.

22 **The deal has pushed up the country's debt load substantially**, and a default would cause big issues for the country given that it uses the euro (despite not being in the EU or eurozone).

23 Maria Abi-Habib, 'How China Got Sri Lanka to Cough Up a Port', *The New York Times*, June 25, 2018, https://www.nytimes.com/2018/06/25/world/asia/china-sri-lanka-port.html, as accessed May 24, 2021.

24 **China has a 99-year lease on the port in Sri Lanka and a 40-year lease on the port in Pakistan**. Kiran Stacey, 'China signs 99-year lease on Sri Lanka's Hambantota port', *The Financial Times*, December 11, 2017, https://www.ft.com/content/e150ef0c-de37-11e7-a8a4-0a1e63a52f9c, as accessed December 6, 2020.

25 **The mosque is Africa's largest**. Abdi Latif Dahir, 'Africa's largest mosque has been completed with thanks to China', *Quartz*, April 28, 2019, https://qz.com/africa/1606739/china-completes-africas-largest-mosque-in-algeria/, as accessed December 6, 2020.

26 Patrick Gathara, 'Berlin 1884: Remembering the conference that divided Africa', *Al Jazeera*, November 15, 2020, https://www.aljazeera.com/opinions/2019/11/15/berlin-1884-remembering-the-conference-that-divided-africa/, as accessed December 8, 2020.

27 'Africa's population will double by 2050', *The Economist*, March 26, 2020, https://www.economist.com/special-report/2020/03/26/

Notes

africas-population-will-double-by-2050, as accessed December 7, 2020.

28 Okuda Hiroko, 'China's 'peaceful rise/development': A case study of media frames of the rise of China', *Global Media and China*, vol. 1, no.1-2 (2016), p121-138, https://journals.sagepub.com/doi/full/10.1177/2059436416646275#articleCitationDownloadContainer, as accessed December 8, 2020.

29 Jack Goodman, 'Has China lifted 100 million people out of poverty?', *BBC News*, 28 February 2021, https://www.bbc.co.uk/news/56213271, as accessed February 13, 2022.

30 **China comes in 175th place out of 180 countries**. 'Press Freedom Index 2022', Reporters Without Borders.

31 Sarah Cook, 'The Chinese Communist Party's Latest Propaganda Target: Young Minds', Freedom House, April 30, 2019, https://freedomhouse.org/article/chinese-communist-partys-latest-propaganda-target-young-minds, as accessed February 14 2022.

32 **A leaked 2021 US Energy Department report suggested that the pandemic likely came from a Wuhan lab**. Edward Helmore, 'Covid-19 likely came from lab leak, says news report citing US energy department', *The Guardian*, February 26, 2023, https://www.theguardian.com/world/2023/feb/26/covid-virus-likely-laboratory-leak-us-energy-department, as accessed April 12, 2023.

33 Ross Andersen, 'The Panopticon is Already Here,' *The Atlantic*, September 2020, https://www.theatlantic.com/magazine/archive/2020/09/china-ai-surveillance/614197/, as accessed February 14, 2022.

34 Lindsay Maizland, 'China's Repression of Uyghurs in Xinjiang', Council on Foreign Relations, September 22, 2022, https://www.cfr.org/backgrounder/china-xinjiang-uyghurs-muslims-repression-genocide-human-rights, as accessed February 14, 2023.

35 John Feng, 'Taiwan's Desire for Unification with China Near Record Lows as Tensions Rise,' *Newsweek*, July 14, 2022, https://www.newsweek.com/taiwan-china-politics-identity-independence-unification-public-opinion-polling-1724546, as accessed February 14, 2023.

36 Sakura Murakami, 'It's 'now or never' to stop Japan's shrinking population, PM says', *Reuters*, January 23, 2023, https://www.reuters.com/world/asia-pacific/its-now-or-never-stop-japans-shrinking-population-pm-says-2023-01-23/, as accessed February 15, 2023.

37 Paul Morland, *Tomorrow's People: The Future of Humanity in Ten Numbers* (London: Picador, 2022), p166.

38 **Some estimates suggest that the population could even fall**

by half by 2100. But Chinese parents have been allowed to have two children since 2016, and in my view the authorities would probably relax the policy further if they faced a huge demographic crisis. Stein Emil Vollset, Emily Goren, Chun-Wei Yuan, Jackie Cao, and Amanda Smith, 'Fertility, mortality, migration, and population scenarios for 195 countries and territories from 2017 to 2100: a forecasting analysis for the Global Burden of Disease Study', *The Lancet*, (July 2020), p1285-1306, https://www.thelancet.com/journals/lancet/article/PIIS0140-6736(20)30677-2/fulltext, as accessed December 6, 2020.

39 Laura Silver and Christine Huang, 'Key Facts about China's declining population', Pew Research Center, December 5, 2022, https://www.pewresearch.org/fact-tank/2022/12/05/key-facts-about-chinas-declining-population/#:~:text=The%20UN%20forecasts%20that%20China's,of%2Dthe%2Droad%20projection., as accessed February 15, 2023.

40 **China's staggering population – over 1.3 billion – would have been over 400 million higher had it not been implemented according to official government estimates.**

41 Hamish McRae, *The World in 2050: How to Think About the Future* (London: Bloomsbury, 2022), p242.

42 Ryan Holiday, *Lives of the Stoics*, (Profile Books, 2020), p51.

PART IV: HAPPINESS

CHAPTER 12: WHY AREN'T WE IN THE WEST HAPPIER?

1 Dan Chisholm, Kim Sweeny, Peter Sheehan, and Bruce Rasmussen, 'Scaling-up treatment of depression and anxiety: a global return on investment analysis', *The Lancet Psychiatry*, vol. 3 (April 2016), p415-424, https://www.thelancet.com/action/showPdf?pii=S2215-0366%2816%2930024-4, as accessed February 16, 2021.

2 Global Burden of Disease and Injury Incidence and Prevalence Collaborators, 'Global, regional, and national incidence, prevalence, and years lived with disability for 354 diseases and injuries for 195 countries and territories, 1990-2017: a systematic analysis for the Global Burden of Disease Study 2017', *The Lancet*, vol. 392 (November 2018), p1789-1858, https://www.ncbi.nlm.nih.gov/pmc/articles/PMC6227754/pdf/main.pdf, as accessed February 16, 2021.

3 John F. Helliwell, Richard Layard, and Jeffrey D. Sachs, The United Nations, *World Happiness Report 2022* (New York: Sustainable Development Solutions Network, 2020), https://happiness-report.

Notes

s3.amazonaws.com/2022/WHR+22.pdf, as accessed February 24, 2023.

4   Vaclav Smith, *Numbers Don't Lie: 71 Things You Need To Know About the World* (London: Penguin Random House, 2021), p41.

5   R. Biswas-Diener and E. Diener, 'The subjective well-being of the homeless, and lessons for happiness', *Social Indicators Research*, vol. 76: no. 2 (2006): p185-205,

6   Results of a survey commissioned in William MacAskill, *What We Owe The Future* (London: Oneworld, 2022), p200.

7   Madeline Stone 'The Happiest Countries In The World, According To Instagram', *Business Insider*, March 20, 2014, https://www.businessinsider.com/happiest-countries-in-the-world-2014-3?r=US&IR=T, as accessed May 29, 2021.

8   **The study was by economist Angus Deaton and psychologist Daniel Kahneman**, who has won a Nobel Prize for Economics. They analysed the responses of 450,000 Americans polled by Gallup and Healthways in 2008 and 2009. Daniel Kahneman and Angus Deaton, 'High income improves evaluation of life but not emotional well-being', *Proceedings of the National Academy of Sciences,* vol. 107: no. 38 (Sep 2010), p16489-16493, https://www.pnas.org/content/pnas/107/38/16489.full.pdf, as accessed December 22, 2020.

9   **For a modern reimagining of Maslow's hierarchy of needs**. Scott Barry Kaufman, *Transcend: The New Science of Self-Actualization* (London: Tarcher Perigee, 2020).

10   **Suicides rate estimates, per 100,000 of the population in 2019**, according to 'Suicide rate estimates, age-standardized estimates by country', World Health Organization, February 9, 2021, https://apps.who.int/gho/data/node.main.MHSUICIDEASDR?lang=en, as accessed February 24, 2023

11   **More data available at** 'Suicide rates, crude', World Health Organization, April 17, 2020, https://apps.who.int/gho/data/view.main.MHSUICIDEREGv?lang=en, as accessed June 11, 2020.

12   **An alternative and fantastic way of looking at our lack of emotional intelligence**. Alain de Botton, *The School of Life: An Emotional Education* (London: Penguin, 2019), p81.

13   **The Institute for Health Metrics Evaluation (IHME) and Global Burden of Disease 'disability adjusted life years' (DALY) metric sums all of the productive years of one's life lost to illness.** In Ibid.

14   'Global status report on alcohol and health 2018', World Health Organization (Geneva: World Health Organization, 2018), p341.

15   **A view shared by Johan Hari, who posits that disconnection from seven factors are the main causes of unhappiness and depression**. Disconnection from meaningful work; other people;

481

meaningful values; childhood trauma; status and respect; the natural world; and a hopeful and secure future. Johan Hari, *Lost Connections: Why You're Depressed and How to Find Hope* (London: Bloomsbury, 2018).

16 **One of the best non-fiction books ever written**, using a deep dive into early history to explain why the world of today is so unequal. Jared Diamond, *Guns, Germs and Steel: A short history of everybody for the last 13,000 years* (London: Vintage, 1997), p11.

17 **As a further example, the fertility rate (births per woman) was 6.9 in Niger compared to 1.6 in the Netherlands in 2018**. 'Fertility rate, total (births per woman)', The World Bank, https://data.worldbank.org/indicator/SP.DYN.TFRT.IN?locations=RW-ZG+%E2%80%8B&most_recent_value_desc=true, as accessed June 8, 2020.

18 **The study has lasted over 80 years**. Liz Mineo, 'Good genes are nice, but joy is better', *The Harvard Gazette*, April 11, 2017, https://news.harvard.edu/gazette/story/2017/04/over-nearly-80-years-harvard-study-has-been-showing-how-to-live-a-healthy-and-happy-life/, as accessed June 9, 2020.

19 **In India, you can be fined for failing to look after your elderly**. Raekha Prasad, 'India's shrinking families', *The Guardian*, April 14, 2007, https://www.theguardian.com/lifeandstyle/2007/apr/14/familyandrelationships.family2, as accessed June 9, 2020. **In China, looking after your old has been ingrained into society and now into law**. Patti Waldmeir, 'China's children are legally bound to respect their elders', *The Financial Times*, April 11, 2016, https://www.ft.com/content/d33fdde0-ffc9-11e5-99cb-83242733f755, as accessed June 9, 2020.

20 **Research suggests that the elderly living in nursing homes report lower life satisfaction and higher rates of depression than community-based elders**. Sarah Hall Guender, Susan Jayne Loeb, Diana Morris, and Janice Penrod, 'A Comparison of Life Satisfaction and Mood in Nursing Home Residents and Community-Dwelling Elders', *Archives of Psychiatric Nursing*, vol. 15: no. 5 (November 2001), p232-240, https://www.researchgate.net/publication/11765885_A_Comparison_of_Life_Satisfaction_and_Mood_in_Nursing_Home_Residents_and_Community-Dwelling_Elders, as accessed February 23, 2020. **And most data suggests nursing-home populations are high and growing in the world's richest countries.** As a starting point, see M. W. Ribbe, G Ljunggren, K. Steel, E. Topinkova, C. Hawes, N. Ikegami, J. C. Henrard, and P. V. Johnson, 'Nursing homes in 10 nations: a comparison between countries and settings', *Age and Ageing*, vol. 26: no. S2 (September 1997), p3-12, https://pubmed.ncbi.nlm.nih.gov/9464548/, as accessed February 23, 2021.

Notes

21 A survey of 4,000 hybrid workers found that 17% said they had a best friend at work in 2021, down from 22% in 2019. Elena Scotti, 'Americans Are Breaking Up With Their Work Friends', *The Wall Street Journal*, August 17, 2022, https://www.wsj.com/articles/forget-work-friends-more-americans-are-all-business-on-the-job-11660736232, as accessed April 14, 2023.

22 The proportion of Americans saying they have 10 friends or more has declined from 33% in 1990 to just 13% in 2021. Daniel A. Cox, 'The State of American Friendship: Change, Challenges, and Loss', *Survey Center on American Life,* June 8, 2021, https://www.americansurveycenter.org/research/the-state-of-american-friendship-change-challenges-and-loss/, as accessed April 14, 2023.

23 An eye tracking study found that Westerners found it harder to detect changes in the background of scenes when compared to Asians. Hannah Faye Chua, Julie. E. Boland, and Richard E. Nisbett, 'Cultural variation in eye movements during scene perception', *Proceedings of the National Academy of Sciences of the United States of America*, vol. 102: no. 35 (2005), p12629-12633, https://www.ncbi.nlm.nih.gov/pmc/articles/PMC1194960/, as accessed February 15, 2021.

24 Some argue that the methods we use to measure happiness should be expanded. Yukiko Uchida and Shigehiro Oishi, 'The Happiness of Individuals and the Collective', *The Japanese Psychological Association*, vol. 58: no. 1 (January 2016), p125-141, https://onlinelibrary.wiley.com/doi/pdf/10.1111/jpr.12103, as accessed June 8, 2020.

25 In my opinion, Harari is the greatest writer of the modern age, with the best mind. His books are Earth-shatteringly prescient. Yuval Noah Harari, *Sapiens* (London: Vintage, 2011), p425.

26 Wilson argues compellingly that the miracle of existence can be explained by science and evolution in quite simple terms. Edward O. Wilson, *The Meaning of Human Existence* (New York: Liverlight, 2014), p21.

27 In the Palaeolithic period (roughly 2.5 million years ago) to 10,000 BCE early humans lived in caves, simple huts, or tepees and were hunter-gatherers. Lesley Kennedy, *History.com*, October 21, 2019, https://www.history.com/news/prehistoric-ages-timeline, as accessed April 14, 2023.

28 All data in paragraph are 2020 estimates from 'Average Household Size', Population Reference Bureau, https://www.prb.org/international/indicator/hh-size-av/map/country/, as accessed February 15, 2020.

29 University of Notre Dame, 'Child rearing practices of

distant ancestors foster morality, compassion in kids', *Science Daily*, September 22, 2010, https://www.sciencedaily.com/releases/2010/09/100921163709.htm, as accessed February 17, 2021.

30   Esteban Ortiz-Ospina, 'The rise of living alone: how one-person households are becoming increasingly common around the world', Our World in Data, December 10, 2019, https://ourworldindata.org/living-alone, as accessed February 15, 2020.

31   Ibid.

32   **A conversation with psychologist and loneliness expert John Cacioppo in** Olga Khazan, 'How Loneliness Begets Loneliness', *The Atlantic*, April 6, 2017, https://www.theatlantic.com/health/archive/2017/04/how-loneliness-begets-loneliness/521841/, as accessed November 3, 2020.

33   Henning Johannes Drews, Sebastian Wallot, Philip Brysch, Hannah Berger-Johannsen, Sara Lena Weinhold, Panagiotis Mitkidis, Paul Christian Baier, Julia Lechinger, Andreas Roepstorff, and Robert Goder, 'Bed-sharing in Couples is Associated With Increased and Stabilized REM Sleep and Sleep-Stage Synchronization', *Frontiers in Psychiatry*, vol. 11: no. 583 (June 2020), https://doi.org/10.3389/fpsyt.2020.00583, as accessed February 17, 2020.

34   **From a meta-analysis review of more than 148 studies on social isolation.** Julianne Holt-Lunstad, Timothy Smith, and J. Bradley Layton, 'Social Relationships and Mortality Risk: A Meta-analytic Review', *PLOS Medicine*, vol. 7: no.7 (September 2010), https://journals.plos.org/plosmedicine/article?id=10.1371/journal.pmed.1000316, as accessed November 3, 2020.

35   **An excellent (and short) background to the key views of the world's most significant philosophers**. The School of Life, *Great Thinkers* (London: The School of Life, 2016), p34.

36   **One of the most clear and accessible reads on our brains by 'the poster child' of neuroscience**. David Eagleman, *The Brain: The Story of You* (London: Canongate, 2016), p9.

37   **A fantastic and comprehensive study of happiness**, by someone who has faced the horrendous loss of the death of a child. Mo Gawdat, *Solve for Happy: Engineer Your Path to Joy* (London: Bluebird, 2017).

38   **For yet more nuggets of stoic wisdom**. Ryan Holiday, *Stillness is the Key* (New York: Portfolio, 2019), p210.

39   Jules Evans, *Philosophy for Life: And Other Dangerous Situations* (London: Rider, 2012), p98.

Notes

CHAPTER 13: TRAVELS FOR THE MIND

1   **And this was in the 1600s**. A study found that in the modern world people detested spending six to 15 minutes in a room alone with nothing to do but think, even to the extent that they'd prefer to give themselves mild electric shocks to pass the time. Timothy D. Wilson, David A. Reinhard, Erin. C. Westgate, Daniel T. Gilbert, Nicole Ellerbeck, Cheryl Hahn, Casey L. Brown, and Adi Shaked, 'Just think: The challenges of the disengaged mind', *Science*, vol. 345: no. 6192 (p75-77), https://www.eurekalert.org/pub_releases/2014-07/uov-dsi063014.php, as accessed December 28, 2020.

2   **The idea that trauma is stored in the body is a central tenant of somatic trauma therapies, as outlined in** Peter Levine, *Healing Trauma: A Pioneering Program for Restoring the Wisdom of Your Body* (London: Sounds True, 2008).

3   **The Dalai Lama offers some surprisingly modern and relevant insights about how to live**. The Dalai Lama and Howard C. Cutler, *The Art of Happiness: A Handbook for Living* (Hodder & Stoughton: London, 1998), p112.

4   **Results from a 2005 National Science Foundation article, quoted in several sources including** Barry Brownstein, 'Why Positive Thinking Doesn't Work', *Intellectual Takeout*, February 21, 2019, https://www.intellectualtakeout.org/article/why-positive-thinking-doesnt-work/, as accessed November 12, 2020. **Further sources suggest that it's lower, at 70%, but it's still high in any case**. Raj Raghunathan, 'How Negative is Your 'Mental Chatter'?', *Psychology Today*, October 10, 2013, https://www.psychologytoday.com/gb/blog/sapient-nature/201310/how-negative-is-your-mental-chatter#:~:text=Even%20though%20people%20claim%20to,referred%20to%20as%20negativity%20dominance, as accessed December 28, 2020.

5   **An excellent book that delves into the evolutionary basis for so many of our emotions.** Randolph M. Nesse, *Good Reasons for Bad Feelings: Insights from the Frontier of Evolutionary Psychiatry* (London: Penguin, 2019), p77.

6   **He has an interesting podcast and several good books.** Tim Ferris, 'The One Routine – Yes, One! – Common to Billionaires, Icons and World-Class Performers', *Observer*, June 12, 2016, https://observer.com/2016/12/the-one-routine-yes-one-common-to-billionaires-icons-and-world-class-performers/, as accessed December 28, 2020.

7   **Further information and news about mindfulness research is available here**. 'Journal articles of mindfulness continue to grow in 2018', *American Mindfulness Research Association*, https://goamra.

org/journal-articles-on-mindfulness-continue-to-grow-in-2018/, as accessed on June 1, 2020 and Misty Pratt 'Trends in Mindfulness Research Over the Past 55 Years', *Mindful*, October 14, 2021, https://www.mindful.org/trends-in-mindfulness-research-over-the-past-55-years/, as accessed February 27, 2023.

8   **There's been an explosion in research in recent years affirming the benefits of meditation**. For a simple background, see Stan Rodski, *The Neuroscience of Mindfulness: The Astonishing Science Behind How Everyday Hobbies Help You Relax, Work More* (Sydney: Harper Collins, 2019). **On stress reduction**, see Madhav Goyal et al., 'Meditation programs for psychological stress and well-being: a systematic review and meta-analysis', *JAMA International Medicine*, vol. 174: no. 3 (March 2014), p357-368, https://www.ncbi.nlm.nih.gov/pmc/articles/PMC4383597/. **On memory loss**, see Dharma Singh Khalsa, 'Stress, Meditation, and Alzheimer's Disease Prevention: Where the Evidence Stands', *Journal of Alzheimer's Disease*, vol. 48: no. 1 (2015), https://pubmed.ncbi.nlm.nih.gov/26445019/. **On insomnia**, see Jason C. Ong, Rachel Manber, Zindel Segal, Yinglin Xia, Shauna Shapiro, and James K. Wyatt, 'A Randomized Controlled Trial of Mindfulness Meditation for Chronic Insomnia', *Sleep*, vol. 374: no. 9 (September 2014), p1553-1563, https://academic.oup.com/sleep/article/37/9/1553/2416992. **On blood pressure**, see Z. Bai, J. Chang, C. Chen, P. Li, K. Yang, and I. Chi, 'Investigating the effect of transcendental meditation on blood pressure: a systemic review and meta-analysis', *Journal of Human Hypertension*, vol. 29: no. 11 (November 2015), p653-62, https://pubmed.ncbi.nlm.nih.gov/25673114/. **On attention span**, see Julia C. Basso, Alexandra McHale, Victoria Ende, Douglas J. Oberlin, and Wendy A. Suzuki, 'Brief, daily meditation enhances attention, memory, mood and emotional regulation in non-experienced meditators', *Behavioural Brain Research* (Jan 2019), https://pubmed.ncbi.nlm.nih.gov/30153464/. **On kindness**, see Julieta Galante, Ignacio Galante, Marie-Jet Bekkers, and John Gallacher, 'Effects of kindness-based meditation on health and well-being: a systematic review and meta-analysis', *Journal of Consulting and Clinical Psychology*, vol. 82: no. 6 (December 2014), p1101-1114, https://pubmed.ncbi.nlm.nih.gov/24979314/, all accessed December 2020.

9   **A comprehensive look at how meditation can change your mind, for the better**. Daniel Goleman and Richard Davidson, *Altered Traits: Science Reveals how Meditation Changes Your Mind, Brain and Body* (New York: Penguin Random House, 2017).

10   **Meditation yields marked changes in electrical activity in the brain**. Jim Lagopoulos, Jian Xiu, Inge Rasmussen, Alexandra Vik, Gin S. Malhi, Carl F. Eliassen, Ingrid E. Arntsen, Jardar G. Saether,

Notes

Stig Hollup, Are Holen, Svend Davanger, and Øyvind Ellingsen, 'Increased Theta and Alpha EEG Activity During Nondirective Meditation', *The Journal of Alternative and Complementary Medicine*, vol. 15, no. 11 (November 2009), p1187-1192.

11 **Stoicism is making a comeback** according to Ryan Holiday, in both Ryan Holiday, *The Daily Stoic: 366 Meditations on Wisdom, Perseverance, and the Art of Living* (London: Profile Books, 2016), p3 and Ryan Holiday, *Stillness is the Key* (New York: Portfolio, 2019). **The most famous example of modern stoicism writing is probably** Mark Manson, *The Subtle Art of Not Giving A Fuck: A Counterintuitive Approach to Living a Good Life* (New York: Harper Collins, 2016), which had sold over 10 million copies as of April 2023..

12 **A staggeringly relevant treatise on how to live, which is almost 2,000 years old**. Marcus Aurelius, *Meditations* (London: Penguin Classics, 2006), pxxxv.

13 **For a simple and at times poetic little introduction to mindfulness**. Thich Nhat Hanh, *The Miracle of Mindfulness: The Classic Guide* (London: Random House, 2008), p52.

14 **As quoted in** Jules Evans, *Philosophy for Life,* p4.

15 **Or the quote often appears as:** 'Reading good books is like engaging in conversation with the most cultivated minds of past centuries who had composed them, or rather, taking part in a well-conducted dialogue in which such minds reveal to us only the best of their thoughts'.

16 Nina Godlewski, 'Who is Carl Sagan? Quotes From the "Astronomer of the People", Cosmos' Host', *Newsweek*, September 11, 2018, https://www.newsweek.com/carl-sagan-quotes-who-birthday-1209600, as accessed March 1, 2021.

17 Lindsey Galloway, 'Five countries where people live the longest', *BBC Travel*, August 9, 2017, http://www.bbc.com/travel/story/20170807-living-in-places-where-people-live-the-longest, as accessed March 4, 2020.

18 Hector Garcia and Francesc Miralles, *Ikigai: The Japanese Secret to a Long and Happy Life* (London: Hutchinson, 2017), p125.

19 Ibid, p123.

20 Hanako Montgomery, 'A National Embarrassment: Japanese Sumo Wrestling is Plagued by Violence', *Vice*, December 30, 2022, https://www.vice.com/en/article/epzwkp/sumo-wrestling-abuse-japan, as accessed April 14, 2023.

21 Emily A. Seward and Steven Kelly, 'Dietary nitrogen alters codon bias and genome composition in parasitic microorganisms', *Genome Biology*, vol. 17, no. 226 (2016), https://genomebiology.biomedcentral.com/articles/10.1186/s13059-016-1087-9#citeas, as accessed March 8, 2021.

22 'Does eating processed and red meat cause cancer?', Cancer Research UK, https://www.cancerresearchuk.org/about-cancer/causes-of-cancer/diet-and-cancer/does-eating-processed-and-red-meat-cause-cancer, as accessed March 4, 2021.

23 **In this study of over 29,000 Americans, intake of processed meat, unprocessed red meat, and poultry was significantly associated with incident cardiovascular disease**. Victor W. Zhong, Linda Van Horn, Philip Greenland, Mercedes, R. Carnethon, Hongyan Ning, John T. Wilkins, Donald M. Lloyd-Jones, and Norrina B. Allen, 'Associations of Processed Meat, Unprocessed Red Meat, Poultry, or Fish Intake With Incident Cardiovascular Disease and All-Cause Mortality', *Journal of the American Medical Association International Medicine*, vol. 180, no. 4 (2020), p503-512, https://jamanetwork.com/journals/jamainternalmedicine/fullarticle/2759737, as accessed March 4, 2021.

24 **If you have a job where you work late hours or nightshifts, probably best not to read this unless you're willing to change careers afterwards**. Matthew Walker, *Why We Sleep* (London: Random House, 2017).

25 Ibid.

26 Diane C. Mitchell, Carol A. Knight, Jon Hockenberry, Robyn Teplansky, and Terryl J. Hartman, 'Beverage caffeine intakes in the U.S.', *Food and Chemical Toxicology*, vol. 63 (January 2014), p136-142, https://www.sciencedirect.com/science/article/pii/S0278691513007175, as accessed March 7, 2020.

27 Ryan Holiday, *The Daily Stoic,* p147.

28 **Several studies show that cold showers can promote fat loss, help reduce the effects of depression, and improve immunity**. Veronique Ouelett, Sebastian M. Labbé, Denis P. Blondin, Serge Phoenix, Brigitte Guérin, François Haman, Eric E. Turcotte, Denis Richard, and André C. Carpentier, 'Brown adipose tissue oxidative metabolism contribute to energy expenditure during acute cold exposure in humans', *The Journal of Clinical Investigation*, vol. 122, no. 2 (February 2012), p545-552, https://pubmed.ncbi.nlm.nih.gov/22269323/, Nikolai A. Shevchuk, 'Adapted cold shower as a potential treatment for depression', *Medical Hypotheses*, vol. 70, no. 5 (2008), p995-1001, https://www.sciencedirect.com/science/article/abs/pii/S030698770700566X, Geert A. Buijze, Inger N. Sierevelt, Bas C. J. M. van der Heijden, Marcel G. Dijkgraaf, and Monique H. W. Frings-Dresen, 'The Effect of Cold Showering on Health and Work: A Randomized Controlled Trial', *Plos One*, vol. 13, no. 8 (September 2016), https://journals.plos.org/plosone/article?id=10.1371/journal.pone.0161749, as accessed March 7, 2021.

Notes

29 **Flow states are a crucial aspect of the Japanese concept of ikigai.** Hector Garcia and Francesc Miralles, *Ikigai*, p70.

30 **Several successful entrepreneurs and CEOs talk about the value and insight provided by their ayahuasca experiences.** Kate Spicer, 'Business leaders' new passion for mind-altering Amazonian retreats', *The Financial Times: How To Spend It'*, May 16, 2019, https://howtospendit.ft.com/travel/206231-business-leaders-new-passion-for-mind-altering-amazonian-retreats, as accessed May 28, 2020.

31 Jacob S. Aday, Christopher C. Davoli, and Emily K. Bloesch, '2018: A watershed year for psychedelic science', *Drug Science, Policy and Law,* vol. 5, no. 1-4, https://journals.sagepub.com/doi/full/10.1177/2050324519872284, as accessed May 15, 2020.

32 **For further reading into the growing science backing up the utility of psychedelic therapy.** Barbara E. Bauer, 'The Top 10 Psychedelic Research Papers of the Last 10 Years', *Psychedelic Science Review*, August 9, 2019, https://psychedelicreview.com/the-top-10-psychedelic-research-papers-of-the-last-10-years/, as accessed May 15, 2020.

33 'Psychedelic Therapeutics Market worth $8.31 billion by 2028 – Exclusive Report by InsightAce Analytic', *Bloomberg*, https://www.bloomberg.com/press-releases/2022-07-18/psychedelic-therapeutics-market-worth-8-31-billion-by-2028-exclusive-report-by-insightace-analytic#:~:text=Money%2DMarket%20Funds-,Psychedelic%20Therapeutics%20Market%20worth%20%24%208.31%20billion%20by%202028,Exclusive%20Report%20by%20InsightAce%20Analytic, as accessed April 14, 2023.

34 Jacob S. Aday, Christopher C. Davoli, and Emily K. Bloesch, '2018: A watershed year for psychedelic science', *Drug Science, Policy and Law,* vol. 5, no. 1-4, https://journals.sagepub.com/doi/full/10.1177/2050324519872284, as accessed May 15, 2020.

35 **A good guide into the method behind the (perceived) madness.** Ryan O'Hare, 'Magic mushrooms may "reset" the brains of depressed patients, study suggests', *Science Daily*, October 13, 2017, https://www.sciencedaily.com/releases/2017/10/171013091018.htm, as accessed May 14, 2020

36 **According to pharmacologist Richard Griffiths,** as quoted in James. S. Romm's introduction to Lucius Annaeus Seneca, *How To Die*, pix.

37 **A thorough journey into the potential use of psychedelics in psychotherapy can be found in** Michael Pollan, *How to Change Your Mind: What The New Science of Psychedelics Teaches Us About Consciousness, Dying, Addiction, Depression, and Transcendence* (New York: Penguin, 2018), p331 onwards.

38 **A large dose can lead to lasting positive changes in your**

outlook on life. The study found that, 'Openness remained significantly higher than baseline more than one year after the session. This is the first study to demonstrate changes in personality in healthy adults after an experimentally manipulated discrete event … Openness includes a relatively broad range of intercorrelated traits covering aesthetic appreciation and sensitivity, fantasy and imagination, awareness of feelings in self and others, and intellectual engagement. People with high levels of Openness are 'permeable to new ideas and experiences' and 'motivated to enlarge their experience into novel territory'. Katherine MacLean, Matthew Johnson, and Roland Griffiths, 'Mystical Experiences Occasioned by the Hallucinogen Psilocybin Led to Increases in the Personality Domain of openness', *Journal of Psychopharmacology* vol. 25, no. 11 (November 2011), p1453-1461.

39   **fMRI brain scanning technology has compared the impacts of long-term meditation or psychedelics on brain activity**, and noted striking similarities. Raphaël Millière, Robin Carhart-Harris, Leor Roseman, Fynn-Mathis Trautwein, Aviva Berkovich-Ohana, 'Psychedelics, Meditation, and Self-Consciousness', *Frontiers in Psychology*, vol. 9, no. 1475 (September 2018).

40   **I can't stress how important preparation and setting are.** In the therapeutic setting, you'll be lying flat, listening to a specially crafted playlist, with an eye mask on, and with a trained professional looking after you. You'll then allow adequate time afterwards to integrate any lessons or experiences you may have had. As Carhart-Harris suggests, 'the experience is carefully prepared for, contained, and mediated. If not done this way, the use of psychedelics can be dangerous'. Robin Carhart-Harris, 'We can no longer ignore the potential of psychedelic drugs to treat depression', *The Guardian*, June 8, 2020, https://www.theguardian.com/commentisfree/2020/jun/08/psychedelic-drugs-treat-depression, as accessed February 26, 2021.

41   **During breathwork, you are instructed to breathe in and out vigorously, filling the lungs and then emptying them completely.** This can lead to non-ordinary states of consciousness, which, like psychedelics, can help you let go of past traumas. This sounds 'out there', but from much personal experience, I can attest to this being true. Christophe Andre, 'Proper Breathing Brings Better Health', *Scientific American*, January 15, 2015, https://www.scientificamerican.com/article/proper-breathing-brings-better-health/, as accessed June 2, 2023.

42   **Every time you remember the hatred, cortisol and adrenaline are released into your body**. Over time, it leads to anxiety, digestive problems, muscle problems, heart disease, sleep problems, and memory concentration impairment. Habib Yaribeygi, Yunes

Notes

Panahi, Hedayat Sahraei, Thomas P. Johnston, and Amirhossein Sahebkar, 'The impact of stress on body function: a review', *Experimental and Clinical Sciences*, vol. 16 (July 2017), p1057-1072, https://www.ncbi.nlm.nih.gov/pmc/articles/PMC5579396/#, as accessed March 4, 2021.

43 **A chilling and vital read, which highlights the degree to which our mortality pervades all that we do**. Ernest Becker, *The Denial Of Death* (London: Souvenir Press, 1973/2020), p27.

44 Quoted in Amanda Blainey*, Do Death: For a Life Better Lived* (London: The Do Book Company, 2019), p33.

45 Quoted in Steven Gambardella, 'Montaigne: To Philosophize is to Learn to Die: Is It Death or Change That We Really Fear?', *Medium*, May 23, 2020, https://medium.com/the-sophist/montaigne-to-philosophize-is-to-learn-to-die-1384f273bfbf, as accessed December 11, 2020.

46 **For a highly relevant and useful approach to understanding our mortality**, see Lucius Annaeus Seneca*, Letters from a Stoic: An Ancient Guide to the End of Life*.

47 Ryan Holiday, 'Memento Mori: The Reminder We All Desperately Need', *The Daily Stoic,* https://dailystoic.com/memento-mori/, as accessed August 24, 2020.

48 Ed Halliwell, 'End-of-life issues', *The Guardian*, December 4, 2008, https://www.theguardian.com/commentisfree/belief/2008/dec/04/buddhism-religion-death, as accessed August 24, 2020.

49 Amelia Goranson, Ryan S. Ritter, Adam Waytz, Michael I. Norton, and Kurt Gray, 'Dying Is Unexpectedly Positive', *Psychological Science*, vol. 28, no. 7 (June 2017), p988–999. https://journals.sagepub.com/doi/10.1177/0956797617701186, as accessed August, 2020.

50 **At times it can slip into the New Age sphere, but on the whole highlights some incredibly important lessons for us all**. Bronnie Ware, *The Top Five Regrets of The Dying* (London: Hay House, 2012).

51 **This is the best introduction to meditation out there**. Dan Harris, *10% Happier: How I Tamed the Voice in My Head, Reduced Stress Without Losing My Edge, and Found Self-Help That Actually Works – A True Story (London: Yellow Kite, 2014)*.

52 **Echoing Socrates' time-honoured statement that the unexamined life is not worth living**. Stephen Grosz, *The Examined Life: How We Lose and Find Ourselves* (London: WW Norton, 2014).

53 Erich Fromm, *The Art of Being* (New York: Bloomsbury, 1989).

54 **His middle name is Ransom, which is pretty cool**. Carl Rogers, *On Becoming a Person: A Therapist's View of Psychotherapy* (New York: Basic Books, 1961), p186.

The Travelling Ape

EPILOGUE

1   **You shouldn't exist**. Dina Spector, 'The Odds of You Being Alive
      Are Incredibly Small', *Business Insider*, June 11, 2020, https://www.
      businessinsider.com/infographic-the-odds-of-being-alive-2012-
      6?r=US&IR=T, as accessed September 21, 2020.

Printed in Great Britain
by Amazon